ANABAPTISTS FOUR CENTURIES LATER
A Profile of Five Mennonite
and Brethren in Christ Denominations

anaBaptists
foUR centURíes LateR

A Profile of Five Mennonite
and Brethren in Christ Denominations

**J. Howard Kauffman
and
Leland Harder**

HERALD PRESS
Scottdale, Pennsylvania
Kitchener, Ontario
1975

Library of Congress Cataloging in Publication Data

Kauffman, J Howard, 1919-
Anabaptists four centuries later.

  Includes bibliographical references and index.
  1. Mennonites — Statistics. 2. Mennonite Church —
Statistics. 3. General Conference Mennonite Church —
Statistics. 4. Mennonite Brethren Church of North
America — Statistics. 5. Brethren in Christ — Statistics.
6. Evangelical Mennonite Church — Statistics.

I. Harder, Leland, 1926-   joint author. II. Title.

BX8121.2.K36   289.7'73   74-30347
ISBN 0-8361-1136-2
ISBN 0-8361-1137-0 pbk.

ANABAPTISTS FOUR CENTURIES LATER
Copyright © 1975 by Herald Press, Scottdale, Pa. 15683.
Published simultaneously in Canada by Herald Press,
Kitchener, Ont. N2G 1A7.
Library of Congress Catalog Card Number: 74-30347
International Standard Book Numbers:
  0-8361-1136-2   (hardcover)
  0-8361-1137-0   (softcover)
Printed in the United States of America

To
The 3,591 church members
who provided the data
for this study

PREFACE

The work of the church goes forward in many ways. Traditionally it has consisted of preaching and worship, evangelism and missions, Christian education, and the production of Christian literature. More recently, special programs of fellowship, counseling, and service have become part of the church's ministry. Research, if found at all in the church's portfolio, is usually at the end of the priority list.

Research plays a servant role in the work of the church. Historical research has long assisted churchmen in their search for contemporary solutions to age-old problems. Survey research has developed only recently, and just as public opinion polls provide a political pulse count, so do surveys of church members provide a reading on the state of the health of the churches.

Not many denominations have found the interest or the resources to conduct a national survey of their membership. Thus it is no small matter for the Mennonites and Brethren in Christ to commit themselves to a two-nation survey of their members. We are grateful to Mennonite Mutual Aid Association for their interest and commitment of major funds to make the study possible. The study reflects an increasing desire of church leaders to base their planning and decisions on some "hard data" in addition to their more informal insights and hunches.

The authors were asked to conduct a study that would yield information of use to church boards and committees, pastors, writers and editors, and others who carry responsibilities for the work of the church. The survey bears some of the marks of eclecticism in trying to gather a wide variety of data that would meet the information needs of many church agencies. However, it became apparent in the early planning that some theoretical framework or integrative theme would be needed as a basis for organizing and interpreting the large quantity of data to be gathered. This was found in the concept of "Anabaptism," a vision of the Christian church that was hammered out in the fires of the Protestant Reformation. The members of the several Mennonite and Brethren in Christ denominations are among the inheritors of that early vision. Therefore, the central theme of this book is to learn how well the present members of these churches reflect that sixteenth-century vision.

In preparing this research report we have had to omit, for reasons of space limitations, many findings that might interest readers. Hopefully, some of these can be published separately. Space given to methodological matters, such as scale construction and testing, has been severely limited. Additional information will be supplied on request. Good counsel was received from a number of Canadian churchmen, but, as Americans, the writers may not have fully represented Canadian interests and concerns in the study. The study reports both strengths and weaknesses in the participating churches, and the writers have attempted to be objective in presenting both.

The study is indebted to several research programs that preceded it, especially the national survey of Lutherans conducted in 1970. We are grateful to Merton P. Strommen and Milo L. Brekke for valuable counsel and for their permission to use certain items from the Lutheran survey instruments. Jarvis Rich and Paul Sheatsley of the National Opinion Research Center provided counsel on data processing. Paul Hiebert served as a consultant at several points in the study.

We gratefully acknowledge the contributions of our colleagues, John H. Yoder, Calvin Redekop, C. J. Dyck, and Ervin Beck. As members of the Administrative Committee, the following assisted in various ways: Paul M. Lederach, Marvin Hein, Lester Janzen, Heinz Janzen, Harvey A. Driver, Merle Brubaker, and Don Shafer. For faithful and efficient secretarial services we are indebted to Winifred Beechy, Dorothy Friesen, and Betty Shenk. Becky Oyer and John Harder provided leadership in data preparation and the preparation of the Index.

We acknowledge with thanks the contribution of time and interest given by over forty church leaders, members of agency and institutional staffs, each of whom traveled as a "research visitor" to a number of congregations to administer the questionnaires. Last but not least, we thank the nearly 3,700 church members who devoted an evening to filling out the lengthy questionnaires.

J. Howard Kauffman
Leland Harder

INTRODUCTION

Anabaptists Four Centuries Later is the product of brotherhood cooperation. It is the result of the labor of many, many persons, freely given, and
the pooling of limited financial resources.

The need for a "Layman's Profile," as the project was called at first,
was expressed by the Curriculum Development Department of the Mennonite Publishing House, Scottdale, Pa., in 1969. How can curriculum materials be prepared for adults in the church, planners asked, unless more is
known about these adults — about their religious practices; about their
theological and doctrinal beliefs; about attitudes and practices concerning
social issues such as war, poverty, and race; about their standards of right
and wrong; about their attitudes toward the church; about their recreational
activities; and about their educational, occupational, economic, and marital
status?

At the same time a similar need was expressed by the Mennonite
Board of Missions, Elkhart, Ind., to plan for more effective educational and
promotional efforts in the congregations concerning missions.

The findings of a youth research in the Mennonite Church (1968) [1]
also gave impetus to the call for a "Layman's Profile." Through a study
of adult members, perspectives would be provided for more fully understanding the results of the youth research.

In 1969 the Fraternal Activities Committee of Mennonite Mutual Aid,
Goshen, Ind., was approached to secure funds for research among Mennonite adults. The proposal captured the imagination of the committee.
However, the committee felt that such research should be done among
adults of all Mennonite groups. The committee appropriated $2,500 to make
a feasibility study for inter-Mennonite research.

Howard J. Zehr, then Executive Secretary of the Mennonite Church,
invited representatives of Mennonite bodies in the "Mennonite Central
Committee constituency" to a meeting March 4, 1970, in Chicago to discuss
cooperation in such a research project. Representatives of the Brethren in
Christ Church, Evangelical Mennonite Church, General Conference Mennonite Church, Mennonite Brethren Church, and the Mennonite Church
responded. This group felt that a "Layman's Profile" would be beneficial
to all. The representatives agreed to secure the approval of the appropriate
agencies in their groups to participate in the research. They agreed to
meet again in June to prepare a budget, a schedule, and a proposal to

submit to Mennonite Mutual Aid for funding, and to set up an administrative group to function once funds were secured.

In June 1970 Merle Brubaker of the Brethren in Christ Church, Harvey A. Driver of the Evangelical Mennonite Church, Heinz Janzen and Leland D. Harder of the General Conference Mennonite Church, Marvin Hein and H. H. Dick of the Mennonite Brethren Church, and Howard J. Zehr and Paul M. Lederach of the Mennonite Church met, prepared a budget of $39,000, and authorized requesting this amount from the Fraternal Funds of Mennonite Mutual Aid. The group agreed to call the research "Church Member Profile" and expressed the hope that more of the groups in the Mennonite Central Committee constituency would be involved. But only the five groups participating in this meeting finally elected to cooperate.

In the June 1970 meeting a schedule was determined and an administrative committee was appointed:

Paul M. Lederach, Scottdale, Pa., Chairman

Marvin Hein, Hillsboro, Kan., secretary

Harvey A. Driver, Fort Wayne, Ind., Treasurer

Merle Brubaker, Massillon, Ohio (replaced by Don Shafer, Nappanee, Ind., July 1971)

Leland D. Harder, Elkhart, Ind. (replaced by Lester Janzen, then Heinz Janzen after Harder became Associate Director of the research project)

Late in 1970 the Mutual Aid Board approved a grant, to be spread across two years, to carry out the Church Member Profile as proposed. While on the matter of finance, it should be noted that were it not for the financial support of Mennonite Mutual Aid and the participating groups, and much donated time, the research would not have been completed. Since the original planning group had not conducted a study of such magnitude earlier, it had no precedents for estimating the budget. Expenses in gathering data and in consulting in the churches exceeded expectations. An additional $10,000 was needed to complete the work. Thanks are in order to the general boards of the participating groups and to the Mennonite Publishing House for funds and also to Mennonite Mutual Aid for matching funds to complete the project.

The first task of the Administrative Committee was to secure a Director and Associate Director. Through the cooperation of Goshen College, Goshen, Ind., and Mennonite Biblical Seminary, Elkhart, Ind., the Administrative Committee was able to secure on a part-time basis the services of J. Howard Kauffman as Director and Leland D. Harder as Associate Director.

J. Howard Kauffman is Professor of Sociology and Chairman of the Department of Sociology, Anthropology, and Social Welfare at Goshen College. He is also Executive Director of the Social Research Service based at Goshen College. Howard is skilled in empirical research and has specialized in the field of marriage and the family. He has been active in a variety of churchwide organizations in the Mennonite Church. He has studied and traveled in Europe and Africa. He received his PhD from the University of Chicago in 1960.

Leland D. Harder is Professor of Practical Theology and Director of Field Education at the Mennonite Biblical Seminary. He, too, is skilled in social research and has conducted significant studies among Mennonites such as *Steinbach and Its Churches* [2] and *Fact Book of Congregational Membership*, [3] Leland is an ordained minister in the General Conference Mennonite Church and has served on many churchwide boards and commissions. He received his PhD from Northwestern University in 1962.

The significance of this research is due, in no small measure, to the competence and dedication of these two men as they gave themselves without reservation to the task. They worked unselfishly many days and long hours beyond those for which they were remunerated. All of us owe a debt of gratitude to them. Thanks are due their secretaries and assistants for careful work — and to their wives for their support and patience as Howard and Leland analyzed mountains of data and wrote the report — this book.

Many others cooperated in this research and deserve a word of thanks:

— the executive officers of the participating groups for their constant support.

— the pastors of the congregations involved in the study. They provided membership lists, arranged meetings for research visitors, and did a lot of planning and follow-up work. There were 174 congregations involved.

— the research visitors. These persons visited the congregations to administer the questionnaire on which this research is based. Space does not permit naming them. Each of the 44 research visitors visited from one to six congregations.

— the members of the congregations involved in the study. There were 3,670 persons who gave an evening to respond to the questionnaire.

— the officers and staff persons of the boards and agencies of the five participating groups who took time to counsel with the research directors about areas to explore and who were so helpful in developing the content of the questionnaire used in the Church Member Profile.

— those who provided counsel to the directors such as their colleagues at the college and seminary and persons outside the participating groups such as Merton Strommen and Milo Brekke, Youth Research Center, Minneapolis, Minn., and Jarvis Rich and Paul Sheatsley of the National Opinion Research Center.

— the Book Division of the Mennonite Publishing House for its cooperation in publishing this report and for the counsel of Book Editor Paul M. Schrock to Howard and Leland as they prepared the manuscript.

— the members of all the participating groups for their expressions of continuing interest in the study and their patience, waiting for the findings to be published.

This book, *Anabaptists Four Centuries Later,* is the first step in reporting the findings of the research. The data can be studied further and analyzed in many more and helpful ways. We hope they will be. This report is important reading for:

— staff persons and members of each board of the participating groups, to know better the persons they are called to serve.

— pastors, to discern the degree to which the persons in their congregations are like or vary from brothers and sisters in the rest of the church.

— students at our colleges and seminaries in courses such as religion, sociology, the church.

— each member, to know better his brothers and sisters, and himself as part of the Mennonite-Brethren in Christ family.

— persons outside the participating groups as an introduction to and analysis of five denominations standing in the radical reformation tradition.

A careful reading of this report, hopefully, will help members of one group see themselves and members of other groups as they are. For too long we have viewed each other through stereotypes that have developed through the decades. Now these stereotypes can be lifted. The strengths and weaknesses of all stand clear. For those evidences of faithfulness to the lordship of Jesus Christ and to the Scripture "four centuries later" we give thanks. Those evidences in our time of falling short in discipleship, in witness, in service, in obedience to Christ and His kingdom remind us anew of our need for repentance, for constant dependence upon His mercy and grace, and for the continued work of the Holy Spirit in our midst.

Paul M. Lederach, Chairman
Administrative Committee
Church Member Profile

CONTENTS

Preface 7
Introduction by Paul M. Lederach 9
List of Tables 14
List of Figures 17

PART I: INTRODUCTION
    1. Anabaptists Yesterday and Today 19
    2. Historical Profiles of the Denominations 31
    3. Characteristics of the Church Members 51

PART II: PATTERNS OF FAITH AND LIFE
    4. Church Participation 64
    5. Religious Experience and Practice 83
    6. Belief and Doctrine 101
    7. Moral Issues 118
    8. Social Ethics 130
    9. Political Participation 150
  10. Marriage and the Family 170

PART III: THE WORK OF THE CHURCH
  11. Leadership in the Congregation 183
  12. Christian Education in the Local Church 199
  13. Denominational Schools 219
  14. The Stewardship of Church Members 233
  15. Parochial and Ecumenical Attitudes 243

PART IV: THE SOURCES AND CONSEQUENCES
        OF CHURCH MEMBERSHIP
  16. Sex and Age Differences 261
  17. Education and Social Class 275
  18. Residence: Rural-Urban, Regional, National 283
  19. Denominational Patterns of Faith and Life, ... 297
  20. The Search for the Key Factors 311

PART V: SUMMARY AND CONCLUSIONS
    21. Summary and Implications for the Churches 333

Notes 344
Appendix: How the Study Was Conducted 386
Index 400
The Authors

LIST OF TABLES

1-1 Baptized Members of Church Bodies, 1972 21

3-1 Membership Distribution for the Five Denominations by Country 52

3-2 Distribution of Sample Members by Country and by Denomination . . 52

3-3 Percentage Distribution of Church Members by Educational
     Attainment and by Denomination 59

3-4 Percentage Distribution of Church Members by Sex and Occupation . . 60

3-5 Percentage Distribution of Employed Church Members and
     Employed United States White Persons, 1970, by Sex and
     Occupation 61

3-6 Percentage Distribution of Church Members by Denomination and
     Household Income 62

4-1 Measures of Associationalism 67

4-2 Measures of Voluntarism 71

4-3 Measures of Communalism · · 77

5-1 Initial Conversion Experience 87

5-2 Types of Conversion Experience 92

5-3 Measures of Sanctification 94

5-4 Measures of Devotionalism 98

6-1 Measures of General Orthodoxy 106

6-2 Measures of Fundamentalist Orthodoxy 112

6-3 Anabaptism Scale Scores 116

7-1 Percentage Distribution of Responses on Moral Issues 123

7-2 Percent Responding "Always Wrong" to Moral Behavior,
by Denomination 124

7-3 Correlations of Various Scales with Moral Attitudes and Behavior . . . 129

8-1 Measures of Pacifism 133

8-2 Relation of Pacifism to Selected Variables 135

8-3 Race Relations as Related to Other Variables 137

8-4 Measures of Race Relations 139

8-5 Denominational Comparisons on Racial Attitudes 140

8-6 Measures of Welfare Attitudes 142

8-7 Measures of Anti-Communism 144

8-8 Attitudes Toward Labor Unions 147

8-9 Miscellaneous Social Concerns Measures 148

9-1 General Attitudes Toward the State and Its Functions 157

9-2 Church and State Relationships 159

9-3 Separation of Church and State as Related to Faith and Life
Variables 160

9-4 Political Participation . . . .

9-5 Political Participation as Related to Faith and Life Variables 162

9-6 Political Party Preferences, 1972 164

9-7 The Political Action of the Church 167

9-8 Political Action as Related to Faith and Life Variables 168

10-1 Attitudes of Church Members on Moral Issues Related to Mar-
riage and Divorce 173

10-2 Marital Status of Church Members, 1972, and of the U.S.
Population 14 Years and Older, 1970 176

11-1 Types of Leadership in the Churches 187

11-2 Type of Leadership as Related to Other Variables 189

11-3 Measures of the Concept of Shared Ministry 191

11-4 Relationships Between the Shared Ministry Scale and Other
Variables 194

11-5 Measures of the Role of Women in the Church 196

11-6 The Role-of-Women Scale as Related to Other Variables 197

12-1 Measures of Sunday School Participation 204

12-2 Sunday School Participation as Related to Congregational and Denominational Self-Identity, for Age-Groups 207

12-3 Scores on the Bible Knowledge Scale, by Denomination 209

12-4 Relationship Between Bible Knowledge and Sunday School Participation 209

12-5 Measures of Evangelism 213

12-6 Differences Between Sunday School Teachers and Nonteachers 216

13-1 Attendance at Church Schools as Related to Other Variables 225

13-2 Type of College Attended as Related to Other Variables 227

13-3 Support of Church Colleges 229

14-1 Per Member Giving for U.S., Canadian, and Participating Churches, 1971 234

14-2 Stewardship Attitudes 236

14-3 Percentage Distribution of Respondents by Support of Various Types of Church Program 241

15-1 Measures of Anti-Semitism and Anti-Catholicism 250

15-2 Correlations Between Anti-Semitism/Anti-Catholicism and Other Variables 251

15-3 Denominational Comparisons on Prejudice 252

15-4 Measures of Ecumenism 255

15-5 Relationships Between Ecumenism and Other Variables 257

15-6 Support of the Mennonite Central Committee 258

15-7 Relationships Between MCC Support Scale and Other Variables . . . 259

16-1 Percent of Respondents Evidencing Selected Religious Characteristics by Age-Groups 268-269

17-1 Distribution of SES Scores by Denomination 276

17-2 Percentage Distribution of Church Members by Education and by Rating on the Anabaptist Vision Scale 278

17-3 Coefficients of Correlation Between Socioeconomic Status and Religious Variables ! 281

18-1 Rural-Urban Residence by Denominations 284

18-2 Demographic Characteristics by Rural-Urban Residence 285

18-3 Style of Life Characteristics by Rural-Urban Residence 287

18-4 Moral and Ethical Variables by Rural-Urban Residence 289

18-5 Religious Orientation Variables by Rural-Urban Residence 290

18-6 Attitude Toward Increasing National Conference Identity 294

18-7 Scale Score Differences by National and Regional Residence 296

19-1 Rank Order of Denominations on Scales 302

19-2 Ratings of Five Denominations on Scales When Compared to Other American Denominations 308

20-1 Intercorrelations Between 15 Independent Variables and 23 Dependent Variables 319

20-2 Intercorrelations of Faith Variables 320

20-3 Overall Average Correlations and Rank Order of Power of Independent Variables to Predict Dependent Variables 323

20-4 Direction of Correlation Between 15 Independent Variables and 19 Dependent Variables 324

A-1 Members, Churches, and Sample Estimates for the Five Denominations, United States and Canada 371

A-2 Congregations in the Sampling Universe by Denonination 372

A-3 Initial Portion of Sample Congregation Selection Table for the Brethren in Christ Church 373

A-4 Computation of Number of Sample Members Needed from Each Congregation 375

A-5 Analysis of Sampling Results 381

A-6 Analysis of Usable Returns 382

A-7 Derivation of Weight Factors for Adjusting Denominational Responses 384

LIST OF FIGURES

3-1 Age-Sex Pyramid for the Sample Members 57

4-1 Village Layout of the Alexanderwohl Mennonite Community in Russia 75

16-1 Age Variations on Church Participation 270

16-2 Age Variations on Moral and Ethical Attitudes 271

Chapter 1

ANABAPTISTS YESTERDAY AND TODAY

It is now four and one-half centuries since the founding of the so-called "Anabaptist" movement. As described by Harold S. Bender,

> The Swiss Brethren movement, commonly called Anabaptism and later known as Mennonitism, was formally initiated on January 21, 1525, in the city of Zurich, Switzerland, or the nearby village of Zollikon. In a prayer service on that night a company of about fifteen earnest Christians, formerly devoted supporters of Ulrich Zwingli's evangelical reformation, were led by what they were convinced was a divine call to establish a brotherhood of believers under the outward sign of adult baptism as a confession of faith and a pledge to live a true Christian life.[1]

The principal founders of the movement, Conrad Grebel and Felix Manz, had joined forces with Zwingli in the Reformation movement in 1522 but began to oppose him several years later. The Anabaptists charged that the Zwinglian reforms stopped short of a true biblical view of the church. Grebel and his associates insisted that the church must be separate from the state and must abandon the notion that church and society are a unity. Only those persons who turn to God in confession and commitment on the basis of responsible understandings and faith, and who are "called out" of the fallen society to live lives of faithful obedience according to the Scriptures are worthy of being called members of the kingdom of God. The seal of their conversion and entrance into the fellowship of the church should be water baptism, that is, adult baptism instead of infant baptism. Hence they were given the reproachful label "Anabaptist," a Greek word meaning "rebaptizer."[2]

The radical ideas of the Anabaptists, the "left wing of the Reformation," spread through various parts of Switzerland, Germany, Austria, and the Low Countries, incurring devastating opposition from both Catholics and reformers. Thousands of Anabaptists were martyred in the attempts of the established churches to root out and destroy these "heretics" and their false teachings. Most of the early Anabaptist leaders lost their lives within a few years.

In addition to the Swiss Brethren, Anabaptist congregations were formed in South Germany, Alsace, and the Tyrol. The Hutterian Brethren developed communal fellowship in Austria and Moravia. In North Germany and Holland Anabaptist teachings took root at various places. In Holland a Catholic priest, Menno Simons, was converted to Anabaptism in 1536. Because of his skills and extensive writings, he became the acknowledged leader of the Anabaptists in northwest Europe. His followers were called Menists, and later Mennonites.[3]

Although the main doctrines of the early Anabaptists still provide a common core of faith for their modern-day descendants, twentieth-century Anabaptists are a house divided. Unhappily, schisms have frequently separated brother from brother. One such cleavage was the sixteenth-century division in Holland between the Waterlanders and the followers of Menno Simons. Another was the seventeenth-century separation between the followers of Jacob Ammann, who came to be known as Amish, and the Mennonites of Switzerland and Alsace. The former was a liberal separation of members who opposed the strict use of the ban, and the latter was a conservative withdrawal by some ministers who insisted on reinstating the practice of "shunning" wayward members.[4]

Other schisms occurred in the nineteenth century notably in the United States and Canada and also among the Mennonites in Russia before many of them migrated to North America. Additional varieties of Mennonites arose in South America, Africa, and Asia as a result of the establishment of mission churches in the past eighty years. The

Mennonite Yearbook for 1973 shows a total of 547,692 members of all Mennonite bodies in forty-two countries, just over half of whom live in the United States and Canada.[5] If children and youth who have not yet joined church were added, the total adherents would probably number between eight and nine hundred thousand.

The focus of this research report is on the members of five of these bodies — four Mennonite denominations and the Brethren in Christ Church, whose roots dip into both Anabaptist and Pietist traditions. The background of these five groups is summarized in Chapter 2. Although all five groups have mission churches on other continents, it was not feasible to expand the scope of the study beyond the borders of the United States and Canada. Table 1-1 is a

TABLE 1-1
Baptized Members of Church Bodies, 1972

Churches	United States	Canada	Total	Percent of Total
PARTICIPATING CHURCHES:				
Brethren in Christ Church	9,145	1,454	10,599	
Evangelical Mennonite Church	3,136	—	3,136	
General Conference Mennonite Church	36,314	20,553	56,867	
Mennonite Brethren Church	14,767	17,982	32,749	
Mennonite Church	89,505	8,984	98,489	
SUBTOTAL	152,867	48,973	201,840	70.5%
OTHER BODIES:				
Beachy Amish Mennonite Church	3,688	320	4,008	
Bethesda Mennonite Colony Conf.	35	100	135	
Church of God in Christ, Mennonite	6,543	2,183	8,726	
Chortitz Mennonites	—	1,800	1,800	
Evangelical Mennonite Brethren Conf.	1,821	1,645	3,466	
Evangelical Mennonite Conf.	—	4,000	4,000	
Evangelical Mennonite Mission Conf.	—	1,850	1,850	
Hutterian Brethren	6,322	14,100	20,422	
Old Colony Mennonites	—	3,193	3,193	
Old Order Amish Mennonite Church	22,375	650	23,025	
Old Order and Wisler Mennonite Church	6,100	2,100	8,200	
Reformed Mennonite Church	553	193	746	
Reinland Mennonites	—	800	800	
Sommerfelder Mennonites	—	4,000	4,000	
SUBTOTAL	47,437	36,934	84,371	29.5%
GRAND TOTAL	200,304	85,907	286,211	100.0%

listing of all church bodies with the number of baptized members in the United States and Canada in 1972.[6] The five bodies who agreed to participate in this study represent about 70 percent of the total membership of Anabaptist groups in the United States and Canada. They account for about 37 percent of the worldwide membership of all Mennonite-related bodies. The three largest North American bodies are included.

The Essence of Anabaptism

What were the essential ingredients of the faith of the sixteenth-century Anabaptists? To what extent do twentieth-century Anabaptists still evidence these ingredients? It is one of the objectives of this survey to answer this second question. The first question can be answered from the considerable body of literature now extant, and an important summary of Anabaptist doctrines will be reviewed in Chapter 6. The Mennonite Central Committee, the relief and service agency in which all five denominations in the study cooperate, adopted the following statement in 1942 concerning "Our Heritage of Faith":

> We are grateful for the noble heritage of faith from our Mennonite and Brethren in Christ forefathers which we most heartily accept and cherish, holding:
> 1. That the whole of life must be brought under the lordship of Christ and that obedience to His will in all things is the ultimate test of discipleship.
> 2. That a way of life is taught by Christ and the Scriptures which is God's plan for the individual and for the race, and that those who espouse discipleship of Christ are bound to live in this way, thus manifesting in their personal life and social relationships the love and holiness of God. We believe that this way of life means the fullest exercise of love, scriptural nonresistance to evil, and complete avoidance of the use of violence, including warfare. We believe further that the Christian life will of necessity express itself in nonconformity to the world in life and character.
> 3. That the Christian Church consists only of believers who have repented from their sins, have accepted Christ by faith, are born again, are baptized on confession of faith, and sincerely endeavor by the grace of God to live the Christ life of holiness and love.

4. That the Church is a brotherhood in which all bear one another's burdens, and in which each considers himself a steward unto God of his life and possessions, and consecrates all that he has to the kingdom of God.

5. That the Church, the Bride of Christ, has a high and holy calling, not only ministering to its own membership, but testifying to the will of God to the world at large.

6. That it is the duty and privilege of all believers to witness for Christ and His Gospel to all men everywhere, to teach all things commanded by Him, and in His name and Spirit to minister to the needs of all men both spiritually and materially.

7. That while, in this world, true believers will suffer tribulation, yet God is faithful to His own and will give the crown of life to all who are faithful unto death, and that accordingly we should always abound in the work of the Lord, forasmuch as we know that our labor is not in vain in the Lord.[7]

In matters of personal piety and daily activities, the Anabaptists endeavored to lead exemplary lives. It may be too much to assume that all adherents achieved such high standards, but the evidence of piety was so strong that it won favorable comment even from their most hostile opponents. In his 1582 publication entitled *Against the Terrible Errors of the Anabaptists* the Roman Catholic theologian, Franz Agricola wrote:

> Among the existing heretical sects there is none which in appearance leads a more modest or pious life than the Anabaptists. As concerns their outward public life they are irreproachable. No lying, deception, swearing, strife, harsh language, no intemperate eating and drinking, no outward personal display, is found among them, but humility, patience, uprightness, neatness, honesty, temperance, straightforwardness in such measures that one would suppose that they had the Holy Spirit of God.[8]

Such reports concerning the sixteenth-century Anabaptists set high standards for twentieth-century Anabaptists to emulate. Would the piety of the twentieth-century descendants be acceptable to their sixteenth-century brethren? Has the passage of time and the absence of persecution eroded the rigors of the Anabaptist ethic so that the tension between church and the world no longer exists? Or has the western world come to accept Anabaptist doctrines (e.g., separation of church and state, freedom of worship, and nonresistance) to such an extent that Anabaptism does not appear in the twentieth century to be a heresy?

Objectives in Studying Church Members

The backgrounds of the church populations on which this report focuses have been well told in a number of denominational histories referred to in the next chapter. Without these painstaking scholarly efforts in reporting the events, the issues, and the emergence of new organizations in past centuries, any attempt to analyze and interpret the faith and life of contemporary church members would be greatly handicapped. The present can only be understood in reference to the past. The sociologist, who observes and analyzes contemporary life, builds on the work of the historian.

There are two general goals in the present study — one *descriptive* and the other *analytical.* The first goal is to describe the members of the five denominations by noting their characteristics on a series of variables or factors which represent the membership. What is the nature of their faith? How is their faith expressed in terms of personal piety and participation in the life of the congregation? Where do they stand on church doctrine and issues that were vital to sixteenth-century Anabaptists? What opinions or attitudes do they hold on contemporary social and political issues? Are their population characteristics similar to, or different from, typical Americans and Canadians? Where do they stand on questions of stewardship and use of resources? On cooperation with other denominations in ecumenical activities? On matters of personal morality? How strongly do they value their denominational identity?

This first goal is to present a profile of people and conditions at a particular point of time. In part, the study provides a portrait of the five groups as a whole. At other points the data offer interesting profiles of the separate groups, making it possible to compare them with each other and with other denominations.

The second goal of the study is to *analyze* the church members by examining the *relationships* between the descriptive variables. What relation does urbanization have to adherence to Anabaptist beliefs and other measures of faith and life? Is there a "generation gap" between the attitudes of young and old? How are church members' attitudes and behavior affected by their education, income levels, or conversion experiences? An examination of the degree to which these variables are interrelated provides tests of a number of theories and hypotheses about religious populations.

Much of the analysis of church members centers around the religion variables: denominational membership, orthodoxy of faith, adherence to Anabaptist doctrines, extent of church participation, devotional practices, attitudes on moral issues, and others. An intriguing part of the analysis is the attempt to discover how religion is affected by other variables, and in turn, how religion affects other variables. For example, a person's faith may be viewed as a *dependent* variable, that is, it depends on, results from, or is influenced by other factors, such as one's family background, one's age, one's educational achievement, or one's marital status. This approach is related to the "social causation" theory of religion. [9]

On the other hand, religion can be viewed as an *independent* variable. This stresses "religion as an autonomous factor," a different theory in the study of religion. [10] It focuses on religious factors as antecedent to various beliefs and behavior. For example, one's faith is seen as affecting or influencing his church attendance, his views on moral issues, his pacifism, or his prejudice toward minorities. This theory is most compatible with a transcendental view of life in which God is seen as the actor and determiner of one's life and walk.

Because both views have validity, some variables will be tested as "antecedent" to religion; others as "consequent." Actually it will not be possible to keep these two approaches neatly separated. In many cases the relationship of a religious variable and some other variable may be interactive, with each variable affecting the other to some degree. For example, a person's religion may affect his decision about getting a higher education, while his higher education (once received) may affect his religious faith. These two modes of interaction between religion and other variables are developed particularly in Part IV, but appear also in Parts II and III.

Theories for Studying Churches

The writings of Ernst Troeltsch and Max Weber have been particularly useful as a theoretical base for the study of churches. [11]

These European scholars developed a "church-sect typology" for comparing religious faiths. The "church type" was the large state-supported denominations — Catholic, Anglican, Lutheran, Reformed. These faiths tended to bring state and church together. The state provided (through its function as tax collector) the financial resources for the church's ministries. The church often utilized the police power of the state to achieve its ends, especially to curb or eliminate the dissidents who did not accept the church's leadership and its canonical laws.

The "sect type" was exemplified by the small, dissident, break-away groups or "free churches" which sprang up in pre- and post-Reformation periods, and the Anabaptists provided a conspicuous example. Sectarian faith tends to be critical of secular society and of the large churches which seem too ready to tolerate the lack of spiritual discipline and commitment in their church members. Sectarian groups have been persecuted by many civil governments with whom the larger denominations were often in league. Thus the sects tend to draw sharp contrasts between church and "world." They do not see their mission primarily as trying to patch up the spiritual and moral condition of the secular society (which responsibility the church type tends to take). Rather they seek to call, through conversion and sanctification, as many individuals as possible out of the world and into the sectarian church which is composed of the redeemed, the "true believers."

Building on the church-sect theory, Niebuhr advanced the thesis that the sects (such as the Anabaptists, Quakers, Levellers, Diggers, and Wesleyans) were movements of the socially and economically deprived.[12] The function of religion for these disinherited was either to give them an acceptable substitute for economic security (if the meek did not inherit the earth, at least they would be first in the kingdom of heaven), or to give them a motivation for dissent or revolt. In either case, the typical result was the eventual accumulation of wealth through hard work and group discipline and the return of the sect to prosperity and mainstream church-type faith.

If Niebuhr's thesis is true, then we would expect the more economically prosperous Mennonites to have less sectarian views. Also, as modern-day Anabaptists rise in the socioeconomic scale, we would expect to find a weakening of commitment to radical Anabaptist faith and practice.

A further elaboration of Niebuhr's theories concerning social and economic factors affecting religion relates to transmitting the faith to succeeding generations:

> Rarely does a second generation hold the convictions it has inherited with the fervor equal to that of its fathers, who fashioned these convictions in the heat of conflict and at the risk of martyrdom. As generation succeeds generation, the isolation of the community from the world becomes more difficult. Furthermore, wealth frequently increases when the sect subjects itself to the discipline of asceticism in work and expenditure; with the increase of wealth the possibilities for culture also become more numerous and involvement in the economic life of the nation as a whole can less easily be limited. *Compromise begins and the ethics of the sect approach the churchly type of morals.*[13]

Anabaptism has now survived at least twelve generations of adherents. How can this be explained? Two somewhat opposing theories, introduced in the previous section of this chapter, provide a basis for exploring this question. According to the social causation theory, supported by Niebuhr, the radical sixteenth-century movement could survive only by compromising with the hard realities of a practical world. One would expect twentieth-century Anabaptism to reflect the social and economic forces that have borne down upon it. If any vitality remains, it must be due to some successful resistance to these forces which lessens their effects.

The other theory (of the "autonomy of religion" type) emphasizes the role which religious commitment plays in the determination of the life of a people. While Mennonites have indeed become acculturated and have assimilated many of the values of the larger culture, they have *not* returned to the "churchly type" of morals and ethics. As long as they continue to challenge the social order by refusing to bear arms, swear oaths, pay war taxes, and discriminate against other minorities, their self-identity as a twentieth-century Anabaptist family of churches will be ideologically as well as historically continuous with their sixteenth-century forebears.[14]

The survey data permit a number of tests of both of these theories. An "Anabaptism Scale" was constructed to measure the church member's degree of adherence to sixteenth-century Anabaptist principles. The respondent's degree of acceptance of Anabaptism can then be correlated with his scores on a number of other scales which measure aspects of his social background and his religious faith and practices. Anabaptism can thus be treated both as an independent and as a dependent variable in relation to the other variables. As a result, two themes provide a thread of thought running throughout the book. These themes can be focused in the form of two hypotheses:

1. A church member's adherence to Anabaptism depends at least in part upon certain social and religious background factors. These may include his age, his parents' denominational affiliation, his educational achievement, his degree of urbanization, and his socioeconomic status. We expect stronger adherence to Anabaptism to be associated with older age, lower educational achievement, rural residence, lower socioeconomic status, and Mennonite parentage.

2. Anabaptism, as an antecedent variable, has a strong positive effect on other beliefs and behavior. This will be demonstrated if high scores on the Anabaptism Scale are found to be correlated with high scores (representing biblical norms) on other religious and social variables. This will test the theory that acceptance of Anabaptist teachings is an identifiable factor in the lives of the church members, moving them in the direction of fulfilling the radical witness of their historic heritage of faith.

Data Gathering and Analysis

It seemed that the best way of gathering the needed information was to administer questionnaires to a valid sample of the church members of each denomination. In effect, five samples were chosen and data were obtained for each so that inter-church comparisons could be made. In some parts of the analysis, the five samples were treated as one, with each denomination weighted according to its proper proportion of the total membership of the five bodies.[15]

The participating denominations, through the Church Member Profile Administrative Committee, specified the basic conditions for the sample selection: (1) only members of churches in the United States and Canada should be included; (2) members of all ages should be included, except those under 13 years of age; (3) inactive and nonresident members should be included; (4) persons should not be included if their congregation is not affiliated with a conference body.

Details on selection of the sample, construction of the questionnaire, field procedures, sampling results, and analysis of data are given in the appendix, "How the Study Was Conducted." A total of 3,670 questionnaires were returned, of which 3,591 were usable for the data analysis. The respondents were members of 174 sample congregations; thus the response rate was 20.6 persons per congregation. About two thirds of the respondents appeared at their church on the appointed evening, where, under the direction of a "research visitor," they took from one to three hours to complete the questionnaire. Absentees were given questionnaires later, to be completed at home and returned by mail. Questionnaires were mailed to the home addresses of nonresident members.

The development and analysis of the survey data involved measuring and correlating a large number of variables. Some variables are easily measured, being *quantitative*, such as age, income, or size of family. Others are *qualitative*, their values being non-numerical, such as occupation, church affiliation, or religious orthodoxy. Special problems arise in the measurement of complex variables such as "devotional practice" or "adherence to Anabaptist doctrines." These generally require the use of a "scale" consisting of several questionnaire items, the responses to which can be scored and combined to produce a continuum of numbers ranging from low to high on the scale. Thus the qualitative variable is transformed into a quantitative scale, and the values can be analyzed statistically by machine data processing.

For the purposes of this study over forty scales were constructed to measure qualitative variables. For example, the Anabaptism Scale (introduced in Chapter 6) consists of eight statements with agree-disagree responses. In general, a concept can be more reliably measured if a number of items are combined into a scale than if the measure depended solely on one or two items.

A list of the scales used in this research report appears in the appendix. Each scale will be introduced and explained in the appropriate succeeding chapter. The scales fall generally into the following categories: (1) scales measuring the respondents' beliefs and Bible knowledge, (2) measures of the respondents' degree of participation in the life and work of the church, (3) measures of the respondents' personal piety, (4) scales indicating the respondents' attitudes on a range of moral and ethical issues, and (5) measures of support of church institutional and extension programs.

A basic objective of the study is to find new clues for answering the questions of what can be done to strengthen and deepen the faith of church members and to strengthen the influence of the church on their lives. Research can be helpful by filling some of the knowledge gaps. But it is not an end in itself. Hopefully the reader will join heartily in the task of answering the question, What does all this mean for the person in the pew, the preacher in the pulpit, and the administrator behind a desk at church headquarters?

Chapter 2

HISTORICAL PROFILES OF THE DENOMINATIONS

Although the five denominations are similar in a great many ways, their differences are sufficient to give each a somewhat unique character. It is the purpose of this chapter to trace the historic origins and developments of each group and to categorize in a phrase each group's most distinctive identity in relation to the other groups. Spokesmen within several of these denominations would claim "missions" as their most distinctive focus. However, that is a distinction shared by all five groups, as can easily be shown by some indicator like per capita giving for missions, and sets them quite apart from mainstream churches in North America. In fact, on eight measures of faithfulness to be summarized in Chapter 19, the five groups are all strongly committed in comparison to non-Mennonite denominations. Such evidence is substantial support for the claim of a fundamental unity in this church-family.

The intent of the present chapter is to try to categorize each group vis-a-vis the other four. The catch-phrase used may not satisfy all members, nor will it necessarily characterize every group at all periods of their history. Nevertheless, there is a considerable amount of documentary evidence to support the validity of the characterizations which follow.

Admittedly, identifying a church by a simple word or phrase

runs the risk of oversimplification. However, for the sake of clarification and interpretation, sociologists frequently are compelled to derive meaningful categories. In deriving a useful category, one needs to avoid a stereotype. A proper category is faithful to reality, whereas a stereotype distorts reality.

The Mennonite Church:
Guardian of the Tradition of the Fathers

Often called the "Old Mennonite Church" in distinction to a number of new Mennonite groups that emerged from it, the Mennonite Church (henceforth, "MC") is the oldest and largest Mennonite denomination in North America. The special identity of the MC has been what Robert Friedmann called "the guardian proper of the tradition of the fathers."[1] The words "proper" and "tradition" present a bit of a problem inasmuch as the other groups also think of themselves as "proper" and the MC has also mixed other traditions with the historic Anabaptist faith-tradition. Nevertheless, H. S. Bender clearly revealed the distinctive self-identity of the MC when he wrote, quoting the Apostle Paul, " 'Prove all things; hold fast that which is good'. . . . We must deliberately and consciously hold our own, not indiscriminately but intelligently, and we must have the necessary resources and means to do this."[2] Bender criticized the "doctrinal importations" into other Mennonite groups such as "baptism by immersion, open communion, second work of grace, entire sanctification, eternal security, premillennialism, dispensationalism," and went on to claim that "none of the above-mentioned imported doctrines are to be found in any historic Mennonite confession of faith, and they never were a part of original Anabaptist-Mennonite theology or practice."[3] He called the MC the "bosom of the old church . . . a living church with great traditions from the past and a great future, the largest single body of Mennonites in America, or even in the world."[4]

Significantly the MC is the only denomination among the five whose name does not include an adjective qualifying the word "Mennonite." It is simply "Mennonite Church," which carries the message that this group is more concerned about being "Mennonite" than about being "General" (ecumenical) or "Evangelical" (missionary) or "Brethren" (fraternal). J. C. Wenger wrote that the members of the MC "have a strong historical consciousness. They are keenly aware that their spiritual forefathers suffered and died for the faith and fled from one land to another in search of religious liberty."[5]

Similarly Grant Stoltzfus characterized the MC as "a people apart, a group that steadfastly resisted the religious currents of North American social history."[6] This self-image is reflected in the group's adoption in 1725 of the Dordrecht Confession of Faith, first written by Dutch Mennonites in 1632 as a basis for consolidation. The content of this Confession will be reviewed in Chapter 6. It is relevant here to note only that it reinforced this group's deep desire to hold fast to the faith of the fathers, "lest in the vast New World under a strange government they may not be free to worship and build their life."[7]

The early Mennonite settlements in colonial Pennsylvania — Franconia and Lancaster — are now two out of nineteen district conferences of the MC. The later westward movement was thoroughly rural, motivated not just by the availability of cheap land but by the earnest belief that the rural Mennonite community was the best basis for the perpetuation of the nonresistant style of life. The westward movement also gave rise to sectionalism, an important clue to an understanding of the character of the MC today. This refers to the unofficial separation of the MC into the older more conservative districts east of the Alleghenies and the younger more progressive districts of the West. Today each section has its own college, seminary, and certain other denominational agencies.

The sectional factor in the development of the MC self-identity centered in the question of how to stand guardian over the tradition of the fathers without becoming static in the work of the church. The way tradition had become authoritative for regulating the lifestyle of members was made vivid in Wenger's history of the Franconia Conference. From records covering about 1830 to 1930, he gleaned over fifty rulings of the bishops, nine of which are the following:

    1. Conference reaffirms an earlier resolution that the sisters shall wear caps (devotional coverings based on 1 Corinthians 11) in the meeting.
    2. The brethren shall be admonished against wearing beards (since the world has them); exceptions: beards worn for humility (if the life and walk correspond) or health . . . in the case of eczema. . . .

3. Brethren shall keep away from taverns for they are for travelers and business people and not for the folks of the community. . . .

4. It is not appropriate for the sisters to wear gold, etc.; and church members shall stay away from surprise parties.

5. The members shall not dress their children so "stylishly."

6. Brethren and sisters shall not attend either the World's Fair at Chicago or the Centennial in Philadelphia. Conference reaffirms its earlier rulings against attending fairs, mass-meetings, political celebrations, etc. . . .

7. All the Conference members except one voted against a General Conference. . . .

8. The organ must be taken from the (Worcester) meetinghouse or no communion will be administered there. . . .

9. Regular prayer meetings are not approved by this Conference.[8]

The pressure brought by the outside influences mentioned in these excerpts caused two types of schism. One stemmed from the persistent concern for guarding the tradition. Often when tradition appeared to be threatened, some members withdrew in order better to resist unwanted change. The other kind of schism stemmed from the opposite desire for more progressive programs. The major schism of this type was later absorbed by the denomination to be sketched next. All together, the MC suffered twenty-five or more schisms in its history.[9] A number of these schisms were concerned with the "plain dress question." A particular garb was one of the ways whereby the MC applied its doctrine of separation from the world.[10] In his enforcement of plain dress, Bishop Daniel Kauffman appealed to "our Anabaptist forefathers"and to the Bible. "If we as a church wish to remain a plain church, the only course open to us is that of adhering strictly to the teachings of God's Word and discipline the Church accordingly. Compromise now means surrender later on."[11]

When those words were written about thirty-five years ago, few members of the MC foresaw how the very concern for the faith of the fathers would prompt changes which would make the old agenda seem like an anachronism. In the spring of 1973 several issues of the *Gospel Herald* presented the agenda for the group's General Assembly in August of that year, using modern methods of group dynamics to rethink the historic norms of their faith, evaluate current programs in the light of those norms, and mobilize the talents of all members to fulfill the historic mission of the MC. In spite of such innovations, however, the distinctive MC commitment remains intact, and the chief aim continues to be the "recovery of the Anabaptist vision." As H. S. Bender wrote,

> The church has in general maintained a strong position in regard to nonconformiy to the world, holding that the full Christian life will of necessity express itself in nonconformity to the world in life and conduct. Its ideals include simplicity in life and costume, rejecting attendance at the theater including motion pictures, the wearing of jewelry, the swearing of oaths, lodge membership, divorce, smoking and drinking, participation in politics and office-holding, membership in labor unions, participation in war or carnal strife of any kind, and advocating simplicity in worship without the use of musical instruments. There is universal observance of the ordinance of footwashing, the prayer veil for women, and close communion. In the application of this principle of nonconformity and simplicity the church in general has maintained a conservative position, with real church discipline, seeking to avoid the evils of legalism and formalism on the one hand and worldliness on the other. . . .[12]

This list of MC characteristics was made on the evidence of the situation in 1956. After nearly two decades some of these principles of nonconformity are no longer universally practiced. The extent to which the members currently adhere to some of these principles will be reported in later chapters.

The General Conference Mennonite Church: Progress Through Mennonite Cooperation

The second largest denomination in the study was actually the first to be organized as a "General Conference" of Mennonites (1860). It is precisely this "first" that gives the General Conference Mennonite Church (henceforth, "GCMC") its most indelible character: progress through Mennonite cooperation.

There are two basic ideas in this description — the idea of progress and the idea of cooperation. The GCMC has always been known as the progressive Mennonite Church. One of its sources of membership was an 1847 schism in the Franconia Conference of MC led by John H. Oberholtzer and sixteen ministers and deacons. Their innovations included democratic processes in church government, more openness to the other denominations, Sunday schools, mission work, the publication of Christian literature, and the formal training of ministers. The "East Pennsylvania Conference of Mennonites" which they formed later became one of six regional conferences of the GCMC.

The formation of the GCMC actually took place, however, in what is now the Central District Conference — the consolidation of three small settlements of progressive Mennonites in Ontario, Ohio, and Iowa. Each of these groups were made up of recent immigrants who had some of the same names and European origins as their Pennsylvania brethren but who "had experienced the spiritual and intellectual freedom which had arisen in Europe after the French Revolution of 1789. They were beginning to be citizens of this world while still being pilgrims on their way to the world beyond."[13]

The other idea strongly associated with the GCMC is its emphasis on unification. The goals that prompted the 1860 plan for a "General Conference of the Mennonite Church of North America" were to unite all Mennonites, to share resources for spiritual renewal, and to cooperate as a general church with a larger mission to the world. Although the aim to unite North American Mennonites was far from realized, a considerable number of congregations affiliated with the GCMC through the decades. This was especially true of nineteenth-century Swiss immigrants in Ohio and Indiana and a larger proportion of some 18,000 Mennonites from Russia who settled in the prairie states and provinces after 1873 and whose descendants now constitute about two thirds of the GCMC membership. Mention should also be made of a number of progressive ministers and congregations of the MC who joined the GCMC because they were excommunicated or could not tolerate the traditional MC emphasis.[14]

The image of the GCMC as progressive and ecumenist partly derives from the charge that they tolerate all manner of deviant behavior and accommodate themselves to worldly styles of living. Certainly, less emphasis on the GCMC was placed on uniformity of behavior than on inter-Mennonite cooperation. The GCMC motto was "unity in essentials, liberty in non-essentials, and love in all things." Heinz Janzen wrote that " 'General' is an apt name for this varied mixture of people and traditions, trying to be faithful to Jesus Christ, listening to many voices for new truth. But this variety has often given the impression that our group doesn't stand for anything."[15] Some Mennonite scholars explain the development of GCMC as the consequence of "liberalizing" and "secularizing" forces at work.[16] These interpretations typically place the MC on one end of a church-world continuum, the GCMC on the liberal end, and other Mennonite groups somewhere between. The data of the present study will provide a test of this old theory.

No doubt its progressive attitudes made the GCMC vulnerable to doctrines of "modernism" and social evolution. The philosophy of progress was one of the intellectual wells from which its leaders drank. Its first historian (1898) began his two-volume work with the sentence, "Mankind is slowly but steadily advancing toward the full reception of those doctrines of our Lord Jesus Christ which apply to practical life."[17] The GCMC joined the Federal Council of Churches in 1908 because many of its leaders felt that the Mennonite teaching on peace and nonresistance would soon be accepted by other member churches.

Some of this optimism was shattered during World War I, when the GCMC affiliation with the ecumenical movement led to a disillusioning experience in peace witness. Most of the denominations in the Federal Council were militant promoters of the war effort, quite intolerant of German-speaking Mennonites not only because their pacifist faith was "wrong" but also because their language was "wrong!" Out of the hurt of betrayal, the GCMC withdrew from the ecumenical organization and henceforth channeled its efforts into a more distinctly Mennonite pattern of faith and life.

One result of this new realism was a more explicit recommitment to historic Anabaptist norms, expressed not in a comprehensive confession of faith but in a series of position statements, beginning with one on war and peace (1941). "We establish no new doctrine among us," it declared, "but merely reiterate an age-long faith in the church which has been held previously by our forefathers from the time that the church was founded in Reformation times in Switzerland (1525) and in Holland (1533). . . ."[18] Following the adoption of this statement, the proportion of the conscripted members of the GCMC refusing military service increased from 25 percent to 63 percent.[19]

The other result of its withdrawal from the wider ecumenical movement was a further strengthening of its historic mandate for inter-Mennonite cooperation. The way this mandate had been stamped into the character of its members is illustrated by a meeting of the Inter-Mennonite I-W Coordinating Board in the early 1960s. This board was established to serve the needs of war objectors from various Mennonite groups doing their mandatory service in the same locality. In Indianapolis twelve couples from the GCMC attended the MC congregation. They were invited to participate fully as "non-members," serve on committees, and take part in the communion and foot washing services. When the wives were asked to wear the devotional head covering and to leave their jewelry at home, some tensions arose. The matter came to the attention of the Coordinating Board, where it was interpreted in light of the distinctive attitudes which GCMC members bring to inter-Mennonite programs:

> The GCMC feel they need to interpret the I-W program on the basis of the kind of church they are. This is largely a polity question, and there are underlying differences that we should acknowledge to each other.
> 1. The GCMC was established as a movement towards Mennonite unity. This great ideal underlies the subconscious thinking of their youth. This is thought of as a group memory and they constantly think and talk out of the background of their conscious efforts toward Mennonite unity. They express the deep concern to do everything together that can be done together, and they feel further that the idea of pulling apart should not be accentuated.
> 2. The GCMC has a permissive attitude to expose their youth to other faiths on almost any occasion. They are anxious to have their youth to see how other people do things.
> 3. The image of the GCMC is that of a wide, welcoming brotherhood. They do not feel that this is the one Mennonite Church, which has the answer to everything. . . . They admit that they have less prescribed church life patterns than some other Mennonite groups.
> 4. The GCMC would offer to their people the privilege of wider accommodation to non-Mennonite cultural patterns. They admit that their dress "is less Mennonite oriented than it is Yankee oriented." They have accepted more of the cultural patterns of the age in which we are living.[20]

On the whole these minutes may be taken as a fair statement of the distinctive character of the GCMC viewed historically — its readiness to accommodate to the cultural patterns of society where issues of Christian ethics are not felt to be at stake and its sense of urgency to work together with other Mennonites as much as possible. Add to this its mid-twentieth-century reaffirmation of Anabaptist principles of peace and nonresistance, and the result is a number of interesting hypotheses to be tested by the church member data.

The Mennonite Brethren Church: Return to Menno and the Bible

The third denomination is the only one of the five that was organized prior to emigration from Europe. The Mennonite Brethren Church (henceforth, "MBC") is even more oriented to its past than the MC or GCMC and especially to the events of its secession from other Mennonites in Russia in order to "return to Menno" and to "the simple, powerful Christianity of the Bible."[21]

The crisis represented by the MBC schism was an inevitable consequence of the conditions under which the Mennonites settled on the Russian steppes. Here, for the first time, they had responsibility not only for the establishment of a church of believers, as in the days of their Anabaptist forefathers, but also for the establishment of law and order in their own isolated communities, which included saints and sinners with the same Low German names. Moral lapse and the failure to share the economic resources of the land created a climate conducive to renewal movements which could not or would not continue to abide in the old compromised Mennonite Church of Russia, called disparagingly the *Kirchliche* (ecclesiastics). One group, the Kleine Gemeinde (loosely translated "minority church") withdrew in 1812 in protest to the way coercion was used to punish deviant members. The MBC was founded in protest to specific types of moral decadence — drinking, dancing, card playing — and to the general lack of emphasis on personal conversion which the seceders had come to experience through the evangelistic preaching of a gifted pastor in a neighboring settlement of German Lutheran Pietists and through small group meetings of "brethren."

In 1859 a cell of Mennonite "brethren" asked the Kirchliche bishop to give them communion separately because they could not partake of the Lord's Supper with dissolute members. When their request was denied, they went to a home for private communion. The re-action in the colony was hostile. Several "brethren" were excommu-nicated and the others were forbidden to hold any more private com-munion services, an order they could not obey. The Document of Secession which they addressed to "the elders of the Molotschna Mennonite Church" lamented the "open godless living" of church members, reported their separation from "this fallen church," sum-marized their articles of belief, and declared their intention to return to Menno and the Bible. These founding events, wrote Elmer and Phyllis Martens, stamped a distinctive identity into the "soul" of the MBC

> to recapture the faith *"wie es im Anfang war"* — "as it was in the beginning." . . . Return to the early Anabaptist vision, they said, and beyond that to the New Testament church, because this is what the early Anabaptist vision was — a return to the simple, powerful Christianity of the Bible. *"Was sagt das Wort?"* — "What does the Word say?" they asked.[22]

Franklin Littell categorized this stance as "primitivism" or "res-titutionism." Indeed, the MBC development was similar to the con-ditions that precipitated the sixteenth-century Anabaptist dissent to which Littell's concept was first applied.[23] Primitivism is the pattern of thought and action in Christian history in which there is an alleged "fall of the church," the rise of a new company of believers who vow to return to the Bible, a series of clashes with established authorities, and a climax in which the group secedes. Rudy Wiebe put it succinctly:

> The Mennonite Brethren movement of 1860 is not a reforma-tion move; it is a revolt. The brethren have despaired of re-forming the church from within; they write themselves out of it even before they are banned; they consciously separate as a wit-ness, a witness to their rediscovery of originally seen clarities now lost in Russia under an eighty-year murk of fat special privilege living.[24]

This emphasis on restitution of primitive Christianity led to several related characteristics. One was their biblicism. This is reflected in the process by which they adopted "backwards immersion" as their form of baptism. The question arose soon after secession, and they searched the Scriptures. They found references indicating that those who were being baptized went "into the water" and came "out of the water."[25] This suggested that baptism should be done in a body of water. They found other passages comparing baptism to being buried and risen with Christ.[26] To be buried suggested to be covered or submerged *backwards* since this was the way bodies were laid out for burial. This way of appealing to Scriptures, wrote A. E. Janzen, has always characterized the MBC. "The conviction has prevailed that for spiritual light, guidance, nurture, and growth, we must of necessity constantly go directly to the inspired Word of God which no other book can equal."[27]

Another emphasis was on the experience of conversion as normative for church membership in contrast to entry by catechetical process in the Kirchliche. "What they desired," wrote Frank C. Peters, "was a 'pure Mennonitism' that was based 'not upon birth but rebirth.' "[28] This experience was defined as a crisis happening rather than a gradual process, and involved conviction of sin, repentance, restitution, and regeneration.

The MBC thrived in Russia until the Communist Revolution, which ended most of their meetings. In spite of severe hardships since World War I, the MBC has never completely lost its identity in Russia. Members worshiped with the Russian Baptists, who received official status, or gathered informally as opportunity presented. One MBC congregation in Soviet Central Asia now numbering 850 members, was officially registered in 1967.[29]

The migration to America began in 1874 when governmental restrictions on Mennonites were first experienced. Unlike the Kleine Gemeinde, who left as a total community, less than half of the MBC emigrated, departing as family units or individuals. So thoroughly had they internalized the distinctive MBC doctrines, however, that they began to form into MBC congregations soon after arrival in the prairie states and provinces. In Steinbach, Manitoba, for instance, they worshiped for a time with an existing Mennonite congregation of another conference (Evangelical Mennonite Brethren). This congregation had some hope that the two groups could unite, and even received permission from their own conference to baptize by immersion for the sake of wooing the new immigrants. The MBs, however, had always assumed that in due course they would withdraw to form their own congregation. This happened on a Sunday in 1927 when

"38 brethren and 7 sisters" met for organization:

> Bro. H. K. Siemens made the opening using for Scripture
> Phil. 2:1-5. . . . Bro. G. H. Unruh was elected chairman and
> Bro. P. J. Martens secretary. Bro. G. H. Unruh explained the
> reason for this meeting, namely, that there were 65 members
> of the M.B. Church in and near Steinbach, and [wondered]
> whether the time had not come to gather these members into a
> local church in order better *to build us up into the most holy
> faith.*[30]

This tendency to withdraw from other Mennonite groups is
characteristic of MBs throughout North America. Pastor William Neufeld of Winnipeg wrote that "a strange fear grips the MBs when the
question of alignment with other Mennonites comes up. We seem to
be afraid of being swallowed up or dominated by other Mennonite
groups, thereby losing our doctrinal identity. Once we walked out
of the Mennonite Church; we do not want to return."[31]

Elmer and Phyllis Martens believe that the MBC stands midway
between the MC and GCMC in its corporate style of faith and life.[32]
As the present study progresses, this hypothesis will be tested by a
number of indicators and the evidence will be summarized in Chapter
19.

The Brethren in Christ Church:
Synthesis of Anabaptism and Pietism

Four church movements cast their shadows across the development of the Brethren in Christ Church (henceforth, "BIC"): the
United Brethren, the Pennsylvania Mennonites, the German Baptists, and the Wesleyans. The distinctiveness of the BIC results from
their synthesis of the Anabaptist vision of the believers' church (via
the Mennonites and German Baptists) with the Pietistic emphasis
on the personal crisis conversion and sanctification experiences (via
the United Brethren and Wesleyans).[33]

The first component of this synthesis was the revival movement in Lancaster County in the 1770s, led by Martin Boehm, co-
founder of the United Brethren in Christ Church (now part of the
United Methodist Church). Boehm was a bishop in the Lancaster

Conference of MC before his expulsion for excessive involvement in ecumenical evangelism. As a leader in the revival meetings connected with the names of Whitefield and Otterbein, he gathered groups of converts at several points — Pequea, Conestoga, and Donegal on the Susquehanna River. The Donegal group became the BIC, first known as "River Brethren" because of their location.

The second element in the BIC synthesis was the Mennonite influence. A number of the Susquehanna brethren had Mennonite background, including Jacob Engle, the group's first bishop. One of its early names was "River Mennonites,"[34] and one tradition asserts that the BIC began as a Boehm-administered Mennonite congregation.[35] This tradition cannot be verified, and it is more likely that the River Brethren were a mixture of backgrounds inasmuch as Lutherans, Reformed, and German Baptists all attended Boehm's meetings. Nevertheless, Mennonite influence was felt in the decisive rejection of Boehm's leadership following the disciplinary action of the Lancaster Conference of MC. Boehm's view of the church was too eclectic from an Anabaptist point of view, with too little emphasis on believers' baptism; and the dissent of the River Brethren indicates a commitment to restitution of the visible church of believers.

A third influence was that of the German Baptists, also called Dunkards and known today chiefly as the Church of the Brethren. This group traces its beginning in 1708 to Schwarzenau, Germany, where eight members of the Reformed Church seceded to form a "true" church of believers. Like the BIC themselves, their sources of influence were the German Pietists and Swiss Anabaptists with whom they made contact. Like the Mennonites, this group also lost some of their old world zeal on the Pennsylvania frontier and were ready for revival. How many Dunkards transferred to the River Brethren is unknown, but Wittlinger believes the Dunkard influence is more apparent than the Mennonite influence. "For example, they [River Brethren] stressed the wearing of the beard, selected church officials by election rather than by lot, held love feasts in connection with communion services, conducted deacon visitations of congregational memberships, and practiced trine immersion baptism. All of these were characteristically German Baptist; none was characteristically Mennonite."[36]

The fourth element in the eclectic faith of the BIC was their acceptance from the Wesleyan movement in the post-Civil War period of the doctrines of holiness and perfectionism. These doctrines stem from Wesley's teaching of "entire sanctification" as a crisis experience subsequent to the conversion experience. "The main teaching of the holiness movement was that the believer could be, and should be, delivered from his sinful nature which caused him, even after conversion, to want to sin. This deliverance was available through a crisis experience — the second definite work of grace."[37] These doctrines caused much controversy in the BIC until they were officially accepted nearly fifty years later when the denomination joined the National Holiness Association.

The BIC synthesis has been a long struggle which Robert Baker compared to a wagon pulled by an unmatched team of horses. For two hundred years "they have been 'geeing' and 'hawing' to keep it in the 'middle of the road.' "[38] Martin Schrag showed in detail how during the nineteenth century the synthesis was "overbalanced in the direction of the concept of the church and its [separatist] relationship to the world."[39] The evangelistic emphasis waned and nonconformity to the world was strictly enforced. The following extracts from early BIC Conference minutes remind one of the Franconia Conference of MC:

> Is it right for members to marry such as are not members of the church? Decided: Only by consent of the church, as decided by by Council of 1843 in Lancaster County, Pennsylvania.
> Is it allowed to receive members into the church who have been baptized by backward immersion without rebaptizing them? Decided: As at former council not allowed.
> Are brethren permitted to foreclose mortgages and sell property by sheriff's sale? Decided: No.
> Is it allowed for members to serve as jurors? Decided: No.
> Is it scriptural to have any given form of dress? Decided: Nothing more than that it should not be in fashion with the world.
> Is it allowable for sisters to go without their heads covered? Decided: It is not consistent.[40]

In the last third of the nineteenth century, the BIC softened their practice of nonconformity by adopting a number of features from evangelical Protestantism — the Sunday school, Christian journalism, mission work, and church schools. With these shifts, the BIC became vulnerable to other influences of American society; and Schrag observed that "the dominant church concept of the nineteenth century, with its emphasis on obedience and a sharp sense of separation from the world, was to a large degree replaced by an individualistic understanding of the faith concerned primarily with personal salvation, personal ethics, and personal evangelism."[41]

Although the BIC joined the National Association of Evangelicals in 1948, they continued to struggle with their mandate for synthesis as an Anabaptist group "in the world" but not "of the world." In 1940 they joined the Mennonite Central Committee and more recently the Mennonite World Conference, and they are cooperating with Mennonites in other ways including the production of a new Anabaptist-oriented Sunday school curriculum. Thus, the historic tension between the influence of their Mennonite connections and the Pietist emphasis of American evangelical Protestantism continues in this group. This means not only that "they decided to keep the best of each," as Norman Bert writes, but also to avoid the worst — the undisciplined individualism of mainline evangelical Protestantism and the unyielding communalism of the Mennonites. As John Zercher put it, "Obedience can become legalism and service to others a frustrating exercise unless we are motivated by the Spirit of Christ and the power of the Spirit. I should not try to outguess the Brethren in Christ historians but I strongly believe that the infusion of Wesleyanism saved us from the legalism of groups closely related to us."[42]

Zercher probably had the Mennonites and BIC historian Martin Schrag in mind. Schrag believes that since 1920 the group has been losing its battle in an over-identification with American culture at the cost of a radical Anabaptist nonconformity. The present study will not measure changes in the BIC between two points in time, but it will certainly reveal much about how this group is presently coping with the church-world dilemma.

The Evangelical Mennonite Church: Search for Self-Identity in the American Environment

The fifth denomination, the Evangelical Mennonite Church (henceforth, "EMC") is the group that has undergone the most adaptation to the American environment and has produced the fewest identity guidelines for coping with rapid change. Its roots were in the

Old Order Amish Church; but after one generation following the Egly schism, during which it clung to cultural traditions more conservative than its roots, it borrowed church-work methods from the Sunday school movement, the revivalist movement, the holiness movement, and the fundamentalist movement. Its ethic was thoroughly nonresistant, as indicated by its first official name — Defenseless Mennonite Church; but today barely one-fifth of its members hold to a pacifist position. Its membership was once entirely Swiss-German Amish stock; but today more than half of its members have come from non-Mennonite backgrounds.

The most distinctive mark of the EMC is its long search for denominational identity in the face of such overwhelming transition. The rest of this sketch will simply document this characterization with a few selected details, first with reference to the group's transformation in the American environment, and second with reference to its quest for denominational alignment.

Like the MBC and BIC, the EMC was a renewal movement in a church that had gotten mired in tradition. Henry Egly was a young Amish farmer in central Indiana in the 1860s when the "lot" fell on him and he was ordained to the office of preacher. By his own testimony, only after he later became bishop did he experience true conversion. It happened in a time of illness through an experience of divine healing after prayer. Straightaway he preached the "new birth" as normative for all members of his church and henceforth a condition for baptism and communion. In fact,

> he rebaptized those, and those only, who had not had this experience before they were baptized, in order to make sure that their baptism could be the answer of a good conscience towards God. . . . His charges against the church were that it was too formal, that applications for membership, especially among the younger element, were received with insufficient preliminary instruction, that the members were lacking in spiritual life and that they *were not strict enough in maintaining the old customs, especially with regard to dress.*[43]

Unlike the other denominations in the present study, the EMC was founded by one man who was paradoxically both an innovator and a traditionalist regarding the old customs. Although it is difficult to sort out the sociological from the personal factors in the schism, it is clear historically that he wanted to renew the old church rather than start a new one. However, he was excommunicated and forced out. About half of the members of that Amish community followed him into the new "Egly Amish" congregation.

His secession sparked a rash of withdrawals in Amish communities in Indiana, Ohio, and Illinois;[44] and in 1883 the first general conference of "Egly Amish" was convened to define their beliefs and polity. The positions taken at that first conference were stricter on beards, the woman's prayer covering, and nonconformity than were those of the Old Order Amish from whom they had separated.

By 1895, however, when the EMC began to meet in annual conference, a significantly more liberal attitude emerged. Within the next decade the new denomination initiated home and foreign missions, Sunday schools, a church periodical, a hospital, a mutual insurance program, a children's orphanage, and a home for the aged. The rapid pace of change posed a threat to the group's self-identity that is felt to this day. In a recent "Statement of Identification," the group's executive officer wrote, "The rigid conservatism of the denomination's early years gradually moderated as the group accommodated itself to the customary standards of dress, accepted the introduction of Sunday schools, dropped the holy kiss among the laity, all but abandoned foot washing, and admitted instrumental music into its worship service."[45] In the 1902 annual conference, the EMC still disapproved the formation of a mutual insurance program, preferring to rely on the traditional custom of direct aid at times of personal disaster. Fourteen years later, the EMC organized the Brotherhood Mutual Insurance Company, which became one of the largest insurance corporations in the Midwest.

In its efforts to find its identity in the face of such rapid assimilation of American socio-religious culture, the group made two assumptions about denominational location. One was that its identity must retain some continuity with its past. Some of the leaders cannot quite forget their Anabaptist roots or discard the Mennonite name. They are mindful of past connections with other Mennonite groups — the Central Conference of Mennonites (with whom they cooperated in operating a hospital, a home for the aged, and a significant foreign mission in what is now the Republic of Zaire in Africa), the All-Mennonite Conventions from 1913 to 1930, Mennonite Central Committee, and Mennonite World Conference.

The other assumption is that sooner or later the EMC will merge with some other denomination to enlarge its base of operation. It is the only one of the five groups with a separate article in its Constitution affirming the principle of denominational merger.[46] Moreover, it has made this affirmation for over three fourths of a century, but a satisfactory merger has never been realized. It has courted many potential brides over this span of time — the Central Conference of Mennonites, the GCMC, the MBC, the Mennonite Brethren in Christ, the Defenseless Mennonite Brethren, and the Missionary Church Association. In 1953, it became engaged to the Evangelical Mennonite Brethren, but this affair broke up after ten years of dating. In 1969 an EMC Commission was appointed to try to bring this process of mate selection to a more lasting resolution. At present the most likely possibility for merger is either with the Evangelical Free Church of America or the MBC.

This historical survey of the EMC reveals a long, rather chronic strain between a distinctly Anabaptist-Mennonite identity and a non-Mennonite conservative evangelical identity. According to Reuben Short, the recognized "theological leader" of the group, the main issue in the struggle is whether the EMC will sacrifice its historic affirmation of nonresistance and pacifism for its historic emphasis on evangelism.[47] The EMC Constitution reaffirms nonresistance, but for the sake of "peace" within its own ranks, it permits "the right of individual conviction" and recognizes "that various positions will be taken on war and military service."[48] Meanwhile, it continues to hear annual reports from its representative to the Mennonite Central Committee Peace Section.

The data of the present study will throw new light on the apparent contradiction between the two historic norms of evangelism and pacifism, on the question of whether this tension is universally troublesome to all twentieth-century Anabaptists, and on the threat to survival of sectarian groups like these caused by rapid social change in the North American environment.

Five Denominations or One?

Lest the historical profiles give the impression that the five denominations are irreversibly divided, one more image of increasing cooperation between them must be sketched. Some of the very experiences that led to disunity also spawned new attitudes and programs promoting unity. Its concern for guarding the tradition of the fathers eventually gave the MC a keen interest in working together with other Mennonite groups. The 1847 schism in the Franconia Conference led to the founding of the GCMC with the primary goal of reuniting all Mennonites of North America. Although the MBC has found inter-Mennonite relations difficult, it has definitely moved in the direction of increased cooperation in certain areas. The separation of the brethren on the river (BIC) from the movement that developed into the United Brethren in Christ Church was not for the sake of schism but for the sake of a larger synthesis between Anabaptism and Evangelicalism. The practical requirements of denominational order were so disconcerting to the Egly Amish (EMC) that they turned immediately to work closely with the Stucky Amish (now part of GCMC) in mission and service projects.

Two inter-Mennonite agencies were especially significant in the increasing rapprochment of these groups. One was the Mennonite Central Committee (henceforth, "MCC"), founded in 1920 to become the joint relief and service agency of nearly all North American Mennonites plus the Brethren in Christ Church. The MC, GCMC, and MBC were charter members, with the EMC joining in 1930 and the BIC in 1940.

The other organization fostering a common Anabaptist identity was the Mennonite World Conference (henceforth, "MWC"). Nine world conventions have been held to date since 1925: Basel, 1925; Danzig, 1930; Amsterdam, 1936; Goshen (Indiana) and Newton (Kansas), 1948; Basel and Zurich, 1952; Karlsruhe, 1957; Kitchener (Ontario), 1962; Amsterdam, 1967; Curitiba, Brazil, 1972. The first three were primarily historical in the content of the addresses, commemorating the 400th anniversary of the origin of Anabaptism in Zurich in 1525 and the 400th anniversary of the conversion of Menno Simons in 1536. Since then, the MWC has grown into large-scale conventions with over 12,000 in attendance at Kitchener, representing twenty-seven countries in which Mennonite and BIC churches are established. Conventions feature addresses and discussions on doctrinal and practical subjects of concern to the common identity and mission of these groups.

Five decades of closer relationships in the MCC and MWC have opened the door to numerous other joint activities. The most recent tabulation lists six categories and over fifty joint projects, including the Church Member Profile reported in this book.[49] In view of this multiplication of joint efforts, it is not facetious to ask whether we are studying five denominations or one. The best answer probably recognizes both their unity and disunity. This dual character of the people in this study will be reflected in the way the information gathered from church members will be represented in the following chapters. The data will be presented in separate columns, one for each group; but the five samples of members will also be combined and properly weighted so that we can treat these members as truly representative "twentieth-century Anabaptists." Behind this method lies the assumption that the five denominations are really one, in distinction from other denominational families of churches in North America.

Various labels could be used to distinguish this particular family of churches — "historic peace church," "believers' church," "free church," "sect-type church," and so on. The most meaningful label for the present study is "Anabaptist." All other labels seem less appropriate than "Anabaptist." For example, "free church" includes the Roman Catholics in America, "believers' church" includes any group with a creed, "peace church" includes the Quakers, and "Mennonite" excludes the Brethren in Christ. The "Anabaptist" label designates the common identity of the five participating groups by pointing to a common historical source for denominational self-identity.

Although these five denominations may not look like sixteenth-century Anabaptists in many ways, there is an undeniable continuity through four centuries of history. Moreover, this continuity is a fascinating subject of study for anyone concerned with the problem of transmitting the faith from one generation to another down to the present. Whatever detours any later generation may take on the historical time line, the norms of the forefathers remain a criterion by which they can chart their own destiny as church members in the twentieth century.

Chapter 3

CHARACTERISTICS OF THE CHURCH MEMBERS

This chapter provides some basic information about the 200,000 Americans and Canadians who belong to the five denominations. An interesting profile of the church members was obtained by analyzing their demographic characteristics (sex, age, residence, occupation, marital status) and comparing them with the national populations of the United States and Canada.

Where Do the Members Live?

About one fourth of the members of the five denominations live in Canada, three fourths in the United States. Table 3-1 shows some major variations between the denominations. Whereas over half (54.9%) of the members of the Mennonite Brethren Church live in Canada, all of the members of the Evangelical Mennonite Church are located in the United States. More than one third of General Conference Mennonites live in Canada.

Substantial numbers of the Mennonite Brethren and General Conference Mennonite churches migrated from Europe to Canada in the 1920s and 1940s. Altogether 202 (5.6%) of the sample members were born in Europe, mostly in Russia, while another 32 (0.9%)

TABLE 3-1
Membership Distribution for the Five
Denominations by Country

	United States		Canada		Total	
	Number	Percent	Number	Percent	Number	Percent
Mennonite Church	89,505	90.9	8,984	9.1	98,489	100.0
Gen. Conf. Mennonite	36,314	63.9	20,553	36.1	56,867	100.0
Mennonite Brethren	14,767	45.1	17,982	54.9	32,749	100.0
Brethren in Christ	9,550	86.7	1,466	13.3	11,016	100.0
Evangelical Mennonite	3,136	100.0	—	—	3,136	100.0
Total	153,272	75.8	48,985	24.2	202,257	100.0

TABLE 3-2
Distribution of Sample Members by Country
and by Denomination*

	United States		Canada		Total	
	Number	Percent	Number	Percent	Number	Percent
Mennonite Church	1,074	89.4	128	10.6	1,202	100.0
Gen. Conf. Mennonite	445	72.5	169	27.5	614	100.0
Mennonite Brethren	348	48.9	364	51.1	712	100.0
Brethren in Christ	567	91.6	52	8.4	619	100.0
Evangelical Mennonite	444	100.0	—	—	444	100.0
Total	2,878	80.1	713	19.9	3,591	100.0

*In the case of nonresident members, classification by countries is for location of congregation where membership is held, rather than for present residence of the member.

were born on other continents.

Table 3-2 shows how the 3,591 sample members are distributed by denomination and by country, according to the location of the congregation in which the church member holds his membership.

At the time of the survey, not all members were living in the country where they hold membership. The table indicates that 713 (19.9%) of the sample members hold membership in Canadian churches, 80.1% in American churches.

An additional 4.3% of the sample should be Canadian if the Canadian proportion (19.9%) were to conform to the Canadian proportion of total denominational membership (24.2 %). This under-representation of Canadians in the sample results primarily from the fact that a dozen Canadian Mennonite Brethren and General Conference Mennonite congregations declined to participate in the survey. The chief reason given was that a large number of their members were German-speaking, unable to complete a questionnaire in English.

Each respondent was asked to report his place of birth (state, province, or foreign country) as well as his present residence. Although 19.5% of the sample were residing in Canada, only 14.3% were born there. Thus about one fourth of Canadian church members were born in foreign countries (other than the United States and Canada). The data indicate that most of these were born in Europe.

Due to migration, Mennonites are increasing numerically more rapidly in some regions than others. In the United States, five percent of the sample respondents were born in the Far West (mountain and Pacific Coast states), but 11% are currently living in that region. The net migration into western states is balanced by a net migration out of midwestern states. Apparently there is no significant net migration into or out of the eastern states, since the proportion born in the East and the proportion currently living there are almost identical (33.2% versus 33.8%). In Canada there appears to be no net migration between eastern provinces (Ont.) and the western provinces. The two major population movements of Mennonites therefore are (1) from Europe to Canada, and (2) from midwestern states to mountain and Pacific states.

The five denominations differ notably in the regions they occupy. Whereas the Mennonite Church and the Brethren in Christ have heavy concentrations of membership in the eastern states and in Ontario, the General Conference Mennonites and Mennonite Brethren are to be found mostly in the midwestern and far western states, and in the western provinces. The Evangelical Mennonite group is limited almost entirely to four states: Ohio, Indiana, Michigan, and Illinois.

Migration between the United States and Canada appears to be small, but favoring the United States. Of the 2,591 respondents who were born in the United States, only 12 (less than one half of one percent) are now living in Canada. However, nearly five percent of those born in Canada (26 out of 554) now live in the United States. Apparently Mennonites are more likely to migrate from Canada to the United States than vice versa.

Rural, But Less So

If someone had studied the Mennonite and Brethren in Christ populations at the beginning of the twentieth century, he would have found almost all of them living in rural areas and primarily on farms. Although a majority still live in rural areas, only a third live on farms. Only 27% of employed males in the sample reported farming as their chief occupation.

Compared to the American and Canadian national populations, twentieth-century Anabaptists are still a rural people. According to the 1970 census, Americans are 73.5% urban (live in cities over 2,500 population) and 26.5% rural; Canadians are 72.4% urban and 27.6% rural.[1] The Mennonite and Brethren in Christ populations, however, as estimated from the sample, are only 35% urban and 65% rural.

In the United States, farm people make up only about five percent of the total population, but the survey shows 33.6% of our church members living on farms. Nearly a third (31.4%) live in towns of fewer than 2,500 population or in the open country but not on farms. It is clear that, as Mennonites have left the farms, they have been slow to shift to cities, preferring to establish their homes in small communities. Of the 35% now in cities, 16% live in places of less than 25,000 while the remaining 19% live in cities larger than 25,000 (nine percent in cities over 250,000).

Conservative rural values clearly persist in Mennonite and Brethren in Christ circles. Even those now residing in cities are in significant numbers only "first generation" urbanites, having lived their early formative years in rural areas. Will the new generations now being born and reared in the city be a different breed? As will be reported later, rural and urban church members were not found to be greatly different. Is this because the urban influence through mass media and advertising has made semi-urbanites out of rural people, or is it that the migrants to cities have not yet "washed the rural mud off their urban boots"? Or is it that, as some sociologists think, the technical advances of modern transportation and mass communication have fused the American and Canadian rural and urban populations into one undifferentiated mass? These questions will be examined in Chapter 18.

The urban proportion varies substantially by denomination. The percentage living in cities, in order of increasing urbanity, is as follows:

Mennonite Church	26
Brethren in Christ	30
Evangelical Mennonite	39
General Conference Mennonite	40
Mennonite Brethren	56

Clearly the Mennonite Brethren Church is the most urbanized and the Mennonite Church least.

Sex and Age

Of the 3,591 fully cooperating respondents, 45.6% were male and 54.4% female. A total of 129 males were arbitrarily added to the sample by virtue of their role as congregational pastor, their names not happening to be selected by the random selection process by which all other sample members were obtained. (See further explanation in the appendix.) Deducting these 129 pastors, the sample proportions became 43.6% male and 56.4% female. These proportions can be compared with the results of recent national studies of Lutherans and American Baptists.[2] Among Lutherans, 42% were male, and among Baptists, 37%. Apparently the Mennonite and Brethren in Christ populations contain a somewhat more even balance between the sexes than is found in the memberships of these two larger denominations.

Some additional data are needed to find the *true* male and female proportions in churches. This can best be estimated by taking into account the nonrespondents as well as the respondents. The process of selecting the original sample yielded a total of 5,141 members (exclusive of the 129 pastors added later), of which 3,405 responded and 1,721 did not. A tally of the 5,141 names by sex, yields 46.4% male and 53.6% female. These figures can be taken as a good estimate of the male and female proportions in the total membership of the five denominations.[3]

It is interesting to note variations among the five denominations. The percentages male and female, based on the original sample list, are as follows:

	Percent Male	*Percent Female*
Mennonite Brethren Church	48.5	51.5
General Conference Mennonite	47.8	52.2
Mennonite Church	47.7	52.3
Brethren in Christ Church	45.4	54.6
Evangelical Mennonite Church	44.7	55.3

Apparently the BIC and EMC churches have a slightly greater sex imbalance than the other groups.

The "sex ratio," defined as the number of males per 100 females, is commonly used as a measure of sexual balance in a population. The population of the United States in 1970 had a sex ratio of 91.4 males per 100 females for all persons 15 years of age and over; in Canada in 1971 the ratio was 98.4. The church member ratio is 86.5 (based on the original sample list, excluding the arbitrarily added pastors, and with denominational weights applied). Thus the shortage of males is significantly greater in the church population than in the national population. As will be noted in Chapter 10, this imbalance has implications for mate selection. The shortage of males is probably due to three factors: (1) more males than females leaving the Mennonite churches, (2) more males than females bringing spouses into the churches from other backgrounds, and (3) the higher death rate of males (normally occurring in populations), leaving more females than males, particularly at the older ages.

Figure 3-1 is a portrayal of the sex and age distribution of the sample members in the form of an age-sex pyramid. Normally an age-sex pyramid for a population includes the children, but these, of course, do not appear among Mennonite church members. Females exceeded males in all categories except the 35-49 and 55-59 age brackets, where the excess of males is probably due to the 129 pastors

Figure 3-1: Age-Sex Pyramid for the Sample Members

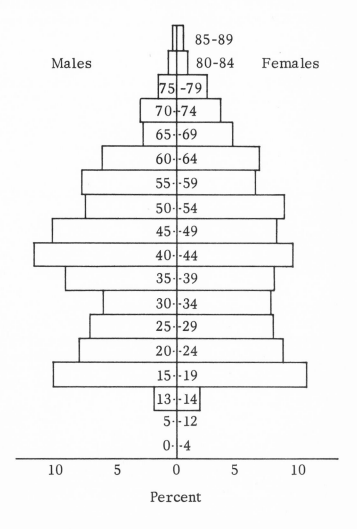

Males   Females

85-89
80-84
75-79
70-74
65-69
60-64
55-59
50-54
45-49
40-44
35-39
30-34
25-29
20-24
15-19
13-14
5-12
0-4

10   5   0   5   10

Percent

added to the respondents. As in the case of national populations, the church member profile reflects the lower birth rates of the Depression years and the years of World War II. That is, there is a shortage of persons aged 25-39 years. The shortage of members aged 20-29 is probably due in part to a somewhat lower response rate at this age level, and partly a result of membership losses, which usually occur in this age range.[4]

The five denominations varied somewhat in the average age of members. EMC members averaged youngest, with a median age of 38.4 years. At the other extreme were the GCMC members with a median age of 45.5. The others were: MC, 39.3; BIC, 40.4; and MBC, 42.4. (The weighted average for all churches was 41.9.) The higher averages for the GCM and MB churches reflect the higher average age at baptism in those two denominations (reported in Chapter 4) as compared to the other three.

Variations in the youthfulness of the church members are evident in the percent of the members under 20 years of age. Teenage members ranged from 7.3% of the GCMC members to 15.9% for the Mennonite Church. Senior members (aged 65 and over) accounted for proportions ranging from 9.1% of the MC and EMC groups to 14.1% of the GCMC.

Educational Attainment

One of the most important and influential social changes that has occurred among twentieth-century Anabaptists is the increase in educational attainment. Among church members 50 years of age and over, 43% did not go to school beyond the eighth grade, compared to only three percent of members aged 20-29. College attendance rates also show striking differences between these two groups: 23% of the older group, but 57% of the younger group, attended college for one or more years.

The distribution of sample members by denomination and by educational achievement is given in Table 3-3. The median number of school years completed for all members is 12.2, ranging from a high of 12.6 in the GCMC to a low of 12.0 in the MC.

Mennonite and BIC educational attainment compares favorably with other populations. The United States census reports that the median number of school years completed by all persons 25 years of

TABLE 3-3
Percentage Distribution of Church Members
by Educational Attainment and by Denomination

Educational Attainment	Percentage distribution for:					
	MC	GCMC	MBC	BIC	EMC	Total
Less than 8 grades	7.5	6.6	9.9	6.5	3.9	7.4
Eight Grades but not more	20.8	12.6	13.8	13.7	10.6	16.7
Some high school	20.8	16.9	25.2	21.8	16.3	20.4
Completed high school but not more	24.9	24.6	15.4	27.4	33.0	23.5
Some College	11.8	16.2	13.4	12.7	14.4	13.4
College graduate but not beyond	4.9	6.1	6.2	6.0	9.6	5.6
Some graduate work but not a degree	3.3	4.8	4.8	2.6	3.4	3.9
Graduate degree	6.0	12.3	11.4	9.3	8.7	9.0
Total	100.0	100.1	100.1	100.0	99.9	100.0
Number of Respondents	1,193	610	710	614	436	3563
Median number of school yrs. compl.	12.0	12.6	12.1	12.3	12.1	12.2

age and older was 12.1 in 1970. This compares with 12.2 years for the sample church members (25 years and older in 1972). Apparently the average educational level of Mennonites and Brethren in Christ is similar to the population of the United States as a whole. On the matter of college attendance, however, the church members appear to be ahead, since 20.7% have completed four or more years of college. Only 11.3% of the United States white population had (in 1970) completed four or more years of college.

Level of education appears to be affected by residence, although not strongly. Somewhat higher educational achievement is associated with increasing urbanity, for the church members as well as the entire population of the United States. A comparison of the median number of school years completed for the white population of the United States and the church members, for persons 25 years and older, is as follows:

	United States	*Church Members*
Urban	12.2	12.7
Rural nonfarm	11.6	12.2
Rural farm	11.0	11.8

Within residence categories, the church members have slightly higher educational attainment than do Americans as a whole.

Occupation and Employment

A look at the occupational distribution of Anabaptists of the twentieth century shows that they are shifting away from farm life. When Mennonites leave the farm, they tend to go into business and professional occupations.

Each respondent was asked to indicate his or her present *chief* occupation. If the respondent was retired or otherwise not employed, he was asked to indicate his *former* occupation.

TABLE 3-4
Percentage Distribution of
Church Members by Sex and Occupation

Occupational Class	Male N=1589	Female N=1858	Total N=3447
Professional and Technical Workers	23.0	9.9	15.9
Business Owners and Managers	7.4	1.1	4.9
Sales and Clerical Workers	5.1	8.2	6.8
Craftsmen and Foremen	10.6	0.0	4.9
Machine Operators	7.7	2.2	4.8
Laborers (farm and nonfarm)	4.8	0.5	2.5
Farm Owners and Managers	23.4	0.2	10.9
Service Workers	2.3	3.6	3.0
Housewives	0.0	60.3	32.5
Students	13.7	13.9	13.8
Total	100.0	99.9	100.0

*In this and later chapters, the letter "N" refers to the number of respondents in that category and therefore the base upon which the percentages were computed.

Among gainfully employed males, 27% have farming as their main occupation. An additional unknown number are part-time farmers while holding down a full-time job elsewhere.

The occupational distribution of the male and female respondents, arranged according to United States census categories, is given in Table 3-4. The data indicate that Mennonite and Brethren in Christ males tend to move most heavily into professional positions (23.0%); business ownership and management accounts for nearly 10%, and skilled craftsmen another 10%. Only small proportions become common laborers and service workers (the latter including such occupations as barber, policeman, fireman, cook, and restaurant waiter).

TABLE 3-5
Percentage Distribution of Employed Church Members
and Employed United States White Persons,
1970, by Sex and Occupation

Occupational Class	Male		Female	
	Church N=1370	U.S.	Church N=479	U.S.
Professional and Technical	26.7	13.5	38.4	14.8
Business Owners and Managers	10.9	10.6	4.2	3.5
Sales and Clerical Workers	5.9	14.0	31.7	39.8
Craftsmen and Foremen	12.3	19.7	0.0	1.7
Farm Owners and Managers	27.0	2.7	1.0	0.2
Service Workers	2.6	7.7	13.8	18.8
Machine Operators	9.0	18.2	8.8	13.2
Laborers (farm and nonfarm)	5.6	7.7	2.1	1.4
Occupation not reported	—	5.9	—	6.8
Total	100.0	100.0	100.0	100.0

Source of United States data: 1970 *Census of Population: General Social and Economic Characteristics, United States Summary,* June 1972, p. 375.

The occupational distribution of the church members differs considerably from the distribution for the population of the United States. Data for the United States population are available for employed persons 14 years of age and over, approximately the same age group as the church members, but with housewives and students not included since they are not gainfully employed. The data, given in Table 3-5, indicate that church members as compared to the United States population are in substantially greater proportions in professional occupations and in farming. They are much less found in nonfarm "blue collar" occupations and in the sales and clerical fields.

Income

Compared to national populations, present-day Anabaptists are relatively prosperous. Table 3-6 indicates the income distribution for

TABLE 3-6
Percentage Distribution of Church Members
by Denomination and Household Income

Income Class	MC N=973	GCMC N=531	MBC N=598	BIC N=523	EMC N=352	Weighted Total N=2977
Below $3,000	6.4	7.9	8.7	4.8	5.4	7.1
$3,000 – 5,999	12.7	17.3	16.1	13.0	9.9	14.7
6,000 – 8,999	21.2	27.9	23.9	27.0	16.8	23.9
9,000 –11,999	22.2	19.2	21.2	23.1	21.9	21.2
12,000 –14,999	15.2	12.4	14.4	14.1	23.0	14.3
15,000 –19,999	12.0	9.4	8.9	9.6	11.9	10.6
20,000 –24,999	4.8	2.3	3.0	5.0	7.4	3.8
25,000 –49,999	3.9	2.8	3.3	3.3	2.6	3.4
50,000+	1.5	0.8	0.5	0.2	1.1	1.0
Total	99.9	100.0	100.0	100.1	100.0	100.0
Median Income	$10,311	8,667	9,184	9,675	11,452	9,608

the five churches. Nine income categories were provided in the questionnaire, and the respondent was asked to "Check the figures that come closest to the combined 1971 net income (before income taxes) of all members of your household living at home." Thus the responses indicate the incomes both of families and of individuals living alone. A total of 614 respondents either did not know how much income the family had, or refused to indicate it. Among the former are many teenagers who were unaware of their parents' income.

Some variation in income levels is observed among the five churches, with the EMC having the highest median income ($11,452) and the GCMC having the lowest ($8,667). The overall median of $9,608 compares with $8,583 reported for the 1971 median income for all households in the United States.[5]

Church member and national households differ even more if comparisons are made within rural and urban categories. The median income for the church member households is substantially higher. It is clear that the financial well-being of twentieth-century Anabaptists is above the average for the United States and Canadian populations.

Home ownership serves as another measure of economic well-being. Eighty-one percent of the respondents report that their families own the homes they live in. According to the 1970 Census of Housing, 62.9% of the families in the United States own their own homes.[6]

To summarize, one might identify the "average" church member — the person who is "typical" on the variables discussed in this chapter. In this sense the average church member is a married female, white, 42 years of age, born in the American Midwest, and still living there. She has completed a high school education but no more. She is currently a housewife and not employed outside the home. She and her family live in a rural nonfarm setting, and enjoy an annual income of around $10,000. Additional characteristics of Mrs. Average Church Member and her family will unfold in later chapters.

Chapter 4

CHURCH PARTICIPATION

The Anabaptists were committed to an idea about the church that many scholars believe was their most distinctive mark. They believed that the church should be a visible gathering of true believers, that it should be voluntary, and that it should be a community in which the totality of life is shared and regulated for the glory of God and highest good of man. Thus, their concept of church participation had at least these three dimensions which can be labeled *associationalism*, *voluntarism*, and *communalism*.

Associationalism and Its Measurement

The first dimension, associationalism, refers to the tendency of religious persons to gather for corporate acts of worship and religious teaching. Under grave danger of arrest by the state, the Anabaptists met secretly in small groups for Bible study and prayer until an evening in January 1525 when they baptized each other as the sign of breaking with the state church of Zurich. Henceforth, their meetings assumed a new mark of seriousness. Their local gatherings were thought to be vested with all of the attributes of the true church of Jesus Christ.[1] As they wrote into one of their early confessions of faith, they pledged "to meet often, at least four or five times [per week]."[2]

In the course of time the character of their meetings became regularized, but the early emphasis upon frequency and simplicity was remembered for many generations. J. C. Wenger describes a typical Mennonite service in Indiana in 1860:

> If one would have dropped into an Amish Mennonite or Mennonite service of 1860 in Indiana, he would have found a small congregation of worshipers in a plain and simple *meetinghouse*. An aisle in the middle would have separated the men and boys, who sat on one side, from the women and girls, who were seated on the other. The *dress* of all would have been plain and simple, with the older men, especially those who were ordained to the ministry, wearing the plain-collared coat without lapels, and in the case of the Amish their coats and vests would have been fastened with hooks and eyes. . . . Likewise the women would have worn long and full dresses, simple and plain in form. On the head of each baptized woman and maiden would have been seen the "cap," now known as the prayer veiling, which veil was regarded as exhibiting and symbolizing the truth which Paul set forth in 1 Corinthians 11:2-16 on the necessity of women being veiled during the services of the church ("praying and prophesying"). Services were formerly held regularly every two weeks, the intervening Sunday being reserved for quiet rest and for visiting with friends and relatives. . . .
>
> The regular worship services were deeply impressive. After the singing of possibly two German hymns one of the ministers would make the "Opening," a sort of preparatory message to get the audience into a reverent and worshipful mood. This was followed by a silent prayer. The deacon would read a chapter from the German Bible, after which another hymn was sung. Then came the main sermon which was followed by the "Testimonies," which were brief statements by the other ordained brethren as they remained seated, that the message was sound and in harmony with the Word of God. The minister who preached then arose and expressed appreciation for the testimonies and the added thoughts which they contained. He then called the congregation to another kneeling prayer. This time he prayed an audible prayer which always concluded with the Lord's Prayer, the *Unser Vater* as it is called in German. After another hymn the congregation arose for the benediction which one of the ministers pronounced.[3]

In the main this description characterizes the early history of at least three of the denominations in our study — MC, EMC, and BIC. Services were always held weekly in the GCMC, MBC, and BIC. In the MBC instead of unison prayer there would have been a number of "spontaneous" unrehearsed prayers by brethren in their seats.[4] In the BIC the "public meeting" was typically preceded by a "private meeting" on the previous Saturday evening for the purpose of sharing and testimony — another aspect of the BIC synthesis of Pietism and Anabaptism.[5] Other features of the Wenger description (such as separation of the sexes for worship) were true of all five groups.

The expectation of association, of course, is universal in religion. As Milton Yinger writes, "There can be religious aspects of private systems of belief and action. A complete religion, however, is a social phenomenon; it is shared; it takes on many of its most significant aspects only in the interaction of the group."[6] In the following paragraphs this dimension will be tested with respect to several of its component elements.

Public Worship. The main test of associationalism in most church member studies is frequency of attendance at public worship. Using this probe, we discovered that 70% of our respondents attended church once a week or more, another 23% attended almost every week and only three percent attended less than once a month (see the first item in Table 4-1). Groups varied from a low of 58% regular attendance in the GCMC to a high of 80% in the MBC.

An important finding is that church attendance in all five groups is very high compared to American denominations generally. Stark and Glock report an overall Protestant rate of 36% attendance. Congregationalists scored lowest with 15%, and Southern Baptists highest with 59%. The attendance rate of present respondents was more like that of the Roman Catholics in their study, which was 70% weekly attendance.[7] In the Detroit study Lenski reported that only 12% of the Jews attended weekly synagogue or temple services, 70% of the Catholics attended weekly mass, and about one third of the white Protestants and 40% of the black Protestants attended church every Sunday.[8] In the Lutheran study, Strommen and his associates reported a 54% weekly attendance,[9] and Campolo reported a 65% attendance for American Baptists.[10]

According to an annual Gallup Poll, weekly church attendance in

America increased to 49% in 1958, and then began a slow decline to 42% in 1970. The drop in Roman Catholic attendance has been twice that for Protestants.

Catholic attendance declined eleven percentage points since 1958 from 74 to 63%, while Protestant attendance dropped from 43 to 37%. Jewish attendance, placed at 30% in 1958, declined to 22% in

TABLE 4-1
Measures of Associationism

Items and Responses	Percentage distribution for:					
	MC	GCMC	MBC	BIC	EMC	TOTAL
1. "On the average, how often have you attended church worship services (on Sunday morning, evening, and/or other days) during the past two years?"						
Less than once a month	2	6	1	5	1	3
Once or twice a month	4	8	2	3	3	5
Almost every week	23	28	17	16	16	23
Once a week or more	71	58	80	77	79	70
2. "How frequently do you attend Sunday School?"						
Most Sundays	11	12	12	7	9	11
Every Sunday possible	76	54	67	82	82	69
3. "How regularly do you attend any youth or adult meetings held on days other than Sunday, that are related to your local congregation?"						
Never/Seldom	36	45	27	26	28	36
Occasionally	28	26	30	26	24	28
Regularly	36	28	43	48	48	36
4. "Do you presently hold, or have you held within the past three years, a position of leadership in your local congregation?"						
Yes	58	54	56	65	58	57
Composite Associationalism Scale:						
7-8 High	16	15	17	25	23	17
5-6 Upper Middle	26	20	29	26	25	25
3-4 Lower Middle	30	23	28	28	29	28
0-2 Low	28	42	26	21	23	31
Total	100	100	100	100	100	101
Number of Respondents	1,157	575	668	593	432	3,424
Mean Score	4.0	3.3	4.2	4.5	4.4	3.9

1970.[11] The present data do not reveal whether church attendance is increasing or decreasing among twentieth-century Anabaptists, since the measurements pertain to only one point in time. We have no reason to doubt, however, that attendance in our groups is also declining somewhat, even though it is still comparatively high.

Other Measures of Associationalism. Table 4-1 shows, further, that 80% of our members attended Sunday school "every Sunday possible," or at least "most Sundays," and 36% attended weekday meetings of the church regularly.[12] Moreover, well over half of the members of these churches have held official positions of leadership in their local congregation during the past three years.[13]

The only comparable figures come from the American Baptist church member study, which showed a low 28% "fairly regular" Sunday school attendance, and 29% attendance at other church activities.[14] Again it is evident that Mennonites and Brethren in Christ score very high in associationalism.

Associationalism Scale. Combining several measures of a person's associational commitment makes it possible to construct a composite scale for the purpose of gauging the degree as well as kind of commitment. Eleven items in the questionnaire seemed to be related to this dimension of faith. By the process of "item analysis," explained in the appendix, it was discovered that eight of the questions were in fact consistently related to each other and could be combined. Therefore, a member was given one point for his associationalism score for each of the following indicators:

1. Attended church worship services once a week or more.
2. Attended Sunday school every Sunday that it is possible.
3. Attended weekday youth or adult meetings of church regularly.
4. Has held an official position of leadership in the church in the past three years.
5. Reported "strongly interested" in serving home congregation in Sunday school teaching, church project leadership, or "other responsibilities for which you have abilities."
6. Reported current participation in the life and work of the church to be "very important."
7. Identified feeling about attending Sunday school as "I wouldn't want to miss any meeting of our Sunday school class."

8. Has served as Sunday school teacher or department leader regularly for more than one year out of the past ten.

Thus, each respondent received a total associationalism score which could be any number from zero to eight. For some parts of the analysis, these scores were collapsed into four classes: high, upper middle, lower middle, and low. The bottom of Table 4-1 shows the percentage distribution of church members for the scale scores, by denomination. Seventeen percent of all respondents were classed as "high." It should be noted that the scale scores were deliberately collapsed so that a sizable fraction of members fell into each class. Thus, the percentage scoring "high" is arbitrary, resulting from the way the scores were collapsed, rather than from some strict definition of "high." The overall mean (average) score is given in a row near the bottom of the table. The BIC scored highest with a mean of 4.5, and the GCMC scored lowest with 3.3.

In this and succeeding chapters additional scales will be introduced, each measuring some dimension of "faith" and "life." In general, the method just presented for developing the Associationalism Scale will be followed in creating other scales. That is, suitable questionnaire items are combined, the items are tested for validity, a total score is derived for each respondent, and these scores are then collapsed into three or four classes to simplify their presentation in tables. Because of space limitations, the derivation of subsequent scales will be presented only in the briefest manner.

Voluntarism and Its Measurement

The second dimension of church participation is "voluntarism," the degree to which a member's choice in joining a church is free and his commitment to the work of the church is uncoerced. Unlike associationalism, voluntarism is not a universal dimension of religion. In his classical study of ancient Semitic religions, W. Robertson Smith wrote that "a man did not choose his religion or frame it himself; it came to him as part of the general scheme of social obligations and ordinances laid upon him, as a matter of course, by his position in the family and in the nation."[15] Voluntarism, according to Troeltsch, is uniquely the characteristic of the sect-type in contrast to the compulsory membership by infant baptism of the church-type; and the Anabaptists were the best historical example of the sect-type.[16] Luther, Zwingli, and Calvin rediscovered salvation by grace through faith; but they did not reorganize the believers' church so as to exclude the mass of marginal members. Religious groups like the Anabaptists, who emphasized the voluntary covenant of their members, rejected any pattern of church establishment or practice whereby Christian allegiance is "affirmed, imposed, or taken for granted without the individual's consent or request."[17]

In the effort to measure voluntarism, attention was given to the age of baptism, the intentional character of the decision on the part of the candidate for baptism, and his present degree of consent and interest in church participation.

Age of Baptism. It was reasoned, first, that the younger the age of a person at baptism, the less voluntary was his formal reception into the church. Support for this assumption was found in the documents of four of the five denominations. In the MBC and BIC, baptism followed the candidate's conversion testimony before the congregation on the basis of which he was specifically approved as ready for membership. They did not expect conversion to occur until one had attained maturity. Norman Bert describes what this meant in the BIC:

> "Maturity" meant twenty to twenty-five years old. In some conservative parts of the church, young people were not expected to "make a start" until they married.
> The Brethren held to this late age for conversion [not] in order to give their young people a chance to sow their wild oats before joining the church. They expected conversion to happen at a mature age because it demanded a serious, responsible decision.[18]

As time moved on and these groups regularized their vision, the age of baptism shifted downward. An MC family census in 1963 revealed that the median age of baptism for the older generation (50 and over) was 16.5; for the middle generation (30-49) it was 14.5; and for the younger generation (20-29) it was 13.6. Melvin Gingerich, the director of the census, asked, "What does this mean in the context of our historic understanding of the responsible decision demanded of those who accept the Christian life?"[19]

Table 4-2 reports an overall median age of baptism of 14.9 years of age. Females are baptized about half a year earlier than males on the average. The median age of baptism is highest in

TABLE 4-2
Measures of Voluntarism

Items and Responses	Percentage Distribution for:					
	MC	GCMC	MBC	BIC	EMC	TOTAL
1. Median Age of Baptism (Years)	14.0	16.4	16.4	14.1	14.5	14.9
2. "As nearly as you can remember, at the time when you first became a member of the church, why did you join?"						
I yielded to pressure	18	16	9	15	7	16
It was my own decision	82	84	91	85	93	84
3. "All in all, how important is it to you to be a member of a church?"						
Fairly important	24	28	27	25	28	26
Very important	69	64	66	67	65	67
4. "Is your present attendance and participation in the life of the church primarily because you want to participate, because you feel you ought to participate, or because you feel you have to participate."						
I feel I have to participate	4	4	2	5	4	3
I feel I ought to participate	26	27	22	26	24	26
I really want to participate	70	69	76	70	72	71
Composite Voluntarism Scale:						
7-8 High	21	42	46	28	31	31
5-6 Upper Middle	53	39	39	49	52	47
3-4 Lower Middle	20	14	12	18	13	17
0-2 Low	6	5	3	5	4	5
Total	100	100	100	100	100	100
Number of Respondents	1,168	587	687	586	423	3,451
Mean Score	5.3	5.9	6.2	5.6	5.9	5.7

the GCMC and MBC (16.4) and lowest in the MC (14.0). The low age of baptism in the MC has been a source of much concern in that group. In 1959 the MC officially adopted a position on "The Nurture and Evangelism of Children" which tried to adapt the old vision to new concepts of "child evangelism." It was an attempt to clarify "age of accountability" and to defend "early adolescence" as the time persons usually become accountable.[20] Critics of the practice of early baptism remained uneasy. Martha Wagner wrote,

> It is a sad but true fact that not all Mennonite young people who are baptized have been converted. . . . I have spoken to several people who say their baptisms were not meaningful because they had not really repented of their sins nor dedicated their lives to Christ. One girl said, "I joined the church because all of my girl friends did." She was twelve. At the age of twenty she really became converted and expressed the wish that she had waited with baptism until it really meant something to her.[21]

The next chapter presents detailed data on the respondents' experience of conversion. At this point we insert a comparison between the median age of conversion and the median age of baptism by generation for the light it sheds on the question of voluntarism.

	Generation 1 (50 & Over)	Generation 2 (30-49)	Generation 3 (20-29)
Median Age of Conversion	15.2	13.8	12.8
Median Age of Baptism	16.2	14.9	14.2

In no generation does median age of baptism precede median age of conversion. The age of baptism is going down, in confirmation of Gingerich's 1963 findings, but so is the age of conversion. This does not deny Mrs. Wagner's claim that in specific cases baptism does precede conversion, but it does suggest that the Voluntarism Scale needs to take into account more than age of baptism.

Reason for Joining Church. No doubt, to put Mrs. Wagner's comment into a larger perspective, one could find members who were baptized at twelve who feel they joined voluntarily. To enlarge the probe of voluntarism, we asked members whether at the time of joining they yielded to pressures put on them by others, or whether it was their own decision. Table 4-2 shows that 84% of the respondents felt that it was their own decision. In part, the data support Mrs. Wagner's thesis in that the MC, which had the lowest median age of baptism, also had the lowest percentage who felt it was their own decision; and the MBC, which tied for highest age of baptism, had the second highest percentage who thought it was their own decision. The GCMC and EMC, on the other hand, do not fit this pattern.

Voluntarism Scale. Two other indicators were added to the over-all scale, both of which gauged present motivation for membership and participation in the church. The scale of eight points was constructed as follows:

	Points
Age of baptism 15 or over	1
Age of baptism 18 or over	1 extra
Joined church because "It was my own decision to do what I felt I wanted to do"	2
To be a member of a church considered "fairly important"	1
To be a member of a church considered "very important"	1 extra
Present participation in church because "I feel I ought to participate, but don't always enjoy it "	1
Present participation in church because "I really want to be a participant and enjoy it"	1 extra
Maximum possible score	8

The distribution of scores of the Voluntarism Scale as they were arbitrarily collapsed is presented at the bottom of Table 4-2. Out of eight points possible, the average score for all respondents was 5.7. The MC scored lowest with an average of 5.3, and the MBC highest with 6.2.

Communalism and Its Measurement

It will come as no surprise to many persons who grew up in rural Mennonite and Brethren in Christ families to read that another form by which their religious life was expressed was in community. Beyond the associational dimension, which meant gathering for religious services, there was the communal dimension, which embraced almost the totality of their existence. By "community" is meant an organization of families who are mutually dependent on one another for the satisfaction of a major part of their daily needs, including social and economic needs. Members of a community have a large proportion of activities, attitudes, interests, and traditions in common. Their "way of life" constitutes what the sociologist calls a "sub-culture" within the larger society.

Within historic Mennonitism, associationalism and communalism were so closely tied together that the terms "Mennonite church" and "Mennonite community" were practically synonymous. As H. S. Bender put it,

> In the sense in which we Mennonites understand the meaning of the words "Church" and "Christian" we might well substitute "church" for "community. . . ." For have we not historically, and in our highest thought, always held that to be "Christian" means to follow Christ in *all* our ways including what the world calls "secular," and that the "church" is a brotherhood of love in which all the members minister to each other in all their needs both temporal and spiritual?[22]

J. Lawrence Burkholder described three forms of community organization which Mennonites have used in their history. First, the "full community" refers to the "community of goods" of the Hutterites, "the most deliberate attempt by Mennonites to find a final and complete Christian social order." Second, the "closed theocratic community" refers to the situations in Russia and Paraguay "where Mennonites have found themselves in almost complete isolation from the world and have consequently been forced to provide for themselves virtually all the services of the church and the state." Third, the "open community" refers to the partially separated Mennonite agrarian communities of North America, which although assuming a considerable degree of interdependence with the total society, nevertheless maintain enough geographic separation "to give the community sufficient autonomy to qualify as 'religious' community and to embody a 'unique way of life.' "[23] Figure 4-1 depicts a thoroughly planned "closed community" in Russia in 1874. When this community moved as a unit to Kansas, an attempt was made to transplant the same village plan. However, within several years, each family moved onto its own farm, which was the American homesteading practice.

Although the formal aspects of communalism are in process of

Figure 4-1: Village Layout of the Alexanderwohl Mennonite Community in Russia

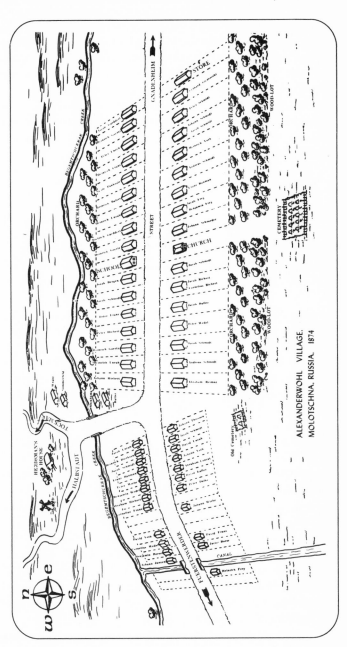

ALEXANDERWOHL VILLAGE.
MOLOTSCHNA, RUSSIA, 1874

dissolution, the more informal aspects of this commitment persist. If "associationalism" is the tendency of religious persons to gather for worship and teaching, "communalism" is the tendency of these same persons to satisfy within the religious group additional needs other than those which are strictly religious in nature. These needs include such things as friendship patterns, mate selection, and economic security. To some degree all religious groups are communal as well as associational. As groups become denominations, however, the relative "strength" of these dimensions shifts. Denominations by definition are formal associations with a minimum of communal characteristics. As religious groups formalize, members often lament the loss of communal bonds that used to give them identity and security. If they fail to grow in numbers, on the other hand, members lament the way communal ties keep outsiders from joining; they cannot "break in."

In his study of churches, Gerhard Lenski attempted to measure a member's communal commitment through a series of questions, the wording of which was varied slightly for Protestants, Jews, and Catholics. The three items that he combined into a communalism index were whether or not one's *spouse*, all or nearly all of one's *relatives*, and all or nearly all of one's *friends*, were *members of the same socio-religious group*.[24] Stark and Glock were also interested in measuring communalism, but only one of their indicators was similar to the Lenski items: "Of the five closest friends, how many are members of your congregation or parish?"[25]

Restricted Friendships. The review of present data will begin with this common item for the sake of making interdenominational comparisons. As Table 4-3 shows, 45% of our respondents reported that three or more of their five closest friends were members of their own local congregation. This compares with 29% for all Protestants and 36% for all Catholics in the Glock-Stark study.[26] In not one of the five groups in our study did the percentage drop that low, which suggests a somewhat stronger communalism than among Protestants or Catholics generally.

Lenski discovered that 38% of the white Protestants in Detroit, 44% of the Catholics, and 96% of the Jews reported that "all or nearly all of their close friends were of the same faith."[27] This, of course, is a different criterion than "same congregation," and the closer comparison in this case is the second item in Table 4-3. It should be noted that 44% of our respondents reported that at least four of their five closest friends were members of the same denom-

TABLE 4-3
Measures of Communalism

Items and Responses	Percentage distribution for:					
	MC	GCMC	MBC	BIC	EMC	TOTAL
1. "How many of your five closest friends are members of your local congregation?"						
Three or more	43	48	52	40	44	45
2. "How many of your five closest friends are members of your denomination?"						
Four or five	48	47	51	35	33	47
3. "Do you and your spouse presently belong to the same church denomination?"						
Yes	94	94	96	89	91	94
4. "Did you and your spouse belong to the same denomination at the time of your wedding?"						
Yes	82	65	75	59	36	73
5. "Do you think it is important that a person marry a member of his own denomination rather than someone from another background?"						
Yes	56	49	55	49	36	53
6. "In your childhood and youth, were your parents members of the church denomination to which you now belong?"						
Yes, both parents	82	77	75	59	43	78
7. "Before you joined a church of your present denomination, were you ever a member of any other denomination?"						
No	89	84	80	73	58	85
8. "How much pleasure or satisfaction do you feel at being known as a Mennonite or Brethren in Christ in the eyes of other people?"						
Very much	13	17	16	19	23	15

Composite Communalism Scale:

	MC	GCMC	MBC	BIC	EMC	TOTAL
6-7 High	8	7	6	5	4	7
4-5 Upper Middle	38	32	36	29	20	35
2-3 Lower Middle	47	51	47	53	47	47
0-1 Low	7	10	11	13	30	9
Total	100	100	100	100	101	100
Number of Respondents	1,145	575	665	582	421	3,388
Mean Score	3.4	3.2	3.2	3.0	2.4	3.3

ination, which is higher than Protestants, similar to Catholics, but not as high as the Jews in the Lenski study.

In-Group Marriage. Although nothing in the historical documents of the five denominations was found that indicated formal restriction of friendships to the primary group, there was considerable evidence of pressure to marry within the group. For two centuries the MC adhered strictly to the Dordrecht Confession which stated that marriage shall be entered into only with those who "have received the same baptism, belong to the same church, are of the same faith and doctrine, and lead the same course of life, with themselves."[28] In the MBC, young people were enjoined to marry "in the Lord," which was usually interpreted as marrying within the Mennonite Brethren fellowship.[29] Although the BIC were somewhat more flexible, the same direction of concern is reflected in the formal action of annual conference in 1874:

> Art. 2. Concerning members marrying out of the church, Conference decided to leave the matter as decided at Conference of 1843, in Lancaster County, Pa. That when a member wishes to marry out of the church, he or she shall make it known to the Brother who is to unite them in marriage. Said Brother is to counsel with two or three brethren, who are to visit the person who is not a member; and if the person is not a despiser of God or of the church, or profligate or light minded, but virtuous, compassionate, a lover of the truth, or repentant, then he may join them in marriage.[30]

These kinds of concerns are recognized by sociologists of religion as universal marks of religious communalism. Lenski asserts that "since endogamy [marriage within one's group] is the background of socio-religious communalism, changes in relevant attitudes or behavior are especially important in assessing trends in communalism."[31] As a gauge of this factor, he collected two pieces of information — one pertaining to whether or not one's spouse presently belongs to the same faith (i.e., Protestant, Catholic, or Jewish faith), the other pertaining to whether or not one thinks it is best to marry within one's faith. He discovered that all of the married Jews in his sample were lifelong Jews married to a lifelong Jewish spouse. Among the Catholics and white Protestants who were married, 84% and 86%, respectively, reported that their spouses were presently of the same faith, but only 68% had been reared in the same faith.[32]

Similar though not identical data were secured for the members in the present study. As Table 4-3 shows, 94% of all our respondents presently belong to the same denomination as their spouses, and 73% did so at the time of marriage. These percentages would be even higher if the wording had been "same faith" rather than "same denomination." The comparative attitudes toward denominational intermarriage present another picture. The question asked in the Detroit study was, "As a general rule, do you think it is wiser for Protestants (or Catholics or Jews) to marry other Protestants (or Catholics or Jews), or not?" Ninety-two percent, 81%, and 75% of Detroit's Jews, Catholics, and Protestants, respectively, think it wiser for members to marry within their own faith.[33] The form of the question in the present study was, "Do you think it is important that a person marry a member of his own denomination rather than someone from another background?" As item 5 in Table 4-3 shows, only 53% of our respondents answered "yes." Seventeen percent indicated "uncertain." One should note that Lenski asked only about intermarriage within the broad categories of faith (Protestant or Catholic or Jewish), rather than one's "own denomination." Had their question been asked, it is likely that most of our respondents would have strong attitudes against mixed marriages with Catholics or Jews. In fact, a declaration adopted by the GCMC in 1962 tried to discourage not only marriage but also courtship with "anyone of a different religious background — for example, Catholic, Jewish, or non-Christian . . . before it is too late."[34] In a prior study of Mennonites of northern Indiana, the writer discovered that 72% of church members thought it best for Mennonites to marry within the Mennonite Church, and another 10% thought it wiser at least to marry Protestants.[35] These figures put Mennonites not as high as Detroit's Jews on this indicator of communalism, but slightly higher than Catholics or Protestants.

Ethnic Solidarity. A third indicator of communal orientation is the transmission of a denominational "way of life" from parents to children. As a rough indicator of such ethnic solidarity, members were asked whether they still shared membership in common with both parents. Overall, 71% of the respondents reported that they still shared membership in common with both parents, and another four

percent with at least one parent. As indicated above, communal indicators like this have a negative as well as positive aspect in the
eyes of in-group critics. On the positive side, 15% of the members
polled had come in from outside — a measure of effectiveness in
evangelism. But this also indicates a high measure of what is called
"birthright membership," a factor that tends to contradict a truly
voluntary membership. Speaking from an MC background, John H.
Yoder writes that Mennonitism has become "a small Christian
body, a Christian corpuscle,"[36] into which most members are born
and into which few converts are won.

> If there has not come into being a "new humanity," made up
> of two kinds of people, some of whom had good strong parents
> and some who did not, of whom some were born under the law
> and some were not, and of whom some have the heritage of
> moral rigidity and some do not, if the marriage of Jews and
> Gentiles is not happening in every generation, then the work
> of Christ as described in Ephesians is not happening.[37]

Yoder's conclusion was that this is not happening in contemporary
Mennonite churches precisely because they are communally oriented.
In a similar vein, Rudy Wiebe writes that "despite the MB stress
on evangelism, mission witness, and church growth, in North America
our church has been no more able to break the ethnic barrier
than any other Mennonite group."[38]

Communalism Scale. With the ambivalences of members concerning intermarriage and ethnicity, a broader set of measures was
needed to gauge the communal dimension of faith. For the construction of a general index, seven items withstood the item analysis
test. The seven achieving the required minimal intercorrelation
were the following, each of which contributed one point to a member's communalism score:

1. Was never a member of any other denomination.
2. Fits in "very well" with the group of people who make up
   his church congregation.
3. At least four out of five of his closest friends are members of
   his denomination.
4. Thinks it is important that a person marry a member of his
   own denomination.
5. Gets "very much" pleasure or satisfaction at being known as

a Mennonite or Brethren in Christ in the eyes of other people.

6. Thinks he will certainly always want to remain a member of his denomination and could never feel right being a member of another denomination.

7. Both parents were members of the denomination to which he now belongs.

Each member was given a score from zero to seven and then placed into a low (0-1), lower middle (2-3), upper middle (4-5), or high (6-7) category. Table 4-3 shows an overall mean score of 3.3 on the scale. The MC scored highest on communalism (3.4), and the EMC scored lowest (2.4). It remains to be seen in later stages of our study whether this communalism scale will prove to be significantly correlated with other dimensions of faith and life and if so, in what direction.

Summary

In this chapter three composite indexes of participation in the corporate life of the church were defined and labeled associationalism, voluntarism, and communalism. On those indicators for which comparative measures were available, Mennonites and Brethren in Christ scored higher in associationalism than Catholics, Jews, and most other Protestants. They also scored higher in communalism than Catholics and other Protestants but not as high as Jews.

Because of the distinct content of each of these concepts, they would appear to be more or less independent (although related) dimensions of religious faith. A positive relationship between associationalism and voluntarism would be expected, but some reason was given to doubt that the relationship between voluntarism and communalism would be similarly positive. In-group spokesmen have criticized the ethic-communal character of these churches on the grounds that members are born into the group and do not join voluntarily. The data of this study, however, do not entirely confirm such suspicions. As the following percentages show, there is a tendency for those scoring high on communalism also to score somewhat higher on associationalism and voluntarism:

Communalism Scale

	Low	Lower Middle	Upper Middle	High
Mean Score on Associationalism	3.3	3.4	4.5	5.1
Mean Score on Voluntarism	5.3	5.2	5.9	6.4

Inasmuch as a positive relationship between all three measures is apparent, the hypothesis of an inverse effect of communalism upon voluntarism can be questioned. This does not mean that John H. Yoder's criticism of twentieth-century Anabaptists for being a "Christian corpuscle" is entirely to be rejected. It means only that Mennonite communalism is not necessarily causing membership to be compulsory rather than voluntary. It is still a membership into which three fourths are born and relatively few outsiders are won. Later chapters will explore the influence of these measures of church participation upon various other attitudes and practices of the members.

Chapter 5

RELIGIOUS EXPERIENCE
AND PRACTICE

Having surveyed the corporate dimensions of church participation, we turn now to several dimensions of faith that are relatively more private and personal. Every variable of faith in this study has both an individual and a collective aspect. The previous chapter pointed out that the formation of the church among Mennonites and Brethren in Christ normally begins with the voluntary choice of the individual to become a member. That more explicitly individual part of the faith response will be examined in greater depth in the present chapter, including especially the dimensions of religious experience and practice.

Religious experience is defined as becoming personally aware of God and experiencing some sense of contact or communication with God. Two types of such experience to be surveyed are conversion and sanctification. Religious practice is defined as performing certain acts or duties as part of one's total faith response with considerable self-initiative although usually with frequent encouragement by the church. Only one type of such practice, devotionalism, will be surveyed here.

Conversion and Its Indicators

In Anabaptist churches conversion has meant a subjective encounter with God accompanied by a more or less personal crisis and resulting in a change of allegiance and behavior. Not only does one forsake the fallen kingdoms of this world and henceforth belong wholly to God and His kingdom, but he also experiences a reorientation of his dominant attitudes and practices from the one realm to the other. The term "conversion" has always implied these deeper behavioral changes but it has frequently been used to refer primarily to the initial crisis episode when the new orientation began. In fact, it was this very conceptual distinction between the *initial experience* of conversion and the *subsequent changes* in behavior that led to the introduction of a second experience called "sanctification" in three of the groups in the study.

In both of these senses conversion was an important part of the faith response in the Anabaptist tradition. The Protestant reformers taught salvation by faith but were unable to develop a practical doctrine of conversion as long as church and state were merged and children of the state were almost automatically baptized into the church at birth. This rite of admission into the membership of the church had long been separated from the factor of moral change, although infant baptism was supposed to be the technical sacrament of regeneration which hopefully sometime later in life would produce the moral fruits of conversion.

The Anabaptists broke with this notion, insisting on the experience of crisis repentance and moral conversion for all persons before baptism and membership in the church. In a tract on the new birth, Menno Simons wrote in 1537, "We must be born from above, must be changed and renewed in our hearts, and must be transplanted from the unrighteous and evil nature of Adam into the true and good nature of Christ, or we can never in all eternity be saved by any means, be they human or divine."[1] In the teaching of Menno, crisis conversion was the key to the reformation of the church.

The conversionist emphasis was modified in several ways by later generations. Mention has already been made of the constant strain to move to a more technical definition of the initial experience and to an earlier age of entrance. An even more serious shift in some groups was the virtual loss altogether of this conversion dimension. In a separatist church over many generations, membership by birth tends to replace membership by "rebirth."

The restoration of concern that every member experience mature conversion came both by way of spiritual renewal within the group and by pietist-revivalist influences from without. As was observed in Chapter 2, three of the five denominations (MBC, BIC, EMC) began with new conversion experiences by their founders. The MBC vowed to return to "our dear Menno" for the express purpose of restoring conversion as the constitutive basis of the church. Sometimes these influences carried a subjective emphasis upon the conversion experience for its own sake, disconnected from the all-embracing obedience to Christ in the fellowship of the church that was so central to the Anabaptists. At other times, they triggered renewal in terms of original norms. In either case, such leaders perceived their own experience as normative for their followers. By the time of the second or third generation, however, the form of the conversion experience became standarized at a certain age or the conversion emphasis died out once more. Children who are reared in Christian homes are somehow not expected to change quite so radically. "Yes, we believe firmly in the new birth," writes MB theologian Delbert Wiens, "but we are becoming more open to discuss how it comes about, and to recognize other types of experience."[2]

Neither the Lenski nor Stark-Glock studies of church membership included the dimension of conversion as we have specifically defined it. To be sure, religious experience was one of the types of religiosity which they defined and measured; but their measurements relate more aptly to what will be called "sanctification" in a later section of this chapter. Sociologists have done little research specifically on the social sources or consequences of conversion, and for this new measures had to be constructed.

Important clues from several older but well-known studies of conversion were gleaned from the literature of the psychology of religion. In the first quarter of the twentieth century such great minds as Francis Strickland and William James focused on two distinct conceptions of conversion:

1. *Initial Conversion.* The experience, more or less abrupt, by which one decides to make a new start in a life of vital faith.[3]

2. *Moral/Ethical Conversion.* The experience, sudden or gradual, by which one changes from sinfulness to righteousness, from selfishness to compassion, by virtue of faith.[4]

These scholars distinguished between the method by which one enters the life of Christian faith and the manner in which the experience affects the subject. The former is the "time-and-place of decision factor," and the latter is the "behavioral change factor."

The more controversial part of the distinction is between a crisis experience and a gradual process of change. Churches in the Anabaptist tradition have a considerable vested theological interest at stake in this issue, which has been with them since the earlier controversies with the Reformers. The early twentieth-century psychologists of religion suggested some ways at least by which one might study these factors one at a time, to see whether or not in fact they are part of the same dimension.

Index of Initial Conversion Experience

In formulating the questions on conversion in the present study, the aspect of initial subjective experience (the time-and-place factor) was separated from the aspect of moral-ethical change. An attempt was made to define the initial experience as a focused episode in life without limiting either the content or the timing of that experience too narrowly. Any one of the following qualified as an initial conversion experience: a definite decision to become vitally committed to God, an explicit acceptance of Christ as Savior, or a clear awareness of making a new start to walk with God. The timing of this experience could be either a "distinct occasion in life" or merely a "period in life" provided a conversion experience occurred in any of these three senses. The aspect of personal crisis, intentionally omitted from this scale, was included in the Moral-Personal and Ethical-Social Conversion scales, to be defined below. Here, the aspect of climax rather than crisis is sufficient to classify respondents as "converted" or "non-converted" in the sense of William James' classic terms, "twice born" and "once born."[5]

Table 5-1 shows that 79% of the respondents reported a conversion experience by this definition. The five denominations

TABLE 5-1
Initial Conversion Experience

Items and Responses	Percentage Distributions for:					
	MC	GCMC	MBC	BIC	EMC	TOTAL

1. "People talk of conversion as a distinct occasion in life when they make a definite decision to become vitally committed to God, when they accepted Christ as Savior, or as a period in life when they became very much aware that they were making a new start to walk with God. Was there a particular point in your life when you had a conversion experience in any of these three senses?"

Yes	80	65	93	89	89	79
No	7	19	3	3	6	12
Uncertain	13	16	3	7	6	10

2. "How many such experiences have you had in your life?"

One	42	52	57	32	56	47
Two	34	27	26	41	28	31
Three	14	10	12	15	10	13
Four or more	10	10	5	12	6	9
Median Number	2.2	2.0	1.9	2.4	1.9	2.1

3. "How old were you at the time of the first such experience?"

Median Age (years)	13.7	14.9	13.1	12.9	13.2	13.8

4. "Where or how did this first experience occur?"

Public Church Meeting	72	55	56	71	67	66
Personal Invitation	10	10	19	8	11	12
Church Camp or School	5	12	6	9	9	7
Private Experience	7	9	7	4	4	6
Small Group	0	4	1	1	1	1
Other	5	10	11	6	8	8

varied from a high of 93% in the MBC to a low of 65% in the GCMC. Although this variation indicates a statistically significant difference related to unique factors in each group, it is evident that conversion is a majority experience in all five denominations. There are no exactly comparable data, but in a well-known study of conversion in 1929, Elmer T. Clark reported that out of a sample of 2,174 persons who considered themselves to be religious, only 34% had a definite conversion experience. They were subdivided into two types — a "definite crisis" type, experienced by seven percent, and an "emotional stimulus" type, experienced by 27%. The rest (66%) referred only to a gradual awakening, but no definite conversion.[6]

A more recent review of thirty-two such studies confirms "that about 30% of religious people report a more or less sudden conversion experience, while the others become gradually more religious as a result of social influences."[7] It is evident that experience of some kind of climactic conversion is much more prevalent in our five denominations than among "religious people" generally.

Frequency of Conversion Experience. Respondents were next asked how many such conversion experiences they have had in their life. Not quite half (47%) reported that they had had only one such experience. The median number of conversions overall was 2.1. Although churches in the Anabaptist tradition tend to think of only one conversion as normative, there are several possible explanations for multiple experiences in these groups, described by Argyle as follows: "The typical sequence for these was for a conversion to last two years, being succeeded four years later by another. . . . Many crisis conversions at revival meetings tend to be temporary, and people who experience a gradual conversion are more religious later on."[8]

A more likely explanation is the peculiar doctrinal emphasis of the groups upon holiness and consistent behavior. In several groups, especially the BIC, this is reflected in a special doctrine of sanctification, an experience of a "second work of transforming grace." This type of religious experience will be surveyed later in the chapter, but it is likely that some respondents were answering the question on the frequency of conversion in the light of what they might have preferred to call subsequent experiences of sanctification.

Age of Conversion. Another question asked was the age of the member at the time of his first conversion experience. As shown in Table 5-1, the median age varied from a low of 12.9 in the BIC to a high of 14.9 in the GCMC, with an overall median of 13.8. On the average, girls are converted six tenths of a year earlier than boys. Moreover, the median age of conversion has been declining through the years. It was 15.2 for the older generation (50 and over), 13.8 for the middle generation (30-49), and 12.8 for the younger generation (20-29).

This same trend has been observed by other students of the subject, and several theories have been given. First, there is some evidence that persons mature earlier than heretofore, through improved nutrition and mass communication. Allport puts it rather bluntly when he writes that "the impact of movies and radio has sharpened the emotional susceptibilities of children, so that the blandishments of evangelists, if responded to at all, are effective at an earlier age than formerly."[9]

Another explanation is the close relationship in many cultures between the phenomenon of conversion and that of adolescence and and puberty. It is the time of transition from childhood to maturity with all the attending physiological and behavioral changes and traumas. Hence it is not surprising to discover that conversion in Anabaptist communities is also predominantly an adolescent experience, although religious commitment attending conversion is supposed to be spiritually mature and above purely naturalistic forces.

Among the five denominations in the study, the MC has worked hardest at this dilemma by formulating a particular theological doctrine of the "age of accountability," grounding adolescent conversion in the order of redemption rather than in the order of creation primarily.[10] This doctrine refers to the age when conversion becomes theologically relevant. It also helps to rationalize the fact that 95% of all conversions in the MC occur between the ages of twelve and seventeen.

The age spread of first conversions is not quite that confined in the other groups. In the MBC, BIC and EMC this is due more to the number of conversions before the age of 9 than to those after the age of 18. In the BIC and MBC, one fifth of all reported conversions occurred before the age of nine.

Place of Conversion. Members were next asked where or how this first conversion experience occurred. Two thirds of all definitely converted members reported some form of a public church meeting — either a revival meeting at church, a regular church service, Sunday school, or vacation Bible school (see Table 5-1). This is especially the context for the experience among MC and BIC respondents, over 70% of whom fell into this place-of-conversion category. In the MBC, nearly one out of five members who experienced definite conversion were led into that experience through a person-to-person relationship with a minister, parent, or friend. Only 14% had their experience at a camp meeting, in a small group of some kind, or by themselves. In the GCMC, however, these latter contexts accounted for one fourth of the reported conversions. In fact, a greater variety of contexts for conversion is represented in the GCMC than in any other group.

Type of Conversion

We turn now to another dimension of conversion, concerned not with time and place of decision but with the deeper effects of the experience. Two types of conversion scales, also newly constructed, were based on the work of A. C. Underwood.[11] An attempt was made to use all three of his types of conversion — "moral," "intellectual," and "emotional" — but the resulting data did not adequately differentiate between the first two, so the "intellectual" type was deleted. Moreover, we chose to test his third category less with the content of the love-emotion than with that of love-ethics in order to make the aspect of social relationships more explicit. The result was the following two type-of-conversion scales:

Moral-Personal Conversion. This was defined essentially in Underwood's terms as

(1) a struggle away from sin and guilt,
(2) a yearning for personal redemption, and
(3) a new empowerment to attain a sense of righteousness.

In this category, a person's basic concern would seem to be inward — a very personal struggle of the soul for peace and holiness.

Ethical-Social Conversion. This was defined as

(1) a despair about human injustice,
(2) a desire for greater love among people, and
(3) a new trust in people.

The basic concern of this type is social rather than individual, outward rather than inward.

A respondent was simply asked whether his experience of each of the three elements in each type was "great" (3 points), "some"

(2 points), "little" (1 point), or "none" (0 points). This produced a range of scores from zero to nine for each type of conversion.

Table 5-2 gives the distribution of scores by denomination for both types. The differences between the GCMC and the other groups are significant for both types, with the GCMC scoring lowest on moral-personal conversion (mean score of 6.6) and highest on ethical-social conversion (mean score of 6.7). The GCMC is also the only group scoring higher on the ethical-social scale than on the moral-personal scale.

These scales are independent of the initial conversion items, and the tabulations just reported include respondents who reported no specific time-and-place conversion experience. The following cross tabulation shows that members who have had a definite conversion score significantly higher on the moral-personal scale than members who have not, but there is no significant relationship between the experience of definite conversion and the ethical-social type:

Definite Conversion Experience

	Yes	Uncertain	No
Mean Score on Moral-Personal Scale	6.7	5.9	5.7
Mean Score on Ethical-Social Scale	6.1	6.1	6.3

Sanctification and Its Indicators

Earlier in this chapter we observed that "conversion," which implies a comprehensive redirection of one's life, came to refer more and more specifically to the point in life at which such redirection was begun. The most common meaning of "sanctification" is the on-going experience of a divine work by which this new life of right-eousness and love is fulfilled. In the history of this doctrine, the Holy Spirit, the third person of the Trinity, is the special source of sanctification. In the New Testament the baptism of the Holy Spirit followed conversion and water baptism (Acts 19:2-6), and the manifestation of such Christian virtues as love, joy, peace, patience, kindness, goodness, and faithfulness was the "fruit of the Spirit" (Gal. 5:22).

Roman Catholic thought defined sanctification as the continual

TABLE 5-2
Types of Conversion Experience

Scales and classes	Percentage Distribution for:					
	MC	GCMC	MBC	BIC	EMC	TOTAL
Moral-Personal Conversion Scale:						
8-9 High	37	33	38	38	40	36
6-7 Middle	46	42	48	44	44	45
0-5 Low	17	24	14	17	16	19
Total	100	99	100	99	100	100
Mean Score	6.9	6.6	6.9	6.9	6.9	6.8
Ethical-Social Conversion Scale:						
8-9 High	28	31	21	22	24	27
6-7 Middle	50	50	46	50	48	49
0-5 Low	22	19	34	28	28	23
Total	100	100	101	100	100	99
Mean Score	6.5	6.7	6.1	6.2	6.3	6.4

experience of miraculous grace through the dispensing of the sacraments. The Protestant reformers separated sanctification from justification by faith, interpreting the former as the divine process begun and assured of fulfillment by justification. Thus, Luther taught that a Christian is continually becoming a Christian under the guidance of the Holy Spirit and that this "becoming" is sanctification. The Anabaptists reacted to this doctrine, which seemed to neglect concern for the transformation of life which the term implies.

Against both Lutheran and Anabaptist doctrines, later definitions coming from the Pietist, Wesleyan, and recent charismatic movements have influenced several of the denominations in our study at various points in their history. Sanctification came to be used in the much narrower sense of moral perfection and instantaneous transformation. The latter was particularly characteristic of BIC doctrine at the turn of the century, as indicated in the following article on sanctification from their official Confession of Faith:

> This experience for believers is obtained instantaneously and subsequent to the new birth. The scriptural terms used to describe the cleansing of the believer's heart imply the same: purifying the heart; crucifixion of the old man; body of sin de-

stroyed; circumcision of the heart; deliverance; creation.

Even though it is possible for a sanctified believer to fall into sin, the Scriptures reveal that by giving heed to the Word, being devoted in prayer, and by rendering loving and obedient service to Christ he is kept from willful transgression by the power of God.[12]

Expressed chiefly in moralistic terms, this definition of the experience of sanctification is best measured not by some new scale but by the Moral-Personal Conversion Scale introduced above. There is evidence, however, that the BIC is shifting to a broader concept of sanctification as the progressive fulfillment of the total gospel in Christian lives. Compare the following sentence which appears to have been added to the article quoted above: "Although sanctification perfects the motives and desires of the heart, the expression of these in terms of accomplishment is a progressive growth in grace until the close of this life.[13]

In the present study, sanctification is defined in this broader sense as implying not just forensic grace or perfectionism, but also such experiences in time and space as the mystic holiness of God, a deeper sensitivity to alien forces of evil, Christ's salvation and healing, delivery from danger, special personal revelation, and a sense of being chosen by God to be His instrument. A number of such experiences (listed in Table 5-3) were utilized as indicators of sanctification. For each item in the questionnaire, there were four possible answers:

	Score
"Yes, I'm sure I have"	3
"Yes, I think I have"	2
"No, I don't think I have"	1
"No, I'm sure I haven't"	0

Most experiences listed were borrowed from the Stark and Glock study, thus permitting denominational comparisons.[14] They contain both experiences of God's benevolence and encounters with a personal devil, known in traditional Christian language as Satan. The argument in favor of putting benevolent and malevolent items into the same scale is that the closer a person's relationship to God, the more aware he becomes of the existence and interference of Satan. Biblical examples of this relationship between benevolent and malevolent experiences would be the character of Job in the Old Testament or the temptations of Jesus in the New Testament.

TABLE 5-3
Measures of Sanctification

	Percentage Distribution for:					
	MC	GCMC	MBC	BIC	EMC	TOTAL

Instruction to respondent: "Listed below are a number of experiences of a religious nature which people have reported having. For each item listed, there are four possible answers. For each item choose the answer that is most accurate for you and place a check mark in that column."

Percent answering "Yes, I'm sure I have":

	MC	GCMC	MBC	BIC	EMC	TOTAL
A sense of being saved by Christ	80	70	92	87	89	79
A sense of being loved by Christ	78	70	85	82	86	77
A sense of being tempted by the devil	75	58	80	76	81	71
A feeling that you were somehow in the presence of God	72	69	74	75	74	72
A feeling that God had delivered you from danger...	65	61	71	73	71	65
An awareness that sin and evil were all around you	64	58	68	64	66	63
A feeling that you were in a holy place	57	58	60	62	59	58
A feeling that the Holy Spirit gave you a special understanding concerning God's truth	45	39	60	53	55	47
A feeling of being filled by the overwhelming joy and power of the Holy Spirit	45	38	52	53	55	45
A sense of being chosen by God to be His instrument	37	30	46	40	43	37
An experience of being healed by God	32	31	29	44	34	32
A feeling that some personal misfortune was caused by the devil	16	11	16	19	23	15
A feeling that the devil was using you as his agent	11	8	13	10	18	11
An experience of speaking in tongues	3	1	2	2	2	2

Sanctification Scale:	MC	GCMC	MBC	BIC	EMC	TOTAL
36–42 High	14	11	15	16	19	13
32–35 High Middle	29	25	31	35	34	29
28–31 Middle	26	25	28	26	25	26
24–27 Low Middle	18	20	15	13	12	18
0–23 Low	12	19	10	10	9	14
Total	99	100	99	100	99	100
Number of Respondents	1,072	537	619	539	398	3,165
Median Score	30.5	29.3	30.9	31.6	31.9	30.5

Stark and Glock predicted that types of religious experience would follow a specific progressive order of increasing intensity and declining frequency.[13] Their specific pattern was not confirmed by our data, but some order of intensity and infrequency seems to obtain. In all, fourteen sanctification experiences were included in the scale, yielding a range of scores from zero to 42. Table 5-3 shows the percentage of members by denomination who checked the response "yes, I'm sure I have." The scores were grouped into five classes, as shown at the bottom of the table. The mean scores vary from a high of 31.9 in the EMC to a low of 29.3 in the GCMC. While 19% of the members of EMC scored "high" on the scale, only 11% of the members of GCMC scored "high." This difference is statistically significant and the scale provides another variable of faith to use in later analyses.

In order to compare present respondents with the Glock and Stark sample of American church members, specific items have to be isolated since not all of their items were used and several new items were added. A comparison of the following three items provides a fair estimate of how Mennonites and Brethren in Christ compare to other Protestants and Catholics in America. The percentage answering, "Yes, I'm sure I have," were as follows:[16]

	Mennonite-BIC	Congregational	Southern Baptist	Total Protestants	Roman Catholic
"A feeling that you were somehow in the presence of God"	72	25	80	45	43
"A sense of being saved by Christ"	79	9	92	37	26
"A feeling of being tempted by the devil"	71	11	76	32	36

The scores of all five groups in our study are closer to those of the Southern Baptists than the Congregationalists and are significantly higher than the totals for Protestants and Catholics generally. Again, it becomes apparent that in one dimension after another

Mennonites and Brethren in Christ as a whole take their faith very seriously indeed.

Devotionalism and Its Indicators

We turn, finally, from religious experience to religious practice, the performance of certain duties as part of the faith response. Numerous personal acts of discipline could be listed — worship, prayer, evangelism, deeds of mercy, almsgiving. Several of these acts will be examined in later chapters in the perspective of the corporate work of the church. Present attention will be focused on the practice dimension usually conceived to be the wellspring of faithful living — personal acts of Bible meditation, prayer, and devotion.

With all their stress upon Christian community and corporate assembly, the early Anabaptists did not overlook the importance of the personal devotional discipline. One of their earliest documents admonished the brothers and sisters to "read their Psalter daily at home."[17] The Mennonite martyrbook reports that it was prayer that gave their Anabaptist forefathers the strength to endure trials and that they even faced execution with prayer on their lips.[18] Long after persecution ceased, prayer was chiefly an individual rather than a corporate expression. When it became a part of corporate worship, prayer usually remained silent. The minister simply admonished his hearers to kneel down and offer their individual prayers to God. Later, when audible prayer was introduced Anabaptists were reluctant to use rote prayers. The worshipers preferred that their ministers simply offer "free prayer." Along with corporate prayer came the development of family worship and the use of devotional literature. Such literature, according to one Mennonite historian,

> included any religious book other than strictly doctrinal or theological works, intended to be used mainly for home devotion, that is, for meditation and prayer and also for uplift (edification). Books of this kind might further be used to strengthen one's own stand in an adverse situation, or to clarify one's faith. . . . In short, all these books *served the practive of an inner rather than an external (ecclesiastical) devotion* of an earnest believer. . . .[19]

This study draws rather fine conceptual distinctions between these various dimensions of faith, and it remains to be seen (in Chapter 20) whether they are really independent factors or whether they measure the same thing. Certainly, devotionalism and the other faith dimensions surveyed so far are related to what in the next chapter will be called "doctrinalism." Anabaptists used the writings of Menno Simons and other leaders both as devotional material and for doctrinal instruction. Later a greater distinction between these commitments developed as some members stressed orthodoxy and others stressed spiritual inwardness.

Devotionalism is also closely related to what was called sanctification above. As pointed out in an early BIC confession of faith, the difference is between the "divine side" and the "human side" in the Christian life. Converting and sanctifying were conceived largely as God's part in the covenant; praying and trusting were man's part:

> Man's part consists in consecration, in submitting his will to the will of God, in resisting the devil, striving against sin, rendering obedience to God, exercising a living faith, praying fervently and trusting. To God belongs the cleansing, liberating, dedicating, and outpouring of the Spirit and sealing.[20]

Attempts to measure a person's devotional commitment were made in both the Lenski and the Stark-Glock studies. Lenski used two questions having to do with the frequency with which the respondent engages in prayer and the frequency with which he seeks to determine what God wants him to do when he has important decisions to make.[21] Stark and Glock used the questions, "How often do you pray privately?" and "How often do you read the Bible at home?" In the present study equivalent forms of all of these questions were used in addition to some items on devotional reading and family worship.

Table 5-4 shows that 77% of the subjects in the present study pray *daily or more*. The practice of daily prayer varies from a low of 73% in the GCMC to a high of 82% in the MBC. Although the differences between the groups are statistically significant, their devotional practices are more similar to each other than to other denominations. Stark and Glock report that 75% of Protestants in America generally pray *"at least once a week"* and the percentage varies from 92 in the Southern Baptist Convention to 62 in the Congregational Christian Church.[22] In the Lutheran study by Strommen and associates, only 53% of the members of the three major Lutheran bodies pray "as a regular part of my behavior."[23]

TABLE 5-4
Measures of Devotionalism

	Items and Responses	Percentage Distribution for:					
		MC	GCMC	MBC	BIC	EMC	TOTAL
1.	"Other than at mealtime, how often do you pray to God privately on the average?"						
	Never or seldom	5	6	3	5	4	5
	Occasionally	17	21	14	16	19	18
	Daily or more	78	73	82	80	77	77
2.	"Do the members of your household have a family or group worship, other than grace at meals?"						
	Yes	41	42	61	51	44	45
	No	59	58	39	49	56	55
3.	"How often do you study the Bible privately, seeking to understand it and letting it speak to you?"						
	Never or seldom	13	17	8	12	11	13
	Occasionally	19	24	15	21	21	20
	Frequently	38	30	35	36	33	35
	Daily	30	28	42	31	35	32
4.	"In general, how close do you describe your present relationship to God?"						
	Close/Very Close	54	48	56	58	59	53
5.	"When you have decisions to make in your everyday life, how often do you ask yourself what God would want you do do?"						
	Often/Very Often	61	55	68	64	61	61

Devotionalism Scale:							
6-7	High	28	27	39	33	32	30
4-5	Upper Middle	34	30	34	35	33	33
2-3	Low Middle	25	26	19	20	23	24
0-1	Low	13	18	8	12	11	14
	Total	100	101	100	100	99	101
	Number of Respondents	1,130	577	656	579	431	3,373
	Mean Score	4.0	3.8	4.7	4.3	4.2	4.1

Family Worship. Family worship is practiced less frequently than private prayer. Table 5-4 shows that not quite half of the members in the sample have a family or household worship other than prayer at meals. A high 61% of the members of the MBC practice family worship. A. E. Janzen calls the "family altar" one of the distinctive emphases of the MBC. He writes,

> In the course of my duties extending over 30 years in connection with conference, educational, and foreign missions administration, I have had the opportunity to visit about 36 countries. My travels have brought me into hundreds of Mennonite Brethren homes in America and into some on four other continents I visited. To God's glory, to the credit of these homes, and as a testimony, I am grateful to be able to verify that in all these years of contact and overnight stops, I have not been in a single Mennonite Brethren home that did not observe family worship. I am sure the family altar is missing in some homes, but these are the exceptions.[24]

Although absence of the practice is not as exceptional as he claimed, the data do tend to verify his observations.

Personal Bible Study. One other item for which comparable data are available concerns the frequency of private Bible study. Table 5-4 shows that 32% of present respondents study the Bible daily, "seeking to understand it and letting it speak to you." The incidence is lowest in the GCMC (28%) and highest in the MBC (42%). Stark and Glock asked a similar question in their national study, and found that only two percent of Roman Catholics and 13% of Protestants in America "read the Bible at home" once a day or more.[25] The Protestant percentages varied as follows:

	Percent
Congregational	3
Methodist	6
Episcopalian	9
Disciples of Christ	12
Presbyterian	10
American Lutheran	11
American Baptist	11
Missouri Lutheran	14
Southern Baptist	35

Again, it is evident that all five of the groups in our study rank near the top in the practice of personal Bible study.

Devotionalism Scale. Table 5-4 reports additional tabulations concerning devotional practices. In all, seven items were combined in the Devotionalism Scale, the five items in Table 5-4 plus two others. Respondents were given one point toward their devotionalism score for each of the following items:

1. Private Bible study once a week or more.
2. Private prayer to God daily or several times per day.
3. The practice of family worship in the home.
4. Daily practice of family worship with Bible reading.
5. Grace spoken before every meal.
6. Petition to God for guidance in times of decision "often" or "very often."
7. Relationship to God reported to be "close" or "very close."

Within a range of possible scores from zero to seven, the overall mean score on devotionalism was 4.1, with a high of 4.7 in the MBC and a low of 3.8 in the GCMC. In later chapters, scores on this scale will be correlated with other faith and life variables.

Summary

In summary, this chapter has introduced five dimensions of religious experience and practice — initial conversion, moral-personal conversion, ethical-social conversion, sanctification, and devotionalism. It has been assumed that these dimensions are independent factors but are positively intercorrelated. Further data to test these assumptions will be presented in Chapter 20 when the selective influences of the faith variables will be analyzed. On those indicators for which comparable data on other denominations were available (definite conversion, experience of the presence of God, a feeling of being tempted by the devil, private prayer, family devotions, personal Bible study) Mennonites and Brethren in Christ rank higher than nearly all other religious groups. We turn next to a third major area of religious orientation, the dimensions of doctrinalism and orthodoxy.

Chapter 6

BELIEF AND DOCTRINE

In the two previous chapters, eight variables of religious faith were introduced. We now turn to several more measures of faith which have to do particularly with religious belief and doctrine. Belief implies intellectual assent to certain theological ideas. Every religion tends to formulate and assent to certain theological doctrines, which usually reflect a collective point of view and style of thought.

This chapter will distinguish between three variables of belief. The first pertains to beliefs which Mennonites and Brethren in Christ share in common with the mainstream of historic Christianity — a dimension to be called "general orthodoxy." The second pertains to beliefs which members of these churches share, more or less, with twentieth-century American fundamentalists — a dimension to be called "fundamentalist orthodoxy." The third variable focuses on particular sixteenth-century Anabaptist doctrines to which Mennonites and Brethren in Christ adhere, more or less, in contrast to alternative Christian views — a dimension to be called "Anabaptism."

General Orthodoxy and Its Measurement

The wellspring of Anabaptism was not some deviant sixteenth-century doctrinal system but the historic Christian confessions and creeds of the ancient church. The doctrinal differences of the Anabaptists pertained not to the central tenets of Christian orthodoxy but rather to the degree of seriousness with which these tenets were applied to daily living. They wanted chiefly to be faithful to the historic revelation of God in Christ, and they wrote several confessions of faith for the doctrinal clarification of what this meant to them. The Schleitheim articles of 1527 presupposed the historic beliefs of the church and treated only the unique emphases of the Anabaptists in their time of persecution. After the worst of the persecution was over, the Dordrecht Confession of 1632 was written to consolidate several branches of Anabaptist-Mennonites in the Netherlands. It included articles of general orthodoxy as well as particular Anabaptist teachings. The MC adopted it as their official articles of faith in 1725, and wrote no other confession until the fundamentalist controversy in the 1920s. The most recent confession of the MC, covering twenty articles, was adopted in 1963.

Another Dutch Mennonite confession was written in 1762 by Cornelis Ris for the dual purpose of consolidating a union of two Mennonite congregations and reversing the numerical decline of these churches by reorienting the members to the apostolic and Anabaptist foundations of faith. Ris' method was conciliatory, both to liberals in his church and to several Calvinist-oriented members. In the 1870s, Carl van der Smissen, a teacher at the GCMC theological seminary in Ohio, made a revision of this confession which was published by the GCMC in 1902 as its unofficial statement of faith.

In the family of Mennonite churches, the Dordrecht articles have been identified as the more conservative and the Ris articles as the more liberal in content. The accuracy of the typical characterization of the GCMC as the most liberal group of Mennonites is supported less by its earlier preference for the Ris confession than by its subsequent minimizing of the value of any such formulations of doctrine. Apart from several brief articles in its official constitution, which were never substantially altered even when the constitution itself was revised three times, the GCMC has never adopted a comprehensive confession — unlike the other four groups in our study. However, nine articles known as the Souderton Statement were adopted by the GCMC in 1941 as the doctrinal basis for opening a new seminary.

An MBC confession of faith was formulated in Russia in 1873 and officially adopted by the MBC in North America in 1902. It was concerned mainly with reaffirming such normative Mennonite doctrines as nonconformity to the world and nonparticipation in military service and with identifying particular MBC doctrines on conversion and baptism by immersion. In its 1972 triennial conference, the MBC gave tentative approval to a new confession, based largely on the text of the MC confession of 1963.

The doctrines of the BIC were first formulated in a historic confession signed by eight of its founding fathers in the latter part of the eighteenth century. It contained three parts that dealt with the conversion experience, the concept of the believers' church, and the Christian's relationship to the world. A later, very brief confession was published with the minutes of General Conferences, 1871-1904. The first comprehensive BIC confession and supplemental statement of doctrine was adopted in 1961 and published in an official *Manual of Doctrine and Government*.

In the EMC, correct doctrine has always been important to the leaders and members. Marie Diller writes,

> It caused the origin of the church, it was the main topic of discussion in the first Conference in 1883, it led to the break in 1898 with the daughter group, the Missionary Church Association, and it was seriously guarded for its young people by the care that was taken in the selection of schools for their attendance.[1]

She notes, however, that until 1917, EMC doctrine was taught only informally and centered primarily on the experience of personal conversion. After the turn of the century certain new views on sanctification, divine healing, and premillennialism were added. In 1917 a 24-article confession was adopted, covering both general and particular issues of theology. This confession was revised in 1937, 1949, and 1960. The latest revision arranges EMC doctrines into nine articles of faith and nine articles of practice.

There is a curious contradiction in the documents pertaining to the function of these various confessions. On the one hand, churches in the Anabaptist tradition are not supposed to be "confessional churches" in the sense of attaching much weight to theological formulations. They write confessions primarily as testimony to their faith, as instructional materials for their members, or as doctrinal bases for mergers or new denominational institutions. On this side of the contradiction, consider these sentences selected from their most recent statements:

> In its beliefs the Mennonite Church is bound ultimately to the Holy Scriptures, not to any human formulation of doctrine. (MC)

> The Mennonite Brethren Church has throughout its history emphasized biblical authority in all matters of faith and practice. This emphasis . . . counsels a proper use of creedal statements and confessions of faith as expressions of our understanding of Scripture. Such documents are to be regarded as descriptive more than normative. (MBC)

> If there is anything herein contained which is not in harmony with the teachings of God's Word, you are under no obligation to receive it; if it is Bible truth, then it is sacred and binding, as though you read it from the sacred page. (EMC)

On the other hand, formal doctrine in these same groups has often been used to test the orthodoxy and loyalty of members and church leaders, as when teachers in a church college were asked periodically to affirm their agreement with some specific conference confession, or members were excommunicated on the grounds of modernism. The rationale for such use of tests of orthodoxy included arguments such as the following:

> We must have . . . a clearly thought out and consistent theological line, not a mixture of confused theologies borrowed from groups and movements. Let us take the lesson from other groups, such as the Church of the Brethren, who are in a considerable dilemma in several respects because of their failure to do this very thing in their theology. It is easy for a whole brotherhood to lose its way. Let it not happen to us.[2]
> God forbid that the Mennonite Church should ever surrender one jot or tittle of the conservative Christian faith — which means strict observance of "all things whatsoever" our Lord commands us.[3]

The "conservative Christian faith" is an affirmation, first of all, of the general historic doctrines of Christianity concerning the personal existence of God, His incarnation in Christ, the opposing kingdoms of Christ, the future return of Christ, life after death, and the future states of heaven and hell. With only one or two exceptions, these basic doctrines are treated in all of the denominational confessions cited above.

Orthodoxy means assenting unequivocally to beliefs like these, the criterion for which is a message of divine revelation expressed in supernatural language. Theologically speaking, a particular "doctrine" of revelation is not identical with the "fact" of revelation or even with the historical "reports" of revelation, but is once or twice removed.[4] What will be measured, then, is not the only way one can think theologically about the Christian revelation, but the way that is most appropriate to the doctrinal style of most churches, gauged by a member's relative acceptance or rejection of such doctrines.

General Orthodoxy Items. As a test of general orthodoxy, six items from the Stark and Glock study were used and a seventh pertaining to the resurrection was added. Each item pertained to a given doctrine and was followed by four or five responses ranging from the most to the least orthodox.

Table 6-1 lists the seven doctrines included in the formation of the General Orthodoxy Scale. For the first four items, the response listed in each case is the most orthodox of the several responses provided for each doctrine. The following question and responses pertaining to the doctrine of God will illustrate the range of responses provided. The distribution of responses for all respondents is also given:

Which one of the following statements comes closest to expressing what you believe about God?

	Percent
I know God really exists and I have no doutbts about His existence.	88.9
While I have doubts, I feel that I do believe in God.	10.0
I don't believe in a personal God, but I do believe in a higher power of some kind.	0.9
I don't know whether there is a God and I don't believe there is any way to find out.	0.3
I don't believe in God.	0.1

For the last three items, pertaining to doctrines of Christ's
return, a personal devil, and life beyond death, the respondent
chose one of the following responses: "definitely," "probably," "pos-

TABLE 6-1
Measures of General Orthodoxy

Doctrine	Percent Responding for:					
	MC	GCMC	MBC	BIC	EMC	TOTAL
Doctrine of God: "I know God really exists and I have no doubts about His existence"	89	86	92	92	94	89
Doctrine of Christ: "Jesus was not only human but also is the Divine Son of God and I have no doubts about it"	91	85	95	93	96	90
Doctrine of Miracles: "I believe the miracles were super- natural acts of God which actually happened just as the Bible says they did"	92	81	95	93	97	90
Doctrine of Resurrection: "I believe Jesus' physical resurrection was an objective historical fact just as His birth was a historical fact"	92	86	96	93	96	91
Doctrine of Christ's Return: "Jesus will actually return to earth someday"	91	83	97	95	98	90
Doctrine of a Personal Devil: "Satan, as a personal devil, is active in the world today"	95	86	97	96	98	93
Doctrine of Life beyond Death: "There is life beyond death"	93	87	97	95	97	92
General Orthodoxy Scale:						
26 High	76	65	87	82	88	75
24–25 High Middle	14	16	9	11	8	14
12–23 Low Middle	9	17	4	5	3	10
0–11 Low	1	2	0	1	1	1
Total	100	100	100	99	100	100
Number of Respondents	1,183	602	689	612	438	3,524
Mean Score	25.2	24.4	25.6	25.3	25.7	25.1

sibly," "probably not," and "definitely not."

In respect to the doctrine of God, as indicated above, 90% chose the most orthodox response. This compares to 81% of Roman Catholics and 71% of all Protestants in the Stark-Glock study. American Protestants vary from a low of 41% in the Congregational Church to a high of 99% in the Southern Baptist Convention. Although the five Anabaptist denominations varied from 86% in the GCMC to 94% in the EMC, all five groups scored considerably higher than the national average for Protestants or Catholics, but not quite as high as Southern Baptists.

Similarly, with reference to the other doctrines, our respondents scored very high indeed, as the following comparison shows:

The Doctrine of:

Percent Most Orthodox:	*Christ*	*Miracles*	*Christ's Return*	*Satan*	*Life After Death*
Mennonites and Brethren in Christ	90	90	90	93	92
Roman Catholics	86	74	47	75	75
Total Protestant	69	57	44	65	65
Congregational Church	40	28	13	36	36
Southern Baptist Convention	99	92	94	97	97

General Orthodoxy Scale. In order to classify respondents along a continuum from those with full certainty in affirming traditional church doctrines to those who reject them, the seven doctrinal items were combined into a scale, giving each member *zero* points for the least orthodox choice, *one* point for the next most orthodox choice, on up to *three* or *four* points, depending on the number of responses in each set. A maximum of 26 points was possible.

The bottom of Table 6-1 shows that the average score for all respondents was 25.1. The denominations varied from a low average of 24.4 in the GCMC to a high of 25.7 in the EMC. Although we are now ready for further tests with this scale, we turn first to a second measure of orthodoxy.

Fundamentalist Orthodoxy and Its Measures

The second test of doctrinal assent is called "fundamentalist

orthodoxy" after the twentieth-century movement that had considerable impact upon four of the five groups in the present study.
Only the BIC escaped serious influence by this system of doctrine, at
least on the levels of conference organization and leadership.[5]

According to Grant Stoltzfus, much of the MC was captured by
it, and although this may be an overstatement, he gives some
strong evidence for his conclusion:

> The 1920s brought to the Mennonite Church a widespread fear
> that liberal Protestant thought was invading the church's life. In
> 1924 John Horsch published a small booklet on *The Mennonite
> Church and Modernism* and set forth the conflicting positions be-
> cause he feared the American Mennonite Church might "go
> the way the church in Holland and North Germany had gone."
> That way he believed was assimilation in life, if not in name.
> In 1921 the Mennonite General Conference adopted a statement
> reaffirming the cardinal doctrines of faith in such a way as to
> counteract liberal Protestant theology. In 1924 a Fundamentals
> Conference at Archbold, Ohio, discussed apostasy, modernism,
> and orthodoxy. The findings committee noted that "a wave of
> blighting liberalism is sweeping over the religious world engulf-
> ing many of the churches of the land, even threatening the unity
> and future welfare of the Mennonite Church. . . ."
>
> In the crisis of the 1920s the church's oldest educational in-
> stitution, Goshen College, closed for the academic year of 1923-
> 24. Its reopening in the fall of 1924 is a chapter in John
> Horsch's *The Mennonite Church and Modernism.* Horsch con-
> sidered the reorganized college to be more in harmony with the
> conservative stand of the church.
>
> The crisis of 1915-30 subsided slowly, though the conservative
> wing's separate educational, mission, and publication enterprises
> showed that the dichotomy in the Mennonite Church was not at
> an end.[6]

The MC was especially vulnerable to fundamentalist dogma according
to Stoltzfus because it was seen as an ally in the preservation of
traditional Mennonite norms of separation from worldliness.

Part of the fallout from the purge of modernism in the MC was
the loss of members and congregations to the GCMC through schism
and expulsion, which reinforced the stereotype of the GCMC as the
liberal wing among twentieth-century Anabaptists.[7] J. C. Wenger
estimates that one eighth of the membership of the Indiana-Michigan

Conference of MC formed new congregations that joined the GCMC. Among the Mennonite leaders attacked by John Horsch for alleged modernism were a number of GCMC teachers at Bluffton College and Witmarsum Theological Seminary, and his polemical tracts sparked a doctrinal controversy at two GCMC triennial conferences.[8] Although fundamentalist-oriented leaders failed in numerous attempts to gain control of the GCMC, they still make their viewpoints felt.

> The year 1968 saw the formation of the unofficial Committee on Christian Concerns to provide a platform for those concerned about fundamental Christian doctrine. The officers and General Board of Conference have repeatedly conferred with members of this group about proposed reforms in conference life. Many of these CCC-ers are alumni of Grace Bible Institute. They assert that they do not want to found a new denomination; rather, to correct faults in our fellowship. Some of them pastor churches which continue support of the conference mission program. They would support our colleges with less enthusiasm, preferring GBI. At this point they are not publishing competitive periodicals and Sunday school literature though some would buy from Gospel Light or Scripture Press.[9]

Fundamentalist infiltration has been greatest in the MBC and EMC. Elmer Martens predicts that the membership of the MBC is on a collision course because of it,[10] and the EMC appears to have become so thoroughly committed to this form of orthodoxy that it has long ceased to be an issue among them.

The term "fundamentalism" refers to a cohesive, militant movement within American Protestantism during the first half of the twentieth century. Although the movement has largely spent itself, it produced reactionary attitudes and moods which continue to affect doctrinal discussions in most denominations. It began as a reaction to so-called "modernism" in the church, meaning a liberal readiness to revise traditional church doctrines in the light of modern science.

The key issue in the fundamentalist-modernist controversy was the authority of the Bible. Liberals tended to reassess the biblical message in the light of historical criticism and such new scientific theories as evolution and to put more emphasis on the ethical aspects of that message than on the doctrines concerning the supernatural. Renowned modernists like Shailer Mathews went so far as

to deny that the Bible had any authoritative, normative significance.[11] Most Christian liberals affirmed that the Bible had an
authoritative function but rejected claims to its infallibility.

Arrayed against the modernists were conservatives and arch-
conservatives who viewed liberalism as a serious threat to the fundamental doctrines of the Christian religion. The so-called "evangelical conservatives" were concerned primarily to safeguard what they
believed to be the basic historic teachings of the church. By 1920 control of the fundamentalist movement was captured by arch-conserva-
tives — a reactionary, polemical faction who were more militant in
their battle with the modernists and who defined the doctrinal issues
more precisely. They came to be known for their "five points of
fundamentalism" — a creedal list of final and absolutely essential
beliefs by which a true Christian could be identified. Actually,
various lists with varying numbers of "fundamentals" were
published, and the list that follows is based on the creed of the
World Christian Fundamentals Association (1919):[12]

1. The inerrancy of the Bible, verbally inspired of God and final
   infallible authority in faith and life.
2. The Virgin Birth of Christ.
3. The substitutionary atonement of Christ.
4. The bodily resurrection of Christ.
5. The imminent, personal, and premillennial return of Christ.
6. The creation of the universe by God in six days according
   to the Scriptures.
7. The bodily resurrection of the just to everlasting blessing and
   unjust to everlasting conscious punishment.

Various theories have been advanced to explain the phenomenon
of fundamentalism. H. Richard Niebuhr interpreted it as a social
phenomenon — an agrarian protest to threats of urbanization and
industrialization upon the church.[13] This theory is certainly pertinent to the impact of the movement upon Mennonites in their
painful transition from rural to urban styles of life.

Stewart G. Cole interpreted fundamentalism primarily as a
political power struggle for the control of American denominations.[14]
The battle was especially fierce in Presbyterian, Baptist, Methodist,
and Disciples of Christ denominations. The fundamentalists lost most
of these battles, but caused a number of denominational shake-ups
and schisms. There were parallel power struggles in the MC, GCMC,

and MBC, related both to the control of conference organization and of the church colleges, especially Goshen (MC), Bluffton (GCMC), Bethel (GCMC), and Tabor (MBC).

Historical theologians have offered two main theories regarding the movement. W. E. Garrison supports the common assumption that fundamentalism was simply an extension of eighteenth-century evangelical conservatism concerned only with the preservation of the basic doctrines of historic Christianity.[15] This was certainly the assumption of influential Mennonite fundamentalists like John Horsch.[16] If we took this view, it would be redundant to construct a measure of fundamentalist orthodoxy because it would measure the same dimension of belief as the General Orthodoxy Scale.

The other theory, which rejects the interpretation of a straight historical line between general orthodoxy and fundamentalist orthodoxy, has been skillfully formulated by Ernest R. Sandeen, who concludes that fundamentalism is "marked by doctrinal innovations and emphases which must not be confused with apostolic belief, Reformation theology, or nineteenth-century evangelism.[17] In a similar vein, MC theologian John H. Yoder has observed that fundamentalist militancy is a serious departure from the Christian pacifism of the Anabaptists, whether it is the assimilation of a quarrelsome attitude toward other members of the church or the tacit approval of explicit military action to defeat atheistic communism.

> Many churches would get a perfect grade on the fundamentalist check list, while holding very unclear, or even wrong, views on separation from the world, the Christian attitude toward nationalism and war. . . . What is the use of having a check list requiring people to accept the biblical view of the cross of Christ if that acceptance does not issue in a biblical view of the cross of the Christian?[18]

A Fundamentalist Orthodoxy Scale. In order to study the extent of commitment to fundamentalism in our groups, a Fundamentalist Orthodoxy Scale was constructed in a manner similar to the construction of the General Orthodoxy Scale described above. The five fundamentalist scale items had to do with the doctrines of the Bible, the virgin birth of Jesus, the creation in six days, the Flood, and hell as a place of eternal punishment. These items, of course, do not cover all the doctrines of fundamentalism. They are a select group, but tend to highlight some of the unique tenets of fundamentalism.

Table 6-2 gives the percent of respondents choosing the most orthodox response for each of the five doctrinal items. The percentages in the last column of the table are lower than the corresponding figures in Table 6-1. Thus the support of fundamentalist orthodoxy is not as great as the support of general orthodoxy among the church members. Only 50% of the respondents held firm to a six-

TABLE 6-2
Measures of Fundamentalist Orthodoxy

	Percent Responding for:					
	MC	GCMC	MBC	BIC	EMC	TOTAL
Doctrine of the Bible: "I believe the Bible is the divinely inspired and infallible Word of God, the only trustworthy guide for faith and life"	84	71	93	88	94	82
Doctrine of the Virgin Birth: "Jesus was born of a virgin"	89	80	96	92	96	88
Doctrine of Creation: "God created the earth and all living things in six 24-hour days"	53	42	54	54	64	50
Doctrine of the Flood: "There was a flood in Noah's day which destroyed all human life except for Noah's family"	84	71	90	87	94	81
Doctrine of Eternal Punishment: "All persons who die not having accepted Christ as their redeemer and savior will spend eternity in a place of punishment and misery"	77	60	85	82	91	74

Fundamentalist Orthodoxy Scale:

		MC	GCMC	MBC	BIC	EMC	TOTAL
20	High	46	34	50	47	58	43
18-19	High Middle	25	21	29	24	29	24
9-17	Low Middle	27	37	21	27	12	29
0-8	Low	2	8	1	2	1	4
	Total	100	100	101	100	100	100
	Number of Respondents	1,188	599	701	614	439	3,541
	Mean Score	17.9	16.4	18.4	18.1	18.9	17.6

day creation, and the 74% who definitely affirmed eternal punishment are less than the 90 to 93% who affirmed every item in the general orthodoxy scale. Nevertheless, the fundamentalism scores are very high. Strommen and his associates, who used a similar fundamentalism-liberalism scale in their church member study, found that Lutherans selecting the most orthodox choice numbered only 24% on their Bible question, 40% on the virgin birth, 37% on the concept of hell, and 27% on the rejection of the theory of evolution.[19] Because the questions used in the different studies are not identical they can serve as a basis only for broad comparisons. In their church member study in the United Church of Christ, Campbell and Fukuyama found that 67% definitely affirmed that "The Bible is the word of God," 58% affirmed the virgin birth of Jesus, and 17% affirmed that "Hell is a just punishment for sinners."[20] Because the responses in the present study were well above all of these percentages, twentieth-century Anabaptists appear to be more fundamentalist than members of these other groups.

Combining the five items, we constructed a composite scale with a range of possible scores from zero to 20. The overall average score was 17.6 (see bottom of Table 6-2). The denominations varied from a high average of 18.9 in the EMC to a low 16.4 in the GCMC.

The Fundamentalist Orthodoxy Scale contains a weakness that needs to be identified. John H. Yoder has pointed out that it is not so much the content of fundamentalist doctrines that makes the difference but the way those doctrines are used to draw lines of separation and break fellowship. He observed that the fundamentalist use of doctrine as a basis for exclusion is a serious departure from the priority placed on discipleship by the early Christians and the sixteenth-century Anabaptists.

> The Anabaptists accepted in their midst men who sometimes were too original and too daring in the attempt to rethink traditional doctrine in the light of discipleship. They accepted them, without accepting their doctrinal deviations, because of their conviction that discipleship mattered first. Likewise, the Anabaptists accepted separation from the state churches, with whom they agreed about everything on the fundamentalist check list, once again because discipleship comes first.[21]

Yoder's interpretation, an important refinement of the Sandeen theory, suggests that the most crucial test of fundamentalist orthodoxy is the factor of exclusion and not the content of belief. Unfortunately, this insight eluded the present researchers who omitted this aspect from the scale. The Yoder thesis suggests, nevertheless, that members who use doctrines as a check-list are selective in the ones they use, and until there is more evidence to the contrary, we will assume a close connection between the attitude of heresy-hunting and the high adherence to precisely the five "fundamentals" in the index constructed for the present study.

Anabaptism and Its Measurement

We turn, finally to a third aspect of doctrinal adherence to be called "Anabaptism." As indicated earlier this study distinguishes between the beliefs which Mennonites and Brethren in Christ share with other Christian denominations and beliefs which relate to their own particular heritage. If we refer to the latter as "particularism" as do several sociologists of religion, we can define particularism as the tendency for divided groups within a world religion to write their own confessions of faith. In so doing, they not only reaffirm the core of doctrine held in common with other groups but also specify those doctrines held as particularly essential or unique. Commitments of particularism have developed in every branch of Christendom following the apostolic age, including the left wing or Anabaptist party of the Reformation.[22] For obvious reasons, the construction of a valid and reliable scale measuring Anabaptist particularism was most crucial for testing adherence of twentieth-century Anabaptists to their own historical tradition. This was the measure of doctrinal belief, moreover, for which we could least depend on the work of other sociologists of religion.[23]

Anabaptism and Its Indicators. The first step in trying to measure the degree of a member's adherence to Anabaptism was to list the principles included in this particular historical heritage. From H. S. Bender's widely accepted paper, "The Anabaptist Vision," twenty-two special doctrines or norms of the movement were identified.[24] Bender had presented these norms in three broad categories which had to do with what it means to be a Christian (six norms), what it means to be the church (ten norms), and what it means to be faithful in the area of Christian ethics (six norms).

Next, these norms were translated into statements calling for one of five responses: strongly agree, agree, uncertain, disagree, strongly disagree. A respondent received a score of 4 if he "strongly agreed," 3 if he "agreed," and so on to 0 if he "strongly disagreed." For variation, an occasional statement was worded in the negative, so that a "faithful Anabaptist" would have to disagree rather than agree. In this case he scored 4 if he "strongly disagreed," and so forth.

Of those statements put into the questionnaire, eight were selected for the Anabaptism Scale on the basis of the item analysis test. These items follow, classified according to the original Bender categories. The percent of all respondents agreeing or strongly agreeing with the statement is given in parentheses.

1. *Christian Being: Discipleship.* "Jesus expects Christians today to follow the pattern which He set in His own life and ministry, including such things as putting evangelism above earning a living, and deeds of mercy above family security." (52%)

2. *Christian Being: Suffering.* "If Christian believers proclaim the lordship of Christ and truly follow Him in all of life they can expect to incur severe criticism and frequent persecution from the larger society." (72%)

3. *Christian Church: Baptism.* "Baptism is neither necessary nor proper for infants and small children." (82%)

4. *Christian Church: Discipline.* "The Mennonite and Brethren in Christ churches should practice a thorough church discipline so that faltering or unfaithful members can be built up and restored, or in exceptional cases, excluded." (60%)

5. *Christians Ethics: Oath.* "It is against the will of God for a Christian to swear the oath demanded by the civil government on occasion." (66%)

6. *Christian Ethics: Nonresistance.* "The Christian should take no part in war or any war-promoting activities." (73%)

7. *Christian Ethics: Separation.* "There are certain offices in our government the tasks of which a true Christian simply could not in clear conscience perform." (74%)

8. *Christian Ethics: Litigation.* "If a Christian has a legitimate claim of property damage against another person, he is justified in bringing suit in a court of law. (disagreed or strongly disagreed: 36%

Scores on this eight-item scale could range from 0 to 32.

As Table 6-3 shows, the mean score for all respondents in our study was 21.8. The MC scored highest with 23.1, and the EMC lowest with 18.6. The differences between the five groups are highly significant, but not as large as they might have been, as the next paragraph will indicate.

TABLE 6-3
Anabaptism Scale Scores

Scale Classes		Percentage Distribution for:					
		MC	GCMC	MBC	BIC	EMC	TOTAL
23-32	High	57	34	40	35	19	46
19-22	Middle	30	34	33	32	31	32
0-18	Low	13	32	26	34	50	22
	Total	100	100	99	101	100	100
	Number of Respondents	1,179	590	685	607	423	3,484
	Mean Score	23.1	20.4	21.2	20.5	18.6	21.8

The validity and reliability of these eight items were tested with two specially selected groups of people. Twenty-two persons, members of the Mennonite Research Fellowship known to adhere closely in personal beliefs to Anabaptist norms, served as a "control" group. Twenty-nine persons, members of a large Presbyterian Church selected by their pastors as fairly representative of a Calvinist (non-Anabaptist) doctrinal point of view, constituted an "experimental" group. The mean score of the "control" group on the eight items in the index was 24.7 (2.9 points higher than the members of the Anabaptist denominations). The mean score of the Presbyterians was 12.7 (9.1 points lower than the Anabaptist members). The fact that this separate test discriminated significantly in the predicted direction between the "experimental" and "control" groups, and did so consistently from one item to another, is further evidence of the scale's validity and reliability. It should be noted that although the five denominations in the study varied significantly on this test, the difference between any two of them was substantially less than the difference between any one of them and the Presbyterian "experimental" group.

Summary

In this chapter, the dimensions of faith related to belief and doctrine (i.e., intellectual assent to certain theological tenets) have been measured by three scales. One, called general orthodoxy, measures adherence to beliefs which Mennonites and Brethren in Christ share in common with the mainstream of historic Christianity. Another, called fundamentalist orthodoxy, tests adherence to the dogmas of the twentieth-century American fundamentalist movement. A third, called Anabaptism, measures adherence to the particular principles of the sixteenth-century movement that provided the main historic heritage and self-identity of the Mennonite and Brethren in Christ groups in the present study.

The members of the five groups in the present study score very high in general orthodoxy, they affirm the doctrines of American fundamentalism to a large degree, and they substantially support the particular teachings of their sixteenth-century forebears. It remains to be seen in later chapters whether and how these variables of belief are related to the attitudes and practices of these church members.

Chapter 7

MORAL ISSUES

From their beginnings, the Anabaptists laid great emphasis on the manner of life as evidence of a person's salvation and regeneration. As H. S. Bender pointed out, the Anabaptists believed that God's spirit in a man's life makes it possible for him to have victory over sin.[1] They rejected the Lutheran view that life in this world, even for Christians, cannot rise above a compromise with the sinful order.

Luther and Zwingli taught that the chief tasks of the church were preaching the gospel and administering the sacraments. To these roles Calvin and Knox added the administration of ecclesiastical discipline. The Anabaptists went further, demanding a disciplined church that admits and retains as members only those who give evidence of being "called out" of the world unto a life of holiness and brotherly love patterned after Christ. The lives of Christ's followers should be distinctive from the general ethical patterns of those Christians who compromise with the ethics of a secular society.

"Anabaptists," wrote John H. Yoder, "believe that to be Christian is to be *different* in the way one relates to his brethren, his neighbors, and his nation." This leads to a moral nonconformity among the Christians that becomes visible in loving their enemies, feeding the hungry, telling the truth, and working for reconciliation between conflicting groups.[2]

Menno Simons saw the holy life as devoid of hatred, vengeance, pride, and unchastity. The Swiss Brethren believed that the "resurrected life in Christ" is one in which the Holy Spirit works with power in continuous growth toward perfection.[3]

This emphasis is in some ways similar to the teachings of John Wesley two centuries later. Wesley extolled the virtues of the holy life, rooting his teachings in the doctrine of sanctification by a "definite work of grace subsequent to regeneration."[4]

The Anabaptists, however, did not teach a "second work of grace." They looked for a process of growth in obedience to God's Word and in love among the brethren. Only those who manifested these qualities of discipleship were fit to be members of the church. Although good works were expected, they were seen as fruits of salvation and not the means to salvation.

Because of the Anabaptist emphasis on these outward manifestations of the Christian life, the Reformers often charged the Anabaptists with preaching a "works salvation." The radical break which the Anabaptists made with what they saw as the compromising ethics of the state churches brought them into all sorts of persecution by the leaders of the state church and secular governments. Despite their ruthless efforts to stamp out the "Anabaptist heresy," they nevertheless admitted that the moral achievements of the Anabaptists were generally superior to those of the members of the state churches. Heinrich Bullinger, head of the Reformed Church in Zurich, long an enemy of the Anabaptists, nevertheless testified of them in 1560,"

> Those who unite with them will by their ministers be received into their church by rebaptism and repentance and newness of life. They henceforth lead their lives under a semblance of a quite spiritual conduct. They denounce covetousness, pride, profanity, and lewd conversation and immorality of the world, drinking and gluttony.[5]

American and Canadian Developments

By the time Mennonites were migrating from Europe to America in the eighteenth and nineteenth centuries, radical Anabaptism had lost much of its rigor. Severe persecutions had led some adherents to forsake the movement. Some were drawn off by the German Pietists, who also stressed the holy life but without the radical world-renouncing elements of the Swiss Brethren and the followers of Menno.[6] A remnant continued to adhere to the church of their fathers, but increasingly adapted themselves to the general cultural mores of the surrounding societies. This was particularly true of the Dutch Mennonites who came under the influence of rationalism and humanism, and who became wealthy leaders in the commercial developments of Holland.

The Mennonite and Amish settlers in Pennsylvania brought with them most of the tenets of early Anabaptism, including the tendency to emphasize a disciplined life free from the excesses of behavior more easily tolerated by other settlers. They stressed the simple life, simple attire, honesty and integrity in business dealings, mutual aid, and opposition to participation in political activities. Since they did not oppose moderate drinking, some Mennonites became brewers. Until the latter part of the nineteenth century there was little opposition to the use of tobacco, and a flourishing tobacco-raising industry developed among Amish and Mennonites in eastern Pennsylvania, which still continues among the Old Order Amish and the more conservative Mennonite groups.[7]

The moral issues which concern Mennonite groups in the twentieth century are in many cases related to the social and technological developments of a modern society. The MC and BIC have been particularly prone to prohibit or discourage their members from participating in such modern developments as lodges, labor unions, county fairs, and carnivals. At certain times and places these churches have opposed new communication media, such as radio, television, and motion pictures. Fashionable clothing and hair dressing have been opposed, along with dancing and certain forms of Sunday recreation. Some groups have opposed life insurance, musical instruments in churches, and betting or gambling of any sort.

Opposition to the use of alcoholic beverages began to occur in the late nineteenth century. The founders of the MBC were vigorous champions of abstinence from both tobacco and alcohol. Although they prohibited liquors of high alcoholic content, wines and beers were tolerated.[8] All of the Mennonite and Brethren in Christ groups were influenced by the temperance organizations that developed in the late nineteenth century. They were also affected by the battle against liquor conducted by the Sunday school and revivalist movements, where Methodist and Baptist influence was particularly strong. Gradually some Mennonite conferences began to legislate against members making or selling liquor or patronizing saloons. By the early twentieth century most Mennonites and Brethren in Christ had become abstainers, and grape juice was being substituted for wine in the communion service.

The Holiness movement, rooted in Wesleyanism and beginning in 1867, was influential in opposition to drinking, smoking, dancing, and certain other behaviors referred to earlier. Some eastern Mennonites were influenced by this movement, but the BIC have been most strongly influenced by virtue of their Wesleyan roots and their membership in the National Holiness Association.

Among the groups in the current study, the MC, MBC, and BIC have been most prone to develop lists of prescribed and proscribed behaviors which members are expected to observe, under threat of discipline for non-observance. The Old Order Amish and Old Order Mennonites (not included in the survey) are most extreme in their **proscription of cultural and technological innovations, including the** use of electricity and telephones, and the ownership of automobiles, tractors, radios, and television. However, they were relatively unaffected by the anti-alcohol and anti-tobacco movements.

From the viewpoint of some Christians, including some Mennonites, these long lists of proscriptions smack of the worst forms of legalism and moralism.[9] In the MC and BIC a form of authoritarian conference structure emerged in the first half of the twentieth century, which made it possible for prescriptions and proscriptions of various sorts to be adopted and enforced by conferences as binding on congregations. Since 1950, however, there has been a renewed emphasis on the primacy of the congregation in determining and maintaining moral standards. Consequently there has been some relaxing of the controls and discipline over individual behavior that characterized the earlier decades of the century. The GCMC and EMC have been less inclined to attempt to regulate moral issues in their confessions and conference action.

At certain times and places Mennonites clearly have been caught in the problems of a legalistic moralism. Emphasis on the "holy life" and the "clean life," with whatever lofty intentions, can easily degenerate into a hardening of rules and discipline. The findings of the 1968 Conference on the Believers' Church pointed to "the danger of imposing our vision of obedience upon the unconvinced, or of defining it legalistically without reference to changes in the ethical context."[10] Some leaders believe that the churches need to consider carefully the extent to which their ministry is to be education and the extent to which it is to be regulation.

Recent years have brought new issues to the attention of the churches. These include the use of marijuana and hard drugs, and issues related to the so-called "sexual revolution" — premarital intercourse, abortion, and homosexuality. The denominations are generally reluctant to deal with these issues by prohibitive legislation. Study conferences, education, and conference-approved standards constitute the present-day approaches to these issues. The most recent specific actions have been taken by the Brethren in Christ. The 1973 revision of their *Manual of Doctrine and Government* states that "the witness of the Christian is hindered . . . by involvement in tobacco, intoxicating drinks, and drug abuse." The *Manual* further states that "marriage is honorable, but premarital sex, adultery, and the practice of homosexuality have no place in the new life in Christ."[11]

Contemporary Attitudes

Our survey did not cover all the moral issues to which the churches have spoken in recent times. However, 25 issues were listed and the respondent was asked to check one of four responses: "always wrong" if he considered the behavior to be wrong under all conditions; "sometimes wrong" (i.e., under some conditions, whether few or many), "never wrong," or "uncertain." Findings related to items on marriage, divorce, abortion, and contraception are discussed in the chapter on "Marriage and the Family." Table 7-1 contains the percentage distribution of responses for all the denominations, for items presented in this chapter.

The respondents are most strongly opposed to the use of hard drugs and to becoming drunken, with 97% and 94%, respectively, checking "always wrong." Next in line come income tax evasion and reckless driving, followed by smoking marijuana (87%), homosexual acts (86%), and gambling (75%). Smoking tobacco is viewed as always wrong by nearly two thirds (64%) of the respondents and moderate drinking by 50%. Social dancing and masturbation elicited the greatest diversity of opinion and the largest percentages "uncertain." Apparently about one third of the church members question the use of tea or coffee, but only under some conditions, possibly such as ill health or addiction to use.

TABLE 7-1
Percentage Distribution of Responses
on Moral Issues

	Issue	Response			
		Always wrong	Some-times wrong	Never wrong	Un-certain
1.	Drinking alcoholic beverages (moderately)	50	36	7	7
2.	Becoming drunken	94	4	1	1
3.	Smoking tobacco	64	26	3	8
4.	Smoking marihuana	87	9	1	3
5.	Use of hard drugs (LSD, heroin, etc.)	97	2	0*	1
6.	Drinking tea or coffee	1	32	57	10
7.	Attending movies rated for adults and children	18	51	22	9
8.	Attending movies rated for adults only	48	41	4	7
9.	Premarital sexual intercourse	85	12	1	3
10.	Extramarital sexual intercourse	86	6	2	7
11.	Homosexual acts	86	6	1	7
12.	Masturbation	46	27	6	21
13.	Gambling (betting, gambling machines)	75	19	1	4
14.	Social dancing	43	35	12	11
15.	Reckless driving	89	9	0*	2
16.	Income tax evasion (not reporting all income as required by law)	90	7	0*	3

*Less than 0.5 percent.

Table 7-2 gives the percentage answering "always wrong" for the denominations separately. Although some important differences between the denominations do appear, on many of the items there is close agreement. We shall refer to the position of greater opposition to the behavior (higher percentages) as the more "restrictive" view and the lesser opposition (lower percentages) as the more "lenient" view. On seven of the 16 items the most lenient and most restrictive churches were separated by only eight percentage points or less.

TABLE 7-2
Percent Responding "Always Wrong" to Moral
Behaviors, by Denomination

| Issue | Denomination | | | | |
	MC	GCMC	MBC	BIC	EMC
1. Drinking alcoholic beverages (moderately)*	56	35	51	68	60
2. Becoming drunken	95	92	98	96	96
3. Smoking tobacco*	66	50	76	75	63
4. Smoking marihuana*	87	85	91	91	93
5. Use of hard drugs (LSD, heroin, etc.)	97	97	99	98	99
6. Drinking tea or coffee	1	2	1	2	1
7. Attending movies rated for adults and children	19	10	25	23	15
8. Attending movies rated for adults only*	54	33	55	60	59
9. Premarital sexual intercourse*	85	79	92	85	90
10. Extramarital sexual intercourse	86	86	86	84	89
11. Homosexual acts*	87	78	91	91	93
12. Masturbation*	47	39	49	52	50
13. Gambling (betting, gambling machines)*	80	66	74	82	78
14. Social dancing*	47	26	57	54	43
15. Reckless driving	88	91	90	87	89
16. Income tax evasion (not reporting all income as required by law)	90	89	94	90	95

*Items used to form the Moral Attitudes Scale.

The greatest denominational differences are indicated for moderate drinking, smoking tobacco, social dancing, and attending movies rated for adults only. For these items the percentage differences between the most restrictive and most lenient churches were 25% or greater. On all four items the GCMC members were the most lenient and the BIC and MBC members were most restrictive, except for moderate drinking, where the MBC is the second most lenient among the five groups.

An overall comparison of the churches can be made by totaling and averaging the percentages in the five data columns of Table 7-2. This indicates that the BIC is the most restrictive, with the MBC a close second, and the EMC a close third. The GCMC is the most lenient, and the MC falls in between, with a position closer to the three more restrictive churches than to the GCMC.

In making interdenominational comparisons, one should remember that these percentages are average and do not reveal the whole range of responses for the members of the churches. In all the churches some members take the extreme positions, so that some members of the more restrictive groups are more lenient in their views than many members of the more lenient groups. In light of the entire range of views of the members within each group, the five denominations do not appear very different. For example, the percentages answering "never wrong" on the "moderate drinking" item are MC, 6.5; GCMC, 9.4; MBC, 5.6; BIC, 5.8; and EMC, 6.6. These differences are so small as to justify the conclusion that the five denominations are really quite similar.

Comparable data for other denominations are difficult to find. Most recent denominational surveys have not included a study of attitudes and behavior related to personal morality. The available data, however, suggest that Mennonites are considerably more restrictive than other groups studied. Whereas about 90% of the Lutheran laymen studied by Kersten said dancing is "not wrong," only 10% of Mennonites responded "never wrong." About half of Lutheran laymen see smoking as "not wrong" compared to three percent for our church members.[12] Kersten's study did not provide data for other items.

Lenski's survey of Protestants, Catholics, and Jews in the Detroit area included a few questions on personal morality to which the respondents were given four options in answering: "always wrong," "usually wrong," "sometimes wrong," and "never wrong." In regard to moderate drinking, the proportions answering "always" or "usually wrong" were: Lutherans, 7%; Episcopalians, 12%; Methodists, 41%; Baptists, 46%; Jews, 5%; and Catholics, 11%. It is clear that Mennonites and BIC are more restrictive than any of these groups. Similarly, our respondents were more opposed to gambling than were any of these Detroit groups.[13]

Attitudes and Behavior Scales

To facilitate cross tabulations between respondents' attitudes on moral issues and other variables, a "Moral Attitudes Scale" was constructed using nine of the moral issues listed in Table 7-2. This provides a more efficient cross-tabulation procedure than attempting to relate each issue separately to all the other scales. The nine issues incorporated into the scale were moderate drinking, smoking tobacco, smoking marijuana, movies for adults only, premarital sexual intercourse, homosexual acts, masturbation, gambling, and social dancing. Each of these nine items "scaled" satisfactorily; that is, each item had an adequate range of responses so that the item discriminated clearly between those who scored high and those who scored low on the scale as a whole. Those respondents scoring high on the scale are those tending to view the behaviors as always wrong.

A second scale, the Moral Behavior Scale, was derived in order to measure the respondent's behavior (or non-behavior) on several moral issues. Measuring behavior is a more delicate matter than measuring attitudes. A respondent may be willing to indicate whether he thinks drinking or gambling is wrong, but he may be offended or reluctant to indicate whether he actually drinks or gambles. In order to avoid the risk of losing the good will and cooperation of the respondents, the questionnaire did not probe for actual behavior, except for three items. These items, the responses provided, and the percentage distribution of responses for the total sample are as follows:

1. Which of the following describes the extent to which you have used tobacco in your lifetime?
       46% "Have never tried it"
       39% "Tried it once or a few times"

    10% "Have used it regularly in the past, but no longer
        use it"
     6% "Am a regular user now"
2. Which of the following describes the extent to which you
  have drunk alcoholic beverages in your lifetime?
    36% "Never drank any"
    46% "Drank some once or a few times"
     5% "Drank occasionally or regularly in times past, but
        no longer"
    13% "Drink occasionally or regularly now"
3. To what extent have you participated in social dancing?
    62% "Never"
    22% "Once, or a few times"
    12% "Occasionally"
     4% "Frequently"

A respondent's score on the Moral Behavior Scale is obtained by adding his scores on the three items. If he responded "never" on all three items, he has scored "highest" on the scale. Rating "low" on the scale means he has regularly or frequently participated in the behaviors. Thus "high" on both scales represents the restrictive view on the issue.

Scholars vary somewhat in their views on the extent to which attitude determines behavior, and vice versa. Having participated in a given behavior may cause a person to change his attitude. On the other hand, his readiness to participate will have been affected by whether he has previously acquired a lenient or a restrictive attitude. In any event, one would expect to find a substantial, although by no means complete, correlation between scores on attitude and behavior scales. Other factors besides attitudes — such as opportunity — will affect behavior. Some persons may have a lenient attitude toward a behavior (*e.g.*, dancing, premarital sex) but have not had or sought out the opportunity to engage in it.

We obtained a correlation coefficient of .55 between scores on the two scales. This indicates a substantial, but not a perfect relationship between the variables, and supports the contention that behavior and attitudes affect each other. This is further illustrated by the relationship between attitude and behavior for a single item. For example, of those saying moderate drinking is "always wrong," 56% report having never drunk alcoholic beverages, and only one percent report being regular drinkers. Of those seeing drinking as "never wrong," 60% are regular drinkers and only 5% have never drunk any.

Variations in Attitudes and Behavior

Significant variations in moral attitudes and behavior appear when these variables are cross-tabulated with age, residence, education, and income. Age makes the biggest difference. The proportion of respondents rating "high" on the Moral Attitudes Scale are teenagers, 68%; 20-29-year-olds, 62%; 30-49-year-olds, 81%; and those over 50, 89%. Thus, in general, increasing age means greater restrictiveness, except that the teenagers are more restrictive than the young adults in their 20s, who evidence the most lenient views.

Scores on the Moral Behavior Scale show similar age variations, with 20-29-year-olds rating lowest and those over 50 rating highest (least participation in the scale behaviors). However, the teenagers rate higher than the 30-49 age group, perhaps in part because of social and legal restrictions, such as laws which prevent teenagers from drinking alcoholic beverages.

Residence appears to have only a small effect on moral attitudes and behavior. Lenient views are slightly more prevalent among urban than among rural church members. In regard to income, attitudes and behavior tend to be slightly more lenient as one goes up the income scale. In general, the higher the educational achievement, the more lenient the attitudes and behavior. Variations between educational levels seem to be greater for attitudes than behaviors.

Finally, some important relationships appear when moral attitudes and behavior are correlated with the variables of doctrine and church participation introduced in the three preceding chapters. The correlation coefficients which were obtained are given in Table 7-3.

These correlations indicate that high scores (restrictive attitudes and behavior) on the morality scales are significantly associated with high scores on the variables of faith and life. This indicates only a general relationship, however, and one cannot conclude that all persons high on the morality scales will also be high on the faith and life scales.

If all persons high on the morality scales were also high on the other scales, then the correlation coefficients would be much closer to a perfect correlation (*i.e.*, 1.00).

We conclude that church members with the most restrictive views on morality tend to be more orthodox in their doctrinal beliefs, hold stronger Anabaptist views, practice a greater personal piety, and are more strongly committed to voluntary church membership and active participation in the life and work of the church.

After four centuries, the followers of the Anabaptists still exercise a rigorous discipline in matters of personal morality. Perhaps some groups have gone too far in the direction of moral legalism, assigning moral definitions to certain customs and technologies of daily life that, some would claim, should not be so defined. On the other hand, some church members have veered off toward very liberal views, easily accepting attitudes and behaviors that the early Anabaptists would have refused to tolerate among the faithful. Apparently the majority of twentieth-century Mennonites and BIC adhere to a fairly rigorous personal ethic, refusing to accept as valid for the Christian many behaviors much more easily accepted or tolerated by general Christendom.

TABLE 7-3
Correlations of Various Scales with Moral Attitudes and Behavior

Scales	Moral Attitudes Scale	Moral Behavior Scale
General Orthodoxy	.50	.33
Fundamentalist Orthodoxy	.57	.39
Anabaptism	.45	.39
Associationalism	.38	.38
Voluntarism	.38	.21
Communalism	.27	.28
Devotionalism	.47	.43

Chapter 8

SOCIAL ETHICS

One of the areas in which the sixteenth-century Anabaptist posture was most decisive was social ethics and witness. The principles of social ethics in the state churches of Europe were based on the necessity of compromise with the hard realities of a sinful world. By accepting social realities (war, the use of force, inequalities of station in life) the Protestant reformers hoped the church would be in a position of influence where injustices gradually could be removed. The Anabaptists rejected this principle of natural strategy and based their social ethic upon an absolute law of love. H. S. Bender wrote, "The third great element in the Anabaptist vision was the ethic of love and nonresistance as applied to all human relationships. The Brethren understood this to mean complete abandonment of all warfare, strife, and violence, and of the taking of human life."[1]

To this day Mennonites and Brethren in Christ are known for their nonresistant commitment and style of life. Although it is a negative concept, the application of which is most conspicuous in a member's refusal to engage in military service or participate in war, this commitment grows out of a positive New Testament way of life founded on love and the cross. The others reformers did not doubt that Jesus was nonresistant, but the Anabaptists went beyond them in their belief that in His nonresistance Jesus gave them an example to follow.

The doctrine of nonresistance has implications for every phase of the Christian's life, first of all in personal relations. The Christian brotherhood is a community of forgiven sinners whose attitude toward one another is that of unbounded forgiveness, unto "seventy times seven." Its members do not seek the highest position; they live in humble subjection one to another out of reverence for Christ who in washing the disciples' feet is their great example in humble, loving service. In the wider social relationships the emphasis is on doing justice, loving mercy, and walking humbly before one's God. Doing that which is just to others takes precedence over seeking justice for one's self or for one's group. Instead of going to law for the settlement of differences the Christian would rather suffer himself to be defrauded. In economic relationships the Christian community does not think in terms of buyer and seller or of management and labor, each seeking his own good; it thinks of itself as a brotherhood whose members are laborers together with God, in honor preferring one another.[2]

In this chapter, adherence to a nonresistant ethic in the "wider social relationships" will be tested with some rather specific probes pertaining to war, race relations, labor-management relations, concern for the poor, and the prophetic witness on several other issues, such as capital punishment. The dimension of "brotherhood ethics" on issues like divorce or the role of women in the church are treated elsewhere (see Chapters 10 and 11). The ethical issues pertaining to church-state relations, voting, and office holding will be covered in Chapter 9. The issue of lawsuits was discussed in Chapter 6 in connection with the Anabaptism Scale.

War and the Peace Position

An absolute position against participation in warfare has always been a distinctive norm of groups standing in the Anabaptist tradition. Following are abstracts from recent official statements of each denomination on this subject:

MC: The peace principles of the Mennonite Church, including

its historic four-century-old witness against all war, are an integral part of the gospel of Jesus Christ and of the discipleship which we believe the lordship of Christ requires of all of His followers. . . . Specifically, we understand this commitment to mean . . . that we can have no part in carnal warfare or conflict between nations . . . and that we can therefore not accept military service, either combatant or noncombatant, or preparation or training therefor in any form.[3]

GCMC: We believe that war is altogether contrary to the teaching and spirit of Christ and the gospel; that therefore war is sin. . . . We cannot approve military service in any form. . . . We are constrained of Christ to take no part in warfare or military service as combatants or as noncombatants because both forms of service have as their ultimate military end the impairment and destruction of life or property of our fellow men.[4]

MBC: We believe that Christians should live by the law of love and practice the forgiveness of enemies as taught and exemplified by the Lord Jesus. . . . The evil, brutal and inhuman nature of war stands in contradiction to the new nature of the Christian. . . . Instead of participating in the military we perform alternate service to reduce strife, alleviate suffering and bear witness to the love of Christ.[5]

BIC: Jesus Christ is our example of the nonresistant way of life. . . . Hence, all acts of violence which seek the injury of of others, whether committed by individuals or groups, and whether physically, socially or psychologically inflicted, are repudiated. Thus, participation in military service is inconsistent with the teachings of Scriptures concerning nonresistance. Jesus sets no limits to our forgiveness.[6]

EMC: We believe that the teaching of Scripture enjoins believers to love their enemies, to do good to them that hate them, and to overcome evil with good. . . . The historic position of the Evangelical Mennonite Church is to oppose the bearing of arms in warfare and the gendering of strife between nations, classes, groups or individuals.[7]

Measures of the Pacifist Commitment. Important differences appear in the official statements quoted above, but before identifying these we will examine data pertaining to a number of questions about the pacifist commitment. Seven such items, listed in Table 8-1, probe (1) participating in war activities, (2) owning stock in companies producing war goods, (3) promoting the peace position, (4) justifying the Vietnam War, (5) justifying the eight-day Israeli-Arab War in 1970, (6) paying war taxes, and (7) choosing a draft position. From a pacifist point of view, the MC ranks *first* on the first, second,

TABLE 8-1
Measures of Pacifism

Items and Responses	Percent of Responses for:					
	MC	GCMC	MBC	BIC	EMC	TOTAL
1. "The Christian should take no part in war or any war-promoting activities."						
Strongly agree/Agree	87	66	54	61	20	73
2. Attitude about the rightness or wrongness of owning stock in companies producing war goods.						
Always wrong	55	39	29	34	16	44
3. "Mennonites and Brethren in Christ should actively promote the peace position and attempt to win as many supporters to the position as possible from the larger society."						
Agree	54	65	47	54	36	56
4. "The Vietnam War was necessary as a means of stopping the spread of communism in Asia."						
Disagree	50	44	22	28	17	42
5. "Israel's victory over the Arab nations is justified because God has promised to restore Israel as a nation."						
Disagree	24	31	12	10	6	23
6. "A member of our churches ought not to pay the proportion of his income taxes that goes for military purposes."						
Agree	12	15	7	8	4	12
7. "Which one of the following positions would you take if faced with a military draft?"						
Regular military service	2	8	8	8	36	5
Noncombatant military service	3	15	23	12	22	11
Alternative service	86	62	48	67	25	71
Refuse registr./induction	3	3	3	1	1	3
Uncertain	7	13	19	12	17	11
Pacifism Scale:						
9-14 High	64	56	26	37	10	54
6-8 Middle	31	33	52	48	41	36
0-5 Low	4	11	21	15	49	10
Total	99	100	99	100	100	100
Number of Respondents	1,084	507	538	509	352	2,990
Mean Score	9.0	8.7	7.1	7.7	5.5	8.5

fourth, and seventh items, and the GCMC ranks *first* on the third, fifth, and sixth items. It is probably the content of these questions that explains the difference between the two groups. On the absolute pacifist position, specifically expressed in the first item, the MC stands firmly for the historic principle; but on promoting that position in society (item 3) or denying the legitimacy of a pagan government waging its pagan war (items 5 and 6) the members of the MC show some pause. The peace ethic of the MC is a two-kingdom ethic, which its official position expresses as follows: "We recognize that in a world where the evil and the good exist side by side, there is a necessary place, authorized by God Himself, for the use of force by the state in the restraint of evil and the protection of the good, though always under restrictions deriving from the higher laws of God."[8] Thus, although 87% of MC members believe a Christian should take no part in war, only 50% denied that the Vietnam War was necessary, 24% denied that Israel's victory was justified, and 12% opposed paying war taxes.

The members of GCMC, on the other hand, are less absolutist on the general pacifist principle but more willing to pronounce against specific wars and the payment of war taxes:

> The levying of war taxes is another form of conscription which, along with the conscription of manpower, makes war possible. We are accountable to God for the use of our financial resources and should protest the use of our taxes in the promotion and waging of war. We stand by those who feel called to resist the payment of that portion of taxes being used for military purpose.[9]

Among the five groups, the EMC is having the greatest difficulty retaining such a thoroughgoing adherence to the doctrine of nonresistance. Its members as a whole were least pacifist on all seven items. Over half of the present membership of the EMC is of non-Mennonite background. While this indicates a good work of evangelism it has made it difficult for pacifism to be accepted. Officially the EMC opposes "the bearing of arms in warfare" but tolerates "the right of individual conviction" on this issue and recognizes "that various positions will be taken on war and military service."[10]

Questions 2, 3, 4, 5, and 7 were combined into a Pacifism Scale having a range of scores from zero to 14. The overall mean score, as reported at the bottom of Table 8-1, was 8.5. Table 8-2 reports a number of cross-tabulations between this index and various "faith," "life," and "work-of-the-church" variables. The table includes several variables that will be introduced later in this and subsequent chapters, and are included here so that their relationship to pacifism can be shown.

TABLE 8-2
Relation of Pacifism to Selected Variables

	Low 1	2	3	High 4	Pearson Coeff. (r)
	(% scoring "high" on Pacifism)				
Anabaptism	33*	50	66		.385
General Orthodoxy	84	65	55	52	-.163
Fundamentalist Orthodoxy	88	62	49	49	-.265
Communalism	40	51	59	67	.177
Ethical—Social Conversion	44	55	64		.162
Socioeconomic Status	63	50	60	71	.172
Education	54	48	60	65	.132
Anti—Communism	77	53	27		-.510
Anti—Semitism	66	54	47	40	-.185
Social Concerns	32	54	77		.439
Welfare Attitudes	40	53	72		.292
Race Relations	43	51	67		.274
MCC Support	37	52	59		.256
Separation of Church & State	68	48	46		-.186
Political Participation	30	28	25		-.112
Shared Ministry	48	52	70		.199
Evangelism	53	52	55	58	.070

*Read percentages as follows: Of those who scored "low" (1) in Anabaptism, 33% scored "high" on Pacifism.

The first five variables in Table 8-2 are "faith" variables which were significantly associated with pacifism — three in a positive direction and two in a negative direction. Since pacifism has a negative correlation coefficient of -.265 with fundamentalist orthodoxy, it is evident that fundamentalists in these churches tend to be non-pacifist. This confirms the fears of the late H. S. Bender that the assimilation of the polemic spirit of fundamentalism was eroding the ethic of nonresistance. In several important articles, Bender pleaded for a sound biblical approach and an evangelical theology that were faithfully integrated with the Anabaptist vision.[11] It will become even more evident on other ethical issues that his concern was attuned to the facts.

Among the other negative correlations with pacifism are anti-communism, anti-Semitism, and the separation of church and state. This evidence would indicate not only that prejudice and pacifism tend to undermine each other, but also that political noninvolvement supports the rejection of pacifism. We can put this in another way by saying that the pacifism of members and the political involvement of their church are not incompatible. The implications of pacifism for a prophetic intervention in society are indicated further by the positive correlation of pacifism with the members' social concern, and their pro-welfare attitudes, race relations attitudes, and support of the Mennonite Central Committee. This evidence underlines the concept of nonresistance as not just a withdrawal from war activity but an application of the way of love in all human relationships.

It is sometimes as interesting to note which variables are relatively unrelated as to note those with high correlations. For instance, the practice of evangelism has little relationship ($r = .070$) to attitudes toward pacifism. The idea in the 1971 statement on "The Way of Peace" adopted by the GCMC that "The way of peace is the way of evangelism" gets relatively little support in the attitudes of the five groups.[12] Although evangelism and peace witness have often worked at cross purposes with each other in these churches, our data suggest that a neutral relationship exists between them.

Race Relations

The church has long been criticized for its prejudiced racial attitudes. Eleven o'clock on Sunday morning (associationalism) has been called the most segregated hour of the week. Numerous studies have reported strong negative correlations between intellectual assent to theological creeds (general orthodoxy and fundamentalist orthodoxy) and uncompassionate attitudes toward persons of other creeds and colors.

Can such indictments be made against Mennonites and BIC? We will start with cross-tabulations of a scale on race relations and then report the items that went into its construction. Of the fourteen most significant cross-tabs in Table 8-3, the first five are with faith variables. With reference to "eleven o'clock on Sunday morning" (associationalism), the attitudes of the respondents are in the positive direction toward racial integration, but with a coefficient of only .092 the relationship is weak. This suggests that persons attending church more regularly tend to be a bit more accepting of persons of other races.

TABLE 8-3
Race Relations as Related to Other Variables

Variable	Score on Scale at Left					Pearson Coeff. (r)
	Low 1	2	3	4	High 5	
	(% scoring "high" on Race Relations)					
Fundamentalist Orthodoxy	61*	44	34	19		-.276
Voluntarism	46	43	32	24		-.156
General Orthodoxy	67	49	37	28		-.150
Associationalism	31	27	33	41		.092
Anabaptism	31	30	34			.056
Anti—Communism	52	23	29			-.345
Anti—Semitism	48	33	21	18	8	-.310
Anti—Catholicism	53	31	19	17	20	-.308
Age (by generation)	40	46	33	20		-.296
Education	18	27	46	53		.257
Socioeconomic Status	23	23	43	50		.248
Social Concerns	20	28	54			.305
Welfare Attitudes	58	24	18			.303
Pacifism	22	24	40			.274
Separation of Church & State	48	40	21			-.262
Shared Ministry	20	29	59			.321
Ecumenism	12	32	43			.233

*Read percentages as follows: Of those who scored "low" (1) on Fundamentalist Orthodoxy, 61% scored "high" on Race Relations. On the age variable, 1 indicates low age, 13-19 years; 2 is age 20-29; 3 is age 30-49; and 4 is age 50 and over.

The other three faith variables, however, and especially fundamentalist orthodoxy, are negatively correlated with attitudes on race relations. This confirms the findings of other studies and troubles the conscience of any Mennonite or BIC who is sensitive to the problem of race prejudice. It is difficult to discover, however, whether orthodoxy causes prejudice, or whether a prejudiced person finds an orthodox religious identification congenial and "voluntarily" turns to the church for "help." Or does a self-doubting, frustrated person grasp at both prejudice and religion to try to resolve his difficulties?

The Anabaptism Scale, which was significantly correlated with pacifism, has only a low correlation (r = .056) with race relations, albeit in a positive direction.

Various kinds of prejudice were negatively correlated with race relations, *i.e.*, the lower the scores on race relations, the higher the scores on anti-communism, anti-Semitism, and anti-Catholicism.

The most favorable attitudes toward other races are found among those church members who are young, who have more education, and who occupy a higher socioeconomic status. Favorable race attitudes are also related to positive attitudes toward other social concerns, public welfare, pacifism, and the concept of the shared ministry.

Race Relations Scale. The five questions that make up the composite Race Relations Scale are listed in Table 8-4. The fact that the MC and GCMC rank highest in the scale among the five denominations may reflect a more concerted effort in these groups to issue official position statements against race prejudice.[13] Both groups' statements, moreover, reflect a deliberate attempt to identify one's attitude toward race with one's attitude toward war. "To refuse participation in warfare," the MC statement declared, "demands that Christians likewise rise above the practices of discrimination and coercion in other areas, such as race relations." The declaration that "racial prejudice is sin" in the GCMC statement was modeled after the similar assertion in its earlier declaration on war, "We believe that war is altogether contrary to the teaching and spirit of Christ and the gospel; that therefore war is sin." Both statements were issued between the time of the United States Supreme Court decision against "separate but equal" schools (1954) and the "open occupancy" legislation by Congress in the area of housing (1968).

As a gauge of influences in the origin and shaping of these declarations, it is significant that both statements supported the prior action of the Supreme Court but neither spoke specifically to the remaining problem of segregation in housing. It should be added, however, that the MC declaration abandoned all "biological objection" to interracial marriage in advance of the Supreme Court decision against state miscegenation laws (1967).

TABLE 8-4
Measures of Race Relations

| | | Percent Responses for: | | | | |
Items and Responses	MC	GCMC	MBC	BIC	EMC	TOTAL
1. "The several races of mankind all share equally in such human qualities as intelligence, physical capacities, and emotional makeup."						
Agree	69	68	65	64	61	68
2. "Although there is no essential difference between blacks and whites, it is preferable for them not to mingle socially."						
Disagree	61	60	55	58	56	59
3. "People (black, red, or white) have a right to keep others out of their neighborhood if they want to, and this right should be respected."						
Disagree	62	56	54	57	51	59
4. "If one's own house were up for sale, he should be willing to sell it to an interested black family regardless of possible neighborhood reaction."						
Agree	60	58	57	54	50	59
5. "There is a biblical basis for the separation of the races."						
Disagree	44	40	29	35	29	40
Race Relations Scale:						
9-10 High	35	32	24	26	21	32
6-8 Middle	44	40	45	44	45	43
0-5 Low	21	28	31	30	34	25
Total	100	100	100	100	100	100
Number of Respondents	1,170	594	685	604	433	3,486
Mean Score	7.3	6.9	6.6	6.8	6.3	7.0

Comparisons of attitudes on race relations between Mennonites and other denominations are possible when similar questionnaire items were used in the different studies. Table 8-5 presents a few comparisons between our church members and the Lutherans in Strommen's study and the Protestants and Catholics in the study by Glock and Stark.

TABLE 8-5
Demonimational Comparisons on
Racial Attitudes

Items and Responses	Mennonite and BIC	Lutheran	Total Protestant	Total Catholic
1. "Although there is no essential difference between blacks and whites, it is preferable for them not to mingle socially."				
Agree	20	56		
Disagree	59	40		
Uncertain	20			
No response		4		
2. "People (black, red, or white) have a right to keep others out of their neighborhood if they want to, and this right should be respected."				
Agree	16	30		
Disagree	59	65		
Uncertain	25			
No response		5		
3. "The several races of mankind all share equally in such human qualities as intelligence, physical capacities, and emotional makeup."				
Disagree	12		30	29

Sources: For the Lutheran data, Merton Strommen, et al, *A Study of Generations* (Minneapolis: Ausburg Publishing House, 1972), p. 374. For the Protestant and Catholic data: Charles Y. Glock and Rodney Stark, *Christian Beliefs and Anti-Semitism* (New York: Harper and Row, 1966), p. 168.

In regard to the first two items in the table, the Lutheran re-searchers forced their respondents either to agree or disagree by not providing an "uncertain" response as was done in the present study. It appears that smaller proportions of Mennonite and BIC members take prejudiced positions on these items. Even if the 20% uncertain were added to the "agree" position (the prejudiced position), the total would not be as high as the 56% agreement of the Lutheran members. On the second item the differences are less significant. On the likely assumption that those answering "uncertain" would be distributed, if forced to take a position, in about the same proportions as those answering "agree" or "disagree," the Mennonite and BIC response distribution would still be less in the prejudiced direction than the Lutheran responses.

On the third item in Table 8-5 the wording of the Glock and Stark question was different: "It's too bad, but in general, Negroes have inferior intelligence compared to whites." Thus, we are comparing a positive statement on the equality of such inborn capacities as intelligence with a negative statement of inborn intellectual inferiority. We note that there were significantly fewer respondents in the present study who denied such native equality than there were respondents in the Glock-Stark study who affirmed inequality. Again, the comparison tends to reveal less prejudice among Mennonites and BIC.

Social Welfare Attitudes

In the attempt to apply the ethic of love and nonresistance to areas of social concern other than peace and race, the denominations have shown a renewed concern for people caught in the problem of poverty. The subject of "ministering to underprivileged peoples" came before the annual conference of the BIC recently, leading to the adoption of a strong resolution to do more to alleviate poverty: "Brethren, we must recognize that this will involve more people, more finances, and more sacrificial giving!"[14] In a "Resolution on Proclamation of the Gospel and Christian Social Responsibility," the MBC noted how the ministry of Jesus was to the physical as well as spiritual needs of man and declared, "We therefore affirm that we recognize Christ's call to His followers to include both proclamation (evangelization) and social action (alleviating human suffering and misery in the world)."[15]

Both the MC and GCMC have collected funds over and above the regular mission budgets for special poverty relief programs, including (in the case of the GCMC) the dual purpose "to involve us, as General Conference Mennonites, in a study of the causes, nature, and effects of poverty," and "to give us, as Christians, an opportunity to meaningfully share our financial and human resources in projects that enable victims of poverty to liberate themselves."[16]

The findings of the present study are especially relevant to the first of these goals. Three questions in particular bore directly on issues of poverty and public welfare: causes of poverty, minimum wage, and welfare subsidies. Table 8-6 shows the responses of the five denominations on these items and on a composite Welfare Attitudes Scale.

TABLE 8-6
Measures of Welfare Attitudes

			Percent Responses for:			
Items and Responses	MC	GCMC	MBC	BIC	EMC	TOTAL
1. "For the most part, people are poor because they lack discipline and don't put forth the effort needed to rise above poverty."						
Disagree	46	50	39	40	35	46
2. "The government should guarantee a minimum annual income for all individuals and families who are unemployed or who receive incomes below the poverty line."						
Agree	24	30	29	22	17	26
3. "With respect to national welfare programs (paying money to individuals and families who lack adequate income), do you feel that your government should increase, decrease, or maintain current levels of welfare benefits?"						
Increase the levels	18	19	12	11	12	17
Welfare Attitudes Scale:						
5-6 High	18	21	15	14	9	18
2-4 Middle	62	61	58	60	57	61
0-1 Low	19	18	27	26	34	21
Total	99	100	100	100	100	100
Number of Respondents	1,160	594	691	596	433	3,474
Mean Score	3.0	3.0	2.6	2.5	2.2	2.9

The latter has a range of scores from zero to six, with an overall average score of 2.9. The MC and GCMC tied for high score among the denominations (3.0), and the EMC was lowest (2.2).

Among three faith variables significantly correlated with welfare attitudes, the direction of association is positive for the Social-Ethical Conversion Scale and negative for fundamental orthodoxy and general orthodoxy. Also associated positively are the shared ministry, pacifism, social concerns, race relations, and higher education variables.

Communism and Anti-Communism

The heading for this section is actually in the title of two official position statements of the MC and GCMC on this subject.[17] In fact, the latter was modeled after the former and states, "We are grateful to find ourselves in wholehearted agreement with the statement adopted by the (Old) Mennonite General Conference in its session of August 24, 1961, in Johnstown, Pennsylvania." These statements begin by recognizing that current anti-communist crusades by leaders in numerous Protestant groups present a serious threat to "our nonresistant position." While affirming the evils of atheistic communist ideology and government, they declare that "the nonresistant Christian witness in this matter must be clearly and unequivocally divorced from any and all advocacy of force and violence, either physical or intellectual."

The members of the five denominations were asked three questions on this subject, which the reader will find in Table 8-7 together with a summary of responses. The Anti-Communism Scale had a range of scores from zero to six. The reader should note that a high score indicated anti-communism, or low adherence to the nonresistant position. The overall mean score was 2.3, with the following low-to-high rank order by denomination: MC, 1.9; GCMC, 2.4; BIC, 2.8; MBC, 2.9; and EMC, 3.5

Out of forty cross-tabulations run on this scale, only two faith variables were in the top fifteen for degree of correlation. Anabaptism was negatively associated with anti-communism, and fundamentalist orthodoxy was positively associated. Other variables related in a positive direction to anti-communism were anti-Catholicism and anti-Semitism. Variables negatively related to anti-communism were pacifism, social concerns, race relations, shared ministry, welfare attitudes, support of MCC, biblical knowledge, and higher education.

TABLE 8-7

Measures of Anti-Communism

Items and Responses	Percent Responses for:					
	MC	GCMC	MBC	BIC	EMC	TOTAL
1. "The national government should take every opportunity (military or otherwise) to stamp out communism at home and abroad."						
Disagree	35	31	19	19	12	30
2. "If communism is to be confronted, it should be with Christian truth and love, and not by military force."						
Agree	84	72	65	69	48	76
3. "Christianity and communism share in common some social and economic ideals and goals."						
Agree	42	40	32	27	22	39
Anti-Communism Scale:						
5–6 High	3	10	15	11	22	8
3–4 Middle	34	37	47	26	54	36
0–2 Low	63	53	39	43	24	56
Total	100	100	101	100	100	100
Number of Respondents	1,181	591	688	603	434	3,497
Mean Score	1.9	2.4	2.9	2.8	3.5	2.3

Industrial Relations

In several respects the issue of industrial relations presents a greater dilemma for conscientious Mennonites than the issues of war, race relations, welfare for the poor, or anti-communism. The principle of love implies a strong identification with the modern industrial worker who bears the brunt of a dehumanizing process that has robbed him of the joy of work. Collective action by unions, which gave the workers a bargaining power lost through the development of mechanization and impersonal division of labor, is not entirely alien to the commitment characteristic of the Anabaptist ethic. The worker's sense of security is strengthened by the knowledge that he and his friends are firmly banded together to defend their common interests against the conflicting interests of the owner-management group. The union serves not only as a means of achieving fairer wages and better working conditions but also as a symbol of the sense of community that was lost in the modern industrial factory.

It is hard for Mennonites and BIC to know whether union membership is right or wrong because of the confusion of two principles applied to ethical decision-making in this area. One is the principle of noncoercion in human relationships which we have been examining so far in this chapter. This calls the legitimacy of union membership into question because labor organizations use power in striving for social justice. The control of local unions by state and national organizations beyond the factory level has bred the kinds of power and intimidation that nonresistant people tend to reject.

The other principle is that of nonviolence. The fact that many of the methods employed by the unions are nonviolent makes it difficult to reject union membership categorically. Their negotiation at the bargaining table, the calling of a strike when bargaining breaks down, even the march in a picket line, are basically peaceful, nonviolent means of addressing grievances.

The GCMC has tended to favor cooperation in programs seeking justice when the methods employed are nonviolent. The MC and BIC have taken a more absolutist nonresistant stand against the use of coercion of any kind in industrial relations, violent or nonviolent. The latter position is reflected in a joint statement on "Industrial Relations" which asserted that "industrial organization in its present form involves a class struggle and conflict which is ultimately due to an absence of the Christian principle of love" and that in their faith and practice Mennonites and Brethren in Christ "have emphasized the principle of love and nonresistance which abjures the spirit of retaliation in all human relations."[18] Specifically, the statement involved four commitments, two of which read as follows:

1. As employers we can have no part in manufacturers or employers associations in so far as they are organized for the purpose of fighting the labor movement, using such well-known methods as the lockout, the black list, detective agencies, espionage, strike-breakers, and munitions. Rather, we consider ourselves under obligation to heed the Scriptural injunction, "Give unto your servants that which is just and equal." We regard ourselves duty-bound to exemplify the industrial way of life herein implied, through the payment of such wages, the maintenance of such working conditions, and the provision of such measures for the social and economic security of the workingman

as shall remove every occasion for grievance, strife, or conflict. . . .

2. As employees we can have no part in labor organizations in so far as their sanctions ultimately rest on force, making use of such well-known methods as the monopolistic closed shop, the boycott, the picket line, and the strike.

The MBC has adopted a statement on "The Christian and Labor Unions" which is similar to the MC-BIC statement in all respects except one. Instead of the prohibition, "We can have no part in labor organizations," it affirmed that "We ought not to forbid union membership."[19]

In view of these denominational positions, we asked our respondents three questions about labor unions, which appear in Table 8-8. These questions were combined to form an Anti-Labor Union Scale with a range of possible scores from zero to six. A high score represents opposition to union membership, opposition to recognizing or bargaining with a labor union, and disapproval of a Christian laborer joining a union in order to exert a Christian influence within. The overall mean score on the scale was 2.3, with the MC scoring high (2.8) and the EMC low (1.5).

Out of forty cross-tabulations, five faith variables (Anabaptism, fundamentalist orthodoxy, sanctification, devotionalism, and communalism) were highly correlated with the Anti-Labor Union Scale, all in the direction of supporting the MC-BIC position. Education and socioeconomic status were negatively correlated with the position statement ($r = -.278$ and $-.216$, respectively). Also negatively correlated were political participation, political action, the Role of Women Scale, and urban residence. It is evident that the more urbanized a member becomes, the more open he becomes to participation in the political process, the more education he has, and the higher he has risen in the socioeconomic ladder, the less he adheres to the official MC and BIC position on labor unions.

A General Measure of Social Concerns

John C. Bennett described the ethic of the Mennonite Church as a "strategy of withdrawal,"[20] and Richard Niebuhr gave it as an example of his "Christ-against-culture" type of Christian ethic.[21] In this final section of the chapter, it is appropriate to test the validity of these labels.

TABLE 8-8
Attitudes Toward Labor Unions

Items and Responses	Percent of Responses for:					
	MC	GCMC	MBC	BIC	EMC	TOTAL
1. "A church member should not join a labor union even if getting or holding a job depends on union membership."						
Agree	25	10	11	12	8	18
2. "A church member who owns or manages a shop should refuse to recognize or bargain with a labor union."						
Agree	31	12	14	18	11	22
3. "The best attitude of a Christian laborer toward a labor union is to join and exert a Christian influence within the union's program and activities."						
Disagree	25	9	10	13	6	17
Anti-Labor Union Scale:						
4-6 High	34	13	14	19	11	23
2-3 Middle	37	38	36	39	35	37
0-1 Low	29	49	50	32	54	40
Total	100	100	100	100	100	100
Number of Respondents	1,193	599	697	611	438	3,538
Mean Score	2.8	1.7	1.8	2.1	1.5	2.3

When asked about such specific involvements as participating in peaceful demonstrations and protest marches for the sake of social justice, taking a stand against capital punishment by one's government, or protesting the use of billions of dollars for space explorations when thousands of Americans live on the poverty level of subsistence, about one fourth of the members were quite uncertain in their responses (26%, 30%, and 21% for the three questions, respectively). On the zero-to-six scale that combined these three questions, 69% of the members scored two to four points (see Table 8-9). Only 11% affirmed all items of protest (with a score of 6), and only 3% rejected all items (with a score of zero). The overall mean score was 3.5 with the GCMC scoring high (3.7) and the EMC and MBC tied for low (2.8).

Only three faith variables were in the top fifteen for correlation with the Social Concerns Scale. Fundamentalist orthodoxy and general orthodoxy were in their typical negative stance and the Ethical-Social Conversion Scale had a high positive relation to the

Social Concerns Scale. Higher education supported social concerns, as did pacifism, race relations, welfare attitudes, shared ministry, ecumenism, and support of MCC. Working at odds with a strong social concerns response were anti-communism, separation of church and state, and anti-Semitism.

The interpretation of the Mennonite ethic as a strategy of withdrawal was mentioned at the beginning of this section, quoting

TABLE 8-9
Miscellaneous Social Concerns Measures

Items and Responses	Percent of Responses for:					
	MC	GCMC	MBC	BIC	EMC	TOTAL
1. "Christians ought not participate in peaceful demonstrations and protest marches even though they may be intended as a means of bringing about social justice."						
Disagree	22	34	24	23	22	26
2. "Capital punishment (the death penalty for a major crime) is a necessary deterrent to crime and should not be abandoned by our national, provincial, or state governments."						
Disagree	46	50	17	33	19	41
3. "Do you think it is desirable that the American government should use large sums of money to carry out space exploration?"						
No	73	66	61	66	59	68
Social Concerns Scale:						
5-6 High	23	34	10	14	9	24
2-4 Middle	72	58	77	77	77	69
0-1 Low	5	8	13	9	14	7
Total	100	100	100	100	100	100
Number of Respondents	1,182	603	695	605	435	3,520
Mean Score	3.6	3.7	2.8	3.2	2.8	3.5

especially the writing of Bennett and Niebuhr. The findings of this study do not support the one-sidedness of that interpretation. Mennonite and BIC declarations simultaneously prohibit and require social services of different kinds; and although the result is not a logical fallacy in theology, it is a precarious combination. The MC Confession of Faith declares, on one hand, that "nonresistant Christians cannot undertake any service in the state or in society which would violate the principles of love and holiness as taught by Christ and His inspired apostles." It asserts, on the other hand, that "we must aggressively, at the risk of life itself, do whatever we can for the alleviation of human distress and suffering." These declarations are not a contradiction, theologically; but they represent a dilemma for Mennonites sociologically.

Summary

In this chapter, the historic Anabaptist emphasis on a radical social ethic of love and nonresistance was reviewed and six scales were constructed to test the degree of adherence to the formal positions of the five denominations in various areas of social ethics. These six scales — Pacifism, Race Relations, Welfare Attitudes, Anti-Communism, Anti-Labor Unions, and Social Concerns — were strongly intercorrelated (average correlation coefficient of .298).

There was a clear ranking of the denominations on these scales, with the MC and GCMC usually ranking first and second for adherence to the expected position, and the MBC and EMC ranking fourth and fifth.

Only one faith variable — fundamentalist orthodoxy — was highly correlated with all five scales, and consistently in a negative relation to the normative Anabaptist position as defined by the denominations. Higher education gives strong support to all of the scales except the Anti-Labor Union Scale. The only work-of-the church scale highly correlated with all five social ethics scales is the Shared Ministry Scale, which shows positive correlations with the social ethics scales. Perhaps the shared ministry concept is related to social ethics because the same quality of radical discipleship undergirds them both.

In this "tug" and "pull" of variables in two directions, the Anabaptism Scale stands somewhere between "low forward gear" and "high gear," having a strong positive correlation with the Pacifism and Anti-Labor Union Scales, a strong negative correlation with anti-communism, and a more neutral association with race relations, welfare attitudes, and social concerns. Nevertheless, its "influence" is in the expected normative direction in all six scales.

Chapter 9

POLITICAL PARTICIPATION

The previous chapter reported data pertaining to various ethical attitudes and positions. Although some of the issues covered bordered on the political arena, the issue of political participation or non-participation will be the central subject of the present chapter. The attitudes of the church members concerning two levels of participation will be explored — the political participation of the individual himself and the political involvement of the church as a group.[1]

The Anabaptist View of Politics

Mennonites and Brethren in Christ have a heritage of ideas regarding politcal affairs that derives from the sixteenth-century Anabaptists. No other aspect of the Anabaptist movement has been researched as fully and with as much consensus on findings by scholars as the Anabaptist view of the state and the Christian's role in it.[1]

The Anabaptist forebears acknowledged that the authority of the state to punish lawbreakers and preserve order was ordained by God, but they asserted the primacy of the claims of God over the claims of government. They firmly believed that a Christian owes obedience to civil laws and authorities insofar as the prior claims of God are not violated by that obedience. But they also believed that the church and church members are not responsible for policies of the state and ought not to presume to direct them. They advocated the structural separation of church and state and were generally convinced that a Christian could not himself become a magistrate. Because they intended to practice a thoroughgoing ethic of love as taught by Jesus and recorded in the New Testament they declined to swear the civil oath, to bring suit in a court of law, to use arms or participate in military service, and in other ways to conform to civil mores.

Thus, the Anabaptist political ethic incorporated both assent and dissent and it can best be interpreted as a "dualism of holding that God ordained the state with its sword, yet claiming that the state's operation involved non-Christian principles."[2] The Schleitheim Confession of 1527 summarized this dualism succinctly in the sentence, "The sword is ordained of God outside the perfection of Christ."[3] On the side of assent, the Anabaptist affirmation of the divine sanction of all governments, good or bad, was no small concession by a group that was severely persecuted by civil authorities. In spite of their treatment, with only a few conspicuous exceptions, they never condoned overthrow of a government by revolutionary means. Full obedience to existing law and order was their stance, except in matters of conscience.

The political dissent of the Anabaptists was on specific occasions a direct challenge to civil authorities concerning matters of alleged injustice. For the most part it was a stance of nonconformity and nonparticipation. In his doctoral dissertation on the subject, Hans Hillerbrand has shown that they had a reasoned basis for their refusal to hold public office or otherwise to participate in government. They found no basis in Scripture for such participation, they observed Jesus' example of nonparticipation, they followed His teaching about not "lording it" over others as meaning primarily in the public realm, and they believed Christians should live loosely in relation to worldly structures.[4]

The Practice of Later Generations

The political ethic of the Anabaptists was formulated in a tyrannical political context in which they were hardly tolerated and seldom granted the privilege of participation in government. Practically the only function of the state was to maintain order and, by police or military force, to defend itself from attack. In Canadian and American contexts, the descendants of the Anabaptists have had the opportunity of being citizens from the outset, and with considerable freedom of conscience. In these North American democracies, moreover, the function of public welfare has been added to that of law enforcement, with new opportunities for citizens to become involved in programs of compassionate concern under government auspices. With these new privileges came new questions about civic responsibilities.

The denominations in our study have taken three positions in their response to these questions, with important shifts in different periods of time and with considerable variation of members within each group.

The Position of Nonparticipation. The first position requires rather complete nonparticipation in government. This is the official position of the MC as indicated by Article 19 of its 1963 Confession which reiterates the historic dualism of the Anabaptist political ethic: "In law enforcement the state does not and cannot operate on the nonresistant principles of Christ's kingdom. Therefore, nonresistant Christians cannot undertake any service in the state or in society which would violate the principles of love and holiness as taught by Christ and His inspired apostles."[5] This was also the position of the MBC and BIC until about World War I.

> Historically, the Mennonite Brethren have refrained from involvement in political activities. At first, even voting at the polls was forbidden (1878). The last resolution, passed in 1890 by the General Conference with reference to political activity, reads, "That members of the church refrain from participation and involvement in the contentions of political parties, but are permitted to vote quietly at elections, and may also vote for prohibition."[6]

The parallelism of the official positions of the MC and BIC until then is illustrated by the following official acts of conference (the former on the district conference level in Pennsylvania, the latter a churchwide statement):

FRANCONIA CONFERENCE OF MC

Brethren shall not use the bankruptcy law. In the case of bankruptcy a member who cannot pay all his debts must in the company of another brother seek the peace of his creditors. Brethren shall be admonished not to claim the $300 exemption allowed them by law in case of bankruptcy.

If a brother has a warrant served on a man he must seek the peace of the one he had arrested before he can be again received as a member.

Members are not to accept any public office. It is considered advisable to abstain from voting. Brethren may quietly vote at the polls but shall not "electioneer," nor attend mass meetings.

No brother may serve as a bank-watchman, or accept any position which involves the bearing of arms, for that violates our nonresistant faith.[7]

BIC ANNUAL CONFERENCE

Is it according to Gospel for a brother to electioneer for political purposes? *Ans.* No.

Is it consistent for members to serve as jurors? *Ans.* No.

Conference decided that it is not allowed for members to take advantage of exemption laws to defraud creditors.

Is it consistent for brethren to attend political elections? *Ans.* It is not consistent.

Whereas the Pennsylvania brethren petitioned General Conference for an expression of its attitude on the prohibition question. Resolved, that inasmuch as the Brethren in Christ do not believe it consistent with their faith as a non-resistant people, to take part in political elections, but since the prohibition question is a moral and not a political one, General Conference submits the question to the conscientious consideration of each brother, but positively forbids any brother, either in sentiment or vote, to give any encouragement to the regular traffic.

Inasmuch as we believe that there is a great danger in opening the door for brethren to hold public offices indiscriminately; and inasmuch as the church is located under different governments, therefore, we would submit the matter to the careful and discriminate consideration of the several Districts, and since we, the committee, cannot point out the various offices which brethren might hold under the different forms of government where they are located, we would advise that brethren should not allow themselves to be used in public offices for fear of becoming involved in political strife, which is contrary to the faith of the church on conscientious principles.

Has a church member the privilege, under the gospel, to go to Law? *Ans.* No. [8]

The Position of Free Participation. The second position encourages rather free participation in government at all levels while affirming nonresistance and nonconformity to the world. About the only participation ruled out by this position would be the police or military function. This position characterizes the GCMC throughout its history and the EMC after World War II. The GCMC has adopted no official position on the subject and typically assumes that each member is competent and responsible to make his own decisions concerning political participation. J. Winfield Fretz expressed this position as follows:

> If one carefully examines the logic of nonparticipation in a political democracy one is forced to the position of abandoning political rule to the evil, and unprincipled and the unscrupulous. Naturally, if the righteous withdraw from participation, only the unrighteous are left. How then can pure, honest, wise, creative government be expected to result? If the logic of the Mennonites were to be followed by all Christians everywhere it would mean that no Christians would be willing to hold public offices. Hence Christians who believed in voting would have to vote for non-Christians only. This type of ascetic withdrawal from assuming full responsibility for the social order in which we live seems to me unrealistic, unwise, and in a sense less than courageously Christian. . . .
> It is becoming increasingly clear to me that the traditional Mennonite attitude toward political nonparticipation is untenable in the kind of political system under which we live. Not only is it possible for a Christian to hold public office and be a dedicated Christian, it is the duty of consecrated Christians to hold public office and thus serve both God and man.[9]

A number of members of the GCMC have been elected to provincial and state legislatures, beginning with H. P. Krehbiel, the first conference historian. Moreover, at least two members have been elected to the United States House of Representatives.[10] Although Fretz did not go into the philosophical implications of his statement, his view seems to echo the early GCMC emphasis on progress — the idea of contributing to the betterment of society through politics or other means, thereby realizing more and more of God's kingdom.

The Position of Selective Participation. A third position accepts the possibility of participation in politics, but maintains a relatively pessimistic view of the nature of government and the political process. It agrees that modern democratic government has a welfare function but it also observes that its primary function is still that of maintaining law and order by securing the obedience of its citizens. This it does by consensus as much as possible and by coercion whenever necessary. In any society with a high proportion of lawbreakers, the use of force will be considerable and nonresistant Christians who participate will have to be on constant guard lest their love ethic be badly compromised. The crucial element in this position, according to Elmer Ediger, is to know the "point of withdrawal."

> Although this . . . point of view would readily agree that we must shift to a positive emphasis toward greater political participation, this view would also underscore the Christian's larger mission and the necessity that every Christian in politics have a point of withdrawal. Rather than being forced into a position of directly doing that which he as a Christian considers wrong, a Christian disciple withdraws with a witness to be relevant in a higher Christian sense. . . . Though different from much in recent Mennonite tradition, this view nevertheless feels akin to early Anabaptism in that this is a narrow path of discipleship which is in the world but not of it.[11]

The denomination that has come closest to this third position in its official stance is the MBC. Historically, as pointed out earlier, the MBC was thoroughly committed to the first position; but a newly adopted position statement has outlined a "Middle Ground" between the "Cross-Bearing Church" and the "Sword-Bearing State," asserting that a Christian's political involvement must be selective, redemptive, and prophetic:

> *Selective Involvement:* "At no time or place can the Christian suspend the exercise of his Christian ethical principles. This means that the believer must be highly selective in his political involvement in order to avoid any compromise of his faith and any restriction of his Christian witness."

> *Redemptive Involvement:* "Political involvement has a tendency to deflect Christians from their primary calling. The areas in which Christians can most effectively serve both their church and their country are the areas within the 'Middle

Ground' which formerly were considered the exclusive territory of the church: public education, public health, public welfare, etc."

Prophetic Involvement: "The prophetic voice of the church will be a vote of protest against racial discrimination, social injustice, economic exploitation, and political corruption."[12]

MBC members have eight specific guidelines for political decision-making. They are encouraged to vote, to exert influence on governmental officials, and even to stand for political office "if neither the attempt to gain the position or the exercising of its functions requires a compromise of Christian ethics." But they are also cautioned against "super-patriotism" and "militant nationalism" and called to a higher allegiance than the state, *i.e.,* a heavenly kingdom. "The Church should not attempt to ally itself with any specific ideology or political party, since none is intrinsically Christian . . . (and) Christians ought not give undivided loyalty to any political unit." Moreover, "the defense of the political order in general or of a specific political system is not the responsibility or duty of the Christian church." The Christian's first concern is "the extension of the kingdom of Christ."[13]

Attitudes Concerning the Function of the State

The survey data regarding the political attitudes and behavior of respondents begins with several questions testing basic attitudes toward government. These questions and the tabulations of answers by denomination are given in Table 9-1. Both questions — one on the idea of the state as an evil force and the other on the issue of capital punishment — are difficult to answer for the thoroughgoing dualist, as the larger number of "uncertain" responses of MC and BIC members seems to indicate. A member who would affirm the traditional Mennonite view of the state as an institution ordained of God could hardly call it an evil force in the world, and yet the Schleitheim Confession called it an institution "outside the perfection of Christ." One fourth of MC and BIC members are uncertain with regard to the first question. Over three fourths of the members as a whole

TABLE 9-1
General Attitudes Toward the State and Its Functions

Items and Responses	Percentage Distribution for:					
	MC	GCMC	MBC	BIC	EMC	TOTAL
1. "The State (national, provincial, and state government) is basically an evil force in the world, an opponent or enemy of the church and its program."						
Agree	7	2	2	4	2	4
Uncertain	25	14	12	23	15	19
Disagree	68	85	86	74	83	77
2. "Capital punishment (the death penalty for a major crime) is a necessary deterrent to crime and should not be abandoned by our national, provincial, or state governments."						
Agree	21	26	57	35	49	30
Uncertain	33	23	26	32	31	29
Disagree	46	50	17	33	19	41

disagree with the assertion, and only 4 percent agree with it.

Similarly, a thoroughgoing Mennonite dualist would affirm the traditional view that the state, while standing outside the perfection of Christ, is ordained nevertheless to punish evildoers by the power of the sword. As a nonresistant Christian, however, he should have scruples against the taking of life by anyone for any reason. We note, again, that a large proportion of MC respondents (33%) are uncertain about whether capital punishment is a necessary means of deterrent for governments. Nevertheless, only 21% (the smallest proportion for any group) agreed with the assertion. This contrasts with the MBC members, 57% of whom approved the use of capital punishment by governments.

Attitudes Concerning Church and State Relationships

As indicated earlier, an important part of the Anabaptist political ethic was the separation of the church from the state, both in terms of auspices and of function. Underlying this view was the assumption that the respective missions of these two institutions are on totally different levels of authority and purpose. Table 9-2 shows that an overall 62% of the respondents agreed that "seeking to improve the moral achievements of secular society is not the central mission of the church." The GCMC agreed least (50%) and the MBC most (71%) with this assertion.

While the spread between these two groups was 21% on this question, there was only one percent difference on the item pertaining to governmental funding of church institutions. Six out of ten GCMC and MBC respondents disagreed with the statement that their church institutions should *not* seek or accept tax money.

For further analysis of attitudes concerning church and state relationships, a scale was constructed by combining the responses to the three items in Table 9-2. The content of the first two questions concerns what the church should or should not do to or for the state, and the third concerns what the state should or should not do to or for the church. It was assumed that persons taking a position of total separation of church and state would strongly agree with all three statements. The scale had a range of scores from zero to twelve.[14] The figures at the bottom of Table 9-2 show that the MC, MBC, BIC, and EMC are quite similar in their mean scores of 5.9, 5.8, 6.1, and 6.0, respectively, in contrast to the GCMC mean score of 4.8.

The scale was cross-tabulated with amount of education, amount of income, socioeconomic status, rural-urban residence, age, and the 10 faith scales defined in Chapters 4-6. Those variables having the greatest association with an attitude favoring separation of church and state were the following: fundamentalist orthodoxy, age, Anabaptism, socioeconomic status, education, and general orthodoxy. The cross-tabulations are summarized in Table 9-3. Note that the three faith variables are *positively* correlated with the scale; that is, the greater the assent to general orthodox doctrines and to Anabaptism, the greater the commitment to church-state separation. Age is also *positively* correlated, except that the association is curved at the younger ages. The commitment to church-state separation is greater for teenagers than for young adults; but then it rises significantly as age increases. The other social background variables are *negatively* correlated: the higher one's socioeconomic status and education, the lower one's commitment to the separation of church and state. Assuming that all of these are independent causative variables, one would select for special attention the opposite effects of Anabaptism and education upon the dependent variable in question. Recalling the three contemporary political positions outlined earlier in the chapter, one can observe that the shift from position one (nonparticipation in politics) to position two (full political involvement) and position three (selective political involvement) appears to be associated with higher education in the denominations. This observation will be tested more directly in the following section.

Political Participation

The attitudes and behavior of church members concerning three

TABLE 9-2
Church and State Relationships

Items and Responses	Percentage Distributions for:					
	MC	GCMC	MBC	BIC	EMC	TOTAL
1. "Seeking to improve the moral achievements of secular society is not the central mission of the church."						
Agree	64	50	71	67	64	62
Uncertain	22	23	16	19	18	21
Disagree	14	28	23	15	18	18
2. "It is not the business of the church to try to influence the actions of government in regard to such issues as war and peace, race relations, poverty, etc."						
Agree	28	18	26	29	26	25
Uncertain	21	14	21	24	28	19
Disagree	51	67	53	47	47	56
3. "Mennonite and Brethren in Christ institutions (high schools, colleges, hospitals, etc.) should not seek or accept tax money or other grants of money from governments."						
Agree	17	15	16	20	22	17
Uncertain	34	25	23	33	37	30
Disagree	48	60	61	46	41	53
Separation of Church and State Scale:						
6–12 High	51	35	51	56	56	46
3–5 Middle	42	49	42	36	37	44
0–2 Low	7	17	7	8	7	10
Total	100	101	100	100	100	100
Number of Respondents	1,173	592	681	604	432	3,482
Mean Score	5.9	4.8	5.8	6.1	6.0	5.6

areas of participation in the political process — voting, writing to legislators, and holding public office — were tested by five items, cited in Table 9-4. Since the responses to these items were highly intercorrelated, four of them were put into a composite scale, the last question on actual experience in public office being omitted. The scores on the scale ranged from zero to ten.[15] A distinct denominational patterning emerged as shown at the bottom of the table. The MC was consistently low on political participation; the GCMC, MBC, and EMC were high on political participation; and the BIC was in the middle.

The Political Participation Scale was cross-tabulated with the independent variables mentioned in the previous section. As Table 9-5 shows, those scales having the highest correlation with political participation were Anabaptism, education, socioeconomic status, rural-urban residence, fundamentalist orthodoxy, and age. Again, the direction of association of the "faith" variables was opposite that of the social background variables with the former *negatively* correlated and the latter *positively* correlated with political participation. This supports our previous conclusion that the shift from the nonparticipation position to a selective or full participation in the political process is the consequence, at least in part, of the higher

TABLE 9-3
Separation of Church and State as Related to Faith and Life Variables

Faith and Life Variables	Position on Scale at Left				Pearson Coeff. (r)
	Low 1	2	3	High 4	
	(% scoring "high" on Sep. of Church & State)				
Fundamentalist Orthodoxy	13	28	49	60	.352
Age	40	30	43	62	.282
Anabaptism	34	43	54		.276
Socioeconomic Status	67	56	38	27	-.248
Amount of Education	65	47	32	33	-.240
General Orthodoxy	30	24	34	52	.223

Note: Age categories are (1) teenagers, (2) young adults, (3) middle age, and (4) older adults. Read percentages as follows: Of those who scored "low" on Fundamentalist Orthodoxy, 13 percent scored "high" on Separation of Church and State.

education of members, and their increasing urbanization and general rise in socioeconomic status.

Of particular interest is the significant inverse correlation between Anabaptism and political participation — the greater the assent to Anabaptist doctrines, the less the participation in the political

TABLE 9-4
Political Participation

Items and Responses	Percentage Distributions for:					
	MC	GCMC	MBC	BIC	EMC	TOTAL
1. "Members of our denomination should vote in public elections for state, provincial, and national offices."						
Agree	56	96	98	79	96	76
Uncertain	28	3	1	16	3	15
Disagree	17	1	0	6	1	9
2. "Members of our denomination should not hold any local, state, provincial, or national government office."						
Agree	24	3	5	9	3	13
Uncertain	33	11	11	23	9	22
Disagree	43	86	84	68	88	64
3. "Church members should witness directly to the state (nation) by writing to legislators, testifying before legislative committees, etc."						
Agree	54	72	60	57	67	61
Uncertain	34	22	30	36	27	30
Disagree	12	5	10	6	5	9
4. "In how many of the elections in recent years have you voted?"						
None	60	14	21	41	25	39
A few/Some	19	10	10	22	12	15
Most/All	20	76	70	37	62	46
5. "Have you ever held an elective office in a local, state, provincial, city, or national government?"						
Yes	1	4	4	2	4	3
Political Participation Scale:						
8–10 High	19	73	66	37	64	44
5–7 Middle	36	23	29	40	29	32
0–4 Low	44	4	6	23	7	24
Total	99	100	101	100	100	100
Number of Respondents	1,160	590	683	599	425	3,457
Mean Score	5.0	8.3	7.9	6.4	7.8	6.6

process. In one sense, this can be interpreted as loyalty to the sixteenth-century position of thoroughgoing separation of church and state processes, but it does not indicate much shift to a selective participation as a fulfillment of the Anabaptists' sense of obligation to bear witness to the state in matters of love and justice.

Political Party Preference

A closer look at the identity of that participation is the next area of investigation. In Canada and the United States, as in most democratic states, the political participation of citizens is filtered through political parties that seek to gain control of the government through popular vote in elections. Canada and the United States have the two-party system. Two major parties alternate in control of the government for varying periods of time, although usually one or more smaller parties are also trying to gain a foothold. Generally, one party tends to be "conservative" and the other "liberal." In fact, these have been the names of the two major parties in Canada for over a century. Although it is sometimes difficult to find much difference between the policies of the two parties, important philosophical distinctions have at times pro-

TABLE 9-5
Political Participation as Related to
Faith and Life Variables

Faith and Life Variables	Position on Scales at Left				Pearson Coeff. (r)
	Low 1	2	3	High 4	
(% scoring "high" on Political Participation)					
Anabaptism	57	48	35		-.332
Amount of Education	32	41	50	73	.283
Socioeconomic Status	36	50	59	82	.239
Rural-Urban Residence	40	39	50	56	.206
Fundamentalist Orthodoxy	61	49	43	41	-.185
Age	2	32	58	52	.181

Note: Age refers to (1) teenagers, (2) young adults, (3) middle aged, and (4) older adults. Residence refers to (rural farms, (2) rural nonfarm, (3) small city, and (4) large city. Read percentages as follows: Of those who scored "low" on Anabaptism, 57% scored "high" on Political Participation.

vided points of political identification. Conservatism is a political philosphy that opposes radical transformation and approves only those changes that are in line with accepted values of the past, especially the federal constitutions that brought the two countries into existence.[16] Liberalism is an alternative political philosophy that seeks substantial changes to solve present-day problems, especially connected with poverty, disease, and social injustice.[17]

Economics becomes a crucial part of the distinction. The conservative clings to the free enterprise system and resists economic controls. The liberal promotes governmental controls and intervention in the production and distribution of economic goods. In the United States both the Republican and Democratic parties have conservative and liberal wings, but the former is generally regarded as more conservative than the latter.

Recognizing that the meaning of the labels changes depending on who is in power, one can nevertheless place existing parties along a conservative-liberal continuum as the basis for studying the political preferences of church members. Using the customary concepts of "left-of-center" and "right-of-center," we have drawn the line accordingly, placing the major and minor political parties of the two countries according to their stated platforms and goals:

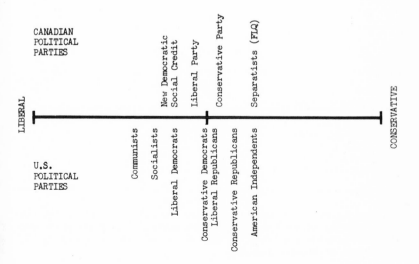

In this survey, American respondents were asked, "With which one of the following American positions do you tend to be most in sympathy or agreement?" Canadians were asked a similar question, with "Canadian" substituted for "American." The answers as of the year 1972, are given in Table 9-6.

Because some respondents might not identify with *any* political position, the response "I take no position at all" was added. Actually

TABLE 9-6
Political Party Preferences, 1972

Party Preference	Percentage Distribution for:					
	MC	GCMC	MBC	BIC	EMC*	TOTAL
Canada:						
"I take no position at all."	43	16	17	40		23
Took a political position	57	84	83	60		77
Total	100	100	100	100		100
Number of Respondents	129	160	350	52		691
Took the following positions:						
Conservative	35	41	39	71		40
Liberal	49	35	23	29		32
Social Credit	5	14	32	0		20
New Democratic Party	10	10	5	0		7
Independent	1	1	1	0		1
Total	100	101	100	100		100
Number of Respondents	74	135	291	31		532
United States:						
"I take no position at all."	47	23	18	25	20	35
Took a political position	53	77	82	75	80	65
Total	100	100	100	100	100	100
Number of Respondents	1,063	441	340	557	432	2,833
Took the following positions:						
Conservative Republican	55	47	63	62	74	54
Liberal Republican	13	14	16	16	10	14
Conservative Democrat	6	11	10	5	4	8
Liberal Democrat	9	15	4	4	1	10
American Independent (Wallace)	2	2	1	2	1	2
Communist	0	0	0	0	1	0
Independent	15	12	6	9	8	12
Total	100	101	100	98	99	100
Number of Respondents	566	340	279	417	346	1,948

*There are no EMC churches in Canada.

23% of the Canadians and 35% of the Americans took no position at all, not even the one that was labeled "Independent," which was designed to catch those who may be politically active but refuse any other political label. As one might predict on the basis of Table 9-4, MC respondents were particularly prone to take no position. This was true of 43% of the Canadian and 47% of the American members of that group.

The breakdown of respondents in Table 9-6 is first of all between those who *did* and those who *did not* take a position. Secondly, a further breakdown is given for those who did take a position. The reader is reminded, therefore, that these latter percentages are not based on the total denominational samples. For example, the table shows that 55% of the MC respondents *who took a position* preferred "conservative Republican" but this accounts for only 29% of the total MC sample.

With respect to those who did take a position, it can be observed that Mennonites and Brethren in Christ tend to be conservative in political leanings. Note, however, that this is much less true in Canada where 58% of the members overall checked Liberal, Social Credit, or NDP parties. The forced-choice question put many Canadian respondents into a quandary because they may vote one of the more liberal tickets on the provincial level and vote with the Conservatives on the federal level of government. Many Russian Mennonites retain a deep sympathy for the Liberal Party because of Prime Minister Mackenzie King's assistance in their immigration,[18] but they believe their agricultural economic interests are better served by the Conservative Party, which has shown more interest in farm issues than the Liberals, who seem preoccupied with eastern industrialism.

The political conservatism of the respondents was especially strong in the United States, with 74% choosing the Republican Party and only 14% the Democratic Party. Historically, one might explain this position by reference to the rugged individualism of Mennonites and their dislike of government interference in their agricultural practices. Sociologically, however, one can examine the political behavior of these church members in the light of their own political ethic. If MBC members really believe their own Anabaptist-oriented position regarding political involvement as outlined above, particularly the principles that "the church should not attempt to ally itself with any specific political ideology or political party" and that "Christians ought not to give undivided loyalty to any political unit," one has to ask what is implied when 79% (of those MBs who took a position) align themselves with the Republican Party and only 6% identify themselves as independent.[19]

Political Action

The issue of political participation for church members involved both an individual response and a group response. John H. Redekop describes the latter as follows:

> A group response could involve an entire denomination, an association of denominations. . . , a group of churches in one area. . . , part of a congregation, parts of several congregations, or an entire congregation. In most situations it will likely be the last mentioned.[20]

Although a group decision in the political sphere is much more difficult than an individual's private choice, Mennonites and Brethren in Christ, with their communally oriented ethic, have not entirely abandoned the idea of corporate witness to the state. The MBC is particularly clear on this mandate for corporate action: "We believe that the church and its members individually should be constructively critical of the political order, always seeking to promote justice, respect for human dignity, and conditions of peace."[21]

In keeping with this mandate, one would expect MBC members to reject the statement, "It is not the business of the church to try to influence the actions of government in regard to such issues as war and peace, race relations, poverty, etc.," but in fact, as we saw in Table 9-2, barely one half of the MBC respondents chose the "disagree" response.

To further test this attitude regarding the initiative of the church in the political process, we asked a series of seven questions with more specific reference to the local congregation. These questions, listed in Table 9-7, were combined into a Political Action Scale, by giving a respondent one point for each "yes" response. The scores in the scale thus ranged from zero, representing disapproval of any involvement of the church in the political process, to seven, representing approval of all seven types of action. The bottom of

TABLE 9-7
The Political Action of the Church

	Percent of Responses for:					
Items and Responses	MC	GCMC	MBC	BIC	EMC	TOTAL
1. "Do you feel it is proper for your congregation to urge citizens to vote?"						
Yes	47	92	94	73	94	70
2. "Do you feel it is proper for your congregation to encourage its members to study political issues and candidates?"						
Yes	52	82	82	68	86	68
3. "Do you feel it is proper for your congregation to encourage groups within the church to engage in political action?"						
Yes	19	48	38	30	41	32
4. "Do you feel it is proper for your congregation to have some effort on the Sunday before political election day to 'get out and vote'?"						
Yes	11	47	44	25	52	29
5. "Do you feel it is proper for your congregation to endorse particular candidates for office?"						
Yes	14	37	32	23	28	25
6. "Do you feel it is proper for your congregation to permit candidates to speak in the church building?"						
Yes	13	31	16	15	13	19
7. "Do you feel it is proper for your congregation to encourage the minister to discuss political issues from the pulpit?"						
Yes	13	23	13	10	12	16
Political Action Scale:						
5–7 High	9	33	21	13	18	9
2–4 Middle	36	53	65	54	72	47
0–1 Low	55	13	14	33	10	34
Total	100	99	100	100	100	100
Number of Respondents	1,118	554	643	576	407	3,298
Mean Score	1.7	3.6	3.2	2.4	3.3	2.6

Table 9-7 shows a mean score of 2.6, which means that overall the respondents approved about two types of action and disapproved the other five. Since the questions have been tabulated in order of the frequency of their approval, the actions approved tend to be the first two listed: urge citizens to vote, and encourage members to study the issues. The actions getting majority disapproval were the last five listed: encouraging groups within the church to engage in political action, helping to get out the vote, endorsing candidates, permitting candidates to speak in church, and encouraging the minister to discuss political issues from the pulpit.

These seven questions were borrowed from the Episcopalian church member study, and it is interesting to note that the order of approval in both studies was about the same, except that the Episcopalians were more permissive with regard to candidates speaking in the church than with regard to endorsing candidates for office. The fact that our respondents were more willing to have the church endorse candidates than to have their minister preach about political issues or to let candidates speak in church reflects their dualistic political ethic and its communal foundation.

The mean scores at the bottom of Table 9-7 are what we would have predicted on the basis of the historical positions of these groups discussed earlier in this chapter. The MC takes a rather non-participatory stance, the GCMC a thoroughly participatory stance, and the other three an in-between position.

Moreover, the cross-tabulations verify our earlier conclusions regarding the sources for the low political participation and high church and state separation. As Table 9-8 shows, of the six faith and social background variables most correlated with the Political Action Scale, the three faith variables listed were all negatively associated with approval, and the three social background variables were

TABLE 9-8
Political Action as Related to Faith and Life Variables

Faith and Life Variables	Position on Scale at Left				Pearson Coeff. (r)
	Low			High	
	1	2	3	4	
	(% scoring "high" on Political Action)				
Fundamentalist Orthodoxy	54	30	12	11	−.375
Anabaptism	33	21	10		−.346
Amount of Education	8	16	28	31	.294
General Orthodoxy	53	41	23	14	−.255
Socioeconomic Status	8	15	22	41	.252
Rural-Urban Residence	13	18	24	25	.208

Note: Residence refers to (1) rural farm, (2) rural nonfarm, (3) small city, and (4) large city. Read percentages as follows: Of those who scored "low" on Fundamentalist Orthodoxy, 54% scored "high" on the Political Action Scale.

positively associated with approval. Such approval appears to be in part a consequence of the higher education and urbanization of the members.

Summary

In this chapter three political positions of contemporary Mennonite leaders were discussed. The political nonparticipation position most nearly reflects the stance of the sixteenth-century Anabaptists, taken in part because of severe persecution by the state. The free participation and selective participation positions reflect recent revisions of the political ethic of Mennonites and Brethren in Christ, one in the direction of rather full responsibility for the political process and the other in the direction of witness to the state but not full responsibility for the actions of the state.

In their present-day attitudes, members of these groups overwhelmingly reject the idea that the state is an evil force in the world or an enemy of the church, an idea that their forebears would have found easy to believe. The average score on a Separation of Church and State Scale was only 5.7 out of a possible 12 points, which also indicates a more ambivalent attitude about separation than their forebears expressed in their writings. The large majority of members (76%) believe that members should vote in public elections. Only 70% actually took a political party position of any kind, including a position labeled "Independent." Of those who took a political party position, three fourths of American members identified themselves with the Republican Party. In Canada the members were more evenly divided between the Conservative and Liberal parties.

The analysis of the association between the independent faith and life variables and political participation did not pertain to the party identification of members but to the degree of their participation. It was discovered that the faith variables are associated with low political participation and the variables of higher education and urbanization are associated with high participation. Although twentieth-century Anabaptists no longer hold to the thoroughgoing separationist stance of their forebears, it is evident they have not yet reconciled their assent to the Anabaptist vision with a more selective and freer participation in the political process.

Chapter 10

MARRIAGE AND THE FAMILY

Marriage and Divorce

From their earliest days, Anabaptists have taken a strongly conservative view of the sanctity and inviolability of the marriage bond. Rejecting a sacramental view of marriage, they nevertheless have grounded their views in the scriptural precepts that marriage should be "in the Lord" and a union of one man and one woman is a lifetime commitment. "What therefore God has joined together, let not man put asunder" (Mark 10:9, RSV).

All five churches cooperating in this study refer to marriage and the family in their confessions of faith and/or in positional statements adopted from time to time by their official conference bodies.[1] Except for minor details, the five bodies express similar positions on the issues related to marriage and divorce: (1) a "believer" should not marry an "unbeliever"; (2) marriage should not be broken except by the death of a spouse; (3) divorce is a violation of God's will and is permissible only in case of adultery; (4) a church member who divorces may not remarry as long as the previous spouse lives, but should remain unmarried with the hope of becoming reconciled with the separated spouse. (The GCMC has no stated policy on this latter point.)

In practice not all church members have adhered to these standards. Divorced and remarried persons have occasionally been received into church membership provided the remarriage occurred before their conversion and entrance into church fellowship. Occasionally in recent years a divorced church member has been permitted to remarry upon confessing as sin the broken vows of his earlier marriage. Such cases have been allowed in the GCMC and, more rarely, in the MC. Currently the MBC is considering a revised policy which would permit a divorced member to remarry if he confesses the sin of his broken marriage. The policy assumes that divorce is "a sin that is forgivable."

The more frequent occurrence of divorce among church members in recent years is forcing a new look at the issues of divorce and the remarriage of divorcees. A slight liberalization of views seems to be occurring, and with it a greater tendency to view cases on their individual merits and to allow congregations more autonomy in dealing with cases.

In view of this current ferment, it is of considerable interest to discover how church members view the issues of marriage and divorce and the extent to which they agree with the official church positions. The question "Which statement best expresses your view of marriage?" yielded the following percentage distribution of responses for the statements provided:

	Percent
A lifelong commitment never to be broken except by death.	76.8
A lifetime commitment, but may be broken only if every attempt to reconcile disharmony has failed.	21.9
A commitment to remain married as long as the couple is compatible.	0.9
A commitment to remain married until one partner wishes to break the marriage.	0.4
	100.0

It is clear that opinion strongly opposes divorce. The proportions responding "a lifetime commitment never to be broken except by death" varied significantly from 64% for the 20-29 age-group to

96% for those 50 and over. No age-group registered more than a total of three percent for the last two responses. Females were slightly more conservative in their responses than males.

The respondents were asked to declare their opinions on the morality (rightness or wrongness) of each of 25 moral issues, noted previously in Chapter 7. Five of these issues related to marriage and divorce. The percentage distribution of responses for these five items are given in Table 10-1.

On the question of whether it is wrong for a Christian to marry a non-Christian, 42% checked "always wrong" and another 45% "sometimes wrong." The weight of opinion seems clearly against such marriages, although a minority see the matter as not of moral concern, at least under some conditions.

A further check on attitudes toward interfaith marriage is provided by the question, "Do you think it is important that a person marry a member of his own denomination rather than someone from another background?" The proportions answering "yes" varied from 36% for the EMC to 56% for the MC, with 53% for the weighted total of all respondents. Opinions vary widely by age-groups, from only 18% of teenagers answering "yes," to 73% of those aged 50 and over. Besides reflecting the greater conservatism of age, the older respondents probably have a greater awareness of the problems of adjustment associated with mixed marriages.

A special case is the matter of interracial marriage. Although 19% see nothing wrong in marriage across racial lines if both are Christian, what can be said of the attitudes of the other 81%? Possibly additional persons would have checked "never wrong" if the item had specified "Christians of different races but of same or similar denomination" which would rule out Protestant-Catholic marriage. Even allowing for this as a complicating factor, there appears to be a lot of opposition to interracial marriage for reasons of prejudice. This is not in line with the statement on Christian race relations, adopted by the General Conference of the MC in 1955, which recommends "That on the question of interracial marriage we help our people to understand that the only scriptural requirement for marriage is that it be 'in the Lord.' "[2]

On the issue of divorce, two conditions were specified, "for cause of adultery" and "for other causes." (See Table 10-1.) In case of the former, one third, and in case of the latter, one half of the church members feel that divorce is "always wrong." Most of the remainder checked "sometimes wrong," that is, under some conditions. We conclude that opposition to divorce among twentieth-century Anabaptists is quite strong, though a substantial minority would not object to it if the circumstances seem to be justifiable. Casual evidence indicates that of the small number who do divorce, many sever their relationships to the church either preceding or following a divorce, probably to avoid expressions of social disapproval that they may encounter.

TABLE 10-1
Attitudes of Church Members on Moral Issues
Related to Marriage and Divorce

Issue	Response			
	Always wrong %	Sometimes wrong %	Never wrong %	Uncertain %
1. Marriage of a Christian to a non-Christian	42	45	4	9
2. Marriage between Christians of different races	15	44	19	22
3. Divorce (for cause of adultery)	33	36	14	17
4. Divorce (for other causes)	49	35	2	14
5. Remarriage while first spouse is still living	60	24	3	13

Among the items in Table 10-1, the remarriage of divorcees tend to be most strongly disapproved, with 60% expressing the opinion that any remarriage while the first spouse is still living is "always wrong." The proportions giving this answer varied from 44% for the GCMC to 70% for the MC. The percentages for the other groups were: EMC, 50%; MBC, 57%; and BIC, 66%. The somewhat more liberal responses of the GCMC members reflects the fact that this denomination has never prepared an official statement regarding the remarriage of divorcees. It has preferred the flexibility of allowing the local pastor and congregation to make the determination in each case, with practice varying from one pastor to another.

To probe the circumstances under which church members would be willing to admit divorced and remarried persons to church membership, the following was asked: "Under what conditions would you approve admitting to membership in your church a person who is divorced and remarried (with first spouse still living)? (Check one.)" The percentage distribution of response was as follows:

	Percent
Under no conditions should he be admitted to membership	10
Only if the divorce was due to unfaithfulness (adultery) by the other spouse	9
If the person has confessed his wrongs and made all possible restitution	38
If the person promises to be faithful to the church's doctrine and teachings from this point on even though not making confession	5
He should be admitted on the basis of his professed belief in Christ without reference to his divorce and remarriage	22
Uncertain	16
	100

These findings suggest that the most common position of present-day church members is to accept the divorced and remarried person on the basis of confession and forgiveness. At least one fourth would support an even more liberal position. Given the present flux of attitudes and the tendency of official denominational policy to be restudied and possibly altered, and given the small but increasing number of couples who divorce and remarry but at the same time seek to retain their fellowship with their congregations, it is possible that the rule against acceptance of divorced and remarried persons will be relaxed.

Family Characteristics of Church Members

Of the 3,580 respondents who indicated their marital status,

23% were single, 70% married and living with the original spouse, 4% widowed, 1.4% widowed and remarried, and 0.3% were divorced, 0.8% divorced and remarried, and 0.3% were separated. Eleven persons were recorded as divorced, and 28 as divorced and remarried. The latter were distributed among all five churches, but with 13 belonging to EMC congregations. Data are not available to indicate whether divorced and separated persons were possibly underrepresented in the sample because they were less likely to cooperate in the study by filling out a questionnaire.

Of those respondents who had ever married and were at least 30 years of age, 0.9% had ever divorced. Allowing for possible underrepresentation of divorced persons in the sample, it is probable that not more than 2% of Mennonite and BIC church members experience divorce. We can assume that additional divorces have occurred among those who formerly were members of Mennonite and BIC churches but who withdrew in the face of strong attitudes disfavoring divorce. Currently more than one third of American marriages are ending in divorce.[3]

The United States census gives data on marital status for persons 14 years of age and over. The age span of the church members is comparable, since the median age at baptism of today's teenagers is 13.8 years. For the population of the United States 14 years and over, 29% of the males and 22% of the females were single in 1970. The figures for the church members were 20% for males and 25% for females.

The tabular comparisons are given in Table 10-2. Both male and female church members apparently are considerably less widowed, less divorced, and less separated than the U.S. population. Mennonite and BIC males tend to marry in larger proportions than their U.S. counterparts, but females 14 years of age and over are married in slightly smaller proportions than females in the national population.

Some Never Marry. A fairly accurate estimate can be made of the proportion of church members who never marry by computing the proportion of older members who are still single. Of the members 45 years of age and over, 1.6% of the males and 9.3% of the females have never married. Clearly more females remain single than males. Inasmuch as at the age of marriage (18 to 29 years generally speaking) the number of males and females in a standard population is just about equal, what is happening to Mennonites and BIC? The discrepancy between male and female marriage rates is probably due to a larger number of males leaving the Mennonite churches or bringing wives into these denominations from other backgrounds.

Landis reports that "in the United States today, 93% of the women and 92% of the men aged 45 and over are married or have been married; these percentages have increased steadily during the past seventy years."[4] Since the figures for the church members are 91% for women and 98% for men, we conclude that Mennonite and Brethren in Christ men marry in unusually high proportions, and women marry in slightly lower proportions than is true for the American population at large.

Among the church members, the proportion of women who marry is apparently increasing. The proportion of women aged 30-44 who have not married is only 6.2% as compared to the 9.3% for women over 45.

Age of Marriage. It may be noted, in passing, that the church members' median age at the time of their first marriage was 23.4 years

TABLE 10-2
Marital Status of Church Members, 1972, and of the U.S.
Population 14 Years and Older, 1970

Marital Status	Church Members		U.S. Population	
	Male %	Female %	Male %	Female %
Single	20.4	24.6	28.6	22.4
Married, not separated	78.4	69.4	64.3	59.0
Married, separated	0.2	0.2	1.5	2.3
Widowed	0.9	5.4	2.9	12.4
Divorced	0.1	0.4	2.7	3.9
Total	100.0	100.0	100.0	100.0

Source of U.S. data: U.S. Dept of Commerce, 1970 *Census of Population: General Population Characteristics, United States Summary,* 1972, p. 311.

for men and 21.7 for women. This compares with medians of 23.1 and 20.9 for the U.S. population in 1971 and medians of 24.9 and 22.1 years for Canadians in 1971.[5] Apparently Mennonites, on the average, are slightly older when they marry than others in the U.S. population but are younger than Canadians at the age of marriage. As is true for the U.S. population as a whole, the average age at marriage has been declining in the long run. The decline is evidenced by comparing church members 50 and over with those 30-49 years of age. For males the median age of marriage declined from 24.6 to 23.1 years of age; for females, 22.8 to 21.4 years.

Mixed Marriages. Among the church members ever married, 73% reported that they and their spouses belonged to the same denomination at the time of their wedding. The percentages varied from 36 for the EMC to 82 for the MC. However, at the time of the survey, 94% of the married respondents reported that they and their spouses belong to the same denomination. Apparently most of the present members who married across denominational lines brought their spouses into membership in their own denomination. Of those couples who did not belong to the same denomination at the time of the survey, nearly half were under the age of 30. Of course, we have no way of knowing how many persons left the Mennonite churches to join their spouses in a non-Mennonite denomination.

Data were not gathered on the church affiliation of the spouse who was not a member of the denomination in question. Probably many of these interdenominational marriages were between persons of different Mennonite and BIC denominations. These could hardly be called "interfaith" marriages because of the similarities of faith in these denominations. "Interfaith" marriages of the Protestant-Catholic or Protestant-Jewish types are rare among the members of the five denominations. Of the 679 respondents who reported having been a member of some other denomination before their present one, only 11 reported having been Catholic, and none reported having been Jewish.

Fertility. Data on size of household corroborates the results of earlier studies showing that Mennonite fertility is significantly higher than the general population of the U.S.[6] The median number of persons in all households in the U.S. in 1970 was 3.06 (3.42 for farm and 3.05 for nonfarm households).[7] The church members reported households with a median size of 4.5 persons (5.0 for farm and 4.3 for nonfarm households). For the U.S. white population the number of children ever born per 1,000 women 35-44 years old and ever married was 3,047 in 1970. The corresponding ratio was 3,796 for the female church members. (For Canadians in 1971 the ratio was 3,253.)[9]

Employment of Women. Mennonite and BIC women are gainfully employed outside the home in significant numbers. According to the U.S. Census, 39.6% of all women were employed (part time or full time) outside the home. The figure for the women in the survey was 45.1%. Counting only housewives, 38% are employed at least part time. Only 14%, however, are employed full time. The percentages of housewives employed at least part time ranged from 23.5 for farm residents to 49.1 for those church members living in cities of over 25,000 population.

Family Worship

Pastors and Christian education leaders of the denominations have generally encouraged newlyweds and parents to make worship a part of their family life. Reliable statistics on the extent to which worship is observed in homes have been difficult to obtain. Several items in the church member questionnaire now make it possible to estimate reliably the extent to which worship is practiced.

The respondent was asked "How frequently do you say grace (offer prayer) at meals in your home?" The responses provided, with the percentage distribution were as follows:

	Percent
Before and after every meal	4
Before every meal	79
At most, but not all meals	13
Occasionally, at least once a week	1
Seldom, or only on special occasions	2
Never, or hardly ever	1
	100

The percentage distributions were very similar for four of the churches. The MBC, however, had about 90% of families having grace every meal, compared to about 80% for the others. Rural-urban differences were negligible, as were differences between levels of educational achievement.

The question, "Are prayers offered audibly or silently at meals?" yielded responses varying considerably between the churches. Respondents checking "always audibly" ranged from 29% of the MC to 75% for the MBC. (BIC, 62%; EMC, 54%; and GCMC, 45%). Nine percent offer prayers "always silently," while the remainder sometimes pray audibly and sometimes silently.

"Family worship" is usually understood to mean something more than grace at meals. It would usually include reading of Scripture and/or other devotional literature, perhaps singing, and normally including prayers. Respondents were asked, "Do the members of your household have a family or group worship, other than grace at meals?" The results indicate that 45% of twentieth-century Anabaptists have a family worship period, whether daily or less frequently. The proportions answering "yes" vary from 41% for the MC to 61% for the MBC. If the priviate worship experience of individuals are added, the proportions of church members experiencing either family or private worship is somewhat higher. Apparently at least a third of church members have neither family worship nor private worship other than prayer at meals and church services. This, of course, is not to imply that prayers are said only in regularly scheduled periods of time.

Sexual Standards

In view of current controversies, three topics related to sexual matters are worthy of attention: sexual intercourse outside of marriage, contraception, and abortion. Church member attitudes on each of these were explored.

With respect to both premarital and extramarital intercourse, 85% of all respondents regard these as "always wrong." The remainder were "uncertain" or checked "sometimes wrong." Such official church pronouncements on the subject as exist have uniformly held that sexual intercourse is to be limited to married partners.

Thus some 15% hold views that would officially be called into question.

Attitudes on sexual intercourse outside of marriage are associated with level of education. Eighty-four percent of the respondents declared that "Sexual intercourse between *unmarried* persons is never justifiable." However, the proportions varied from 90% for those with no more than elementary education to 75% for those who went to college. Age was even more strongly related to the responses to this item. The proportions answering "is never justifiable" ranged from 66% for the 20-29 age-group to 95% for the group 50 years and over.[10]

Only one item in the questionnaire referred to contraception. On the item "Use of birth control devices or pills by married spouses" the church members responded as follows: "always wrong," 11%; "sometimes wrong," 25%; "never wrong," 47%; and "uncertain," 17%. Apparently about half of the church members are unwilling to give a blanket approval to the practice of contraception, despite the fact that the MC and GCMC churches have adopted statements indicating approval of contraception by methods that are approved by the medical profession.

Abortion poses difficult problems and decisions for church members and for church boards carrying responsibilities for hospital administration. The recent Supreme Court decision allowing women to choose abortion within the first third of the fetal period has thrust the issue into the public forums. Many states have revised their abortion laws, and local hospitals, physicians, and nurses have had to face the question of the extent to which they will participate in performing abortions for clients who request them.

The attitudes of church members on the rightness or wrongness of abortion were tested with several items. Two items were "Therapeutic abortion (for mother's health)" and "Non-therapeutic induced abortion (at mother's wish, not later than third month)." In a general way, the first item reflects the legal basis for abortion in most states *before* the Supreme Court decision; the second reflects the legal basis *since* the decision. The percentage distribution of responses to these two items is shown in the chart at the top of the next page. Clearly the majority opinion is against non-therapeutic abortion as currently approved by the Supreme Court and most state laws. The sizable minority which is "uncertain" reflects the complexity of the

Response	Non-therapeutic abortion	Therapeutic abortion
Always wrong	10	57
Sometimes wrong	27	23
Never wrong	36	4
Uncertain	27	16
Total	100	100

issues and the confusion that many people consequently feel.

Another questionnaire item probed the various circumstances under which the respondent would "think it should be possible for a pregnant woman to obtain a *legal* abortion." "Yes," "no," and "uncertain" responses were provided. The percent answering "yes" for each item is as follows:

	Percent "yes"
If there is a strong chance of serious defect in the baby	49
If the woman's own health is seriously endangered by the pregnancy	73
If the family has a very low income and cannot really afford any more children	12
If she became pregnant as a result of rape	46
If she is not married and does not want to marry the man	9
If she does not want the baby	8

Again it appears that majority opinion favors abortion only in case the mother's health is threatened. However, about half the respondents approve legalizing abortion when the baby is likely to be defective and when pregnancy has resulted from rape. There is strong opinion against legalizing abortion for economic reasons or for reasons of personal preference.

Some statistically significant variations between the denominations were registered, although the differences were not great. Slightly more "liberal" responses were given, on the average, by members of the GCMC. The most "conservative" responses were registered by the MC and MBC members. Variations by age were moderate, with 20-29-year-olds evidencing the most liberal attitudes. Variations by educational levels were substantial, with college educated persons taking more liberal positions. Male and female responses were so similar that statistically significant differences were not obtained on most abortion items. On two items where statistically significant differences were obtained, men evidenced the more liberal views.

Summary

As seen through the survey data, contemporary Anabaptists are strongly conservative in their views on marriage, divorce, mixed marriages, sexual standards, abortion, and contraception. Three fourths believe marriage is "a lifelong commitment never to be broken except by death." Apparently less than two percent of the church members ever experience divorce. The scope of the study unfortunately did not permit an investigation of the quality of interpersonal relations in Mennonite and BIC families.

The attitudes of the church members are considerably divided on the rightness or wrongness of divorce, of the remarriage of divorcees, of interracial marriages, and of the marriage of a Christian to a non-Christian.

Compared to the U.S. population as a whole, Mennonites and BIC tend to marry at slightly older ages and have more children. Males marry in larger proportions than American males generally, and females in slightly smaller proportions. Women are employed outside the home in slightly larger proportions than American women generally. Nearly half of the homes practice some form of family worship.

Five-sixths of the church members view any form of sexual intercourse outside of marriage as "always wrong." The use of contraceptives for the control of fertility in marriage was not opposed by most respondents. On the issue of abortion, the majority view as wrong the non-therapeutic abortions currently legalized in the United States as a result of the recent Supreme Court decision.

Chapter 11

LEADERSHIP IN
THE CONGREGATION

In the preceding seven chapters various dimensions of faith and life were defined and tested with the survey data gathered from church members. For the next five chapters the subject matter shifts to the dimensions of church work. In all, twelve dimensions of church work will be explored in this third part of the book: type of leadership, shared ministry, the role of women in the church, Sunday school participation, Bible knowledge, evangelism, support of church colleges, stewardship attitudes, stewardship performance, ecumenism, anti-Semitism, and anti-Catholicism.

The analysis of attitudes and behavior concerning the work of the church properly begins with the factor of leadership in the church. The discussion begins with the Anabaptist view of ministry and proceeds with the first three dimensions of church work listed above: classification of leadership, a shared ministry scale constructed for the purpose of testing assent to the Anabaptist view of ministry, and a role-of-women scale that measures attitudes regarding the "equal" participation of women in the work of the church.

The Anabaptist View of Ministry

As commonly defined, the term "leader" was foreign to the

vocabulary of the sixteenth-century Anabaptist. They spoke of ministers, shepherds, teachers, and preachers, but not of leaders as such. They emphatically rejected the established distinction between clergy and laity and considered every member to be a minister of one kind or another. As Franklin Littell wrote, "In Anabaptism there began that . . . ministry of the whole people by virtue of their ordination in Christian baptism."[1] He called this phenomenon "spiritual government," and described it as follows:

> We are confronted with a primitive Christian brotherhood in which each believer has his definite role and responsibility in reaching a statement of the community decision. The social scientist may be justified in considering this one of the first manifestations of government by consensus. The church historian finds it one of the first patterns of lay government in Christian history, a historical movement when the professional monopoly of theologians and canon lawyers was broken in favor of the priesthood of all believers.[2]

Luther had made much of the concept of the priesthood of believers, but as Hendrik Kraemer pointed out, his concept "to the present day . . . fulfills [more] the role of a flag than of an energizing, vital principle."[3] The Anabaptists were one of the earliest Protestant groups to put the concept into practice in the restitution of the believers' church.

It is known from their earliest Confession of Faith that the **Anabaptists ordained certain members for the shepherding of local** congregations and the carrying of the faith to unbelievers.[4] "Not that they have no clergy but that they have no laity," Littell explained. "At least in their classical periods the restitutionist movements have had no laity of the sort that Christendom, until the coming of the 'post-Christian era,' counted by the millions."[5] Their set-apart leaders were supported by voluntary contributions rather than by tithes or taxes as in the state-church system. Menno Simons wrote that he had lived for years "from brother to brother and had never gone hungry nor in want."[6]

By the middle of the sixteenth century, however, a more traditional definition of leadership authority was developing. In the local congregation, in addition to the pastor (shepherd), the offices of elder (sometimes called bishop) and deacon became the pattern, producing the threefold ministry that has been traditional in the Mennonite Church for four centuries and that has once again relegated the laity to a more passive role.

In the five denominations, various attempts to recover the more radical concept that every member is a minister can be noted. In the MBC, which began as a deliberate return to a more brother-hood-type pattern of authority, David Ewert and Delbert Wiens have recently pleaded for a continued faithfulness to this vision of a congregation in which every member is "charismatically endowed" with a "call to service and the ability to perform it."[7] Both the MC and BIC are shifting from a synodal polity in which regional conferences through their bishops exercised considerable authority over local congregations to a more brotherhood-type of congrega-tional polity.[8] The GCMC, on the other hand, began its history by celebrating the autonomy of the local congregation and is now moving toward a modified congregationalism with regional pastors and denominational secretaries trying to stir up local churches to more active participation in the total work of the larger church.

Another indication of return to a more radically Anabaptist view of the ministry is the new curriculum of the Associated Menno-nite Biblical Seminaries sponsored jointly by the MC and GCMC. This institution, entrusted with the training of ministers for the work of these churches, has drawn the following conclusions about the na-ture of the Christian ministry:

> We can say on the basis of New Testament authority that every member has a ministry (Romans 12:4-9; 1 Corinthians 12:4-31; Ephesians 4:4-16), that this ministry is not just his gainful employment in the secular realm but a job to be done in the corporate life of the congregation, in its worship, in its teaching, **its preaching, its discernment of God's will, in its government, and** in its diakonia [service] in the world. These tasks are specifically assigned, multiple in the sense that one function might be shared by several members, and diverse in the sense that the church's mission requires a variety of persons to work in unity rather than a variety of functions to be assigned to one "minister." Some of the elements in a contemporary pattern of ministry would be the following:
>
> (a) The expectation that prior to the call of a professional minister, a congregation exists in viable form that does not make its survival or its authenticity dependent upon the presence of

the professional. This implies a recognition that the centraliza-
tion of responsibility in one man is neither possible nor desirable,
the expectation that the spiritual gifts in the congregation are
being discerned and exercised, the sharing of leadership responsibility by a number of mature persons in the congregation, and
the assumption of responsible roles in the congregation by
women as well as by men.

(b) The call of men and women as professional ministers,
when the presence of specialized skills requiring formal preparation is desired for the greater faithfulness and effectiveness of the
congregation's ministry of preaching, teaching, counseling, evan-
gelizing, etc. The way or ways in which the professional
minister fulfills the role of facilitating the total ministry in which
other members have a function is not susceptible to generaliza-
tion, but depends upon the situation and the gifts and training
which the professional brings to his role.[9]

Three Role Categories in the Churches

The quotation above spoke of several types of roles in the congregation — the role of every member, the role of women, and the
role of the professional minister. Sociologically speaking, a role is
simply the part a person plays in the organization of any human
group. It is the specific participation that is expected of a member
as the group works to achieve its purposes. In this respect the
church is no different from other groups; it must have a system of
roles if it wants to achieve its purposes. How a member's role is
defined, of course, depends on the concept of the church and its
polity. In the normative Anabaptist sense, every member would be
a minister or "leader" whether officially so designated or not. On
this basis members could be classified by three role categories: unofficial leaders, official leaders, and ordained leaders. These labels
were not used, however, because they presuppose an adherence to
the shared ministry vision that has not yet been verified in the
study.

A less presumptuous division of members into the following
three role categories was made: lay member, lay leader, and ordained minister. This will be referred to as the "Type of Leadership"
variable. As Table 11-1 reveals, two questions were used to develop
these categories. The respondents were first asked whether they had

held a position of official leadership in the local congregation and were given seven examples of what was meant by this. They were next asked whether they had ever been ordained as a minister or deacon. These questions established the distinction between *lay leader* and *ordained minister*, and those who answered negatively to both of these questions were classified as *lay members*. The table shows that 57% of the respondents are leaders (or have been within the past three years), including the 9% who are ordained ministers. This leaves 42% who are in the lay member category.

The proportion (49%) who serve as lay leaders in Mennonite and BIC churches can be compared to that of several other denominations in America for which roughly comparable figures are available. In a study of Roman Catholic parishes, Fichter reports that only 6% of Catholics carry leadership roles in the parish.[10] Campbell and Fukuyama report that 36% of the members of the United Church of Christ have held an office or served on an official board or committee of their local church during the past three years.[11] In a study of eight urban Lutheran churches, Kloetzli found that 39% of the members were presently serving on the church

TABLE 11-1
Types of Leadership in the Churches

Items and Responses	Percent of Responses for:					
	MC	GCMC	MBC	BIC	EMC	TOTAL
1. "Do you presently hold, or have you held within the past three years, a position of leadership in your local congregation (minister, elder, council member, officer, S.S. teacher, committee chairman, youth group officer or sponsor, etc.)?"						
Yes	58	54	56	65	58	57
2. "Were you ever ordained as a minister or deacon?"						
Yes	7	11	10	12	6	9
Type of Leadership:						
Lay Member	41	45	43	34	42	42
Lay Leader	52	44	48	55	52	49
Ordained Minister	7	11	10	11	6	9
Total	100	100	101	100	100	100
Number of Respondents	1,192	609	700	615	443	3,559

council, on a church committee, as an officer of a church organization or as a teacher in the Sunday school.[12] Strommen and associates report that 55% of Lutherans in America had an office, special job, or committee assignment in the congregation or denomination during the past year.[13] The proportion of respondents in the present study who serve as leaders equals or exceeds the figures just quoted. This is especially true for the BIC, in which about two thirds of the members serve as leaders in the congregation.

The survey data suggest that the size of congregations has something to do with the proportion of members who serve as lay leaders. Small churches tend to call on a larger proportion of their members to serve in leadership roles. The GCMC has the largest congregations, with an average of 194 members per congregation, but has the smallest proportion (44%) in the role of lay leader. At the other extreme, the BIC have only 61 members per congregation, but have the largest proportion (55%) serving as lay leaders. If maximum involvement of laymen in congregation leadership is an objective, congregations should not become large. Among congregations with less than 100 members, 69% of the members had served in leadership roles in the past three years, compared to only 45% for congregations of over 500 members.

For the sake of analyzing factors associated with the selection of leaders and ministers, the Type of Leadership variable was cross-tabulated with the faith and life variables in the study. Nineteen of these variables having the highest correlation with type of leadership are listed in Table 11-2 in the rank order of their correlation. As would be expected, a higher percentage of leaders and ministers than lay members score high on associationalism. The influence is probably two-way: leaders are selected because they rank higher in church participation, and they participate more when they are given leadership. The same is true for the other faith variables: evangelism, biblical knowledge, and devotionalism. There appears to be little difference between lay members and lay leaders on sanctification and communalism. On fundamentalist orthodoxy, leaders are significantly less orthodox than members, and ministers still less than leaders. The latter would indicate either that fundamentalism is not a test for leadership in these churches or that other factors are more influential in the selection of leadership, in which case there might be considerable potential for role conflict.

TABLE 11-2
Type of Leadership as Related to Other Variables

Variables	Member	Lay Leader	Minister	Total	Contingency Coeff.
	(Percentages unless otherwise indicated)				
High on Associationalism	0	24	52	17	.541
High on Evangelism	11	13	63	16	.394
High on S. School Participation	37	74	85	60	.381
Occupation "Professional"	19	26	67	30	.355
Median School Years Completed	10.6	11.7	15.9	11.4	
Attended College	24	34	66	33	.323
High on Bible Knowledge	27	43	80	40	.315
High on Stewardship Attitudes	18	33	48	28	.289
Females	58	58	6	53	.285
High on Devotionalism	22	29	64	29	.284
Age 30-49	25	45	56	37	.274
Median Age	40.8	39.0	47.0	40.6	
Upper/Upper Middle Socio-economic Status	40	52	74	52	.267
High Anti-Communist Attitude	25	37	62	34	.248
High Sanctification	13	11	25	13	.207
High on Moral Behavior	58	64	73	62	.180
High on Communalism	6	5	17	7	.171
High on Race Relations	26	35	47	32	.166
High on Political Participation	36	49	60	45	.164
High on Fundamentalist Orthodoxy	49	39	28	42	.160
High on Anabaptism	41	44	66	45	.148

The evidence for the influence of other factors is seen in the variables of age, education, and socioeconomic status. Fifty-six percent of all ministers and 45% of all leaders are in the middle years (30-49), compared to only 25% of the lay members. Amount of education is an even greater factor in leadership selection. Thirty-four percent of lay leaders have been to college compared to only 24% of the lay members. The socioeconomic status scale, which combines education, income, and occupation, further confirmed the selectivity of leaders on the basis of social factors operating alongside the factors of religious qualification. These findings are not new in the literature of the sociology of the church.[14] Leiffer points out that "there is greater probability that a school superintendent, doctor, or businessman will be given a leadership post than a man who earns his living by manual labor. The reasons are obvious, though perhaps not fully justifiable. Men with better education, who are able to express their

ideas with clarity, and whose work constantly brings them into contact with people, have more confidence in themselves and less hesi-
tancy to accept responsibility."[15] Leiffer was speaking from a
mainstream American Protestant perspective; but from a radical
Anabaptist perspective it would seem that the selection of leaders
from the socially favored classes represents something of a deviation
from the normative vision outlined earlier in the chapter. At least it
would seem to face a challenge by John H. Yoder's assertion that

> The ministry of the Believer's Church honors the weaker mem-
> ber. The church's decision-making processes must not put a pre-
> mium on rationality or articulateness, as much parliamentary,
> group and committee process does. It must not put a premium
> on intellectual correctness; often the right position can be ex-
> pressed in terms which are "wrong" when measured technically
> by the norms and phrasings of academic or dogmatic theology.[16]

The Concept of Shared Ministry

One of the most distinctive marks of the Anabaptist conception of
roles in the church was a radical sharing of functions pertaining to the
church's ministry in the congregation and mission in the world. As
Littell put it, "Among the restitutionists . . . the Great Commission
was held binding on all members of the covenant. The rule applied
to both men and women: among the restitutionists, women too were
speakers and missioners."[17] Or as John H. Yoder wrote,

> The ministry in the church of the believers is universal. No one
> is not a minister. By virtue of her definition of membership, the
> church of believers is freed from the need to create a category
> of the non-involved "lay" status in order to accept as members
> everyone within a given society, regardless of the degree of their
> commitment.[18]

In order to test adherence to so radical a vision, a number of
questions probing this concept were included. The responses are tabulated in Table 11-3. Just over half of the members of the five denominations (58%) affirmed the concept that "all members are
ministers." The members of the MC adhere most closely to the radical
vision (61%) and the members of the EMC the least.

The next question raised the difficult issue of ordination among twentieth-century Anabaptists. In Roman Catholic and Protestant churches with a "high" view of church organization, the ordination of priests or ministers confers an indelible authority to administer the sacraments — the central mark of the church in these communions. The meaning of ordination is one of the most unresolved issues in at least two of the denominations: MC and GCMC. Article 10 of the MC Confession of Faith states that

> It is the intention of Christ that there should be shepherds in His congregations to feed the flock, to serve as leaders, to expound the Word of God, to administer the ordinances, to exercise, in cooperation with the congregation, a scriptural church discipline, and in general to function as servants of the church. Ordination is accompanied by a laying-on of hands, symbolic of the church assigning responsibility and of God imparting strength for the assignment.[19]

TABLE 11-3
Measures of the Concept of Shared Ministry

Items and Responses	Percent of Responses for:					
	MC	GCMC	MBC	BIC	EMC	TOTAL
1. "A proper view of congregational organization and leadership is that <u>all members are ministers</u> and should share, as they are able, in the ministerial functions of the congregation."						
Strongly agree/Agree	61	55	54	54	48	58
2. "A church congregation cannot be complete unless there is an ordained minister to lead the congregation and perform the ministerial functions."						
Strongly disagree/Disagree	26	31	36	29	31	30
3. "How important is it, in your opinion, that the pastor in your congregation be on full-time salary rather than earning all or part of his income through other employment?"						
Of little importance/Quite unimportant	23	11	12	10	4	17
Shared Ministry Scale:						
10–16 High	18	19	12	14	6	17
5–9 Middle	65	60	60	62	58	63
0–4 Low	17	21	28	24	36	20
Total	100	100	100	100	100	100
Number of Responses	1,187	596	701	604	437	3,525
Mean Score	7.0	6.9	6.2	6.4	5.5	6.8

But in the attempt of his teaching faculty to recover the normative universality of ministry, the Dean of the Associated Mennonite Biblical Seminaries (MC and GCMC) wrote that

> The concept of ordination, in the perspective of the view of church and ministry outlined above, needs either to be redefined or dropped altogether. The term "ordination" in the modern ecclesiastical sense does not occur at all in the New Testament. The "laying on of hands" as a form of religious gesture in the New Testament signifies blessing, healing, baptism, and consecration, but in no sense does it transmit an indelible character to the recipient. In view of various and frequent usages of this gesture, we draw three conclusions: (1) It was not basically regarded as an essential channel of ministerial authority, but was used to consecrate all sorts of persons; (2) one person could be so consecrated more than once, as was Paul at the time of his baptism and the time of his commissioning to missionary service; and (3) it was regarded primarily as an act of intercessory prayer. Relating this to the modern view of ordination would call for ordaining many people each to his specific ministry, or abandoning altogether the practice of ordination as it is commonly understood. Certainly if we reject the concept of a sacramental distinction between clergy and laity, we reject the concept of ordination on the basis of which this distinction survives.[20]

It is evident in the second item in 11-3 that the majority of members adhere to the more traditional view of the centrality of the ordained "shepherd" in the congregation. Only 30% disagreed with the assertion that a congregation cannot be complete unless it has an ordained minister. While 61% of MC members affirmed that "all members are ministers" (first question), only 26% denied that a congregation needs an ordained minister to be complete.

The third question pertained to the concept of self-supporting ministers in the churches. There has been more continuity between sixteenth and twentieth centuries on the practice of lay ministry than on the matter of the universality of ministry. H. S. Bender wrote that

> in Anabaptism . . . lay preaching attained its full right, and the principle is still firmly held in the Mennonite churches in various countries and continues to be widely practiced in more than one group. In fact in the first quarter of the 20th century at least three fourths of all Mennonite congregations were served by lay preachers, and in 1955 at least half.[21]

Bender was speaking primarily of the MC, inasmuch as the other four denominations had moved much farther in the direction of the professional ministry with nearly all congregations having salaried pastors. These variations in practice produced larger interdenominational differences in the third item in Table 11-3 than in the other two. Nearly one fourth (23%) of the MC members feel it is of little or no importance that the pastor be on full salary, in contrast to only 4% in the EMC who feel that way.

The three questions just reviewed, plus two on the role of women in the church (see below), were combined into a composite Shared Ministry Scale, with scores ranging from zero to 16.[22] The overall average score was 6.8 with a high of 7.0 in the MC and a low of 5.5 in the EMC. The construction of the scale made it possible to test correlations with other variables. For example, the following crosstabulation shows that ordained ministers scored significantly higher on the Shared Ministry Scale than lay leaders or lay members:

	Member	*Leader*	*Minister*	*Cont.* *Coeff.*
Mean Score on Shared Ministry Scale	6.9	7.1	8.2	.110

Out of a total of over forty such intercorrelations examined, the highest twelve are given in Table 11-4. Although its correlation coefficient is much less than the first twelve, Anabaptism is added because the association is still significant and in a direction opposite to what we would have expected. Those scoring *high* on Anabaptism score *low* on shared ministry.

The only faith variables that fell into the top twelve having highest correlation were fundamentalist orthodoxy, voluntarism, and general orthodoxy; and the correlations were all in reverse direction. In fact, all of the scaled faith variables except ethical-social conversion were negatively correlated with Shared Ministry, which indicates that the higher the scores on these faith variables, the lower the score on the Shared Ministry Scale. Thus support for the shared ministry concept must be found elsewhere. Support is stronger among those with higher education and those of younger age. It seems also to come from persons who are less moralistic, less prejudiced in relation to Negroes, Communists, Catholics, and Jews, and who are favorable to ecumenical relations and greater social concerns. It is unknown, of course, whether these factors promote favorableness toward a shared ministry, or whether persons committed to the shared ministry concept tend to get these other attitudes as a consequence of that commitment.

TABLE 11-4
Relationships Between the Shared Ministry Scale
and Other Variables

Variables	Position on Variable at Left					Pearson Coeff. (r)
	Low 1	2	3	4	High 5	
	(Mean Score on Shared Ministry Scale)					
Fundamentalist Orthodoxy	10.4	8.2	6.9	5.9		−.418
Age (by Generation)	8.6	8.2	6.8	5.9		−.352
Moral Attitudes	10.1	9.1	8.2	6.6		−.324
Race Relations	5.8	6.8	8.3			.321
Voluntarism	9.1	8.1	6.9	6.1		−.309
Anti-Communism	5.2	6.5	7.2			−.294
General Orthodoxy	11.1	9.3	7.8	6.4		−.294
Ecumenism	5.6	6.8	8.1			.277
Social Concerns	6.2	6.7	8.5			.269
Anti-Catholicism	8.3	6.9	6.3	6.1	5.3	−.261
Amount of Education	6.0	6.7	11.7	8.4		.253
Anti-Semitism	7.9	7.2	6.3	6.0	5.5	−.241
Anabaptism	7.3	7.2	6.7			−.075

Note: Read scores as follows: Respondents who scored "low" in fundamentalist orthodoxy scored an average of 4.7 on the Role-of-Women Scale.

Note: Age categories are (1) teenagers, (2) young adults, (3) middle aged, and (4) older adults. Read scores as follows: Respondents scoring "low" on fundamentalist orthodoxy scored an average of 10.4 on the Shared Ministry Scale.

The Role of Women in the Church

Two of the items in the Shared Ministry Scale pertained specifically to the role of women in the church, and they will now be examined as a separate issue. H. S. Bender wrote that

> In the early Anabaptist movement women played an important role. The Anabaptist emphasis upon voluntary membership, adult baptism, and personal commitment inevitably opened up new perspectives for women. The court records in the Swiss-South German areas as well as in Holland show that they could and did give vigorous and intelligent independent testimonies

of their own to their faith, and shared martyrdom unflinchingly with men, although the number of male martyrs reported generally outnumbered the women two to one.

Bender added, however, that "Later, after the creative period of Anabaptism was past, the settled communities and congregations reverted more to the typical patriarchal attitude of European culture."[23] Twentieth-century Anabaptists are considerably more known for their vestiges of patriarchalism than for their sharing of ministerial functions with women. In the MC and BIC Confessions of Faith, for instance, the traditional view of a woman's place in the church is expressed as follows:

> We believe that in their relation to the Lord men and women are equal, for in Christ there is neither male nor female. But in the order of creation God has fitted man and woman for differing functions; man has been given a primary leadership role, while the woman is especially fitted for nurture and service. Being in Christ does not nullify these natural endowments, either in the home or in the church. The New Testament symbols of man's headship are his short hair and uncovered head while praying or prophesying, and the symbols of woman's role are her long hair and her veiled head. The acceptance by both men and women of the order of creation in no way limits their rightful freedom, but rather ensures their finding the respective roles in which they can most fruitfully and happily serve. (Article 14, MC Confession of Faith.)
>
> The teaching in 1 Corinthians 11:1-16 presents the use of the head covering . . . as an external symbolism to indicate that men and women recognize and accept their divinely appointed relationship to Christ and to each other. . . . In recognizing this God-ordained relationship, the man when praying or prophesying should have his head uncovered and the woman should have her head covered. (Article XI, BIC Manual of Doctrine.)

The responses of the samples of members of the five denominations to three questions probing the role of women indicates considerably more adherence to the traditional patriarchal view than to the radical Anabaptist view. Table 11-5 shows that only 32% believe that more women should serve on church boards and committees of the church, only 17% believe that women should be ordained, and only 16% believe that women in Canadian and American societies are being denied certain basic rights. When these three items are combined into a composite Role-of-Women Scale, we note that the GCMC scores highest (2.6 mean score in a range of zero to six), and the EMC and MBC score lowest (mean score of 1.6). Although the status of women in the GCMC is relatively higher, in no denomination is her status very high.

TABLE 11-5
Measures of the Role of Women in the Church

Items and Responses	Percent of Responses for:					
	MC	GCMC	MBC	BIC	EMC	TOTAL
1. "In the future should larger numbers of qualified women be elected or appointed to church boards and committees at denominational, district, and congregational levels?"						
Yes	29	40	26	36	22	32
2. "Should the policy on ordinations in your denomination be changed to allow for the ordination of women to the Christian ministry?"						
Yes	12	30	12	17	12	17
3. "Do you believe that women in Canadian and American societies are being discriminated against and denied certain basic rights?"						
Yes	15	20	14	12	10	16
Role of Women Scale:						
5-6 High	9	18	8	9	7	12
3-4 Upper Middle	20	27	17	26	18	22
1-2 Lower Middle	43	34	38	37	41	39
0 Low	26	21	37	27	34	27
Total	99	100	100	99	100	100
Number of Respondents	1,185	601	697	600	437	3,520
Mean Score	1.9	2.6	1.6	2.0	1.6	2.0

As in the case with the Shared Ministry Scale, the following cross-tabulation shows ordained ministers to be significantly more open to an enlarged role of women in the church than lay leaders or lay members:

	Member	Leader	Minister	Cont. Coeff.
Mean Score on Role-of-Women Scale	2.0	2.0	2.5	.150

In Table 11-6, the twelve faith and life variables having the highest correlation with the Role-of-Women Scale are listed in rank order. Again, the faith variables (fundamentalist orthodoxy, general orthodoxy, and Anabaptism) are all negatively associated with the scale. Like the shared ministry concept, the more open attitude toward the role of women in church and society has a relationship to higher education, greater social compassion (welfare attitudes, political action, and social concern) and less prejudice regarding Negroes, Catholics, and Jews. It is especially interesting to note that male respondents scored slightly higher on the Role-of-Women Scale than females. Thus, women struggling against tradition for the cause of equal participation in the work of the church should be aware that their own sex is the greater supporter of the traditional view on this issue.

TABLE 11-6
The Role-of-Women Scale
as Related to Other Variables

Variables	Position on Variable at Left				Pearson Coeff. (r)
	Low 1	2	3	High 4	
	(Mean Score on Role-of-Women Scale)				
Fundamentalist Orthodoxy	4.7	3.0	1.9	1.3	−.523
Moral Attitudes	4.2	3.6	3.1	1.9	−.443
Political Action	1.4	2.2	3.2		.379
General Orthodoxy	4.8	3.8	2.6	1.7	−.373
Ecumenism	.9	2.0	3.0		.362
Separation of Church and State	2.9	2.4	1.5		−.339
Welfare Attitudes	1.4	1.9	3.2		.326
Social Concerns	1.5	1.8	3.2	3.1	.320
Anti-Catholicism	3.0	1.8	1.4		−.303
Amount of Education	1.4	1.8	2.6		.299
Race Relations	2.3	1.9	2.8		.296
Socioeconomic Status	1.7	1.7	2.5	3.8	.294
Anabaptism	2.7	2.1	1.7		−.230
Sex	Male: 2.3 Female: 1.9				

Note: Read scores as follows: Respondents who scored "low" in fundamentalist orthodoxy scored an average of 4.7 on the Role-of-Women Scale.

Summary and Conclusions

A review of the teachings and practice of the sixteenth-century Anabaptists regarding ministerial leadership revealed a strong emphasis on a broad sharing of leadership responsibilities among all the members of a congregation. The survey data produced in this study provided a test of whether present-day Mennonites and BIC accept this radical doctrine of lay participation in the leadership roles of the church. It was found that support for this radical doctrine is not very strong.

Three measures were used in the analysis. The first measure indicated the extent to which lay members participated in leadership roles in the congregations. Over half were found to be filling one or more leadership positions in the work of the church, a proportion somewhat larger than was found for the members of a number of non-Anabaptist denominations on which studies have been made. On a series of faith and life scales, ordained ministers tended to score substantially higher than other members and lay leaders scored somewhat higher than non-leaders.

In spite of the substantial proportion of members serving as lay leaders, nearly half of the members rejected a statement that "all members are ministers," and only 15% scored above 9 in a 16-point Shared Ministry Scale, constructed to test assent to the Anabaptist doctrine of leadership. Scores on this scale were negatively correlated with most of the faith variables, including the Anabaptism Scale. However, there was a positive association with the social ethics scales, indicating that those most favorable toward a shared ministry in the church also tend to support ethical concerns.

Attitudes regarding the role which women should take in the leadership of the church were tested, using a "Role-of-Women Scale." The results on this scale were generally similar to those of the Shared Ministry Scale but were more pronounced. Traditional attitudes unfavorable toward increased participation by women in lay leadership and ministerial roles appear to persist among both male and female church members, with men evidencing slightly less traditional attitudes than women.

The discrepancy between the normative Anabaptist vision and the present attitudes of church members appears to be greater in this area than in any other covered in the study so far.

Chapter 12

CHRISTIAN EDUCATION IN
THE LOCAL CHURCH

The Church Member Profile had its origin in a concern of professional Christian educators for more accurate information about the faith and life of the members whose Christian education was their primary responsibility. Although every chapter in this book speaks to this concern, the dimension of Christian education to be covered in this chapter is limited primarily to the church's program of formal instruction. The probes have to do with attending Sunday school and some consequences of the Sunday school program — increased Bible knowledge, incorporation of young people into the church, holy living, lay leadership, and lay evangelism. A profile of the Sunday school teacher and several probes of attitudes pertaining to the production of curriculum for Christian education will also be reported. This focused treatment, however, needs to be placed within a larger context of Christian education, which in Mennonite and BIC history and theology has at least three dimensions of meaning.

Dimensions of Christian Education

Informal Nurture. One dimension of meaning is the Christian nurture of members, especially of children. Long before these churches had a formal program of education, they carried on an informal Christian nurture that more or less effectively transmitted the faith to each succeeding generation of members. Although informal nurture can be a powerful means of transmitting the faith, there are serious drawbacks in an educational system centered exclusively in the unplanned, almost unconscious assimilation of the group's beliefs and attitudes through habitual association in the congregation, the church-controlled community, and especially the member's family. Faith quickly becomes traditional, and it is difficult for succeeding generations to embrace the inherited convictions with the same fervor as their parents unless those convictions can somehow become their own. Sooner or later this seems to require a more formal program of Christian instruction, with a curriculum of written materials, especially concerning the Holy Scriptures.

Formal Instruction. The primary agency of formal Christian education adopted by these churches was the Sunday school. The idea of the Sunday school was borrowed from the so-called Sunday school movement that began with Robert Raikes in England in 1780 and spread rapidly in America and Canada in the early nineteenth century.

> By 1815 it had become a powerful popular movement, and by 1824 a national organization, called the American Sunday School Union, had been organized to promote Sunday schools on a nation-wide scale. In 1830 this organization undertook a great missionary compaign "within two years to establish a Sunday school in every destitute place where it is practicable throughout the valley of the Mississippi," and in 1839 it resolved to establish a Sunday school in every place in the West.[1]

Some prominent MC and BIC leaders attended union or denominational Sunday schools during their youth and found them helpful.[2] John F. Funk wrote of his early Sunday school experience in Pennsylvania, "This . . . proved to be one of the greatest blessings of my life."[3] Attempts to introduce this agency into MC and BIC churches met with considerable resistance and even hostility for more than a quarter of a century. It was not approved for adoption until 1867 in the MC (Ohio Conference)[4] and 1885 in the BIC.[5] In 1867 the Virginia Conference (MC) voted against it.

There were two reasons for the opposition to the introduction of the Sunday school. One was simply stubborn resistance to change itself. In Chapter 2 reference was made to the schism in the Franconia Conference (MC) that first caused the division between the MC and GCMC. Among the innovations that sparked this schism was the Sunday school that John H. Oberholtzer started in the Swamp Mennonite Church in 1847. According to his own testimony, his opponents had said that "they would rather see their children go fishing or to the saloon on Sunday than to the Kinderlehre."[6] The introduction of the Sunday school was also the direct cause of the withdrawal of the conservative group known as the Old Order (Wisler) Mennonite Church. Bishop D. D. Miller summarized this reason for resistance in a talk at the first Sunday school conference in Indiana in 1892: "Opposition to the Sunday school work has existed in a great measure because of adherence to custom, without investigating the propriety or necessity of just such work for our young people as is done by the Sunday school."[7]

The other type of opposition was considerably more sensitive to the risks involved in borrowing forms from alien religious movements. The American Sunday School Union promoted a type of Christian education and piety that was foreign to the Anabaptist view of the church and of discipleship,

> a Methodist sort of emotional religion which our people were instinctively unwilling to accept and which they, with good reason, feared. Sometimes the Sunday School Union missionaries used devious devices to secure attendance, such as picnics which were not always carefully conducted, financial rewards, light music, and similar attractions. Again these Sunday schools were seldom in sympathy with the Mennonite principles of nonresistance, simplicity, and nonconformity to the world.[8]

This, of course, was not an argument against Sunday schools under Mennonite or Brethren in Christ auspices, but rather an argument against indiscriminate copying of the methods of others. Some critics were alert to the need to develop a kind of Christian education that was uniquely Anabaptist and that would use appropriate methods to serve that end.

Corporate Discernment. A third dimension of Christian education in the Anabaptist tradition cannot be simply identified with either informal nurture in the family and community or formal instruction in the Sunday school. It is a process of corporate discernment in the congregation that has been called "discipleship." This involves a dynamic relationship with Jesus Christ as Lord in the fellowship of His church through which the believers learn to live together now as members of Christ's eternal kingdom. This is an elusive definition largely beyond the bounds of scientific inquiry, but it enlarges the context for our study in the present chapter. As Harold Bauman writes, the Anabaptist style of Christian education

> is found in the believers under the guidance of the Holy Spirit searching the Word until a consensus is reached. In the Believers' Church the laity comes into its own, for discipleship is "talked up" among the members and gains its strength at the point where a consensus is obtained. This is in contrast to discipline which is determined by professionals and levied upon the members. In the voluntary gathered church, the only constraint that can be used to gather persons into the fellowship is soul-force, the persuasive power of the Spirit. Within the congregation, the educational methods are to be consistent with the suffering love of Christ.[9]

Some evidence in both the MC and BIC prior to the adoption of the Sunday school supports a view of Christian education as discipleship with corporate discernment as its chief focus and Christ as revealed in the New Testament as the epistemological norm. In the earliest confessions of faith of these groups, the corporate search for Christ's way extended to economic and social aspects of daily living.[10] No important matters such as marriages, change of address, or buying of real estate were to be decided without congregational discernment. This very discernment process was conceived to be the teaching mandate of the church. When the BIC met in General Conference, they gathered to talk through specific questions and arrive at consensus. Martin Schrag shows, however, that the Sunday school and five other methods of church work borrowed from American culture altered the historic concept of corporate discernment by minimizing the importance of the church and emphasizing the sovereignty of the individual before God.[11]

With a renewed appreciation of the fuller meaning of Christian education in all three dimensions, the MC, BIC, and GCMC are now engaged as publishing partners in the production of a new cooperative Anabaptist curriculum to be called the Foundation Series. The initial production will be limited to unbaptized children (nursery, kindergarten, and grades one through eight) with the prospect of adding baptized members (grades nine through twelve, plus adults) at a later date. The curriculum will be designed with the Sunday school as the primary agency of teaching and learning. It remains to be seen whether it can help the BIC and its Mennonite partners recover the teaching-learning style of corporate discernment which has been largely lost, in part because of the alien doctrines and emphases that came in by way of the Sunday school during the past century.

The Sunday School and Its Effectiveness

H. S. Bender attributed the "great awakening" in the MC between 1890 and 1910 largely to the effects of the Sunday school.

> It was not so much the specific contribution of the Sunday school organization or the weekly Sunday school lesson that produced this, as it was the whole complex life that the Sunday school evoked and symbolized. The Sunday school made the Great Awakening possible. It was largely grown-up Sunday school boys [and girls?] who carried it forward and built the new Mennonite Church.[12]

Bender discussed nine major contributions of the Sunday school, some of which can be tested with the data gathered for the present study:

1. It was an important factor in holding the young people for the church.
2. It has greatly increased Bible knowledge.
3. It elevated the level of spiritual life.
4. It raised the level of moral life in the church, especially through the teaching of temperance.
5. It provided activity and expression and thus contributed to new life in the church.
6. It created lay leadership.
7. It was largely responsible for the missionary movement.
8. It was a factor in the great awakening of the Mennonite Church.
9. It helped to give the Mennonite Church a new vision.

Measures of Sunday School Participation. Six of these claims will be tested with contemporary data, but first the construction of a Sun-

TABLE 12-1
Measures of Sunday School Participation

Items and Responses	Percentage Distribution for:					
	MC	GCMC	MBC	BIC	EMC	TOTAL
1. "How frequently do you attend Sunday school?"						
Seldom or never	6	23	11	6	4	11
Occasionally/Half the time	8	12	10	6	5	9
Most Sundays	11	12	12	7	9	11
Every Sunday possible	76	54	67	82	82	69
2. "Which statement best expresses your situation and feeling about attending Sunday school at your church?"						
I don't attend Sunday school.	4	23	10	6	3	11
I generally dislike Sunday school and skip it whenever I can.	2	2	1	2	1	2
Sunday school class is all right sometimes, but usually I attend only because someone expects or requires me to attend.	6	5	5	4	8	5
Although I generally enjoy Sunday school class, I have no regrets if I must be absent occasionally.	46	36	38	39	36	41
I wouldn't want to miss any meeting of our Sunday school class.	43	34	46	48	52	41
3. "To what extent are you interested in serving your home congregation in Sunday school teaching, church project leadership, or other responsibilities for which you have abilities?"						
No interest	5	7	4	4	4	5
A little interest/some interest	26	30	22	24	26	26
Interested	41	40	44	39	40	41
Strongly interested	28	23	31	33	30	27
Sunday School Participation Scale:						
10-12 High	65	49	62	71	70	60
7-9 Middle	24	21	23	19	22	23
0-6 Low	11	30	15	10	8	17
Total	100	100	100	100	100	100
Number of Respondents	1,190	590	687	606	439	3,512
Mean Score	9.5	7.9	9.1	9.7	9.8	9.0

day School Participation Scale must be reported. Table 12-1 summarizes the responses to three questions concerning participation in Sunday school — frequency of attendance, degree of interest in attending, and degree of interest in helping to lead Sunday school. The five possible responses for each question were scored zero to four, yielding a range of scores from zero to twelve. The bottom row of the table indicates an overall average score of 9.0, with the EMC scoring high and the GCMC low. The differences between the denominations were highly significant. Compared to other major denominations in America, however, all five of our denominations rank high in attendance (and probably also, therefore, in interest). In the American Baptist Church, only 28% of the members report a "fairly regular" attendance at Sunday school,[13] and a study of eight urban Lutheran churches revealed that only 16% of the members attended Sunday school as often as once a month.[14]

A review of the consequences of participation in Sunday school will be preceded by a brief look at the "causes" (who "stays" for Sunday school and why). This information results from examining the scale correlations with Sunday school participation as a dependent variable. Although there is a slight negative correlation between Sunday school participation and amount of general education, after a person graduates from college there is a significantly renewed interest. Urbanization definitely works at cross-purposes with Sunday school participation: the more urbanized a member becomes, the less he is involved in Sunday school. Among the "faith" variables, associationalism, general orthodoxy, Anabaptism, fundamentalist orthodoxy, sanctification, voluntarism, communalism, and moral-personal conversion are highly correlated with Sunday school participation, in that order, and all in a positive direction. Apparently Sunday school participation and all these types of religious commitment are mutually reinforcing.

Age and Sunday School Participation. H. S. Bender claimed that the Sunday school was an important factor in holding the young people for the church.

Before the time of the Sunday school, large numbers of young people from Mennonite homes were attracted to other denominations, often through the influence of Sunday schools. The increase in the Mennonite church in those years was very slow, and many churches of other denominations were built up in Mennonite communities largely from the material furnished by Mennonite homes. The Sunday school gradually led to a radical change in this situation. *Today almost one hundred percent of Mennonite youth are being won for the church.* The Sunday school is not the only factor in this change, but it has without doubt played a major role in it.[15]

Bender was undoubtedly claiming too much to say that nearly all Mennonite youth were being won for the church, to say nothing about the Sunday school participation of those who do become members. By age-groups, the members in our study responded as follows to the three questions in the Sunday School Participation Scale:

	Age Group			
Percent who . . .	*13-19*	*20-29*	*30-49*	*50 Plus*
Attend Sunday school every Sunday	75	48	73	72
Wouldn't want to miss	26	23	42	55
Are strongly interested in teaching	18	21	33	27

Sunday school attendance hits a low ebb among people in their 20s, but the teenagers in the sample attended more frequently than those over 30. However, on the attitude variable, esteem for Sunday school is significantly lower both for teenagers and young adults than for members over 30.

A precise test of Bender's claim would be a comparison of young people who drop out with those who continue their membership to see whether Sunday school participation was a factor in the difference. The nearest we can come to such a test is to compare young people who score high on the Sunday School Participation Scale with those who score low to discover whether there is a present difference in their denominational or congregational self-identity and plans to remain a member or discontinue. As Table 12-2 shows, the answers given to two questions provide strong support for Bender's claim.

Members of all ages, including those under 30, who score *high* in the Sunday School Participation Scale, tend much more frequently than those who score *low* to say (1) that their current participation in the life of the church is very important and (2) that they prefer to remain a member of their denomination. High scores on the scale are no guarantee that members might not drop out, but low scorers tend much more frequently than high scorers to indicate thoughts in that direction.

TABLE 12-2
Sunday School Participation as Related to Congregational and Denominational Self-Identity, for Age Groups

| Items and Responses, by Age | Sunday School Participation | | | |
	LOW	MIDDLE	HIGH	TOTAL
1. "How important for you is your current participation in the life and work of the church?"				
Percent who answered "very important":				
13-19 years	7	9	44	26
20-29 years	8	19	55	31
30-49 years	23	25	66	52
50 years and over	26	31	72	57
2. "Which statement best reflects your present opinion about your future relationship to your denomination?"				
Percent who plan always, or would at least prefer to remain a member				
13-19 years	42	65	73	65
20-29 years	49	68	74	64
30-49 years	70	76	81	78
50 years and over	78	81	87	84
Percent who are considering another denomination or discontinuing altogether				
13-19 years	26	10	5	10
20-29 years	26	12	4	13
30-49 years	11	8	4	6
50 years and over	5	3	3	4

Sunday School and Bible Knowledge. The early approval of the adoption of the Sunday school in the local congregation was given by district or general conferences of the MC and BIC on condition that the Bible be the chief or only subject of study. At first even lesson helps were ruled out. Probably there was more emphasis on Bible study in Mennonite and BIC Sunday schools than in most other denominational or union Sunday schools. Bender wrote that

> Year after year it has taught children from their earliest years the Bible story from Adam to Paul, from Eden to the New Jerusalem. Two generations and more of church members have learned Bible history, Bible doctrine, Bible characters, and thousands of choice Bible verses through the Sunday school. Before the Sunday school, in spite of numerous faithful parents who gave home instruction, there was a lamentable lack of Bible knowledge in the church.[16]

In order to test this claim, we incorporated a Bible knowledge test consisting of eight multiple choice questions. Respondents were asked simply to identify Gethsemane, the Exile, Bartholomew, Zacchaeus, the Ruler under whom Jesus lived, the Samaritans, Pentecost, and the Macedonian Call. These particular items were selected because they were shown in a pre-test to discriminate among Mennonites better than eleven other items did, and because these items had been given to the members of a large Methodist congregation in California, and thus provided opportunity for a direct comparison.[17] The overall median score in the Methodist congregation was 30% correct, compared to 81% for members of the Mennonite and BIC churches. Only 37% of the Methodists had half or more right, compared to 88% of the Mennonites and BIC.

For ease of presentation, the scores (ranging from 0 to 8) on the Biblical Knowledge Scale were collapsed into four classes. As Table 12-3 shows, the overall mean score was 5.7. A test of Bender's claim that Sunday school participation results in greater Bible knowledge is now possible, given the data in Table 12-4. Members whose Sunday school participation is high, score significantly higher on the biblical knowledge test than do other members, thus supporting Bender's claim.

Sunday School Participation and Spiritual Maturity. Bender's third claim was that

> *The Sunday school elevated the level of spiritual life.* By its emphasis upon Bible study, particularly in childhood and youth, and by its aggressive teaching of Bible doctrine and spiritual and moral truth in personal contact and through stimulating and practical discussions freed from the tradition of the hortatory sermon and the custom-bound forms into which many preachers of the past century had fallen, the Sunday school undoubtedly did much to elevate the level of spiritual life. As a new generation of young people came to maturity who had been taught for years in the Sunday school, they had higher standards of spirituality and a deeper appreciation of the meaning of personal religion and high personal Christian ethics than had been the case earlier.[18]

Although the definition of spirituality in this statement is a bit vague, it clearly refers to two types of consequence — personal religion and Christian ethics. By using the sanctification and devo-

TABLE 12-3
Scores on the Bible Knowledge Scale by Denomination

Ranking on Bible Knowledge	Percentage Distribution for:					
	MC	GCMC	MBC	BIC	EMC	TOTAL
7-8 High	40	38	43	39	32	40
5-6 High Middle	36	36	40	39	41	37
3-4 Low Middle	19	20	14	16	21	18
0-2 Low	6	6	3	6	7	5
Total	101	100	100	100	101	100
Number of Respondents	1,165	590	682	598	431	3,466
Mean Score	5.7	5.6	6.0	5.7	5.4	5.7

TABLE 12-4
Relationship Between Bible Knowledge
and Sunday School Participation

Ranking on Bible Knowledge	Sunday School Participation		
	Low	Middle	High
7-8 High	23	32	48
5-6 High Middle	41	38	35
3-4 Low Middle	27	22	14
0-2 Low	9	8	3
Total	101	100	100
Number of Respondents	574	763	2,047
Mean Score	5.0	5.3	6.0

tionalism scales as measures of "personal religion" (see Chapter 5) and the pacifism and race relations scales as gauges of Christian ethics (see Chapter 8), it is possible to test the claim that Sunday school participation makes a significant difference in the predicted direction. Following are the mean scores for the characteristics in question:

Sunday School Participation

	Low	Middle	High	Corr. Coeff.
Mean Score on Sanctification	27.1	29.4	30.2	.296
Mean Score on Devotionalism	2.6	3.2	4.8	.459
Mean Score on Pacifism	8.6	8.6	9.2	.076
Mean Score on Race Relations	6.6	6.6	6.7	.013

The correlations are highly significant and in the predicted direction on the first two variables, but not on the third or fourth. Participation in Sunday school seems to make little difference on race relations or pacifism. One must turn to other factors to account for "right" or "wrong" attitudes regarding other racial groups. Moreover, the correlation between Sunday school attendance and ethical concern is negligible also with regard to tolerance toward Jews, compassion for the poor, and scores on the Social Concerns Scale. Sunday school attendance correlates positively with the more personal aspects of Bender's understanding of "spiritual life."

Sunday School and Morality. Bender's fourth claim was that "the Sunday school raised the level of moral life in the church, especially through the teaching of temperance." By moral life, Bender meant emphasis upon clean and holy habits of living, with specific reference to smoking and drinking. Even more specifically, Bender believed that "it was the quarterly temperance lesson in the Sunday school that contributed more to driving tobacco and liquor out of the Mennonite Church than any other single factor."[19]

The Moral Attitudes Scale and the Moral Behavior Scale defined in Chapter 7 provide rather specific measures of morality in these areas, the former gauging whether or not a member feels such personal practices as smoking, drinking, attending X-rated movies, homosexual acts, masturbation, gambling, and social dancing are wrong; and the latter specifying whether or not a member actually engages in smoking, drinking, and dancing. As the following table shows, Sunday school participation has a significant effect on morality as Bender claimed.

| | **Sunday School Participation** | | | |
	Low	*Middle*	*High*	*Corr. Coeff.*
Mean Score on Moral Attitudes	19.0	21.1	22.7	.424
Mean Score on Moral Behavior	4.9	6.4	7.3	.447

Holy living is certainly one aspect of an Anabaptist vision of Christian education, but it is not the only goal or even the primary goal. The leaders responsible for planning the new Anabaptist curriculum might well review in this regard James Smart's warning about "the suffocating fog of moralism" in American Sunday schools.[20]

When the conduct of children becomes the main concern in Christian education, the dynamic source of holy living is usually undermined by the moralistic emphasis. In Anabaptist theology, this source is the participation in a process of corporate discernment under the guidance of the Holy Spirit that makes a distinction between the question of conduct and the question of truth.

Sunday School and Shared Ministry. Part of the question of truth with high priority in the goals of an Anabaptist Christian education is the nature of the church in which "all believers are fully franchised citizens of the kingdom, having accepted knowingly the responsibilities of membership and functioning in them."[21] Bender claimed that the Sunday school led the MC in a renewal of the church in precisely this respect:

> Before the time of the Sunday school, the lay members of the church had practically no avenue for expression or activity. The sole activity of the church was the biweekly or even four-weekly church service, at which only the ordained men took part. . . . But in the Sunday school there was opportunity for activity, expression, and responsibility. Many teachers were needed, and they often faced a more difficult and challenging task in attempting to teach the Bible to restless youngsters than the preacher did when he gave the traditional admonition to an audience who were compelled to take what he gave whether they wanted to or not. . . . All the members of the Sunday school had a chance for expression in the class discussions, and often in the review period. . . . As generation after generation of boys and girls grew up in the Sunday school, a new type of church member was created who not only possessed more within himself but was able to give more to others and who demanded more of the preachers and the church in general.[22]

The present church member data leave no doubt that the Sunday school created new opportunities for lay leadership. Sunday school participation is much higher among lay leaders and ordained ministers than among the members. The percentage scoring "high" on the Sunday School Participation Scale was 37 for lay members, 74 for lay leaders, and 85 for ordained persons.

Whether or not Sunday school participation produces favorable attitudes toward the concept of a shared ministry is another question. Chapter 11 reported that the recruitment of leaders in the church is a very selective process, with deference to the middle-aged and those with higher education. A Shared Ministry Scale was also defined in that chapter, and it is possible to test the question posed above. As the following data show, there is a slight negative correlation between Sunday school participation and commitment to the concept of the shared ministry. Those whose participation is highest are somewhat less committed to a shared ministry. Apparently one of the most crucial goals of an Anabaptist Christian education has not been achieved by the contemporary teaching in the Sunday school.

Sunday School Participation

	Low	Middle	High	Corr. Coeff.
Mean Score on Shared Ministry	7.4	7.4	6.7	-.092

The Sunday School and Evangelism. The last hypothesis formulated by Bender regarding the effects of the Sunday school in the MC was that it promoted evangelistic and missionary work.

> The new life and new leadership produced by the Sunday school movement was bound ultimately to lead to a new and larger sense of responsibility for spreading the Gospel and evangelizing the multitudes without Christ, both at home and abroad. Before the Sunday school came, the Mennonite Church was not known as a missionary church. . . . The reasons for this are not far to seek, and do not concern us at this point, but lie largely in the persecutions of the past. But the Sunday school brought a new knowledge of the Bible, a new appreciation of the message of salvation, and a new sense of responsibility for the spread of the Gospel. The International Sunday School Lesson Series emphasized missions. The Sunday school movement as a whole was evangelistic and missionary in spirit and practice. But most of all, perhaps, the young generation of lay members who were growing up under the stimulus of the Sunday school began to get a vision of the church at work for the kingdom of God as it had not been before.[23]

The present researchers decided that an appropriate test of Bender's claim today would be not so much the financial support for the missionary enterprise largely carried on by others (professional missionaries), but the member's own involvement in witness and evangelism. Three questions along these lines were asked and the answers combined into a composite Evangelism Scale. The questions and scale are summarized in Table 12-5. The high-to-low rank order of the denominations on evangelism is BIC, EMC, MBC, MC, and GCMC. It is interesting to compare this to the high-to-low rank order for success in winning members from non-Mennonite (or non-BIC) background[24]: EMC, BIC, MBC, GCMC, MC. The correlation is obviously very high. The more a group evangelizes, the greater the number of members brought in from the "outside."

Before examining the question of whether the Sunday school is linked with evangelism, a brief look at other sources and consequences of evangelistic involvement is appropriate. One highly significant finding is that all of the "faith" variables discussed in Part II of this study are positively correlated with evangelism in the following order of influence: devotionalism, associationalism, sanctifi-

TABLE 12-5
Measures of Evangelism

Items and Responses	Percentage Distributions for:					
	MC	GCMC	MBC	BIC	EMC	TOTAL
1. "How frequently do you take the opportunity to witness orally about the Christian faith to persons at work, in the neighborhood, or elsewhere?"						
Never/Seldom	32	40	31	27	34	34
Sometimes	51	44	49	48	44	48
Often/Very often	17	16	20	24	22	18
2. "How frequently have you invited non-Christians to attend your church and/or Sunday school services?"						
Never/Seldom	59	62	54	42	50	58
Occasionally	34	34	39	40	43	35
Frequently	7	4	8	18	7	7
3. "Have you personally ever tried to lead someone to faith in Christ?"						
No, never	25	26	13	18	17	23
Yes, a few times	67	66	74	68	72	68
Yes, often	8	9	13	13	11	9
Evangelism Scale:						
7-10 High	16	14	20	25	21	17
5-6 Upper Middle	33	30	38	36	37	33
3-4 Lower Middle	32	34	28	25	27	31
0-2 Low	20	22	14	14	15	19
Total	101	100	100	100	100	100
Number of Respondents	1,183	596	695	606	441	3,521
Mean Score	4.4	4.1	4.8	5.1	4.8	4.6

cation, general orthodoxy, Anabaptism, fundamentalist orthodoxy, voluntarism, moral-personal conversion, communalism, and ethical-social conversion. All of the dimensions of faith (church participation, Christian experience, Christian practice, and doctrinal adherence) are tied to evangelism, not just in theory but in practice. From the standpoint of the goals of Christian education, these are encouraging signs.

The social background variables are also encouraging in this respect. As one matures in life, he takes evangelistic witness more seriously. Contrary to the suspicions of some members, higher education does not undermine evangelistic witness but promotes or reinforces it. The group with the greatest involvement in personal witness are those who have had postgraduate study. Moreover, evangelism goes with urbanization, with the one exception that church members in large cities are not as active as are members in small cities. The three "weaknesses" in evangelistic practice are with young people, rural farm people, and high income earners.

Apart from the immediate "fruit" of evangelism, which is leading people to faith in Christ, we can examine several other consequences, particularly those with which there have been troubling tensions in past Mennonite and BIC history. The data indicate that churches have not yet succeeded in integrating evangelism with social concern. High scores on evangelistic witness are associated with anti-Semitism, anti-Catholicism, and race prejudice. They are negatively related to women's rights, welfare attitudes, and ecumenicity. They are neutral with respect to pacifism and support of MCC service programs. It is perhaps better to be neutral than to be negative, but this does not yet achieve the aim of "The Way of Peace" statement, newly prepared by the GCMC, which proclaims that "the way of peace is the way of evangelism."[25] The task of integrating evangelism and Christian social ethics is unfinished.

On the prior question of Bender's claim, however, the data strongly verify that Sunday school participation is positively correlated with evangelistic involvement. The following data summarize this finding:

	Sunday School Participation			
	Low	*Middle*	*High*	*Corr.* *Coeff.*
Mean Score on Evangelism	3.3	3.6	5.2	.385

The Sunday School Teachers

Writers of curriculum materials will be particularly interested in the characteristics of the Sunday school teachers for whom they write. The survey data provide a profile of these persons. Each respondent was asked "Within *the past ten years,* how frequently have you served as a Sunday school teacher or department leader?" The responses indicated that 36% had never taught, 19% taught "a few times, or as a substitute," 8% "served regularly for a period of less than a year," 25% "served regularly for one to five years," and 10% "served regularly for all or most of the past ten years." If the second and third, and fourth and fifth categories are combined, then 27% have taught "occasionally," and 37% "regularly" during the ten-year period. The BIC has the largest percentage of regular teachers (45%), followed by the EMC (40%), MBC (39%), MC (36%), and GCMC (34%).

A profile of "regular" Sunday school teachers shows that 45% are males and 55% females, almost the same proportions as in the sample at large. Middle-aged persons are most strongly represented among regular teachers. One percent are teenagers, 13% are ages 20-29, 52% are 30-49, and 32% are 50 and over.

Eight percent of the regular teachers are single, 87% married, and 4% have some other marital status. Twenty-three percent of all church members were single, but of course that included a large number of teenagers. The teachers were somewhat more likely to have had a definite initial conversion experience, 85% versus 75% for all other members.

The educational achievement of regular teachers is only slightly higher than that of all other members. The median number of school years completed for the teachers was 12.6 years; for other members it was 12.1 years. The percent attending (but not going beyond) each educational level was:

	Regular teachers	Other members
Elementary School	19	27
High school	40	46
College	21	18
Graduate school	20	9

Table 12-6 provides average scores on a series of scales for the regular teachers, the occasional teachers, and the non-teachers. The regular teachers differed most from other members on the Bible knowledge, evangelism, and devotionalism scales, as is indicated by the highest contingency coefficients. On most scales the regular teachers were consistently higher than others. However, differences were negligible on the race relations, political participation, shared ministry, role of women, anti-Semitism, and anti-Catholic scales.

TABLE 12-6
Differences Between Sunday School Teachers and Non-teachers

Scales	Regular teachers	Occasional teachers	Non-teachers	Cont. Coeff.
	(mean scores on scales)			
Bible Knowledge	6.3	5.9	4.9	.303
Evangelism	5.1	4.4	3.7	.255
Devotionalism	4.7	4.1	3.5	.241
Political Participation	7.0	6.2	6.4	.181
Moral Behavior	7.1	6.8	6.3	.176
Race Relations	7.3	7.4	6.5	.161
Anabaptism	22.4	22.1	20.9	.162
Voluntarism	5.9	5.5	5.5	.154
Moral Attitudes	23.1	22.1	21.5	.154
General Orthodoxy	25.4	25.1	24.6	.130
Pacifism	8.8	8.6	8.2	.117
Anti-Catholic	1.2	1.1	1.4	.113
Role of Women	2.0	2.1	2.1	.111
Social Concerns	3.5	3.6	3.4	.097
Anti-Semitism	1.2	1.2	1.4	.095
Fundamentalist Orthodoxy	17.7	17.4	17.5	.092
Communalism	3.4	3.2	3.2	.084
Shared Ministry	6.7	7.2	6.6	.083
Ecumenism	10.5	10.4	10.2	.073

The Production of Curriculum

We turn now to several items concerning the production of curriculum — attitudes regarding cooperative curriculum and the willingness to increase expenditures for this purpose. The samples of members of the five denominations were asked the following question: "Some church leaders say that in order to gain certain advantages, Mennonite and Brethren in Christ denominations should join their church literature preparation and publication efforts. Others argue for separate publishing of most pieces of church and Sunday school literature. Which would you favor?" The choices given and the percentages of members selecting each choice were as follows:

	MC	GCMC	MBC	BIC	EMC	Total
Each denomination should produce its own literature	36	24	35	44	33	33
Joint publishing of literature should be maximized	32	52	36	27	29	38
Uncertain	32	24	28	29	38	29

Members as a whole seem evenly divided between separate and joint denominational production of curriculum. The concept of a cooperative curriculum receives most support in the GCMC and least support in the BIC. Although the reasons for these choices probably vary in the several groups, the joint Publishing and Editorial Councils currently planning the Anabaptist Curriculum Project will discern from these figures the kind of promotional effort that will be needed if their project is to be accepted.

The church members were asked how the total denominational budget should be apportioned among a list of twelve areas of church work. For each area they were asked to indicate whether the budget should be increased, decreased, or maintained at the current level. A tabulation of responses for all areas will be reported in Chapter 14. It is sufficient here to note only the three areas pertaining to Christian education. The following are the percentages of members who preferred to increase or to decrease budgets in four designated areas of Christian education:

	Budget Increase	*Budget Decrease*
Church and Sunday school literature for use in congregations and homes	15	13
Education on peace and social issues	19	16
Home and family life education	34	5

Of the four areas listed, it seems that members would be most likely to support new programs in home and family life education — the first dimension of Christian education defined earlier in the chapter. This area ranked third out of twelve for budget increase. There is also more support for increasing the budget than for decreasing it for Sunday school literature and education on peace and social issues — the second and third measures described at the beginning of the chapter.

Summary

Three dimensions of Christian education were defined: informal nurture, formal instruction, and corporate discernment. Most of the probes of this chapter related to the second of these dimensions. It was shown that the Sunday school program has achieved a considerable success in most of the areas listed in H. S. Bender's centennial booklet. The Sunday school has been instrumental in winning many of the young people for the church, although it is probably less effective in this area now than in prior generations. It has increased the Bible knowledge of members. It has promoted high personal morality among the members but there has been less success in the area of social ethics. It has helped members to experience the personal reality of the Holy Spirit and to practice the disciplines of prayer. It has provided many new opportunities for lay leadership and more active involvement of members in the church, although it has not inculcated the doctrine of the shared ministry. Finally, it has promoted an interest in evangelism and missionary outreach with considerable evidence of lay involvement at home rather than just professional missions abroad.

The present chapter revealed mixed attitudes of members concerning the joint production of curriculum, although it also indicated a considerable support either for maintaining present levels of expenditures or budget increases for curriculum development in three areas of Christian education.

Chapter 13

DENOMINATIONAL SCHOOLS

In contrast to European tradition, the doctrine of separation of church and state has been strongly developed in the American and Canadian settings. Consequently churches have had less influence and control over government-operated schools, colleges, hospitals, and welfare institutions than has been true in Europe, where state and church have been more closely linked. Not being willing to yield full control of educational and welfare programs to the secular (governmental or public) arm of society, many American and Canadian denominations have established private institutions under their own control. The proliferation of denominations in the United States has contributed to this development, as many denominations have sought to establish institutions, particularly schools, where attention could be given to their own unique doctrines or ethical practices.

Mennonite and BIC bodies have mirrored this development. They have established a considerable number of colleges, seminaries, high schools, elementary schools, general hospitals, mental hospitals, children's homes, retirement homes, service agencies, mutual aid societies, camps, and publishing houses. No attempt has been made in this survey to assess church members' participation in and attitudes toward all of these church-related institutions. However, one section of the questionnaire did inquire into members' attendance at, and support of, the church colleges.

This chapter will report findings relative to the following ques-\
tions: What proportion of the church members have attended church\
schools? Are there any important differences between those who
have, and those who have not attended church schools? Do church
members think the churches should continue to operate colleges? What
kind of church members most strongly support the church colleges?

The five participating denominations operate twelve colleges,
each of which has less than 1,100 full-time students, and also four
seminaries.[1]

Attendance at Church Schools

Forty-five percent of the church members answered "yes" to
the question, "Did you ever attend an elementary school, secondary
school, college, Bible college or institute, or seminary operated by a
Mennonite or Brethren in Christ denomination?" The range was
from 7% for the EMC to 53% for the MBC respondents (MC,
45%; GCMC, 44%; BIC, 38%). The proportion coming under the
influence of one or more of these types of schools is apparently increasing. Among respondents aged 20-29, 53% have attended a church
school, compared to only 39% for those aged 50 and over. This reflects the fact that new church-sponsored elementary, secondary,
and Bible schools have been established, particularly by the MC,
since World War II. Older persons had less opportunity to attend
church schools, and also attended school fewer years.

Attendance at church schools varies greatly by type of school.
Following is the percent of respondents having attended each type
of school (some attended more than one type), by denomination:

Type of School	MC	GCMC	MBC	BIC	EMC
Elementary	10	6	7	5	3
Secondary	20	14	19	16	1
Winter Bible School	12	6	15	4	0
College	17	24	16	21	2
Bible Institute	2	4	10	0	1
Seminary (graduate level)	2	5	2	1	0
Did not attend a church school	56	56	48	62	93

The data indicate that attendance at elementary and secondary church schools is highest in the MC, college and seminary attendance is highest in the GCMC, and attendance at Bible schools and institutes is highest in the MBC. Low attendance among the EMC reflects the fact that the denomination operates no schools of its own.

Trends in attendance at church schools are difficult to assess accurately. Only the MC has gathered details on the attendance at college by persons of college age. For this denomination the numbers of Mennonites attending MC colleges as a percent of all members aged 18 to 21 grew gradually from 12% in 1951 to a peak of 19% in 1966, and has since declined to 14% in 1972.[2] Meanwhile the number and percent of MC college-aged persons attending non-MC colleges and universities grew from 8% in 1962 to 15% in 1969, declining to 12% in 1972. Thus, for the MC, about half of those attending college are in MC colleges, whereas 10 years ago at least two thirds were attending MC colleges. The trend is clearly toward greater attendance at non-church colleges and universities, at least until 1969.

This trend reflects the national situation. Until the mid-twentieth century, higher education in the United States was mainly private and mainly Protestant. In 1950, for the first time, the number of students enrolled in public institutions exceeded the number in private institutions. By 1970 three fourths of college students were in public institutions, with only one tenth attenting Protestant colleges.[3]

Should Mennonite and BIC youth be expected to prefer their church colleges? Forty-nine percent of the respondents agreed with the statement, "In general, every Mennonite young person who goes to school beyond high school should take at least one year of study in a Mennonite college or Bible institute." Thirty percent disagreed and 21% were "undecided." The percent agreeing ranged from 34 for the EMC to 60 for the MBC. By age groups, agreement was expressed by 33% of the teenagers, 36% of the young adults (20-29), 54% of those aged 30-49, and 58% of those over 50.

With the decline in the proportion of young people attending church colleges, and with smaller proportions of youth favoring attendance at church colleges, trends seem to be definitely against church-sponsored higher education. Can the church colleges expect to survive in the next generation? Should they survive?

The Impact of Church-Related Colleges

These concerns prompt further questions: What are the goals of church colleges? Are these goals being achieved? One would expect the chances of survival to be greater if the colleges are serving the purposes which the churches have for them.

Regarding goals, a recently completed study by one of the participating denominations (MC) offers some insights. Focusing broadly on "A Philosophy of Education for the Mennonite Church" at all levels of education, including Christian education in the local congregation, the report concludes that:

> For the Christian church, Jesus is the chief model and authority figure. The ultimate educational mission of the church is to lead persons to accept and commit themselves to Him.[4]

The report does not overlook the general objective of education as the transmission of the cultural heritage. However, in respect to the "people of God" (the churches), there are the additional unique objectives to:[5]

1. Transmit their history and make their identity clear.
2. Train in the skills needed to carry on the work they consider important.
3. Teach the values they consider important.

If Mennonite colleges are meeting these objectives, at least in part, one would expect church members who attended church colleges to differ on some of our scales from those who did not attend church colleges; that is, they could be expected to score "better" on the relevant scales. Before turning to the data, however, we will examine the results of research in other denominations.

The limited data available refer mainly to the effects of church-school attendance at the elementary and secondary levels rather than the college level. Kersten compared Lutherans who had attended a Lutheran parochial school with those who had attended only public schools. He found that those attending parochial schools scored significantly higher on indexes of "Religious Beliefs," "Religious Practices" and "Religious Knowledge," but not on the indexes of "Associational Involvement" and "Communal Involvement."

In a study of Lutheran youth reported by Strommen, those youth attending parochial schools scored higher on a series of doctrinal questions than did other youth. In a footnote the author suggests that "the kind of parents who send their children to a parochial school may serve as a selective factor to partially account for the differences."[6] This should caution us against a conclusion that too eagerly assumes that any differences are specifically the result of the school experience.

Lederach reports the results of a 1968 survey of 1,232 Mennonite (MC) high-school-aged youth. When youth attending church high schools were compared with other youth on a series of scales and items, few significant differences emerged. The study gave no evidence that youth attending the church-related schools have any higher spiritual attainment, at least when they were in school.[7]

In a study of residents of Detroit, Lenski compared Catholics who had received most of their education in Catholic schools with Catholics who had received most of their education in public schools. Those with mostly Catholic school education were doctrinally more orthodox, evidenced somewhat greater devotionalism, and were stronger in their belief that the Catholic Church is the "only true church."[8]

Other major studies of Catholics have been made. Greeley reported Catholic data from a national survey of college and university graduates in 1961. Catholics attending Catholic colleges, as compared to Catholics attending other colleges, were more likely to think of themselves as religious, may be more service oriented, are less likely to leave the church, and are somewhat more likely to attend church regularly. He concluded that "Catholic colleges apparently produce a more conservative and conventional Catholic than do the other colleges."[9] One wonders, however, whether it is simply that the more conservative and conventional Catholics choose to attend the Catholic colleges.[9] We will have to ask the same question about Mennonites who attended Mennonite colleges.

In a later survey, Greeley suggests that the differences between Catholics attending and those not attending Catholic schools may be due to differences in kinds of parental influences. Variations in a person's adult religious beliefs and behavior may be more affected by the intimate settings of home, neighborhood, friendship, and workplace than by formal indoctrination.[10] In this later study,

Greeley found that attendance of Catholics at Catholic colleges is significantly associated with doctrinal orthodoxy, ethical orthodoxy, religious knowledge, participation in the sacraments, and attendance at mass.[11]

Mennonite Differences

We turn now to the survey data to see whether attendance at Mennonite or Brethren in Christ schools yields any observable relationship to the variables of faith and life. As noted earlier in this chapter, 45% of the respondents had attended one or more schools operated by the five denominations. These can be compared with the 55% who never attended any Mennonite or BIC school. We shall refer to the first group as the "attenders" and the second as the "nonattenders."

The attenders scored substantially higher than nonattenders on the Bible Knowledge Scale (55% versus 31% in the "high" category on the scale) and on the Support-of-Church-College Scale. Attenders were substantially lower on social prejudice measures. The attenders scored slightly higher — a difference great enough to be statistically significant, however — on the scales of associationalism, Anabaptism, ecumenicity, moral behavior, and percent of income given to church and charity.

A small difference between attenders and nonattenders was observed also on the Communalism Scale. Apparently attendance at church schools has a slightly positive relationship to the strength of "in-groupness" as measured by the Communalism Scale. In the modern world many forces and factors bring church members into communication and association with members of the larger society. Perhaps attendance at a church school no longer provides sufficient isolation from the larger society to cause any significant increase in the strength of religious in-groupness. These findings are little different from those regarding Catholics as reported by Greeley and Rossi. Catholics attending Catholic schools were compared with those not attending Catholic schools on a number of "divisiveness" items. No significant differences in the degree of association with, or involvement in, non-Catholic society were found.[12]

Among the observed relationships between church school

attendance and other variables, only in one area did a negative relationship occur. This was with respect to the religious orthodoxy scales. The attenders were somewhat lower than nonattenders on the General Orthodoxy Scale and substantially lower on the Fundamentalist Orthodoxy Scale. On the latter scale, 34% of the attenders but 56% of the nonattenders ranked "high." Further analysis (in Chapter 17) will suggest that this negative association is probably due not so much to specific church-school attendance, but to the liberalizing impact of education *per se*.

The foregoing comparisons between those attending and those not attending church schools are deficient in that there is no discrimination on the basis of *type* of church school attended, or *length* (number of years) of attendance at church schools. To partially compensate for this deficiency, the data in Table 13-1 provide further comparisons. The table reports the percentage scoring "high" on a number of scales, for three types of respondents: (1) those who did not attend any church school, (2) those who attended a Mennonite or BIC high school, and (3) those who attended a Mennonite or BIC college. There is some overlap in the last two categories, since some respondents attended both church high schools and church colleges.

In general, the data confirm the findings reported above on the

TABLE 13-1
Attendance at Church Schools as Related
to Other Variables

Scale	Never attended church schools N=2131	Attended church high schools N=558	Attended church colleges N=605
	(Percent in "high" category)		
Associationalism	15	17	26
Communalism	7	9	8
Anabaptism	44	52	46
General Orthodoxy	81	71	59
Fundamentalist Orthodoxy	56	27	13
Bible Knowledge	31	57	66
Ecumenicity	18	21	29
Stewardship Performance	58	66	69
Moral Attitudes	81	75	70
Moral Behavior	40	40	38
Support of Church Colleges	38	54	58

differences between church school attenders and nonattenders. In addition, important differences are revealed between those attending church high schools and those attending church colleges. In general, church college attenders are more extreme — *i.e.*, more different from nonattenders than are church high school attenders. College attenders are "higher" than high school attenders on associationalism, Bible knowledge, ecumenicity, and support-of-church-college scales. College attenders are lowest on the religious orthodoxy and moral attitudes scales. Church college attenders are lower on the Anabaptism scale than are church high school attenders, and are not significantly higher than those who never attended a church school.

Why should persons who attended church colleges be more extreme on scale scores than those attending church high schools? One possible reason is that those attending church colleges probably have, on the average, a larger number of total years spent in church schools. This would create a larger cumulative impact in the direction of values implanted by the influence of the church school. It is also possible that college experience is more "intensive," and thus makes a greater impact in favor of church values than do church high schools. Finally, it is possible that religious attainment prior to church school attendance may be higher for those attending church colleges than those attending church high schools. Although this selectivity differential is possible, one would expect those persons choosing to attend church high schools and those choosing to attend church colleges to be similar in their religious attainment prior to church school attendance.

Type of College Attended

A further question to be answered is, "Do those who attend church colleges differ from those who attend other colleges and universities?" Can we say that those who attend church colleges are "better" (have higher attainment scores) than those who attend colleges and universities which have no relationship to a church?

Data in Table 13-2 provide a basis for tentative answers to these questions. A different set of respondents appears in each column of the table. In the first column are the members who attended college at Mennonite or BIC colleges only. In the second column are those who attended a Mennonite college and also some other church college (Bible college, other Protestant college, etc.). The third column contains those who attended some other church college, but who did not attend a Mennonite or BIC college. In the fourth column are those who attended both a Mennonite college and a public college or university. In the last column are the students who attended a public college or university but did not attend any church-related college.

"Attendance" in this table refers only to undergraduate, not graduate, school. Also "attendance" includes not only those who obtained a college degree but also those who attended one or more years without earning a degree.

The data in Table 13-2 reveal that on most scales students attending only Mennonite colleges scored midway between those who attended "other church colleges" and those who attended public institutions only. Students who attended only Mennonite and BIC colleges scored highest only on the Anabaptism scale. They scored lowest on none of the scales. Students who attended only public institutions scored lowest on 11 of the 14 scales and highest on

TABLE 13-2
Type of College Attended
as Related to Other Variables

Scale	Menn. only N=364	Menn. + other church N=55	Other church only N=68	Menn. plus public N=154	Public only N=214
	(Mean score on scale at left)				
Associationalism	4.1	4.9	4.9	4.2	3.1
Communalism	3.4	3.5	2.4	3.2	2.5
Devotionalism	4.0	4.4	4.8	4.1	3.6
Evangelism	4.4	5.6	5.6	5.0	4.0
General Orthodoxy	24.0	24.8	25.2	23.9	24.2
Fundamentalist Orthodoxy	15.2	15.3	17.4	14.5	15.8
Anabaptism	21.8	21.4	20.8	21.4	20.1
Bible Knowledge	6.6	6.9	6.8	6.9	5.8
Pacifism	9.6	9.3	7.7	9.7	8.1
Moral Attitudes	20.5	21.8	22.9	20.5	20.2
Moral Behavior	6.4	7.2	6.6	6.4	5.4
Stewardship Performance	2.8	2.6	3.0	2.7	2.4
Ecumenicity	11.2	11.3	10.6	11.7	10.9
Support of Church Colleges	6.7	6.8	6.0	6.6	6.0

none of them. Students who attended other church colleges (either solely or with part attendance at Mennonite colleges) scored highest on all scales except Anabaptism, pacifism, and ecumenicity.

Assuming these scales are valid measures of religious attainment, we must conclude that those students who attend Mennonite and BIC colleges do not have as high an average religious attainment as those who attend other church colleges. What can explain this finding that the church's own schools appear not to perform as well as other church schools? The data do not provide an answer to this question, so we can only speculate on the reasons.

One possible explanation would assume selectivity, at the time of college entrance, in who attends "other church colleges" and "public colleges." Those who enter Mennonite colleges may include the whole range of students from the highest to the lowest "attainers." But of those Mennonite youth who choose non-Mennonite schools, it is possible that a larger proportion of the higher attainers choose to go to other church schools, and a larger proportion of the low attainers choose to go to the public institutions. If this were true, it could account for the observed differences.

An alternative explanation would assume that Mennonite college entrants at all types of schools have average or similar attainment at the time of college entrance, but are differentially affected by the school experience. This would assume that the "other church schools" have a more effective program of teaching religious values than Mennonite schools, and that attendance at public institutions leads to a decline in religious attainment. Supporters of Mennonite schools might readily accept this assumption regarding public colleges but might have difficulty accepting the assumption about other church colleges.

Our data do not indicate what type of "other church schools" are attended. Probably they are more fundamentalistic, stressing religious orthodoxy, Bible study, personal piety, and moral restrictiveness.

Who Supports Church Colleges?

Three questionnaire items were used to assess church members' loyalty to the denominational colleges. The items and percentage distributions of responses are given in Table 13-3.

A majority of the church members seem committed to the maintenance of the colleges. However, about a third of the church members are uncertain about the need to maintain the colleges, and a small minority would favor discontinuing them.

Responses to these three items were scored and combined to form the Support-of-Church-Colleges Scale. Scores on the sacle did not vary much between denominations, but MBC respondents were strongest in support of church colleges and GCMC and EMC members averaged lowest.

Correlations between the Support-of-Church-Colleges Scale and other scales indicate what types of church members are most

TABLE 13-3
Support of Church Colleges

Items and Responses	Percentage Distribution for:					
	MC	GCMC	MBC	BIC	EMC	TOTAL
1. Do you think the benefits derived from our present church colleges justify the costs of maintaining them?						
Yes	47	40	50	54	43	45
No	8	14	11	7	9	10
Uncertain	45	46	39	39	48	44
2. In general, every Mennonite young person who goes to a school beyond high school should take at least one year of study in a Mennonite college or Bible institute.						
Agree	49	46	59	43	34	49
Undecided	24	17	15	27	23	21
Disagree	27	37	26	30	43	30
3. In view of the increasing gap between costs of an education at church colleges and the lower costs of education at tax-supported universities, we should gradually close out our church-related colleges in the years ahead.						
Agree	4	5	4	3	4	4
Uncertain	28	31	26	26	24	28
Disagree	68	64	70	71	72	68
Support-of-Church-Colleges Scale:						
7-8 High	46	38	48	43	36	44
5-6 Middle	42	43	42	48	50	43
2-4 Low	12	19	9	9	14	13
Total	100	100	99	100	100	100
Number of Respondents	1,165	595	687	592	434	3,473
Mean Score	6.3	5.9	6.4	6.3	6.0	6.2

likely to view church colleges favorably. The data, not presented here in tabular form, indicate that church members most favorable toward church colleges tend to score high on the devotionalism and Anabaptism scales. They also are relatively high on the scales measuring church participation (church and Sunday school attendance, church leadership), Bible knowledge, stewardship attitudes, and moral attitudes. Support of church colleges is also related to communalism, which is to say that persons favoring church colleges have somewhat stronger "in-group" feelings about their own religious affiliation.

As the age and socioeconomic status of church members increase, there is a slight tendency for support of church colleges to increase. There is no difference between rural and urban members in loyalty to church colleges. Church leaders, particularly ordained men, are substantially stronger in support of church colleges than are other members.

The respondents were asked, "In your mind, what, if anything, would justify a Mennonite young person's attending a church college if his costs were $1,000 more per year than at a state college or university?" The question was aimed at finding out what values or reasons are uppermost in church members' minds as a rationale for supporting church colleges. A checklist of responses was provided. The percent of respondents checking each item follows:

	Percent
To have the opportunity to study Bible and religion	72
To have the opportunity of developing a Christian value system	58
To obtain preparation for a Christian vocation in some academic area	56
To form friendships with other church young people	54
To be exposed to a Christian philosophy of service	49
To get a Christian viewpoint on academic subject matter	46
To get a higher quality education	39
To learn to know Christian teachers and church leaders	31
To study the Christian beliefs of Anabaptists	30
To support a church institution	18
To satisfy the parents who want their son or daughter to attend a church college	13

Conclusion

Mennonite and BIC church members appear to show majority support for the continuation of the denominational colleges. A substantial minority, however, question whether the costs of maintaining the colleges justify their long-range existence. But this minority does not appear to be growing. The relation of the Support-of-Church-Colleges Scale scores to the variables of age, residence, socioeconomic status, and church leadership suggests that support of church colleges is not likely to weaken in the years ahead. As church members grow older, move up the social class ladder, and assume positions of leadership in the church, their support of church colleges appears to strengthen slightly rather than weaken.

Clearly a major factor in support of church colleges is attendance at church colleges. Those who attended the denominational colleges are substantially more loyal to church colleges than those who did not attend them. Even allowing for the probability that those who chose denominational colleges were more loyal in the first place, it seems that attendance generates additional loyalty to the colleges attended. One development, however, may cause some concern. The current decline in the proportion of college-aged youth attending denominational colleges seems to work against the growth of loyalty resulting from attendance at the church colleges.

Are the church colleges achieving their goals? Insofar as the colleges are promoting the values of service, pacifism, love and concern for minorities, stewardship, Bible knowledge, and church participation and leadership, there is evidence of goal achievement. Those having attended the denominational colleges rank higher on scales measuring those variables, when compared with church members who attended public universities or who did not attend college at all.

Insofar as Mennonite colleges promote understanding and acceptance of the Anabaptist heritage and doctrines, their success is limited. Perhaps they need to strengthen their programs designed to promote acceptance of the basic Anabaptist doctrines. On the matter of doctrinal orthodoxy, experience in Mennonite colleges results in diminished orthodoxy. Perhaps since members of Mennonite and BIC churches are extremely orthodox in beliefs, any change resulting from college experience could only be in the liberal direction. Those who expect our colleges to bolster the most orthodox beliefs will be disappointed. Those who see college as a process of testing and evaluating orthodoxy, requiring a greater openness to alternative viewpoints, may regard the results of college education as positive. Even with some liberalization of beliefs, church members having attended Mennonite colleges are still considerably more orthodox than members of most Protestant denominations.

In discussing American nonpublic schools, Otto F. Kraushaar concludes that the evidence "does not support the contention that religion is withering away and the church schools are becoming or are due to become irrelevant."[13] However, he cautions that church schools will need to attain and maintain quality education and "keep abreast of the educational times." Given the substantial church support that currently is evidenced, if they keep abreast of educational movements for quality education, the Mennonite colleges should remain a relevant part of denominational programs for some time.

Chapter 14

THE STEWARDSHIP OF CHURCH MEMBERS

A steward is someone who takes care of the property belonging to another person. Christian stewardship begins with the awareness that "the earth is the Lord's" (Psalm 24:1) and that we are the caretakers of what God has entrusted to us. Although stewardship involves nonmaterial as well as material resources, this chapter will be limited to a report on the monetary aspects of stewardship and attitudes related to giving.

From their very beginning in New Testament times, the Christian churches have given attention to finances, supporting both their missionaries and their brethren in need. When three thousand persons were filled with the Holy Spirit at Pentecost, "all who believed were together and had all things in common; and they sold their possessions and goods and distributed them to all, as any had need" (Acts 2:44). The Apostle Paul praised the Macedonians for their liberal gifts in support of his ministry. (See 2 Cor. 8:3.)

The Stewardship of Denominations

Church finance in the United States and Canada today is big business, although perhaps not nearly as big as it should be if all church members were faithful stewards. The American Association of Fund-Raising Council reports an estimated total giving to religious causes of 8.6 billion dollars in 1971 in the United States.[1]

The *Yearbook of American Churches* annually reports on church finances for those denominations who supply financial data. Table 14-1 summarizes data on per member giving for our five particular

TABLE 14-1
Per Member Giving for U.S., Canadian, and
Participating Churches 1971

Denominations	Per Member Giving		
	Total Giving	For Cong. Finances	For Benevolences
42 U.S. Denominations	$103.94	$ 83.88	$ 20.06
21 Canadian Denominations	78.89	60.10	18.79
Mennonite Church (U.S.)	171.79	92.31	79.48
Mennonite Church (Canada)	147.29	50.93	96.36
General Conference Mennonite (U.S. and Canada)	170.78	92.75	78.03
Brethren in Christ (U.S.)	336.07	246.89	89.18
Brethren in Christ (Canada)	309.60	234.79	74.81
Mennonite Brethren (U.S. and Canada)	198.60	111.40	87.20
Evangelical Mennonite Church	255.51	149.85	105.66

Weighted average (mean) for the 5 participating denominations: $184.81.
Source: *Yearbook of American and Canadian Churches*, 1973, and denominational yearbooks.

denominations, with comparative data for U.S. and Canadian churches.[2]

Of the 21 Canadian denominations for which data are reported, the BIC had the highest per capita total giving. In the United States, the BIC was fourth among the 42 reporting denominations, being exceeded only by the Seventh-Day Adventists, the Missionary Church, and the Berean Fundamental Church. The MC and GCMC rated sixteenth and seventeenth among the U.S. churches. All five of the churches in this study were above the average in their respective countries in total giving and especially in benevolences.

The higher giving by members of the BIC and the EMC may be the result of more emphasis on giving in their churches. The EMC "Articles of Practice" devotes several paragraphs to stewardship including the sentence, "Believers are encouraged to adopt the system of tithing their income as a minimum expression of their stewardship."[3] Likewise the BIC emphasize tithing in their *Manual of Doctrine and Government:*

> The scriptural method for the gathering of money for support of the church and her program is by the means of tithes and offerings (Num. 18:21; Mt. 23:23). Special blessing is pronounced upon those who not only pay the tithe, but also give freewill offerings in addition to their tithe (Mal. 3:10).[4]

The MC, GCMC, and MBC do not refer to stewardship in their official statements of faith and practice. However, tithing is favorably mentioned in occasional articles in church papers, in some pulpits, and in the personal testimonials of some church members. Perhaps the leadership in these groups has been less inclined to promote tithing, fearing reaction from members who feel that a strong emphasis on tithing is "legalistic."

Stewardship Attitudes

Attitudes toward tithing were probed in the survey with a series of statements expressing different views on the subject. The respondent indicated his views by checking each statement that he agreed with. The items, and proportions checking each item, by denomination are given in Table 14-2.

Several conclusions can be drawn from these data: (1) Although a majority of the members are favorable, a small proportion in each denomination are unfavorable toward the promotion of tithing. (2) The churches that officially emphasize tithing have members most favorable toward tithing. (3) In view of the data of giving, the churches with members most favorable to tithing receive the highest per member contributions. These findings lead logically to the conclusion that a teaching program on tithing will increase denominational giving. The findings suggest that a large proportion of the church members would support a stronger emphasis on

TABLE 14-2
Stewardship Attitudes

Items	Percent of Responses for:					
	MC	GCMC	MBC	BIC	EMC	Total
	(percent agreeing)					
1. The church should urge all members to tithe.	46	38	55	70	57	47
2. Tithing is legalistic and not in harmony with the ideal of Christian freedom.	4	6	6	3	3	5
3. The tithe is a biblical standard which all Christians should accept as a guide for giving.	53	46	65	70	69	54
4. God expects the tithe and any sacrificicial giving begins only when one goes beyond the tithe.	34	23	34	47	51	32
5. Although tithing is a worthy goal, no one should feel guilty if he gives less.	28	27	21	14	16	26
6. In prompting giving, the church should not refer to tithing.	7	8	7	3	5	7
7. What a church member gives is his own business and the church should not urge any standard upon him.	14	19	13	12	14	15
8. It is not right to expect all members to give similar proportions.	37	39	34	18	24	36
Stewardship Attitudes Scale:						
9–11 High	28	20	33	49	44	28
7–8 Middle	42	50	43	34	37	44
1–6 Low	30	30	23	17	19	28
Total	100	100	99	100	100	100
Number of Respondents	1,143	576	676	590	424	3,409
Mean Score	7.4	7.1	7.7	8.2	8.0	7.4

tithing, but that some opposition would be felt from five to ten percent of the members.

A recent study of stewardship attitudes and practices in 15 Protestant denominations in the United States and Canada affords some interdenominational comparisons. Although about half of Mennonite and BIC members support tithing as a biblical standard, Johnson and Cornell report that the traditional view of tithing as a minimal standard "is upheld in the United States by only 27 percent of the laity and 20 percent of the pastors, and in Canada, by only 10 percent of the laity and six percent of the clergy."[5]

Stewardship Attitudes Scale. A six-item scale was constructed to assess the respondent's favorableness or unfavorableness toward several stewardship principles. Three items on tithing were used (items one, three, and four in Table 14-2), plus items assessing the respondent's attitude toward his having a planned (rather than an unplanned) pattern of giving to the church, toward the frequency of the congregation's asking for money (offerings), and toward the congregation's use of an annual budget as a basis for deciding on allocations to causes. These latter three items are reported in a later section of this chapter. Total scores on the Stewardship Attitudes Scale ranged from one to 11. The percentage distributions of scores and the mean scores for the denominations are given in the lower portion of Table 14-2.

Estimated Giving

What proportion of incomes do church members actually give to church and charitable causes? Respondents were asked to report their most accurate estimate. Response categories, and the percent checking each, are shown in the chart at the top of the next page.

On the basis of these estimates it would seem that church members contribute around eight percent to church and charity. However, evidence that these self-reported estimates may be upwardly biased comes by checking with the actual dollar amounts given in 1971. Each respondent was asked to report how much he or she, " . . . together with the other members in your household, gave to church and charitable causes in 1971." The median amount re-

Amount Reported	MIC	GCMC	MBC	BIC	EMC	Total
Less than one percent	11	9	6	7	7	9
At least one but less than 3%	12	14	7	9	8	11
At least three but less than 5%	11	14	8	7	9	11
At least five but less than 10%	26	34	32	23	27	29
Ten percent or more	40	29	47	54	50	39

ported was $635. This, of course, being a *per household* amount, can be expected to be larger than the $185 *per member* weighted average based on denominational statistics reported in Table 14-1, since the average household will contain at least two or three members.

The median reported (household) giving of $635, when divided by median household income of $9,608 yields an estimated giving of 6.6%, which is about 1.4% lower than the respondents themselves estimated. There may be several reasons for this discrepancy, one of which would be inaccuracy of recall, both of income figures and amounts given to church and charities. Another reason may be due to variations in the way the proportion given is computed. Some church members may compute their giving as a proportion of net income *before* income taxes, others *after* income taxes. A tithe of income *after* taxes would be a lesser amount than if it were based on income *before* taxes. If a respondent reported the amount of his income *before* taxes (as requested in the questionnaire) but estimated his tithe as percent *after* taxes, this would contribute to the discrepancy. The discrepancy may also be due in part to a human tendency, in the absence of accurate data, to make larger estimates of giving than is actually true.

Stewardship Performance Scale. The procedure of dividing reported household giving by reported household income yields for each respondent a "proportion given," which is a measure of how well he (his household) performs on stewardship. The proportions ranged from zero to over 10% and constitute a Stewardship

Performance Scale which can be correlated with other variables. Perhaps this is a better measure of actual stewardship than the Stewardship Attitudes Scale, on the grounds that performance is a more reliable indicator of stewardship than attitudes.

The stewardship performance scores were collapsed into five classes: (1) under 1%, (2) 1-3%, (3) 3-5%, (4) 5-10%, and (5) over 10%. In subsequent tables, mean scores are given in terms of the class number instead of actual percentages. However, for the denominations, the proportional giving was 6.8% for the MC, 5.8% for the GCMC, 7.5% for the MBC, 7.1% for the BIC, and 7.3% for the EMC.

Congregation Program

Each respondent was asked, "How do you feel about the number and frequency of askings for money (offerings) that come to the members of your congregation?" For the total respondents, two-thirds felt the askings "are about right," nine percent indicated the "askings could be greater and more frequent than they are," and eight percent replied that askings are "too many and too frequent." Another 18% checked "no opinion." On balance, the status quo appears acceptable. There was little variation in responses between the denominations.

The use of an annual budget as a means for the congregation to decide on how its contributed funds should be used appears to be well accepted by church members. Seventy-five percent of MC members and 81-84% of members of the other groups indicated that they favored using a congregational budget. Only 14% were unfavorable. Favorableness toward use of a budget was greater the higher the respondent's educational attainment.

The question, "Do you feel you have a choice or a voice in what your church offering money goes to?" elicited a "yes" response from two thirds of the church members. By denominations, the percent "yes" ranged from 61 for the BIC to 72 for the EMC. About 20% replied "no" to the question, and the remainder were "uncertain." The findings do not indicate why some members feel they have no say in how the money is appropriated. Perhaps in some congregations the decisions are not shared sufficiently with the congregation. Perhaps some members do not avail themselves of the opportunities that do exist for expressing their preferences.

The data do show that larger proportions of respondents at the higher educational levels and in the older age-groups (especially the 30-49 group) feel they have a voice in decisions on where the money goes. No doubt these persons exercise more leadership in the congregational decision-making process.

An attempt was made to determine the extent to which church members actively plan their giving to the church budget or offerings. In response to a probe on this, 78% indicated that they "give a planned amount (per week, month, or year)." Although this does not clarify exactly how the planning is done, it does suggest that most members are not haphazard in their approach to giving.

Support of Denominational Programs

An attempt was made to determine the extent of support which members show for the various types of programs to which the local contributions are given. A dozen types of programs were listed and the respondent was asked, for each program, whether he thought "the *proportion* or share of total resources that goes for that program should be increased, decreased, or maintained at current levels." The respondent was reminded that any increase in the *proportion* (of total resources) that goes to one program would have to be offset by a corresponding decrease elsewhere. Thus any "decrease" does not necessarily imply a cutback in absolute dollars for a specific type of program; it implies a relatively smaller expansion of program, if not an absolute decrease. However, despite the reminder, more programs were checked "increase" than were marked "decrease."

Strongest support for program increases was shown for home missions and service, foreign relief and service, mass communications outreach (TV, radio), home and family life education, and overseas missions, in that order. (See Table 14-3.) Only three programs elicited opinion favoring a net decrease in expenditures: elementary education, secondary education, and local congregation expenses.

Some important variations between churches were noted. Opinion

TABLE 14-3
Percentage Distribution of Respondents by Support of
Various Types of Church Program

Program	In-crease	De-crease	Maintain current proportion	Un-certain
	(percent)			
1. Home missions and service	37	3	50	10
2. Overseas missions	30	9	49	11
3. Relief and service programs	33	4	50	13
4. Mass communications outreach (TV, radio)	36	8	37	20
5. Church and Sunday school literature for use in congregations and homes	14	14	61	11
6. Education on peace and social issues	20	16	43	21
7. Home and family life education	32	5	46	16
8. Higher education (church colleges)	22	11	48	19
9. Secondary education (church high schools)	14	19	45	23
10. Elementary education (church grade schools)	10	24	40	25
11. Church seminaries	20	8	52	21
12. Local congregation expenditures (buildings, equipment, salaries, etc.)	11	20	55	14

favoring overseas missions expansion was weaker in the GCMC than in the other four groups. Opinion in favor of net decreases in expenditures on secondary schools appeared in all denominations except the MC, which has most of such schools. Support for mass communications outreach is strongest among the MBC. Percentages favoring increases in expenditures for relief and service programs ranged from 38% among MC members to 18% in the EMC. Differences in support of programs in higher education were minor (although statistically significant) with favorableness toward increase in money going to seminaries a bit higher in the MBC and BIC groups. In regard to local congregation expenditures, in the BIC and EMC opinion favoring increases was greater than that favoring decreases. The reverse was true among other groups, particularly in the MC.

What kinds of church members have the strongest stewardship attitudes and give the largest share of their incomes to charities? The Stewardship Attitudes Scale and Stewardship Performance Scale were cross-tabulated with the variables of faith and life. In general, those who scored higher on the Attitudes Scale also rated higher on the Performance Scale ($r = .374$). Both attitudes and giving tend to increase as age increases. Stewardship attitudes were slightly stronger among those with higher educational and occupational rank. However, the proportion (not the amount) given to charity is higher among lower income than higher income persons. Rural-urban differences on both scales were insignificant.

The church members who are stronger on stewardship tend also to be stronger on other religious attainment scales, particularly the associationalism, devotionalism, and evangelism scales. Their support of church and Sunday school programs is higher, and they score higher on the Bible knowledge, orthodoxy, and Anabaptism scales.

We conclude that stewardship is not an isolated criterion of religiosity, but is a well-integrated aspect of the life of the committed Christian. Given a strong faith in God and an earnest commitment to the church and its mission, stewardship flows as naturally as water from a deep and abundant well.

Chapter 15

PAROCHIAL AND ECUMENICAL ATTITUDES

Throughout the history of Christianity the faithfulness of Christians has been troubled with divisiveness. There is a curious kind of correlation between commitment and separation in the Christian experience. On the one hand, the Apostle Paul lamented divisiveness in the churches he established. "For it has been reported to me by Chloe's people that there is quarreling among you, my brethren. What I mean is that each one of you says, 'I belong to Paul,' or 'I belong to Apollos,' or 'I belong to Cephas,' or 'I belong to Christ.' Is Christ divided?"[1] On the other hand, Paul rebuked the "mismating" of believers and unbelievers in the church. Or what fellowship has light with darkness?" Quoting Isaiah 52:11, he wrote to the same church whose divisiveness had earlier concerned him, "Come out from them, and be separate from them."[2]

The dilemma of the early church was also the dilemma of the sixteenth-century Anabaptists and their descendants. The concern for avoiding defilement was an unwitting cause of numerous schisms. One of the questions asked of the respondents was, "Do you believe that the teachings of your denomination more accurately reflect the Word of God than the teachings of any other denomination?" Three fourths of these twentieth-century Anabaptists answered affirmatively, 29% saying "Yes, *definitely*." It is true to the radical

Anabaptist vision for a member to be unreserved in his assent to the Word of God, but many members think it scandalous that this commitment has led to over twenty-five schisms in one branch (MC) alone. A prominent leader of this group wrote recently on "Church Practices We Can Do Without":

> There are many other church practices, past or present, that we could do without. Let me close with this one — starting new branches of the church. Mennonite history has many examples, from the Amish schism in 1697 down to the latest one that you have heard of. Few of them involve basic theology. Many are related to personal differences; people don't like each other, or can't work together. Most are related to social change: what changes shall be accepted, and how fast shall they be allowed to come. We have differed, often very sincerely and very violently, over methods of church discipline and what we shall discipline about: the ban, cuts of garments, shapes of headgear, the use of such inventions as automobiles, electric current, radio and television; about Sunday schools, evening meetings, moving pictures, higher education, and athletics.
>
> Sometimes we have had the Christian grace and character to discuss our differences and gradually to find a way to understanding and tolerance and cooperation. But too often we splinter up our congregations and conferences. And because the seceding persons are so individualistic, the splinters keep asplintering.
>
> We have enough branches of the church that it would seem any dissatisfied person or group could find another group sufficiently like themselves so that they would not need to start a new branch. I strongly feel that dividing and subdividing is a practice we can do without.[3]

Position Statements on Ecumenism

The Anabaptist doctrine concerning the unity of the church has recently been a subject of special inquiry by scholars.[4] One way to approach such inquiry is to assume that the Anabaptists had no such doctrine. They were sectarians, meaning schismatics. They broke with the mainstream Protestant Reformation in order to be faithful to their own vision. This assumption, however, has been shown to be false. John H. Yoder has studied some forty serious "conversations" between early Anabaptists and Reformed churchmen before there was ever a permanent break.[5] These were conversations about the nature of the church, the state, believer's baptism, holy communion, and the use of images in the church. Only at the point of expulsion by the state church did the founding group meet on January 21, 1525, to institute baptism on confession of faith and and to establish a separate church. Yoder derives the following principles of ecumenism from the Anabaptist witness.

First, they never claimed that they were the only true Christians. "Once, in fact, when Zwingli asked Felix Manz why he didn't go ahead on his own to set up the kind of church discipline he wanted, Manz answered that he could not because Zwingli was the bishop."[6]

Second, the unity they sought was a common search for God's truth through serious conversation and dialogue.

> For conversation to be more than a talking-past-one-another, there are two formal prerequisites. There must be an epistemological norm, under the authority of which both parties stand in the common search for truth; and each party must recognize the other party's right to exist. The Reformed and the Anabaptists agreed as to Scripture's being the touchstone of truth, fulfilling the first requirement. The Anabaptists stood consistently, and the Reformed occasionally, usually with reluctance and for a limited time, for the principle of tolerance.[7]

Third, there must be a willingness to change positions when the proof has been brought. "If there is not such movement, talking about the differences only serves to harden them."[8]

Fourth, if there must be a break within the church between those who are faithful and those who are unfaithful, the initiative must come from the unfaithful side. "The faithful church will discipline; she will expel, if necessary, one at a time, disobedient individuals. She will not, insofar as the choice is hers, withdraw from the body of believers."[9]

Fifth, the congregational polity of the Anabaptists dictated a specific style of ecumenical relations.

> This is not the spiritualized concept of a purely invisible unity. Nor need it be denied that councils, boards, conventions, associations, and synods may have any ecclesiological significance. The import which congregationalism has for these other agencies means rather that their authority is that of the "congregational" character, procedures, and unity of conviction which is

given them as they meet. They cannot authoritatively bind other, local congregations which meet more frequently, whose members know one another better, and whose responsibilities are for the total life of their members.[10]

Yoder was aware that these principles of ecumenism judge the twentieth-century heirs of the Anabaptists as much as it judges the modern "ecumenical movement" whose organizational approach by-passes the local congregation. The issues of disunity, not only between Mennonites as a whole and the rest of Christendom but also between the five denominations, were discussed in Chapter 2. What remains to be reviewed here are the present positions of these groups and the probes concerning the attitudes of members about the problem of interchurch relationships.

The MC has just recently declared itself on interchurch relations and moved more deliberately toward cooperative programs with other groups. Grant Stoltzfus writes that "in the 1920s and 1930s and beyond, the Mennonite Church was critical toward interchurch movements such as the Federal Council of Churches and it refused to identify with pacifist movements, largely because it was not in accord with the theology which sponsored these groups. Cooperative ventures have often been difficult and seemingly dangerous to the unity, identity, and ongoing life of the Mennonite Church."[11] This apparent lack of concern for the issues of division and unity was thoroughly amended in the MC General Conference of 1965 when an Interchurch Relations Committee was established for the specific purpose of guiding the MC in a thorough-going renewal of its ecumenical responsibilities. Two positional statements prepared by this committee were approved in 1967, one on "The Challenge of the Divided State of American Protestantism" and the other on "Christian Unity in a Divided Mennonitism."[12] A third was presented for discussion in 1969 on "The Organizational Expression of Christian Unity."[13] These statements try to take seriously as norms for inter-church relations the five principles of ecumenism outlined above. Specificially, they recommend efforts toward functional unity rather than toward structural unity, and advise against "solidifying the lines of organizational cooperation at those points where this is easiest (*e.g.*, a given ecumenical organization or a given Mennonite denom-ination) at the cost of rendering more difficult relationships with others."[14] These statements also provided the content for Article

XVIII in the new MC By-Laws on Inter-Mennonite and Interdenominational Relationships.

The GCMC began with Mennonite unification as its preeminent goal and from 1913 to 1937 its leaders spearheaded a series of All-Mennonite Conventions attended by representatives from nine branches of this family of churches with the hope of moving them toward closer identity and cooperation. Its inter-Mennonite initiatives were often characterized as being too aggressive and lacking an adequate theological foundation. Some evidence for this characterization can be found in a strongly worded resolution concerning "unity among Mennonites" adopted at the time of GCMC's one hundredth anniversary in 1959.[15] The subject was on the agenda for the next three GCMC triennial conferences. In 1962 MC-GCMC relationships were singled out as particularly hopeful. In 1965 a GCMC Interchurch Relations Committee was established parallel to that of the MC, and in 1968 a two-day joint meeting of the two committees was reported and it was said quite candidly that "the Interchurch Relations Committee has been somewhat disappointed that the discussions we had with the (Old) Mennonite Church . . . have not progressed as far as we had hoped."[16]

The MBC, after its withdrawal from the mainline Mennonite Church in Russia, found inter-Mennonite relations most difficult. One of its pastors wrote recently that "a strange fear grips the MBs when the question of alignment with other Mennonites comes up. We seem to be afraid of being swallowed up or dominated by other Mennonite groups, thereby losing our doctrinal identity."[17] On the other hand, the MBC has felt greater affinity with a number of non-Mennonite groups (Baptists, Billy Graham Associates, Campus Crusades, etc.) than with other Mennonite bodies. For the sake of these wider ecumenical contacts, "some MBs are quite ready to drop the name Mennonite."[18] Out of this attitudinal background the MBC Board of Reference and Council, with the approval of the MBC General Conference, dispatched a letter to the officials of the MC and GCMC in response to overtures of their respective Committees on Interchurch Relations. The letter reaffirmed the traditional MBC stance on withdrawal:

> We are . . . aware that more often than we realize we as Mennonite Brethren have failed to express in Christlike attitudes and actions our professed desires for love and unity. . . . It is

our studied opinion, however, that the consensus of our brotherhood at the present is not such that we could engage actively
in meetings and discussions having to do with mergers or other
bold steps to achieve church unity organically.[19]

The BIC *Manual of Doctrine and Government* contains no
article on interchurch relations, nor has this group issued any position
statement on ecumenism.

The EMC is the only one of the five groups whose Constitution
(*Manual of Faith and Practice*) contains articles, not just on "Cooperation" but also on "Affiliation," indicating openness to consider
merger with "groups of like faith and emphasis." The 75-year
search for wider affiliation by this group came to a reverse climax
in the spring of 1974, when a formal resolution was adopted to
"relieve the Commission on Fraternal and Social Concerns of all
responsibility to assume initiative in merger negotiations and that
the subject of merger be tabled." This action came after findings
of the Church Member Profile (the present study) were reported
showing that the EMC constituency was opposed to merger by a
five-to-one ratio.[20]

As indicated above, the MC has refrained from affiliating with
any national or world ecumenical organization. The GCMC was
a charter member of the Federal Council of Churches in the United
States, but withdrew in favor of closer relationships with other Mennonite groups. The MBC, BIC, and EMC have affiliated with the
National Association of Evangelicals. As the MC positional statements warned, such affiliation only made it more difficult to achieve
the goal of unity among all five groups. In fact, the MBCs affiliation threatened the unity between its Canadian Conference and its
U.S. Area Conference and required specific reconciling action.[21]

Enough has been said to show how delicate is the whole issue
of ecumenics among Mennonites and BIC. Although denominational
position statements on the subject so far have concerned mostly
inter-Mennonite relations, our study has a broader range of inquiry
covering three dimensions: attitudes toward Jews and Catholics,
attitudes toward non-Anabaptist Protestants, and attitudes toward
Anabaptist churches.

Attitudes Toward Jews and Catholics

The factors that influence the attitudes of Mennonites and BIC to Jews and Catholics are complex and paradoxical. One, of course, is pure religious prejudice — the opposite of ecumenical concern. Another is the difficult question of how to apply the Anabaptist principles of ecumenism listed earlier in this chapter. With regard to Catholicism, for instance, the principle of conversation is hindered by the traditional Roman Catholic view that it is its own final authority for Christian truth. It is also hampered by ignorance among Mennonites of the new ecumenical stance of Catholicism following the Second Vatican Council.[22]

Our questions were intended mainly to tap prejudice against Jews and Catholics rather than to investigate these more complex factors. Their wording and responses are summarized in Table 15-1, together with the composite scales. Among scores ranging from zero to four on both scales, identical overall mean scores of 1.3 were obtained for both measures. The EMC and MBC were the most anti-Semitic and anti-Catholic by these indices, and the GCMC and MC the least prejudiced.

Table 15-2 summarizes the factors associated with religious prejudice. Out of nine faith variables that correlate significantly with anti-Semitism and anti-Catholicism, all but one are associated in the positive direction — high religious commitment associated with high religious prejudice. It is particularly disturbing from the normative point of view to note that high scores on the Anabaptism Scale are associated with anti-Semitism and anti-Catholicism. Only Ethical-Social Conversion is inversely associated with religious prejudice. Less prejudice is also associated with higher education, higher socioeconomic status, and youthful idealism, but older members tend to express more anti-Semitic and anti-Catholic attitudes. All four social-ethical variables listed in the table are negatively associated with religious prejudice, as are also the Shared Ministry Scale and the Ecumenism Scale (to be defined below). High scores on all these scales are associated with low prejudice. The correlations just observed resemble those reported for racial prejudice in Chapter 8, except that Anabaptism in that connection functioned slightly to counter prejudice. In their research, Glock and Stark found data to support their hypothesis that "orthodox Christian belief" is a cause of anti-Semitic prejudice.[23] Strommen and associates rejected the hypothesis that prejudice (including anti-Semitism) is related to "the belief system

TABLE 15-1
Measures of Anti-Semitism and Anti-Catholicism

Items and Responses	Percent of Responses for:					
	MC	GCMC	MBC	BIC	EMC	Total
1. "The reason Jews have so much trouble in the world is that God is punishing them for rejecting Jesus."						
Agree	14	14	31	24	28	18
2. "Jews are probably just as honest and fair in their business practices as Christians are."						
Disagree	12	9	18	15	14	12
Anti-Semitism Scale:						
4 (High Anti-Semitism)	4	4	7	5	6	4
3	8	8	15	12	15	9
2	28	21	32	31	32	27
1	29	31	25	28	27	29
0 (Low Anti-Semitism)	31	36	21	24	20	30
Total	100	100	100	100	100	99
Number of Respondents	1,187	602	697	602	435	3,523
Mean Score	1.2	1.1	1.6	1.5	1.6	1.3
3. "Being a Catholic does not give a person any less favor in God's eyes than being a Protestant."						
Disagree	5	4	5	5	8	5
4. "It would not be good for this country if more and more Catholics get into political leadership positions."						
Agree	26	28	44	41	39	31
Anti-Catholicism Scale:						
4 (High Anti-Catholicism)	2	2	4	3	5	3
3	8	6	7	8	9	7
2	26	28	41	37	37	30
1	36	35	28	31	33	34
0 (Low Anti-Catholicism)	28	29	20	21	16	26
Total	100	100	100	100	100	100
Number of Respondents	1,186	602	698	605	437	3,528
Mean Score	1.2	1.2	1.5	1.4	1.5	1.3

most central to Lutherans."[24] Our data support the thesis of Glock and Stark. It cannot be said that anti-Semitism and anti-Catholicism are unrelated to the belief system most central to Mennonites and BIC.

TABLE 15-2
Correlations Between Anti-Semitism/Anti-Catholicism and Other Variables

Scales	Anti-Semitism	Anti-Catholicism
	(Pearson correlation coefficients)	
Fundamentalist Orthodoxy	.292	.323
General Orthodoxy	.198	.199
Voluntarism	.161	.168
Anabaptism	.146	.141
Sanctification	.132	.101
Moral-Personal Conversion	.129	.118
Devotionalism	.126	.150
Communalism	.103	.114
Ethical-Social Conversion	-.063	-.076
Education	-.261	-.273
Socioeconomic Status	-.255	-.274
Age	.173	.234
Race Relations	-.310	-.308
Welfare Attitudes	-.204	-.218
Social Concerns	-.199	-.178
Pacifism	-.185	-.144
Shared Ministry	-.241	-.261
Ecumenism	-.180	-.226

Another way to examine the data is to compare the extent of prejudice among Mennonites and BIC with that of other denominations. Such comparisons were reported for the Race Relations Scale in Chapter 8 and the respondents were found to be somewhat less prejudiced against Negroes than Lutherans, other Protestants, and Catholics. This is not the case for the Anti-Semitism and Anti-Catholic Scales. The comparative responses for specific items in the questionnaire are given in Table 15-3.[25]

Because the questions and the response choices were not exactly comparable, an effort was made to make the comparisons as objective as possible. On the first question, for instance, the wording of the item was identical but the percentage figures had to be re-computed to eliminate "no response" from the Glock-Stark table. The wordings of the other two questions were not identical. The second question was put as follows in the Strommen study: "Jews are just as honest as other businessmen." It was put in the negative sense in the Glock-Stark study: "Jews are more likely than Christians to cheat in business." Because researchers generally assume that it takes slightly more candidness to disagree with a positive statement than to affirm a negative one, the comparisons reported above do not put the Mennonite respondents into an unfair position. The wording of the third question by Kersten was, "Do you feel that Catholics have been trying to get too much power in this country?"

TABLE 15-3
Denominational Comparisons on Prejudice

	Mennonites and BIC	Lutherans	Total Protestant	Catholic
1. "The reason Jews have so much trouble in the world is that God is punishing them for rejecting Jesus."				
Agree	21		14	12
2. "Jews are probably just as honest and fair in their business practices as Christians are."				
Disagree	14	16*	17	14
3. "It would not be good for this country if more and more Catholics get into political leadership positions."				
Agree	34	29**		

° ALC, MSLC, and LCA.   °°LCA only.

In conclusion, it must be said that the extent of anti-Semitic and anti-Catholic prejudice among the members in the present study is as great as or greater than that revealed among the members of other denominations in the studies cited.

Relations with Other Anabaptist and Protestant Churches

Type of Ecumenical Attitude. One question was asked to gauge the style of ecumenicity preferred by members of the five denominations:

> The ecumenical concern for the unity of a divided church can best be expressed by . . .
> (A) . . . having more and deeper meetings of Christians from

separated denominations, demonstrating by those meetings the truth of Jesus' promise that whenever two or three are gathered together in His name, He is there also, empowering them to speak to one another about His teachings.

(B) . . . making spiritual unity primary, since the unity in Christ is not an organizational matter, but a spiritual oneness across denominational divisions.

(C) . . . working toward greater cooperation and doctrinal agreement among existing denominations leading to their eventual union.

The authors assumed that choice "A" was most in keeping with the five Anabaptist principles of ecumenism listed earlier in the chapter, that choice "B" was a "spiritualist" interpretation with too little regard for organizational unity, and that choice "C" was a "theocratic" interpretation with too much prior concern for doctrinal agreement and organizational union. The choices of members follow:

Percent choosing:	MC	GCMC	MBC	BIC	EMC	*Total*
Ecumenical Type "A"	38	45	38	44	40	40
Ecumenical Type "B"	50	43	54	45	50	49
Ecumenical Type "C"	12	12	8	11	10	11

The unembodied "spiritualist" conception of ecumenicity was chosen most often by four out of the five groups. The only group that chose Type "A" most often was the GCMC. This type, the Anabaptist style, was preferred by four out of ten members, and there was considerable rejection of Type "C," which identifies ecumenical concern with cooperation, doctrinal agreement, and eventual union.

Five Measures of Cooperative Attitude. The author's assumption that ecumenism for Mennonites means inter-Mennonite cooperation leading gradually toward a reunion of Mennonite groups influenced the formulation of the next five questions that probed attitudes concerning inter-Mennonite and interdenominational cooperation. We will examine the questions and responses first and then return to the matter of interpretation in relation to Anabaptist norms. The responses to the first question about "cooperation between various Mennonite and BIC denominations" (see Table

15-4) indicate overwhelming support for the practice of cooperation. Only 4% of the members want "fewer joint activities" than presently undertaken. In fact, 70% favor an increase in the present degree of cooperation, with 18% desiring an outright merger of programs and institutions. The GCMC had the largest percentage favoring merger.

The second item asked a similar question about cooperation with churches of other denominations on the level of the local community. The responses followed a similar pattern except that they were somewhat more cautious. Still, one in five (21%) felt that their own congregation should take the initiative in promoting programs of interdenominational cooperation.

The third and fourth questions raised the issues of organizational union on the inner-Mennonite and interdenominational levels, respectively. The responses reflect the warnings about premature merger in the official documents of MC and MBC reported earlier in the chapter. Only 15% favored denominational merger within the Mennonite-BIC family of churches, and only 5% within the wider Protestant family. Again, it is GCMC members especially (24%) who desire inter-Mennonite union. In light of the historic EMC struggle to decide its own denominational alignment, it is interesting to note that only 10% of EMC members (9% in items 3 and 10% in item 4) favor any merger at all, and that they are divided nearly 50-50 between union with another Mennonite group or union with some other denomination.

The fifth question concerns joint or separate programs of "relief and service." This question introduced the issue of cooperation developed since 1920 through the Mennonite Central Committee, which will be treated separately in the next section of this chapter. A discrepancy seems to exist between the answers to questions five and one. While only 4% preferred fewer joint activities in answer to the first question, 16% answered the fifth question by choosing "each denomination its own" relief and service program. Probably the words "pooled into one" frightened some members who had earlier rejected retrenchment as the answer. Nevertheless, 67% preferred either that all resources be pooled or at least that there be some pooling as presently practiced through MCC.

Composite Ecumenism Scale. The five questions (plus one on Canadian-American conference cooperation to be presented at the

TABLE 15-4
Measures of Ecumenism

Items and Responses	Percentage Distributions for:					
	MC	GCMC	MBC	BIC	EMC	Total
1. "Which of the following best expresses your opinion about cooperation between various Mennonite and Brethren in Christ denominations?"						
Prefer fewer joint activities	4	2	5	2	4	4
Maintain present cooperation	28	20	32	40	41	27
Increase cooperation gradually	53	52	49	49	45	52
Merge programs & institutions	15	26	14	9	10	18
2. "Which statement best expresses your opinion about your congregation engaging in cooperative programs with churches of other denominations in your local community?"						
Avoid such activities	8	3	4	5	6	6
Cooperate with caution	43	26	41	43	52	38
Cooperate actively	32	44	34	35	28	36
Initiate cooperation	17	27	20	17	15	21
3. "Would you like to see your own denomination unite with some other Mennonite or Brethren in Christ group?						
No	42	33	50	55	48	41
Uncertain	47	43	40	40	43	44
Yes	12	24	11	6	9	15
4. "Would you like to see your own denomination unite with some other Protestant denomination (not Mennonite or Brethren in Christ)?"						
No	68	58	64	68	57	65
Uncertain	28	35	30	26	33	31
Yes	3	6	6	6	10	5
5. "Should each Mennonite and Brethren in Christ denomination develop its own relief and service program or should all resources be pooled into one inter-Mennonite relief and service agency?"						
Each denomination its own	18	14	14	12	19	16
All resources pooled	30	39	39	38	24	35
Combine both approaches	32	33	30	34	33	32
Undecided	20	14	17	16	24	17
Ecumenism Scale:						
13–18 High	16	30	16	10	13	17
7–12 Middle	74	66	79	86	79	76
3–6 Low	10	4	5	4	8	7
Total	100	100	100	100	100	100
Number of Respondents	1,115	563	657	567	400	3,302
Mean Score	10.2	11.2	10.2	9.9	9.8	10.4

end of Chapter 18) were combined into an Ecumenism Scale, with a range of scores from three to eighteen. The reader should note that a high score on this scale reflects ecumenical Type "C" above, emphasizing cooperation eventually leading to union, rather than Type "A," emphasizing fellowship and conversation. As the bottom of Table 15-4 shows, the overall average score was 10.4, with the GCMC far to the top and the other four groups below the overall average.

Factors associated with high Type "C" ecumenism scores can now be reported. The correlations are summarized in Table 15-5. None of the faith variables is positively correlated with pro-ecumenism attitudes. Four faith variables especially tend to undermine ecumenical attitudes: fundamentalist orthodoxy, general orthodoxy, Anabaptism, and communalism.

On the other hand, the variables of social background — youthfulness, urbanization, and especially socioeconomic status and higher education — have a positive influence on ecumenism. Restrictive moral attitudes tend to go with anti-ecumenical attitudes; and "liberal" ethical attitudes (political action, racial tolerance, etc.) tend to go with pro-ecumenical attitudes, as does the concept of a "shared ministry."

How are these findings to be explained? First, the responses probably include an expression of the historic Judeo-Christian dilemma between particularism and universalism mentioned in the first paragraph of the chapter. One principle calls for separation and in-group covenant. The other principle calls for cooperation and the reunion of mankind. In addition the authors admit that the Ecumenism Scale fails to sort out the finer issues of a style of ecumenicity (ecumenical Type "A," above) that would reflect the Anabaptist and New Testament paradox. Hence, the scale is not strictly a test of the five Anabaptist principles of ecumenism with which we began.

Nevertheless, the issues of programmatic cooperation and merger may be an accurate indicator of a member's willingness to get in touch with his brother across denominational lines. To put it negatively, a questionnaire that would have evaded the issues of merger would have enabled the respondents to avoid one of the most troublesome aspects of the present divisions: the way the five denominations maintain nearly duplicate sets of machinery to ad-

TABLE 15-5
Relationships Between Ecumenism
and Other Variables

Variable	Position on Scale at Left				Pearson Coeff. (r)
	Low 1	2	3	High 4	
	(% scoring "high" on ecumenism)				
Fundamentalist Orthodoxy	48	27	17	13	−.317
General Orthodoxy	46	38	27	16	−.207
Anabaptism	25	20	16		−.205
Communalism	25	23	16	11	−.186
Socioeconomic Status	17	18	22	37	.254
Education	15	17	24	30	.240
Political Action	11	22	33		.341
Moral Attitudes	41	47	31	16	−.324
Shared Ministry	13	18	33		.277
Race Relations	12	20	26		.233

Read percentages as follows: Of the members who scored low in Fundamentalist Orthodoxy, 48% scored high in Ecumenism.

minister a work that could probably be effectively handled by a single set of agencies. The self-perpetuating character of their separate programs makes the vision of an Anabaptist style of ecumenicity rather remote, at best.

The Mennonite Central Committee

Efforts at inter-Mennonite relations in the twentieth century reflect two approaches. The All-Mennonite Conventions from 1913 to 1937 represent Ecumenical Type "A." The cooperative programs of the Mennonite Central Committee, founded in 1920, represent Ecumenical Type "C." The attempt to work at ecumenicity through doctrinal dialogue broke down after twenty-four years and seven conferences; but when ecumenical efforts centered in a common relief and service mission throughout the world, a new fraternal trust and rapport resulted that dialogue alone could not achieve.

Three questions gauged support for the present program of the

Mennonite Central Committee. The responses are summarized in Table 15-6. Sixty-nine percent of the members of all groups are generally satisfied with the MCC program, and only 2% are dissatisfied. A somewhat greater proportion of members are satisfied with one specific program called Mennonite Disaster Service, and a somewhat smaller proportion of members favor the lobbying offices of MCC in the Canadian and American capitals.

When the three questions were combined into an MCC Support

TABLE 15-6
Support of the Mennonite Central Committee

		Percentage Distribution for:				
Items and Responses	MC	GCMC	MBC	BIC	EMC	Total

1. "How satisfied or dissatisfied are you, in general, with the program and emphases of the Mennonite Central Committee?"

	MC	GCMC	MBC	BIC	EMC	Total
Very satisfied/satisfied	71	73	58	69	55	69
Partly satisfied/no opinion	28	26	38	30	42	30
Dissatisfied/very dissatisfied	2	2	4	1	4	2

2. "The Mennonite Disaster Services (MDS) has gradually developed as a major program under the Mennonite Central Committee. How satisfied or dissatisfied are you with the MDS program as it presently exists?"

	MC	GCMC	MBC	BIC	EMC	Total
Very satisfied/satisfied	79	77	62	68	54	75
Partly satisfied/no opinion	21	22	37	31	45	24
Dissatisfied/very dissatisfied	1	1	1	1	1	1

3. "Opinions vary on the question of whether the Mennonite Central Committee should maintain an office in Washington, D.C., and in Ottawa, Canada, to be in close contact with government officials in order to keep aware of matters that affect our churches on matters of war and peace, the draft, and various social issues. Do you tend to favor or to disfavor this type of contact with the national government?"

	MC	GCMC	MBC	BIC	EMC	Total
Favor it	52	59	56	56	50	55
Neutral/no opinion	36	29	31	36	36	34
Do not favor it	12	12	13	8	15	12

MCC Support Scale:

	MC	GCMC	MBC	BIC	EMC	Total
6 High	36	43	30	37	25	37
4-5 Middle	51	44	48	47	50	48
0-3 Low	13	14	22	16	25	15
Total	100	101	100	100	100	100
Number of Respondents	1,176	604	696	587	432	3,495
Mean Score	4.9	5.0	4.6	4.8	4.4	4.8

Scale, with scores from zero to 6, the overall average score was a high 4.8. According to the attitudinal tabulations, GCMC, MC, and BIC are the best supporters of the MCC program.

In contrast to the cross-tabulations of Table 15-5, in which all faith variables were negatively correlated with the Ecumenism Scale, we find in Table 15-7 that Anabaptism, associationalism, and communalism are positvely correlated with the MCC Support Scale. The

TABLE 15-7
Relationships Between MCC Support Scale and Other Variables

Variable	Position on Scales at left				Corr. Coeff. (r)
	Low			High	
	1	2	3	4	
	(% scoring "high" on MCC Support)				
Anabaptism	33	37	40		.136
Associationalism	30	37	41	45	.125
Fundamentalist Orthodoxy	50	46	36	31	-.106
Communalism	33	36	40	40	.094
Education	27	32	51	51	.165
Socioeconomic Status	21	36	48	55	.154
Pacifism	23	34	46		.256
Social Concerns	28	35	53		.230
Ecumenism	24	37	44		.131

Read percentages as follows: Of the members scoring low in Anabaptism, 33% scored high in MCC Support.

only "faith" variable that is negatively correlated with MCC Support is fundamentalist orthodoxy, which by now should surprise none of our readers.

Conclusion

Not strictly a test of the Anabaptist principles of ecumenism as defined at the beginning of the chapter, the Ecumenism Scale measures the favorableness of church members toward increasing cooperation between denominations, including possible eventual merging of denominational programs. The "MCC Support Scale" also measures an aspect of interdenominational cooperation, but the Anti-Semitism and Anti-Catholic Scales represent counter opinion, that is, attitudes unfavorable toward interfaith understanding and cooperation.

All of the faith variables including Anabaptism, but excepting Ethical-Social Conversion, are associated positively with anti-Semitic and anti-Catholic attitudes and low commitment to ecumenism as defined by the Ecumenism Scale. Fundamentalist orthodoxy was associated negatively with all four of the ecumenical scales presented in this chapter; Anabaptism with three of them, but less negatively.

This chapter brings Part III, "The Work of the Church," to an end. Twelve variables related to the work of the church were introduced in Part III, and it may be of interest to compare Anabaptism and fundamentalism with respect to their relationships to these 12 variables. In terms of the norms implicit in these scales, as constructed by the authors, Anabaptism emerged positively on seven of the variables, and fundamentalism on five of them. Whether the correlations were negative or positive, Anabaptism scores were closer to the norms than fundamentalism on all 12 variables.

In Part IV the faith, life, and work-of-the-church variables will be explored further in a search for the impact of social background factors on them. Part IV will then conclude with a search for the key factors in the lives of Mennonites and BIC, thus bringing the issues hopefully to a more definite conclusion than has been possible to this point.

Chapter **16**

SEX AND AGE DIFFERENCES

What causes a person to believe and act as he does? This fascinating question provides grist for the discussion mills all the way from coffee klatch gossip to the intricate research designs of the social psychologist. Research on explaining human behavior is most complicated, and the results are far from precise. Yet the search goes on.

The study of religious beliefs and behavior is no less difficult than the study of other dimensions of the human personality. Nevertheless one constantly seeks, by formal or informal methods, to explain why a particular church member's faith is weak or strong, why his attitudes are liberal or conservative, or why he conforms or does not conform to the moral norms that his religion prescribes.

Treated as a *dependent* variable, a person's religion can be seen as the end product of many conditions and influences that have affected his life. First of all, religion is to a considerable extent "inherited." That is, whether a person is a Catholic, a Jew, a Methodist or a Mennonite is in most cases determined by the religion of his parents. The individual was not offered a smorgasbord of faiths from which he could pick and choose. His religious training was parental faith and its virtues, and alternative faiths were not given equal treatment.

Secondly, for many Christians, God has a hand in determining their faith and life. It may not be so dramatic as in the case of the Apostle Paul, but God's Spirit "moves in a mysterious way His wonders to perform." The religious life may be fashioned by unusual, even cataclysmic, events, but usually the forces of change render their effects quite gradually, even imperceptibly.

This research does not focus on *why* the church members belong to their respective denominations, but on why given members of a particular church vary so remarkably in their beliefs and practices. How can the differences between members be explained?

This chapter begins an investigation of the relation of certain background factors to the religion of church members. Factors of family background (such as parent-child relationships) have generally not been incorporated into the study design, and the methods of survey research are inadequate to probe the mysteries of the Holy Spirit's work in the lives of church members. But there are other significant variables that beckon investigation.

Two important biological variables — age and sex — are the subject of this chapter. No person can control these variables, in the sense that he can control (choose) his residence, his occupation, or his marital status. Nevertheless we may ask if there are any significant differences between the religion of males and females, between the religion of young persons and older persons.

How Different Are Males and Females?

The survey data indicate that male and female church members are quite similar in their beliefs and attitudes. But, first, let us note what other researchers have discovered.

Writing in the late 1950s, Argyle summarized the findings about sex differences in religion from the studies done in Britain and America up to that time.[1] He concluded that "women are more religious than men on all criteria." He observed that women are in larger proportions members of churches, they attend church more faithfully, and their attitudes are more favorable toward church and religion. While women are more conservative in beliefs than men, he noted that the differences in belief are small. Men are closer to women on scales measuring beliefs than they are on scales measuring practices, such as attendance and prayers.

Glock, Ringer, and Babbie, examining data on members of the Episcopal Church in the United States, noted that "Episcopal women are more likely to attend church on Sundays, and more likely to become deeply involved in the church's organizational life than are men." They also found that women were more "intellectually involved" in the church and religion than men.[2]

In a survey of members of the United Church of Christ, women scored higher on all religious indexes except "organizational involvement." Although women attended church more faithfully, men tended in larger proportions to get into positions of leadership in the organizational structure of the churches.[3]

The authors of the Lutheran study (*A Study of Generations*, 1972) focused heavily on the age factor but did not report findings on male and female differences. Studying a different sample of Lutherans, Kersten found no difference between males and females on his indexes of Associational Involvement, Religious Knowledge, and Religious Beliefs, but females scored higher on the measure of Religious Practices.[4]

The Roper data reported by Campolo indicated that among American Baptists larger proportions of men than women attend worship services and "other church services or meetings." However, women's groups were more strongly supported by women than men's groups were supported by men.[5]

How do Mennonites and BIC compare? Seventy-one percent of males and 68% of females report attending "church worship services (on Sunday morning, evening, and/or other days) once a week or more often on the average during the past two years." Male church members were also slightly higher in proportions involved in positions of congregation leadership.[6] Since church attendance is almost universally on a "whole family" basis, possibly the slightly lower attendance rate for females is due to the necessity of mothers to stay home on occasion to care for infants or members of the household who are ill.

On many of the scales used in this study, male and female differences were insignificant. Some interesting differences did emerge, however, and merit attention. Women scored consistently higher on the scales measuring orthodoxy of beliefs. They also scored higher on the Devotionalism Scale and on specific items testing frequency of prayer and Bible study. They were higher on stewardship attitudes. Women are apparently somewhat more conservative or restrictive on moral issues, such as abortion, sexual relations outside of marriage, masturbation, and use of tobacco and alcohol, but were less restrictive than men on contraception.

On the other side, men evidenced less social prejudice in respect to other races and other religious groups. Men were slightly stronger in support of pacifism and other Anabaptist principles and men scored higher on political attitudes and participation. These differences were minimal, although statistically significant.

Major differences between males and females were discovered only in respect to the use of tobacco and alcohol. As reported in Chapter 7, males and females were similar in their attitudes opposing the use of alcohol and tobacco, but apparently males in much larger numbers than females actually deviate from the moral norms opposing their use. The proportions of regular users of tobacco now or in the past were 27% for men but only 6% for women. Hence men differ little from women in their attitudinal support of the Mennonite norms, but differ significantly in their rate of deviation from some norms. This agrees with those findings that led Argyle to conclude that "men are closer to women on scales measuring beliefs than they are on scales measuring practices," except that patterns of Mennonite male church attendance do not agree with Argyle's findings.

Do we conclude that, among Mennonites and BIC, women are more "religious" than men? If religion is measured in terms of orthodoxy of beliefs, the practice of personal piety, and a conservative stance on moral issues, the answer is "yes." If church participation and leadership, loyalty to Anabaptist teachings, and position on social and political issues are used as the criteria, the answer is "no." Twentieth-century Anabaptists fit the general stereotype of women's greater religiosity only in part.

Various theories have been advanced to explain the greater church participation of females, but these are not relevant here since our males had the stronger participation.[7] However, our findings agree with other studies which rather uniformly indicate that women are stronger on religious orthodoxy and moral behavior. We are inclined to reject theories that women are inherently more religious. The factors would seem to be sociological and cultural rather than biological.

Women seem to undergo more social pressure than men to conform to the social norms and cultural values of a given society. From early childhood, girls are more strongly channeled into "proper" behavior patterns than boys. Society seems to tolerate male deviancy more readily than female deviancy from social expectations. Girls should be "nice" but "boys will be boys." Hence, even though men may be in essential agreement with women on what doctrinal and ethical standards should be upheld, men nevertheless are under less compulsion than women to live up to the standards.

Another possible explanation of the higher female conformity to religious norms is that women are less in contact with alternative patterns of belief and behavior than men. This is particularly relevant to a unique ethnic minority group such as Mennonites. Because of their occupational roles, more men than women rub elbows with people outside the minority "in-group" whose values (*e.g.*, on smoking or drinking) are different from those of the in-group. On the theory that deviancy from minority group norms is a function of the degree of communication and interaction with members of the *majority* system (the "out-group"), males would be expected to deviate more than females from the norms of the minority group.

Age Differences

Gordon Allport provides a framework for understanding age differences.[8] He describes the natural changes in religious interest as a person moves through the life cycle. Children tend to imbibe the religion of their parents, although its meaning for them is conditioned also by their temperament and imagination, and by the sincerity or insincerity of their parents' piety. The first serious reverses begin at adolescence, when religious attitudes must be transformed "from secondhand fittings to firsthand fittings of his personality." The transition of the teen years is usually characterized by a certain amount of alienation and rebellion and by the fact that youth is encouraged by their culture to question authority. This critical attitude reaches a peak after high school with the result that "the early and middle twenties are . . . the least religious period of life." Religious interest begins to return after marriage and the arrival of children with its attending concern to give them the benefit of the religious influence they had in their own childhood. Especially is this true of persons who recall with appreciation the sincerity and piety of their parents. From then through the middle years, most people feel the need for a religious orientation to life. These shifts through the life-span, according to Allport, have been observed repeatedly for more than a century.

Allport's thesis is supported by the results of a number of empirical studies. In reviewing religious behavior in England and America, Argyle included observations on age variations. He noted a decline in religious interest and activity from age 16 (the modal age for conversions) to approximately age 30, although the low point for some people comes earlier than age 30. After the age of 30 and continuing until death there is a steady increase in religious activity and interests.[9]

Likewise Glock and his associates observed that "whatever index is used, the general pattern for both sexes is the same: a decline from the original level of involvement followed by a recovery which is more marked for women than for men."[10]

The most exhaustive analysis of age variations in religious beliefs and behavior has been made by the authors of the Lutheran study.[11] Variations between the "generations" were noted on 52 scales used in the study. Six age-groups were compared: 15-18, 19-23, 24-29, 30-41, 42-49, and 50-65. On many of the scales the college age-group (19-23) scored lowest, with scores gradually increasing to the oldest group. These scales included "Religious Experience," "Personal Evangelism," belief in "A Personal, Caring God," "Congregational Activity," "Need for Religious Absolutism," and avoidance of "Questionable Personal Activities."

On other scales both 15-18 and 19-23 groups were lowest with gradual increases through successively older groups. Some of these scales were "Emotional Certainty of Faith," "Life Purpose," "Attitudes Toward Life and Death," "Transcendental Meaning in Life," and "Acceptance of Middle-Class Norms." However, these youngest age-groups were lowest on "Generalized Prejudice" and "Social Distance — Racial and Religious Groups." That is, the young groups were least prejudiced and expressed fewest feelings of social distance toward other groups, whereas the 50-65 group had the most prejudiced feelings.

Some interesting comparisons between the Lutheran data and the Mennonite and BIC data are now possible. Table 16-1 summarizes data on age variation for 32 scales and individual questionnaire items used in the study. Figures 16-1 and 16-2 provide a visual interpretation of eight of the scales and items. Comment will be made only on the more salient findings.

For purposes of analysis, the church members were divided into four age-groups: the teenagers (13-19 years of age), the young adults (20-29), the "middle-age" group (30-49 years), and the oldest group running from age 50 to the nine respondents aged 85 or over. This breakdown facilitates a comparison of teenagers with their generation of parents, most of whom fall within the 30-49 category, as well as a comparison of the young adults with their parent generation, which is mostly over 50 years of age. Of course, many in the 30-49 group will also have parents in the older age level. For most purposes it did not seem important to subdivide the "50 and over" group.

Table 16-1 shows that 21% of the "middle age" group, and 43% of the oldest group rated "high" on the Associationalism Scale. Thus the middle-age church members have the highest, or most intense participation, in the life of the church.

The Associationalism Scale was composed of eight questionnaire items. Data on three of these items, presented in Table 16-1 and Figure 16-1, show three different patterns of change associated with increasing age. Regarding attendance at church services, the teenagers have the highest proportion attending at least once a week. The lowest attendance rate is evidenced by the young adults, which is in line with the pattern in other denominations noted above. Church attendance of the oldest group (aged 50-85) drops off slightly from the middle age-group, probably due to health reasons.

Chapter 4 reported that rates of church attendance for Mennonites and BIC are higher than for other Protestant denominations for which data are available. Attendance rates *within age-groups* are not reported in most other studies. However, the Lutheran study shows attendance "weekly or more" ranging from 41% for the 19-23 age-group to 64% for the 50-65 age-group. High schoolers (15-18) had a percentage of 60. The Mennonite and BIC attendance rates are thus higher at all age levels, and exhibit similar variation between age-groups except that our teenagers have relatively higher rates in comparison to middle and older age-groups than do Lutheran teenagers.

Since church attendance is a family affair among Mennonites and BIC, it is not surprising that attendance rates for teenagers and

TABLE 16-1
Percent of Respondents Evidencing Selected Religious
Characteristics by Age-Groups

(Lowest scores have single underlining; highest scores, double underlining.)

| | Age | | | | |
Characteristics	13–19 N=483	20–29 N=609	30–49 N=1323	50+ N=1167	Total N=3582
	(percent)				
I. Church Participation Variables:					
High on Associationalism Scale	21	27	53	43	41
Attend services at church once a week or more	79	54	74	68	69
Attend Sunday school at least "most Sundays"	85	65	82	82	80
Held congregational leadership positions within past three years	43	53	72	48	57
Participation in church is "very important"	35	46	71	85	67
High on Evangelism Scale	5	4	20	24	17
II. Beliefs and Bible Knowledge					
High on General Orthodoxy	62	60	77	87	75
High on Fundamentalist Orthodoxy	27	25	41	62	44
High on Bible Knowledge	22	32	46	43	40
High on Anabaptism Scale	32	40	45	54	46
III. Personal Piety					
High on Devotionalism Scale	15	16	31	42	30
Daily private prayer (excluding grace at meals)	66	62	78	88	77
Bible study "daily" or "frequently"	49	46	70	81	67
Relationship to God is "close" or "very close"	37	37	52	68	53
High on Stewardship Attitudes	9	24	33	32	18

TABLE 16-1 (Continued)

	Age				
Characteristics	13–19 N=483	20–29 N=609	30–49 N=1323	50+ N=1167	Total N=3582
IV. Attitudes on Social Issues					
High on Pacifism Scale	45	53	56	56	54
Would take Alternate Service if drafted	66	70	72	71	71
High on Race Relations Scale	40	46	33	20	32
High on Political Participation	2	32	59	52	44
Low on Anti-Semitism Scale	28	40	34	22	30
Favor more women in church leadership positions	16	23	11	5	12
High on Ecumenism Scale	20	24	22	15	20
High on Welfare Attitudes	13	21	25	20	21
High on MCC Support Scale	54	68	70	64	66
V. Moral Attitudes and Behavior					
High on Moral Attitudes Scale	68	62	81	89	78
Smoking tobacco is "always wrong"	52	52	65	73	64
"Have never tried" tobacco	53	35	40	54	46
Drinking (moderately) is always wrong"	45	30	49	62	50
"Never drank any" alcoholic beverages	53	20	31	43	36
Sexual intercourse outside of marriage "is never justifiable"	68	66	87	95	84
Use of hard drugs is "always wrong"	95	94	99	99	97

their parent generation (30-49) are similar. The main gap, although not large, is between the young adults and their parent generation, which is similar to the results from the Lutheran study. When the young adults become the age of their parents, will their attendance rate rise to their parents' present rate?

The extent to which church members hold leadership positions in the congregation is an important dimension of associationalism.

Figure 16-1: Age Variations on
Church Participation

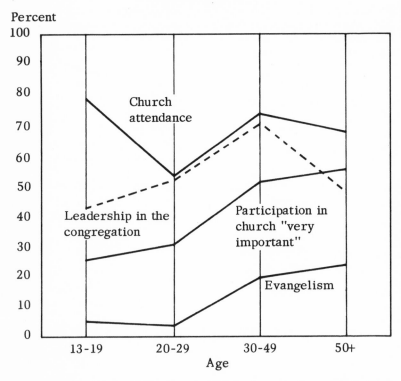

Percent

100
90
80
70
60
50
40
30
20
10
0

Church
attendance

Leadership in the
congregation

Participation in
church "very
important"

Evangelism

13-19   20-29   30-49   50+

Age

Data in Table 16-1 and Figure 16-1 show that persons in the middle age-group hold positions of responsibility in the local congregation in substantially larger proportions (72%). Teenagers are least involved in leadership, although a surprisingly large minority (43%) have held positions of responsibility within the most recent three years. These results parallel the findings on the United Church of Christ where an "Index of Organizational Involvement" yielded scores of highest involvement for the age-group of 35-49 years.[12]

Another measure of church involvement is how important the member feels in his "current participation in the life and work of the church." The differences show a steady growth from the youngest to oldest age-groups in the proportion who feel that participation is "very important." Perhaps the church plays an increasingly significant

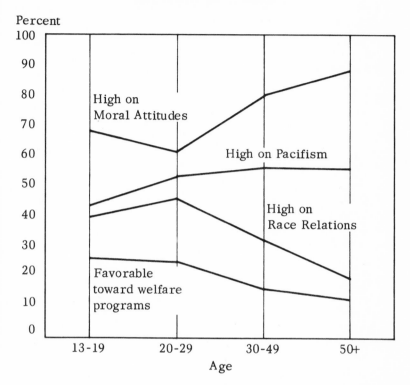

**Figure 16-2: Age Variations on
Moral and Ethical Attitudes**

role in the lives of its members as they grow older, both in an absolute sense and also relative to the significance of other groups and institutions with whom the individual has a relationship.

In respect to orthodoxy of beliefs, increasing age is associated with increasing orthodoxy, particularly from age 30 onward. Although young adults were typically lowest in orthodoxy, they were not significantly lower than teenagers. Acceptance of Anabaptist principles, as indicated by scores on the Anabaptism Scale, steadily rises from the youngest to the oldest ages. Bible knowledge also rises significantly from one age-group to the next older.

On matters of personal piety, or devotionalism, such as prayer, Bible study, and relationship to God, there is also a direct relationship between age and piety. On private prayer and Bible study the young adults rank lowest, but not much below the teenagers. Of course, the whole range of scores in personal piety, as in the case of orthodoxy of beliefs and measures of church participation, varies more *within* age-groups than between them.

The Lutheran researchers found that college age youth tend to be more liberal than other age-groups on social issues and tend to show less prejudice toward blacks and other social and religious minorities.[13] Our data yield similar results. Young adults scored considerably higher on Race Relations and lower on Anti-Semitism (*i.e.*, they had less prejudiced attitudes) than did the older groups. The oldest church members evidence considerably more prejudiced or unaccepting attitudes toward blacks, Jews, Catholics, Communists, poor people, long-haired youth, and labor unions. Hopefully the more tolerant attitudes of the young people will increasingly prevail, so that the social and legal repression of minority groups will diminish in the years to come.

Attitudes favorable to ecumenical relationships between denominations differed little among age-groups, except that the oldest group was significantly lower. Young adults were slightly more favorable.

There appears to be little difference between age-groups in respect to attitudes favorable to pacifism and alternative service programs, and unfavorable to participation in military services. The denominational emphasis on opposition to any type of participation in war-related programs appears to be accepted by young persons almost as strongly as by older persons. On the other hand, fewer than five percent of the respondents were favorable toward "absolutist" positions of refusal to register or to be inducted under the Selective Service System (in U.S.), and these were sprinkled across all age levels.

The Moral Attitudes Scale and related items provide a test of how closely the church members agree with the official teachings of the churches against certain behaviors often defined as wrong: smoking, drinking, gambling, dancing, sexual relations outside of marriage, use of hard drugs and marijuana, and so on. (See Chapter 7.) Age variations on all these items followed a rather consistent pattern. The oldest group was most opposed; the middle age, less so; the teenagers even less; and the young adults, least opposed to the behaviors. Teenagers were somewhat more "liberal" on these items than their parents (the 30-49 age-group), but the big gap was between the young adults and their parental generation. This gap is probably too large to lead one to expect that the young adults will become as conservative as their parents when they get to be as old as their parents are now. The church's teaching and discipline on these matters is less vigorous now than it was a generation ago. This, plus more interaction and communication with "outside groups," probably leads young people to take a less restrictive view than their parents did a generation ago. This may lead to a gradual diminution of restrictiveness along these lines within the next decades.

Conclusions

In summary, four age-groups were compared on 32 scales and individual questionnaire items that measured aspects of religious faith and practice. Teenagers rated highest only on regularity of church and Sunday school attendance, but were lowest on many of the other measures. Young adults (aged 20-29) are least prejudiced toward minority groups and are most favorable toward ecumenical relationships. They tend to rate low or lowest on church attendance, orthodoxy of beliefs, measures of personal piety, and moral attitudes and behavior.

Middle-age members rated highest on measures of congregational leadership, Bible knowledge, stewardship, pacifism, political activity, and attitudes toward programs in public welfare and church service. They did not rate lowest on any scales. The oldest age-group rated highest on half the scales — chiefly the measures of orthodoxy of beliefs, personal piety, and moral issues. They evidenced the greatest social prejudice and the least interest in ecumenicity. These observations must not obscure the fact that large variations occur *within* age-groups, so that many respondents in each category are not typical of their age level.

Is the "generation gap" a serious one? We conclude that the differences between those under 30 and those over 30 are normal and not serious. Youth is a time of questioning the traditions of the parental generation, a time of doubting, of testing even deviant paths. Many individuals have a psychological need to "free" themselves from norms that were superimposed on them by the parental generation. Even though they will not abandon most of these norms, they must come to feel that they are their own, not someone else's.

Commitment to an abiding faith depends in part on the resolution of emotional and social problems associated with youth. As the individual moves through the stages of completing an education, deciding on an occupation, getting married, establishing a home, achieving financial independence, and becoming the parents of children, problems of faith and religious practice begin to clear up. As he takes the role of parent, he begins to insist on the same standards that his parents did. His views on moral issues become more conservative as his own children move into the turbulent high school and college years. He may develop a greater feeling of dependence on God, as some of the self-confidence, optimism, and idealism of his earlier years diminish. Perhaps 25 years from now the young adults in our study will score as high on measures of orthodoxy, personal piety, and moral issues as the parental generation scored in 1972.

What will the church in the next generation be like? Although predictions are hazardous, we risk the following: Church members will be less prejudiced toward minority groups and more ready to cooperate in church programs that cut across denominational lines. Although orthodoxy of beliefs and conservatism on moral issues may decline somewhat, the next generation of Anabaptists will still be very conservative relative to other mainline Protestant bodies. They will probably be as strong as the present generation in personal piety, in social concerns, and in adherence to the pacifist teachings of the Anabaptists.

Chapter 17

EDUCATION AND
SOCIAL CLASS

All modern societies tend to develop a social class system based on the inequalities of economic and social status among the members of the society. In some societies, notably India and medieval Europe, class lines are fixed and social interaction across class lines, as well as movement from one class to another, is severely restricted. In the more "open class" system of the United States and Canada class lines are diffuse and relatively easy to cross. Because of this "openness" some even insist on the delightful fiction that we are a one class society. Such notions are far from the truth, of course. Even churches evidence wide variations in wealth and in the access which people have to the things that money will buy.

A Socioeconomic Status Scale

Accumulated wealth and current income are primary factors in determining the social status of a person or his family. Other factors are occupation and education. A person's social status is normally not immediately evident, but if his occupation is known some estimate can be made of his income and his education. In a face-to-face situation it would be a social indiscretion to ask a man the amount of his wealth or the size of his income, and in some circumstances even his age or education, but no harm is done in inquiring about his occupation or profession.

The anonymity of a social survey, however, enables one to obtain information on many of the "status characteristics" of the respondent. The current study utilized a Socioeconomic Status Scale (SES Scale) in order to assign a social ranking to each respondent. The SES scale was constructed by combining the respondent's income, occupation, and education. Nine income categories (ranks) were used, from "$50,000 and over" to "below $3,000." Nine levels of "formal schooling" were used, from "none" to "graduate or professional degree." Occupations were grouped into eight ranks, following census categories, from "professional" to "laborer."[1]

The three rankings were then added for an overall SES score. The scores were collapsed into four "classes," designated "upper," "upper middle," "lower middle," and "lower." These labels are relative rather than absolute. That is, the 8% of respondents who are arbitrarily classed as "upper" rank high relative to the others, but few of them would meet the status requirements to be called "upper class Americans."[2]

The distribution of church members by SES and by denomination is given in Table 17-1. Mean scores on the scale range from a low of 11.7 for the MC to a high of 12.8 for the EMC. The five groups are quite similar in their SES distributions, the differences not being statistically significant.

The use of a socioeconomic scale makes it possible to test the

TABLE 17-1
Distribution of SES Scores by Denomination

SES Scale		MC	GCMC	MBC	BIC	EMC	Total
19–23	Upper	6	10	10	9	6	8
12–18	Upper Middle	43	43	43	42	58	43
6–11	Lower Middle	45	42	41	42	34	43
1–5	Lower	6	5	6	7	2	6
Total		100	100	100	100	100	100
Mean Score		11.7	12.1	12.1	12.0	12.8	12.0

hypothesis that a person's religious faith and practices depend, in part, on his social station in life. We can also test the assimilation hypothesis that upward mobility is associated with loss of unique sectarian religious characteristics. These hypotheses can be tested partly by looking separately at the effects of education, occupation, and income on faith and practice, but the SES scale provides efficiency in looking at the factor of social class, since none of the three separate variables is by itself an adequate measure of social class.

Radical Christianity has tended to be very critical of class differentiation. Rejecting the accumulation of wealth as a valid goal for the sincere Christian, many individuals, like St. Francis of Assisi, have spurned the pursuit of material goods and have looked upon wealth as incipient evil. Likewise whole colonies of Christians have sought to maintain or restore the true Christian community through the communal sharing of all income and consumption goods. Although the Anabaptists emphasized mutual sharing of goods, the followers of Jacob Hutter, from 1528 to the present, have done most to maintain equality of economic goods within the community. On a Socioeconomic Status Scale, all adult Hutterian Brethren would have almost identical scores, since no individuals or families have private incomes, and all share the same communal consumption goods. Likewise nearly all Hutterites are farmers (the schoolteacher may be an exception), and nearly all terminate their education with the eighth grade or slightly beyond.

The Impact of Education

Before looking at the general effects of SES on religion, we will examine the relation of educational achievements to Anabaptism. The "church-sect" typology developed by Weber and Troeltsch, referred to in Chapter 1, is helpful in thinking about the possible impact of social status on adherence to Anabaptist beliefs. The "church type" philosophy accepts the status quo of the social order and sees the church and the civil government as embodying and serving the same population. Thus any improvement in the "church community" is *ipso facto* an improvement in the civil and economic community.

The "sect type" ideology draws a sharp line between the church and the larger society. The sect develops its own "subculture," which contains rigid behavioral requirements for its own members. The sect sees itself as a "called out" group, achieving religious excellence and purity by avoiding the excesses of immoral behavior which it thinks the state-church philosophy too readily tolerates.

Dynes tested the church-sect typology on a sample of residents of Columbus, Ohio. He found that the degree of acceptance of the church-type beliefs increases with an increase in the amount of education.[3] If this result generally prevails, then we should expect twentieth-century Anabaptists to show less support for the sectarian beliefs of their forefathers as their educational levels increase. Table 17-2 indicates support for this hypothesis. Church members who did not go beyond the eighth grade scored somewhat higher on the Anabaptism Scale than those in all categories of higher educational achievement. However, differences between the other three educational categories are slight, with respondents attending graduate school showing slightly greater acceptance of Anabaptism than those attending high school and college but not beyond. This slight reversal of trend is possibly due to the presence in the graduate school group of seminary-trained pastors who scored higher than laymen on the Anabaptism Scale.

Limitations of space do not permit a detailed presentation of the statistical data on the relation of education to the religious variables. However, this is unnecessary in view of the data on the

TABLE 17-2
Percentage Distribution of Church Members by
Education and by Rating on the Anabaptist Vision Scale

Rank on Anabaptism	Educational Achievement			
	Grade School N=805	High School N=1525	College N=673	Grad. School N=453
High	57	42	40	45
Middle	31	33	32	31
Low	12	25	28	24
Total	100	100	100	100

$X^2 = 81.51$. P is less than .001.

SES variable which follows, since the results of inter-variable correlations for education and for SES are similar.

Social Class and Religion

The relation of the social status of church members to their church participation and their religious beliefs and practices is a subject which has gained the increasing attention of serious research in recent decades. Although a body of evidence is slowly accumulating, the findings are inconclusive and sometimes contradictory. Most of the surveys have probed church attendance and other "associational" variables, but little information is available on the relation of beliefs and personal piety to social status.

Combing the evidence from church history, Niebuhr concludes that "the religion of the disinherited" (the lower class) is more fundamentalistic in beliefs and is expressed with greater emotional fervor.[4] Lower class churches are more sectarian and more critical of the social order, and are the spawning ground for social revolutions or reform movements. If Niebuhr's analysis holds for twentieth-century Anabaptists, we would expect to find that our church members with higher social status will have lower scores on the scales measuring fundamentalist orthodoxy, communal commitment (strength of in-group feelings), and support of Anabaptist principles (sectarian identity).

Glock summarized empirical findings from several studies on the relation of church participation to social class.[5] Most surveys indicate that, with increasing social status, both church membership (the proportion of persons belonging to church) and church attendance tend to increase. Among Episcopalians, however, Glock found that increasing social status was associated with *decreasing* church attendance and involvement in church activities.[6] Argyle's review of research on religion in the United States concludes that the middle classes are slightly more active (in religion) than those above or below.[7]

Lenski reports that, in Detroit, white Protestant church members of higher status attend church more regularly, but score lower on scales of orthodoxy and devotionalism.[8] Among Catholics, however, increasing status is associated with *increasing* devotionalism but with unchanging orthodoxy. The Strommen study on Lutherans does not report data on the basis of social class, but a few observations are made on the effects of education. Larger proportions of the less educated reflect a conservative or fundamentalist viewpoint, and show more social prejudice.[9] Using a combination of income and education as a measure of social class, Kersten found that Lutherans of higher class have more liberal religious beliefs.[10]

The findings on Mennonite and BIC church members are compressed into Table 17-3. Correlation coefficients are given for each variable correlated with the Socioeconomic Status Scale. For samples of this large size, statistical significance (at the .01 level) is yielded by a coefficient of .04 or more, positive or negative. However, an "important" relationship between two variables can hardly be assumed unless the coefficient is at least .20 (plus or minus). A correlation is not "high" unless the coefficient is at least .50.

In regard to church participation, higher SES has a slight positive correlation with church attendance and other aspects of church participation. In this respect, twentieth-century Anabaptists are like most other groups that have been studied, but not like the Episcopalians reported on by Glock and his associates. Sentiments of communal commitment are slightly greater among lower status members (r = -.05). Higher status persons apparently perceive their commitment to the church as somewhat less voluntary (= -15).

Although higher status members have a greater knowledge of the Bible, they are less orthodox in doctrinal beliefs. The negative association is strongest in respect to fundamentalist beliefs. (r = -.18). As in the case of church members of higher educational attainment, those of higher SES show slightly less support of Anabaptist principles. Thus an increase in SES results in a slight diminution of sectarian loyalties.

Apparently expressions of personal piety bear no significant relationship to SES. We conclude that church members of all class levels have similar behavior patterns in respect to their devotional life and personal relationship to God. Higher status persons have slightly more favorable attitudes toward tithing and planned giving (r = .17 for Stewardship Attitudes) but the proportion of incomes actually given to church and charitable causes is no greater (r = -.03).

Socioeconomic Status seems to have its greatest effect in relation to attitudes favoring pacifism and political participation, more favorable attitudes toward other races, and more favorableness toward women playing a larger leadership role in the churches. Church members of higher SES show less prejudiced attitudes toward Communists, toward religious minority groups, and toward labor unions. Slightly less favorable attitudes toward government welfare programs are correlated (r=-.09) with higher SES. In general, higher SES is associated with more liberal views on social issues, whereas lower status church members are more conservative.

TABLE 17-3
Coefficients of Correlation Between
Socioeconomic Status and Religious Variables

I. Church Participation Variables:		IV. Social Ethics:	
1. Associationalism Scale	.17	17. Pacifism Scale	.16
2. Church Attendance	.04*	18. Political Participation	.24
3. Congregational Leadership	.21*	19. Race Relations Scale	.25
4. Sunday School Participation	.05	20. Anti-Communism Scale	-.28
5. Support of Church Colleges	.15	21. Anti-Semitism Scale	-.26
6. Communalism Scale	-.05	22. Anti-Catholic Scale	-.27
7. Voluntarism Scale	-.15	23. Anti-Labor Union Scale	-.22
		24. Welfare Attitudes Scale	-.09
II. Beliefs and Bible Knowledge:		25. Role-of-Women Scale	.29
		26. Capital Punishment	.15*
8. General Orthodoxy Scale	-.20	27. Euthanasia	-.12*
9. Fundamentalist Orthodoxy Scale	-.38		
10. Anabaptism Scale	-.11	V. Moral Issues:	
11. Bible Knowledge Scale	.30		
		28. Moral Attitudes Scale	-.20
III. Personal Piety Variables:		29. Moral Behavior Scale	.01
12. Devotionalism	-.01		
13. Frequency of Prayer	.00*	VI. Church Extension Variables:	
14. Relationship to God	-.01*		
15. Stewardship Attitudes Scale	.17	30. Evangelism Scale	.08
16. Stewardship Peformance Scale	-.03	31. Ecumenism Scale	.25
		32. Social Concerns Scale	.18
		33. MCC Support Scale	.15

*Kendall's Tau C. All other coefficients are Pearsonian r.

Increasing SES is negatively associated with attitudes of restrictiveness on moral issues. That is, the higher the SES, the weaker the opposition to smoking, drinking, gambling, dancing, premarital sexual relations, and other "vices" against which the churches have traditionally taught.

With regard to church extension or outreach to people beyond the borders of Mennonite and BIC congregations, higher status persons show more favorable attitudes. On the scales measuring evangelism, ecumenicity, witness, and service, higher status persons scored consistently higher.

Conclusions

The relative importance of socioeconomic status among the various background factors affecting religion will be demonstrated more clearly in Chapter 20. Data presented in this chapter lead to the conclusion that the socioeconomic status of church members does have some important effects on their faith and attitudes, albeit not as much as age.

SES was more strongly related to fundamentalism than to any other variable. The correlation was -.38, indicating that lower class members tend to be more fundamentalistic. This agrees with Strommen's findings on Lutherans and Niebuhr's more general theories.

As twentieth-century Anabaptists increase in socioeconomic status, their commitment to Anabaptism and its related sectarian characteristics (such as non-participation in political affairs) can be expected to diminish slightly. However, little change in church participation and personal piety is expected. Increased SES can be expected to result in diminished prejudice towards minorities and persons of other faiths, and in increased support of ecumenical programs.

Three major forces in the assimilation of minority groups are increased education, increased income and wealth, and urbanization. We have looked at the first two, and now turn in the next chapter to the third. After that some conclusions can be drawn about the probable future assimilation of Mennonites and BIC into the mainstream of American and Canadian national life.

Chapter 18

RESIDENCE: RURAL-URBAN, REGIONAL, NATIONAL

In the previous two chapters the influence of sex, age, education, and socioeconomic position upon the religious behavior of church members was explored. Another important variable is residence. The members of the groups under study are distributed over the landscape in residential configurations — isolated farmsteads, rural towns, larger cities, metropolitan regions, nation-states. This prompts us to ask whether and how religious commitment varies as place of residence shifts. It is known that all these residential units are linked together by transportation and communication networks that tend to reduce differences and subject nearly all residents of a country and continent to the same urbanized influences.

The purpose of this chapter is to discover in what ways church members do or do not vary by differences in place of residence. Contradictory points of view among leaders of these churches will be reviewed concerning the effects of urbanization and nationalism upon Anabaptist faith. These viewpoints will be tested especially by the scores of members with varying places of residence on the scale measuring assent to Anabaptist doctrines.

Rural-Urban Place of Residence

Rural and urban differences in residence were studied using

standard Canadian and United States Census definitions. Church members were first of all divided into the following four categories: *rural farm* (residence on a farm of three acres or more), *rural non-farm* (residence on a plot of less than three acres outside a village or

TABLE 18-1
Rural-Urban Residence by Denominations

| Place of Residence | Percentage Distribution for: | | | | | |
	MC	GCMC	MBC	BIC	EMC	Total
Rural Farm	38	33	25	22	31	34
Rural Nonfarm	36	28	19	8	30	31
Small City	14	16	20	16	24	16
Large City	12	23	36	13	15	19
Total	100	100	100	99	100	99
Number of Respondents	1,195	611	703	613	440	3,562

city, or in a village or town under 2,500 population), *small city* (population of 2,500 to 24,999), and *large city* (population of 25,000 and over). In 1970 the percentage of the population of the United States having rural residence was 26.5, with 5.2% rural farm and 21.3% rural nonfarm.[1] In Canada in 1971, 27.6% of the population was rural by this definition, with 6.6% living on farms.[2] The respondents in the present study are considerably more rural than both of these national figures. As shown in Table 18-1, 65% are rural, with 34% living on farms. Among the five groups, the MC is the most rural (74%) and the MBC least rural (44%). The BIC has the lowest percentage of members living on a farm, but is still the second most rural group by virtue of a 48% rural nonfarm membership.

Demographic Characteristics. Since Aristotle wrote his *Politics* it has been recognized that as the number of inhabitants in a settlement increases, the relationship between them changes. Mennonites and BIC are aware that urbanization is rapidly changing their communities, which were once predominantly rural. As members get more formal education, they tend to enter nonagricultural oc-

TABLE 18-2
Demographic Characteristics by
Rural-Urban Residence

Demographic Characteristic	Rural Farm	Rural Nonfarm	Small City	Large City	Total
	(percent unless otherwise indicated)				
Median school years attained	11.8	12.2	12.6	12.9	12.2
% college graduates	9	18	24	32	18
Median family income (dollars)	9,293	9,431	10,100	9,889	9,623
% lived in present community less than five years	6	18	22	28	16
% nonresident members	4	8	14	18	10
% "professional" occupation	5	19	20	28	16

cupations and move to the cities for gainful employment. Thus, we would expect to find significant differences between rural and urban places of residence on such demographic indices as education, occupation, income, age, and mobility.

It can be observed in Table 18-2 that there are differences in all of these respects. For members, the city is associated with the opportunities that come by way of education, professional employment, higher income, and great mobility. The rural farm member has 1 1/2 years less schooling than the large city member and earns $800 less family income. By both indices, these people reflect the situation in the society as a whole, in which the education and income of rural residents are considerably below that of urban residents. Past generations of Mennonites and BIC have experienced poverty in various ways, and their newest threat to economic subsistence may come with members who remain on the farm, 9% of whom had less than $3.000 family income in 1971, compared to 4% for large city members. Nevertheless, in comparison to rural farm residents in the United States generally, rural farm Mennonites and BIC have a 29% higher median family income;[3] so these income differences *within* the church must also be seen in the larger societial perspective.

Style of Life. Sociologists continue to find systematic differences between rural and urban communities while noting that these differences are becoming smaller. The usual way to study differences and similarities is by reference to historic types representing extreme contrasts, even though such contrasts are seldom found anymore. What one actually finds between the extremes is a continuum along which existing communities may be placed on the basis of their relative "urbanity" or "rurality." The following summary of contrasting types is based on the works of three rural sociologists:[4]

Item of Comparison	Rural Society	Urban Society
1. Social Unit	Family	Individual
2. Social Roles	Integrated	Compartmentalized
3. Social Bond	Custom	Contract
4. Social Values	Traditional	Permissive
5. Social Welfare	Direct Action	Referral to Agencies
6. Social Environment	Nature	Technology

Activities related to work, recreation, and religion historically have been family matters in rural society; but in urban society the social unit is the individual. The roles of urban society are divided between the realm of residence and the realm of work, with hardly any connection between the two, while the rural worker is known more in the totality of his existence. Rural residents are united by the bond of custom. "Their relationships are predicated, not upon formal agreement or legal enactment, but upon those unwritten laws which have been the evolution of centuries of human practice."[5] Moral values in rural society are traditional and conservative, but in urban society they are decided on more permissive and pragmatic grounds. Rural people rely on direct action for mutual aid while urban people refer needy persons to social welfare agencies of many kinds. Finally, there is a contrast in environment, rural people being more conscious of nature than of technology.

The church member questionnaire was not designed to test the relative rural or urban character of the societies represented in the study, but in retrospect, certain items can be seen to apply to the typology. Four items summarized in Table 18-3 reveal small differences in the direction indicated by the *social unit*. Rural farm households are significantly larger in size, indicating larger families. Rural members tend to own their own houses and to believe marriage is a lifelong commitment. Nearly twice as many urban housewives as rural farm housewives are employed outside the home. In spite of these contrasts, there appears to be little difference between rural and urban members on the items that compose the Communalism Scale — city members look to the church as much as rural farm members for friends, mate selection, and family solidarity.

Four items seem to lend some support to the *social roles* and *social bond* theory of differences. A greater percentage of rural members dislike the compartmentalization of labor unions, preferring the old custom of employer and laborer working side-by-side. Urban members emphasize the contract more than custom in such matters as settling grievances by suit of law, guaranteeing a minimum wage, and recognizing women's rights.

Rather clear differences obtain also on some of the items related

TABLE 18-3
Style of Life Characteristics
by Rural-Urban Residence

Style of Life Characteristic	Rural Farm	Rural Nonfarm	Small City	Large City	Total
	(Percent unless otherwise indicated)				
Social Unit					
Median no. people in household	4.9	4.3	4.0	5.4	4.4
Home is rented	8	10	15	20	12
Marriage a lifelong commitment	80	79	74	70	77
Housewife employed outside home	24	43	48	49	38
Scored high in Communalism Scale	6	10	4	7	7
Social Roles					
Against joining labor union	22	19	14	10	17
Social Bond					
Justifies personal law suits	29	28	36	43	33
Favors guaranteed income	22	28	27	31	26
Believes women's rights denied	11	14	20	24	16
Social Values					
Believes long-haired youth are rejecting Christian values	28	21	22	16	22
Believes divorce always wrong	39	33	32	24	33
Believes attending X-rated movies always wrong	54	51	48	33	48
Believes premarital sex always wrong	87	87	82	78	84
Social Welfare					
Believes mutual aid still needed	87	85	86	84	86
Favors Mennonite Mutual Aid plans	54	57	58	44	54
Scored high in Welfare Attitudes	30	36	41	38	35
Social Environment					
Median hours per day watching TV	1.0	1.3	1.4	1.3	1.2
TV commercials influence purchases	28	29	26	24	27

to *social values.* Rural members are significantly more conservative on such matters as premarital sex, X-rated movies, divorce, and long hair on youth.

On the matter of *social welfare* in the face of emergencies, the best indicator available did not confirm the classical contrast between direct aid and referral to agencies. The percentage of respondents considering mutual aid within the framework of the church to be preferable to commercial insurance policies was no less for urban members than for rural. In fact, a greater proportion of the members in small cities are favorable to Mennonite Mutual Aid programs than is true for rural farm members; but there appears to be some doubt in this regard among large city members. Urban members are rather more favorable to government-sponsored welfare programs than are rural farm members.

The number of hours per day spent watching television might be an indicator of the difference, if any, in *social environment.* Urban members spend slightly more time in front of the tube than rural farm members, but the latter admit to slightly greater influence of TV commercials on their purchasing behavior.

Overall, the lifestyle characteristics that have been summarized support Richard Dewey's findings about the classical rural-urban continuum: "real but relatively unimportant."[6]

Personal and Social Ethics. Closely related to the differences in lifestyle are variations in personal and social ethics. As summarized in Table 18-4, urban members exhibited two types of liberation from the stricter social controls of a rural social system. On scales of moral attitudes and behavior containing questions on such traditional Mennonite and BIC taboos as smoking, drinking, dancing, movies, and extramarital sex, urban members were less absolutist in their responses, a trend that rural members lament as worldliness and secularization.[7]

At the same time, the urbanized members scored higher on the Social Concerns Scale that affirmed peaceful demonstration to attain social justice, questioned the priority of space exploration in the allocation of public funds, and favored the abolition of capital punishment. Rural respondents evidenced more prejudice toward racial minorities, a greater anti-Catholic attitude, less participation in local and national politics, and less interest in a women's rights move-

TABLE 18-4
Moral and Ethical Variables
by Rural-Urban Residence

Moral–Ethical Variables	Rural Farm	Rural Nonfarm	Small City	Large City	Total
Percent who scored:					
High on Moral Attitude Scale	83	81	74	69	78
High on Moral Behavior Scale	46	47	42	32	43
High on Social Concerns Scale	19	24	31	27	24
High on Welfare Attitudes Scale	30	36	41	38	35
High on Race Relations Scale	29	30	37	37	32
Low on Anti–Catholic Scale	22	26	28	33	26
High on Role of Women Scale	18	20	29	30	23
High on Political Action Scale	13	18	24	25	18
High on Political Participation	40	39	50	56	44

ment. Thus, urbanization can be seen both as a threat to local community discipline in the moral realm and as a liberation from some of the traditional controls of rural society that prevent needed change, what Harvey Cox called "some of the cloying bondages of preurban society."[8] The urbanized member may well be more open than his rural brother to some of the radical ethical viewpoints that characterized his sixteenth-century Anabaptist forebears. To this question and to other possible differences in religious commitment we now turn.

Religious Orientation Variables. Sociologists of religion have long observed that religion functions differently in urban and rural environments. Urban areas have historically provided the setting for new religious breakthroughs and reformation movements, but rural areas have provided the stronghold for the perpetuation of a religious movement once begun and its transmission from one generation to another.[9] This was the case with the Anabaptist movement, which was born in the city centers of Switzerland but survived in the rural hinterlands.

It is with no small interest, therefore, that we explore the effects of ruralization of Mennonites and BIC upon their religious attitudes and behavior. Table 18-5 shows that urban church members scored slightly lower on scales measuring church and Sunday school attendance, and are less orthodox and "fundamentalistic" in their doctrinal beliefs. On the other hand, they have more interest in ecumenical efforts and are more involved in personal evangelism. Here again, there are contradictory signs of responsibility and irresponsibility concerning the establishment of Christian community in the

TABLE 18-5
Religious Orientation Variables
by Rural-Urban Residence

Religious Orientation Variable	Rural Farm	Rural Nonfarm	Small City	Large City	Total
Percent who scored "high" on:					
Associationalism Scale	17	19	15	14	17
Sunday School Participation Scale	64	65	59	47	60
General Orthodoxy Scale	79	77	74	67	75
Fundamentalist Orthodoxy	48	48	41	31	43
Ecumenism Scale	18	16	21	27	20
Evangelism Scale	11	20	22	16	17
Stewardship Attitudes	22	31	32	30	28
Stewardship Performance	28	26	24	17	24

city. Urban members are in a position to avoid the mistake of confusing rural society with the Christian concept of community, but it is far from clear that they have found more meaningful forms of Christian fellowship in the city. This contradiction is indicated also in their higher scores on the Stewardship Attitudes Scale but lower scores on the Stewardship Performance Scale.

Anabaptism and the Rural-Urban Question. On sabbatical leave from a teaching position, the writer recently had the opportunity to make a pilgrimage to places of early Anabaptist history in Europe, both rural and urban. I went to the village of Pingjum in Friesland where Menno Simons, the local Roman Catholic priest, was so moved by the testimony of roving Anabaptists that he converted to become the "shepherd" of the movement at a time when it might have died because of persecution and decimation of leadership. I went to Zurich where in 1525 the movement had its beginning as the radical wing of the Zwinglian Reformation. I stood on the portico of the Grossmünster Church where the leaders of the Anabaptist schism first became inspired by Zwingli's preaching; and I looked out over the Limmat where Felix Manz was executed by public drowning.

Two scholars[10] working independently with documents related to court trials of early Anabaptists noted their places of residence and occupations and came to similar conclusions that (1) Anabaptism was initially an urban movement, (2) there was no proletarian common denominator in the movement contrary to the claims of other scholars,[11] and (3) the movement was heterogeneous in character with adherents from all social classes and vocations. Both writers puzzled over the shift in the center of gravity from the bourgeois classes of clergy, nobility, university students, and merchants, to the rural peasantry, and with the rise of persecution, to a rural phenomenon with an agricultural type of social organization.[12]

The only exception to the ruralization of Anabaptism in Europe was in the Netherlands, where Mennonites survived in Amsterdam, but even in this part of continental Europe ruralization was the trend. By 1544 Menno Simons was writing to his scattered brethren, "Rent a farm, milk cows, learn a trade if possible, do manual labor as did Paul, and all that which you then fall short of will doubtlessly be given and provided you by pious brethren."[13] This so-called radical wing of the Reformation fled the cities and perpetuated themselves only in small tightly knit agricultural communities in eastern Europe, Poland, Russia, North America, and South America.

The unresolved question is how and why a renewal movement within Protestantism, urban and heterogeneous at birth, turned rural and homogeneous in its transmission. Was the movement by its very nature adapted only to a society that offered the possibility of rural withdrawal? Or was there something peculiar to the sixteenth century which was so hostile to the movement that it was forced to become agrarian to survive and can now effectively return to the city because persecution has ceased?

Among the scholars who have reflected on these questions, two contradictory hypotheses have been presented. The traditional perspective has fostered the "rural life hypothesis" that community agrarianism is an integral part of Mennonite faith and life because it reinforces the central doctrines of nonconformity to the world and nonresistance to inevitable persecution in the world.[14] One scholar, under whose leadership the annual Conference on Mennonite Community Life was founded, expressed this point of view as follows: "Certainly no environment is more favorable for the perpetuation of the nonresistant faith than the rural community; and for this reason the Mennonite churches will do well to keep themselves established in such communities, with a high percentage of their members directly engaged in agriculture."[15]

An alternative "urban life hypothesis" was formulated in the wake of two developments within this community — the movement of members to the city in increasing numbers and the rediscovery of the "Anabaptist vision" and its original urban impetus.[16] This is not to say that movement to the city and renewal of the vision were directly related. These rural people were not prepared to cope with "what the city does to people" as Murray Leiffer described it.[17] Attempts to reestablish Mennonite and BIC congregations in the city were fraught with handicaps. Nevertheless, perceptive leaders in the back-to-the-city movement took note of how certain normative elements of the vision were being denied by rural withdrawal, such as evangelism and prophetic witness to the power centers of the world. The "rural life hypothesis" became less credible upon such deeper reflection. At an important stage of the search for alternatives, another ingroup scholar formulated the urban life hypothesis. "Mennonites must be told simply and bluntly: not everything that is rural is for that reason Christian. . . . If the genius of Anabaptism is the creation and perpetuation of the distinctly religious community, and is thus involved in social heterogeneity, then the urban environment provides a more congenial setting for a vital Anabaptism than does the rural."[18]

The following cross-tabulation of Anabaptism and rural-urban residence provides an empirical test of the rural life and urban life hypotheses defined above — the relationship between normative Anabaptist faith and rural or urban environments:

	Rural Farm	Rural Nonfarm	Small City	Large City	Total
Mean Score on Anabaptism Scale	19.7	20.0	18.5	17.2	19.1

Although there is little difference between the two categories of rural residence, the movement of members to the city does not appear to be conducive to commitment to Anabaptist doctrines.[19] The data which are statistically significant, tend to support the rural life hypothesis rather than the urban life hypothesis.

It is concluded that the rural-urban residence variable is not a powerful predictor of the faith and life variables overall. More precise comparisons in this respect will be given in Chapter 20, but it can be noted here that among fifteen independent variables including age, education, income, socioeconomic status, and ten faith variables, rural-urban residence ranked only 13th in its effect on other variables.

Regional and National Place of Residence

In their historical development, the denominations in this study organized along regional and continental but not national lines. Regional differences as the basis for the organization of district conferences were taken for granted from the start. The various waves of Mennonite migration to North America coincided with various stages of land settlement, and both factors made regional conferences fairly homogeneous. The predominant source of membership for the eastern conferences was "Pennsylvania-German" of early eighteenth century immigration, settled into what is now the urban-industrial region of the eastern seaboard. The mid-American conferences were composed largely of Swiss-South German immigrants of the nineteenth century who settled into the great "corn belt" of the United States. The wheat-growing areas of the Midwest with their dry-farming characteristics were settled largely by the Mennonites from Russia after 1874. The first Mennonite and BIC settlers in Canada came from the United States, the eastern and central immigrants moving to Ontario and the midwestern settlers to Manitoba and Saskatchewan. Regional conferences were formed in these provinces also. The idea of forming conferences along national lines divided by the border between the United States and Canada was slow to emerge.

The fact that most of the institutional headquarters of these continental denominations were south of the border was also taken for granted — conference offices, publishing houses, colleges, and seminaries. It has been only in the past few years that Canadian members have begun to protest ways in which these institutional programs developed roles, expectations, and identities that were national (American) rather than continental (American and Canadian) in character. In one denomination (the MBC), this growing national awareness resulted in the formation of parallel conferences along national lines, and there are similar pressures in the GCMC also. The main argument for such reorganization is what Frank Epp described as "an unequal structural yoke tied to dissimilar [national] psychological expectations.[20] By this he meant that members inevitably reflect a national as well as a regional and continental character, and a denominational reorganization should reflect the tri-level identity.

The assumption that the national identity is as great among members as the regional identity can be tested with the survey data of the present study. This was done by re-tabulating all of the scales and controlling simultaneously for regional and national places of residence to determine which seems to have the greater influence. But first, let us examine the answers to a general question on the subject, worded as follows: "There appears to be some tendency for American and Canadian church conferences and boards to develop increasing national identity and separate programs, with decreasing joint activity across national boundaries. Assuming such a tendency exists, do you tend to favor it or disfavor it?" We note in Table 18-6 that the majority of members are uncertain about this issue. Among the minority who have an opinion, nearly three times as many members disfavor increasing national identity as favor it. The EMC, 14% of whose members favor increasing national identity, has no membership in Canada. The BIC Canadian membership is confined to Ontario and shows the least desire to increase identity along national lines. Otherwise, the MBC, which has already moved to national conference structures, shows the greatest national identity; but even in this group, over half of the members are uncertain about this trend.

TABLE 18-6
Attitude Toward Increasing National Conference Identity

Response	MC	GCMC	MBC	BIC	EMC	Total
"I favor it"	12	11	14	10	14	12
"I disfavor it"	33	34	32	35	24	33
"I am undecided"	55	55	54	55	62	55
Total	100	100	100	100	100	100
Number of Respondents	1,173	596	699	604	431	3,503

For a further analysis of the issue, the members were divided into four national-regional categories: *USA East, USA West, Canada East* and *Canada West.* The dividing line between USA East and USA West is roughly the border between Pennsylvania and Ohio, and the border between Ontario and Manitoba is the division between Canada East and Canada West.

Table 18-7 summarizes the cross-tabulations between this regional-national classification and thirty-three scales with which the classification had a significant relationship.[21] If the national difference between *Total USA* and *Total Canada* exceeded the regional difference between *Canada East* and *Canada West* for each scale, there is a plus sign (+) in the last column. We note, for example, that the percentage (34) of members who reside on a farm is identical for the USA and Canada, while the percentage varies from 29 to 37 between the two Canadian regions, making the national difference smaller than the regional.

It turns out that for 18 out of 33 scales, the national differences are smaller than for the regional differences within Canada; for 14 of the 33, the national differences are larger. When the four regions are ranked from high (1) to low (4) for each scale, the overall average ranks are Canadian West *first,* USA East *second,* USA West *third,* and Canadian East *fourth.* Five of the scales follow this pattern and others approximate it.

Moreover, for 20 out of 33 scales, the national differences are the same or smaller than the regional differences within the USA. This greater variation between the USA regions than between the Canadian regions is probably related to the fact that most of the pressure for reorganizing along national lines is coming from the Canadian side of the border.

These figures indicate that the case for national conferences is less compelling than the case for regional conferences. The differences among Canadian members themselves between East and West are considerable for such variables as Voluntarism, Moral-Personal Conversion, Devotionalism, Orthodoxy, Social Concerns, Political Participation, and the Role of Women; and it would appear on these issues that many Canadian West members would find more in common with US East members than with their fellow-Canadians of the East.

Compared to the factors of age, education, and socioeconomic status discussed in the previous two chapters, the variables of

TABLE 18-7
Scale Score Differences by National and Regional Residence

Designated Scale	USA East	USA West	Total USA	Can. East	Can. West	Total Can.	National Difference*
	(mean scores unless otherwise indicated)						
Social Background Variables:							
Percent farm residents	35	34	34	29	37	34	−
Median Age	37.2	42.9	40.9	40.8	41.8	41.5	−
Median school yrs. completed	12.1	12.5	12.4	10.8	11.5	11.2	+
Percent "professional" occup.	33	25	28	37	24	29	−
Median annual income (dollars)	8530	10177	10240	8908	7829	8271	+
Faith Variables:							
Associationalism	4.1	3.8	3.9	3.4	3.9	3.7	−
Voluntarism	5.4	5.5	5.5	5.9	6.7	6.4	+
Communalism	3.4	3.1	3.2	3.4	3.5	3.5	+
Percent having initial conv.	80	76	77	79	88	84	−
Moral-Personal Conversion	6.9	6.6	6.7	6.7	7.2	7.0	−
Devotionalism	4.1	3.9	4.0	3.9	4.8	4.4	−
General Orthodoxy	25.2	24.9	25.0	25.1	25.5	25.3	−
Fundamentalist Orthodoxy	18.1	17.2	17.5	17.4	18.1	17.8	−
Anabaptism	23.0	21.0	21.7	22.1	22.5	22.3	+
Moral-Ethical Variables:							
Moral Attitudes	23.0	21.9	22.2	22.1	22.9	22.6	−
Moral Behavior	7.1	6.7	6.8	6.1	6.7	6.5	−
Race Relations	7.3	6.8	7.0	7.3	7.2	7.2	+
Anti-Semitism	1.3	1.2	1.2	1.4	1.6	1.5	+
Anti-Catholic	1.3	1.2	1.2	1.3	1.4	1.4	+
Anti-Communism	3.9	3.7	3.8	3.7	3.5	3.6	o
Social Concerns	3.4	3.6	3.6	3.5	2.9	3.2	−
Welfare Attitudes	3.2	3.1	3.1	2.8	3.1	3.0	−
Separation of Church & State	6.2	5.4	5.7	5.0	5.3	5.2	+
Political Participation	4.9	7.1	6.3	6.8	7.9	7.5	+
Political Action	1.7	3.0	2.6	2.4	2.7	2.6	−
Work of the Church Variables:							
Shared Ministry	6.9	6.8	6.9	6.5	6.4	6.4	+
Role of Women	1.8	2.3	2.1	2.1	1.6	1.8	−
Stewardship Attitudes	7.4	7.4	7.4	7.3	7.6	7.5	−
Stewardship Performance	2.6	2.6	2.6	2.5	2.7	2.6	−
Sunday School Participation	9.5	9.0	9.2	8.0	8.5	8.3	+
Ecumenism	9.6	10.5	10.2	10.8	10.8	10.8	+
Support of Church Colleges	6.3	6.1	6.2	5.9	6.4	6.2	−
Support of MCC	4.8	5.0	4.9	4.7	4.6	4.6	+

*National difference greater (+) or smaller (-) than regional difference *with Canada*, or the same (o)

residence explored in this chapter are not very significant overall in their association with matters of faith, ethics, and church work. The chief concern of the remaining chapters will be to discern whether denominational affiliation and assent to the Anabaptist vision are relatively more significant in their influence on these church members.

Chapter **19**

DENOMINATIONAL PATTERNS OF FAITH AND LIFE

The preceding eighteen chapters reported the average scores of church members on numerous scales. Eleven of the scales pertained to dimensions of their faith, thirteen to moral and ethical attitudes and behavior, and ten to involvement in the work of the church.

In this chapter, the patterning of these scales by the five denominations will be described first in comparison to each other and then in comparison to other denominations. In Chapter 20, the scales themselves — including the social background variables of age, education, income, and urbanization — will be intercorrelated in the search for the key factors that explain the faith and ethics of the Mennonite and BIC churches.

Secularization Theories of Denominational Position

The historical interpretation of the five denominations in Chapter 2 examined the distinctive patterns of development and adaptation to the North American environment. In that connection the concept of "secularization" was mentioned as supplying one interpretation of these denominational patterns in relation to each other.

Robert Friedmann used this concept to contrast the MC, "the guardian proper of the tradition of the fathers," with the GCMC, "the way of adjustment and greater conformity to the general pattern of American Protestantism . . . a way toward full secularization and loss of substance."[1]

Employing similar concepts of a "secularization process" and a "conservative-liberal continuum," John A. Hostetler put the MC in the " 'middle of the road' position among about twenty 'species' of Mennonites."[2] In his study of membership gains and losses in the MC, he discovered that by far the largest source of new members was the Old Order Amish and similar Mennonite groups "more traditional in religious practices than the Mennonite Church." He also found that the destination of nearly all ex-members of the MC who remain in this family of churches was "other Mennonite denominations which are more liberal in religious practices than the Mennonite Church." Among those Hostetler included on the more liberal side were the GCMC, BIC, and EMC.

Elmer and Phyllis Martens employed this same scheme in the interpretation of the MBC. "In matters of culture and dress," they wrote, "Brethren stand perhaps midway between the Old Mennonites and General Conference; organs and an occasional orchestra in church services are OK, but members don't altogether approve when the young people decide to put on Shakespeare."[3]

Before these interpretations are tested with the survey data of the present study, the fuller implications of the secularization and conservatism-liberalism concepts must be explored.

Sect-Cycle Theory. One way to talk about denominational position is by the concept of stages in the so-called re-entry or re-assimilation of sectarian groups into the mainstream of society. The "sect," according to Park and Burgess,[4] typically emerges as a schism from a "church," and then progressively moves back toward the church-type as accommodations are effected. Karl Baehr applied this concept to Mennonites as follows:

> Stage *one* is the conflict which first drives the sect into isolation, to escape persecution. Farming becomes the chief occupation of members because it provides a maximum of self-sufficiency and a minimum of contact with the hostile world. The sect becomes a closed community, characterized by distinctive

dress, in-group marriage, and other devices.

Stage *two* is the cessation of overt conflict and the granting of formal religious freedom. Contact with the out-group is cautious, and comes primarily through the purchase and sale of commercial products.

In stage *three*, contact between the sect and society becomes more frequent. Through hard work and frugality and the peace that toleration brings, members become prosperous and begin to adapt their style to the ways of those around them.

Stage *four* is marked by differentiation within the sect between the conservatives, who fear the loss of the community's sacred values and want to enforce the old ways, and the liberals, who advocate change. There is also a new division between the "haves" and the "have-nots," and the former begin to deal with the latter according to the economic principles (rent, interest, mortgage, wages, foreclosures) of the larger society.

The *fifth* stage is the splintering of the sect, so that its variant groups, all claiming the same original label, contain all shadings along a continuum from withdrawal to accommodation. The most liberal group cannot be distinguished from the larger society, except by name. The moderate group retains some distinctives from the world but finds the doctrine of nonconformity increasingly difficult to preserve. The conservative group maintains the old ways through strict discipline and the practice of excommunication.[5]

In the sect-cycle theory, as in all secularization concepts, contact with the outside world is identified as the beginning of adverse change within the group. In fact, most ingroup scholars who use these terms identify culture-borrowing *per se* with secularization and loss of original and sacred norms.[6] In so doing, however, they usually overlook the fact that the Anabaptist movement was not borne from heaven but was itself in large part the product of cultural diffusion. A more precise definition of terms is therefore needed in order to analyze the data of the present chapter.

Cultural Diffusion. Diffusion is the process by which cultural traits and values are spread from one individual or group to another, for better or for worse. It can be the source of a group's renewal or the cause of its decline. In either case diffusion is inevitable because people are universally interdependent and cultural contact therefore unavoidable.[7] Although cultural borrowing moves more often from the majority group to the minority, it often occurs in the other direction. The words of Jesus to His followers, "You are the salt of the earth" (Mt. 5:13), was a counsel concerning cultural diffusion.

In the process of cultural diffusion, the minimal adjustment of two or more individuals or groups is known as *accommodation*. When one group borrows cultural traits or tools from another, that is *acculturation*. When in addition, the group adopts the basic values underlying those cultural traits, that is *assimilation*. *Secularization* refers to the exchange of sacred for profane values — the church's assimilation of the "world," defined theologically as a profane social reality fallen from the creative purposes of God.`

Assimilation does not inevitably follow accommodation or acculturation, nor does it necessarily lead to secularization. It does so only if the values adopted require ethical compromise on the part of the church. In his study of cultural diffusion among Mennonites, Calvin Redekop observed that some types of acculturation lead to assimilation and secularization, others do not. The borrowing of agricultural tools, he believes, is an example of acculturation without assimilation, but the adoption of educational methods usually leads to some assimilation and secularization. Whether it will do so depends, he adds, on whether the techniques or values adopted through education are compatible with historic Anabaptist norms. The adoption of a voluntary service program for young people has included some degree of assimilation, requiring personal identification and not merely contact with other cultures; but in the main the program has reinforced Mennonite identity and provided a new expression of the Anabaptist vision.[9]

Like Redekop, E. K. Francis observed many indications of acculturation among the Mennonites of Manitoba which had not led to any significant assimilation or secularization. He explained this by citing "a core of religious principles and practices which differentiates all branches of the Mennonite church from non-Mennonite religious bodies and . . . draws them together, once the chips are down."[10]

Rank Order of Denominations

The secularization theories defined above can be tested in two ways with the data of the present study. The validity of the sect-cycle theory can be gauged by examining the rank order of the five denominations along every scale to discern whether there is a pattern of location, whether that pattern conforms to the expectancy, and whether it does so consistently. According to the writings of Friedmann, Hostetler, Baehr, and others, one would expect the MC to rank at one end of the scale, the GCMC at the other end, and the other three groups in between.

The deeper question of whether or not cultural diffusion leads to loss of faith (secularization) requires specification of the direction of each scale in relation to the Anabaptist vision. The summary of data in the present chapter will be limited primarily to the prior issue of rank order *position*. The deeper question of the *direction* of that position in relation to Anabaptist norms. will be discussed in the next chapter.

In Table 19-1 the five denominations have been ranked for each of thirty-four scales. The denomination having the highest mean score for each scale was ranked in first position, and so forth. The size of the contingency coefficients in the last column indicate that the differences associated with denomination are significant. They are greater on the average than the differences associated with education, income, or urbanization, but not as great as the differences associated with age.

Rank Order on Faith Variables. In the upper portion of Table 19-1, the five denominations are ranked on eleven faith variables. In several respects the patterns conform to what one would have expected on the basis of the historical interpretations in Chapter 2. The MC, the "guardian of the tradition of the fathers," ranked first on the Anabaptist vision scale. The GCMC, characterized as the most intentionally progressive, appears to be the most secularized, in conformity to its image in the other groups, ranking fifth on seven out of the eleven scales. Two notable exceptions are its second rank on voluntarism (the degree to which church participation is free and uncoerced) and its first rank on ethical-social conversion. In view of the prominent place given to ethics by the sixteenth-century Anabaptists, as well as to voluntarism, these are curious findings that bear watching as we move into the deeper analysis.

TABLE 19-1

Rank Order of Denominations on Scales

Variables	High Rank 1	2	3	4	Low Rank 5	Cont. Coeff.
The Variables of Faith						
Anabaptism	MC	MBC	BIC	GCMC	EMC	.291
Initial Conversion	MBC	BIC	EMC	MC	GCMC	.260
Communalism	MC	MBC	GCMC	BIC	EMC	.235
Fundamentalist Orthodoxy	EMC	MBC	BIC	MC	GCMC	.231
Voluntarism	MBC	GCMC	EMC	BIC	MC	.223
General Orthodoxy	EMC	MBC	BIC	MC	GCMC	.206
Associationalism	BIC	EMC	MBC	MC	GCMC	.167
Sanctification	EMC	BIC	MBC	MC	GCMC	.141
Devotionalism	MBC	BIC	EMC	MC	GCMC	.135
Ethical-Social Conversion	GCMC	MC	EMC	BIC	MBC	.125
Moral-Personal Conversion	MBC	EMC	MC	BIC	GCMC	.094
Average Rank and Contingency	MBC	EMC	BIC	MC	GCMC	.192
The Variables of Ethics						
Political Participation*	MC	BIC	EMC	MBC	GCMC	.454
Pacifism	MC	GCMC	BIC	MBC	EMC	.428
Political Action*	MC	BIC	EMC	MBC	GCMC	.401
Anti-Communism*	MC	GCMC	BIC	MBC	EMC	.318
Social Concerns	GCMC	MC	BIC	EMC	MBC	.293
Anti-Labor Union	MC	BIC	MBC	GCMC	EMC	.278
Moral Behavior	BIC	MBC	MC	EMC	GCMC	.204
Moral Attitudes	BIC	MBC	EMC	MC	GCMC	.196
Welfare Attitudes	GCMC	MC	MBC	BIC	EMC	.182
Anti-Semitism*	GCMC	MC	BIC	EMC	MBC	.176
Anti-Catholicism*	GCMC	MC	BIC	MBC	EMC	.162
Church-State Separation	BIC	EMC	MC	MBC	GCMC	.164
Race Relations	MC	GCMC	BIC	MBC	EMC	.138
Average Rank and Contingency	MC	BIC	GCMC	MBC	EMC	.261
The Work of the Church Variables						
Stewardship Attitudes	BIC	EMC	MBC	MC	GCMC	.247
Sunday School Participation	EMC	BIC	MC	MBC	GCMC	.210
Role of Women	GCMC	BIC	MC	EMC	MBC	.198
Ecumenism	GCMC	MBC	MC	BIC	EMC	.190
MCC Support	GCMC	MC	BIC	MBC	EMC	.189
Shared Ministry	MC	GCMC	BIC	MBC	EMC	.166
Support of Church Colleges	MBC	BIC	MC	EMC	GCMC	.147
Evangelism	BIC	MBC	EMC	MC	GCMC	.139
Stewardship Performance	MBC	EMC	BIC	MC	GCMC	.126
Bible Knowledge	MBC	BIC	MC	GCMC	EMC	.117
Average Rank and Contingency	BIC	MBC	MC	GCMC	EMC	.173

Note: Rankings are based on mean scores on each scale, except for the unscaled Initial Conversion classification, for which the percentage of members answering "Yes" to the experience of conversion question is used. The mean scores for these scales were reported in earlier tables. Ties, which occurred infrequently, were broken by using additional decimal places. The contingency coefficient is a measure of the degree of association between the two variables (denomination and scale). Scales marked with an asterisk (*) have ranking reversed (low to high).

The first ranking of the MBC on four out of eleven faith variables reflects its restorationist self-image and historic concern "to return to Menno and the Scriptures." The tendency of the BIC to find the "golden mean" along these faith dimensions reflects its historic concern for synthesis and balance. The uneasy, largely unsuccessful search for synthesis in the EMC is reflected in its high scores on orthodoxy and low score on Anabaptism.

Although the correspondence between the survey data and the historical profiles is reasonably close, the average rank of the groups on the variables of faith overall do not exactly verify the sect-cycle theory of denominational position as earlier interpreted. Friedmann and others would not have been prepared for the fact that the group that emerges as second most "liberal" overall (4th rank) is the MC, notwithstanding its historic convervatism. It appears that the cultural gap between the MC and GCMC is closing fast and that they have more in common with each other than with any other group, as indicated by the fact that in seven out of eleven faith variables the two groups are positioned side by side.

Table 19-1 also provides the first empirically controlled test of Elmer and Phyllis Martens' guess that the MBC stands midway between the "conservative" MC and the "liberal" GCMC. Although they were referring more to moral-ethical and work of the church variables than to the dimensions of faith, on the eleven faith variables their theory holds for only two scales: communalism and Anabaptism. On the other nine dimensions the MBC is positioned at the end of a linear relationship to MC and GCMC.

Rank Order of Moral and Ethical Variables. As the middle of Table 19-1 shows, when compared with the top, the denominations differed more widely on the moral and ethical scales (overall average contingency of .261) than on the faith variables (.192 average contingency). That may indicate that "discipleship" in the historic Anabaptist sense of moral and ethical behavior is more difficult for the church member to integrate into his life than are the explicit acts of piety and belief.[11] The MBC and EMC, which were in first and second positions on the faith scales overall, moved to fourth and fifth positions on the moral and ethical scales.

Eight times out of thirteen, the MC and GCMC rank side by side in their ethics, as they did on the faith variables. They are in first and second positions on pacifism, poverty welfare concerns, social concerns, interracial tolerance, and the rejection of anti-Communism, anti-Semitism, and anti-Catholic attitudes. They are least strict with respect to moral attitudes, a finding that may surprise some MC readers. On the moral behavior scale, however, the two groups part company, the GCMC remaining in fifth position. It is only on the political action of the church, the political participation of the member, and the anti-labor union dimensions that the MC and GCMC are on opposite ends of the scale, thus reflecting their more "traditional" images.

Rank Order on Work of the Church Variables. The five denominations vary least in their average scores on the work of the church scales (mean coefficient of .173 at the bottom of Table 19-1). Nevertheless, the scale differences between them were all significant (P < .01) except for the biblical knowledge scale (.01 < P < .03).

The BIC and MBC have achieved the highest overall participation of members in the work of the church according to the ten indicators listed. The GCMC was either in first or fifth position eight times out of ten. It was in first position on support of Mennonite Central Committee, support of women's rights in the work of the church, and ecumenism. These are hardly the positions one would assign on the basis of a sect-cycle theory without attempting to untangle the deeper issues in the relation between acculturation and recommitment to Anabaptist norms.

Doctrinal Norms. The ambiguities which a secularization theory leaves unexplained can be specified by examining one scale from each of the three groupings in Table 19-1. At first glance, the position of the GCMC on the General Orthodoxy Scale seems to fit its liberal image. It has not invested much time and talent in the writing of confessions of faith. Its motto has been "unity in essentials, freedom in non-essentials, and love in all things." The "unity in essentials" part of that formula was confined to one paragraph in the group's written constitution and referred to the teachings of Menno and the Anabaptists, the way of love and non-resistance, and the lordship of Jesus Christ, the Son of God.

The MC has worked harder at the task of defining its doctrines in detail, and has formally written and adopted two confessions of faith in the twentieth century in keeping with H. S. Bender's plea, "We must have . . . a clearly thought out and consistent theological line, not a mixture of confused theologies borrowed from groups and movements."[12] A direct result of its doctrinal formulation of 1921, in the heat of the fundamentalist-modernist controversy, was the transfer to the GCMC of twelve congregations and fifteen ministers.[13] Today, however, this earlier image of the MC as the conservative wing of the movement that excommunicates its liberals is no longer supported by the facts. One finds about as much dissent expressed and welcomed at general assemblies of the MC as at general conferences of the GCMC. In the data of the present study, the MC ranks first in adherence to the Anabaptist vision but fourth in doctrinal orthodoxy.

The MBC ranked second in orthodoxy, being significantly more conservative in its doctrinal norms than the MC. In their recent appraisal of the MBC, Elmer and Phyllis Martens wrote that "theologically, there are emerging tensions between individual Brethren with more liberal views and the orthodox majority. If ethics was the problem of the sixties, theology may well be the problem of the seventies."[14] The MBC stands, not midway between the MC and GCMC as they had supposed, but clearly on one side of the conflict, for these battles have long been waged in the other two groups, both of which have achieved a certain mediating stance beyond the point of impending crisis.

It has not yet been discerned, of course, whether this mediating stance in the MC is a kind of liberal toleration that comes from living in a pluralistic society whose values have been assimilated and exchanged for rigorous commitment, or whether it represents a genuine desire to keep human formulations of doctrine secondary to a sound biblical faith, "profiting from the best that comes to us from the outside, rejecting the harmful, moving forward in our witness and ministry in accord with God's historic purpose for us since 1525."[15]

Behavioral Norms. On the question of moral attitudes and behavior the MC has usually specified by corporate disciplinary process the actions of members that are approved or censured; and in its official statement on Christian separation and nonconformity to the world (1955), those norms prohibited attendance at movie theaters, smoking, drinking, and dancing. The GCMC has been more reluctant to prescribe moral behavior and has given freedom to the member to work out his own style of life on the principle that "each believer stands before God Himself in faith as a free individual, uncoerced by other believers."[16]

Today, on the Moral Attitudes Scale, the MC and GCMC stand together in fourth and fifth rank, while the MBC ranks second for restrictiveness. MBC writings show that this group is struggling to maintain taboos against smoking, drinking, dancing, and card-playing. Elders like A. E. Janzen and J. H. Quiring teach and write with the purpose of transmitting these norms to their youth,[17] while younger leaders protest the rigidity with which this has been done in the past. "For years," write Elmer and Phyllis Martens, "the defining of sin, or sins, was something of a conference pastime. . . . A long and changeable list of things to avoid was the frequent result. The circus, theater, county fair, life insurance, radio, television, movies, square dancing, cutting of women's hair, and lipstick all made the blacklist at one time or another."[18] A new policy adopted at MBC General Conference in 1969 says that the church will "continue to set guidelines to assist all members to walk before the Lord in holiness and truth" but that the church "will not consider the guidelines once laid down as binding for all times."[19] This was clearly meant to be a mediating position and was so identified by its authors.

Is the trend in all of these groups to assimilate the ways of the world and exchange profane values for those that were once sacred? The variables will have to be further intercorrelated and analyzed before it is possible to speculate about that; but it is already evident that the concept of a secularization ladder among these groups is no longer tenable in the way it was once defined.

Ecumenical Norms. On the face of it, the denominational mean scores on the Ecumenism Scale conformed to the sect-cycle expectancy more than those on the scales of doctrinal orthodoxy and moral attitudes. The historic GCMC concern for interchurch and inter-Mennonite cooperation was indicated by its first rank on the Ecumenism Scale. The MC has been rather more cautious in its steps toward cooperative ventures, which, Grant Stoltzfus writes, "have often been difficult and seemingly dangerous to the unity, identity, and ongoing life of the Mennonite Church."[20] Its significantly lower mean score on the Ecumenism Scale (third rank) correctly gauged this contrast in ecumenical attitudes, and is reflected also in the practice of "close communion" in the MC (reserved for members only) and open communion in the GCMC (visiting Christians are welcome to participate).

The second rank position of the MBC between the GCMC and MC does not fully represent its ecumenical stance. A reexamination of the MBC responses to the six questions that made up the scale reported in Chapter 15 reveal that the MBC scored higher than the MC on the "interdenominational" questions but considerably lower on the "inter-Mennonite" questions. In its withdrawal from mainstream Mennonitism, the MBC has exhibited as great an affinity with various non-Mennonite groups like the Baptists as with other Mennonite groups, and some members would like to drop the name Mennonite.[21]

By now, this selective ecumenical point of view is rather alien to the other two groups, both of whom are committed to retain their name, renew its normative meaning, and work together except insofar as deep differences of history or conviction compel them to work separately. They have come to reject the earlier "break-to-be-faithful" principle,[22] and there is considerable consensus on both sides that the 1847 schism that first divided them was regrettable. Members know that the risk of cooperation is the assimilation of worldly values, but they prefer to resist secularization by the new strategy of cooperation rather than by the old strategy of withdrawal.[23]

Comparison to American Denominations

The patterns of faith and ethics in the five denominations can be summarized in two ways. One way, just concluded above, is to compare them to each other, ranking them from high to low along each scale. The other way, the focus of the present section, is to compare them to American denominations generally as gauged by other church-member studies. The first approach highlighted their differences. The present approach will highlight their similarities in contrast to Catholics, Protestants, and Jews, insofar as comparable data are available.

In previous chapters, the reader will recall, a number of such comparisons were made when each new scale was first presented. The measures used for these comparisons were not always identical, but they were usually sufficiently close in content to provide reliable assessments. This was the case for seven of the faith variables and seven of the moral-ethical and work-of-the-church variables.

Table 19-2 presents the authors' ratings of the five denominations on the basis of a review of these comparisons. The groups as a whole (and individually, with only six exceptions) scored high on all seven of the faith variables, when compared with Protestants and Catholics in the Glock and Stark national sample, with Protestants, Catholics, and Jews in Lenski's Detroit sample, or with other church-member samples cited throughout the study.[24]

The five groups scored generally high also on the scales of moral attitudes, race relations, Bible knowledge, and stewardship performance. Only two exceptions to this trend could be identified. One pertained to the personal evangelism scale, on which one group must be rated low and another medium in comparison to three Lutheran bodies studied by Strommen and associates. Moreover, three of the groups must be rated as more anti-Semitic and

TABLE 19-2

Ratings of Five Denominations on Scales When Compared to Other American Denominations

Variables	MC	GCMC	MBC	BIC	EMC	TOTAL
Associationalism	High	Medium	High	High	High	High
Communalism	High	High	High	High	Medium	High
Initial Conversion	High	Medium	High	High	High	High
Sanctification	High	Medium	High	High	High	High
Devotionalism	High	High	High	High	High	High
General Orthodoxy	High	Medium	High	High	High	High
Anabaptist Vision	High	High	High	High	Medium	High
Race Relations	High	High	High	High	Medium	High
Anti-Semitism*	Medium	Medium	Low	Low	Low	Medium
Anti-Catholicism*	Medium	Medium	Low	Low	Low	Medium
Moral Attitudes	High	Medium	High	High	High	High
Stewardship Performance	High	High	High	High	High	High
Personal Evangelism	Medium	Low	High	High	High	Medium
Bible Knowledge	High	High	High	High	High	High

*Scale reversed so that "low" means highly anti-Semitic or anti-Catholic.

anti-Catholic than four Lutheran bodies studies by Lawrence Kersten.

Apart from these exceptions, the five groups present an obvious "unity" of high level faith commitment and ethical response. Stark and Glock made a similar observation but were at a loss to explain it. An unknown number of Mennonites fell into their national sample, and they were totaled with the members of the Assemblies of God, Church of Christ, Church of God, and similar groups under the label "sects." On their scales the sects scored highest of any denomination on orthodoxy, highest on ritual involvement, second highest on devotionalism, second highest on religious experience, highest on religious knowledge, highest on particularism, second highest on communal involvement, and highest on ethicalism. The researchers were so surprised to discover the sects to be high on ethicalism when on all other indexes they "behaved like other conservatives," that they simply wrote them off with the comment, "The answer lay in their unselectivity on the criteria of salvation. A reexamination of sect members' responses to the salvation items reveals that for all practical purposes these people think everything bears on salvation."[25]

This judgment, while true empirically, fails to explain the sectarian scores in any meaningful way. Given the classical sociological definition of sect, these otherwise knowledgeable researchers should not have been surprised at the high sectarian scores on ethicalism. As Benton Johnson points out, the sect type is "an association of ethical virtuosos who attempt to realize in their own conduct the principles in terms of which they are united."[26] Any attempt to understand the religious behavior of a group like the Mennonites will have to take the process of ethical justification more seriously than do Stark and Glock.

It will also have to go beyond the sect-cycle theory, as the present chapter has pointed out. While some aspects of that behavior, such as liberal doctrine, ecumenical attitudes, and permissive morals, can be understood in terms of cultural contact and perhaps also secularization, other aspects which may be more significant for ethical rigor cannot be explained in these terms. "What is needed now in this field," Johnson concluded, "is an understanding of how particular kinds of ethical belief systems affect the overall structure and development potential of sects."[27]

It is to that analysis, with particular references to Mennonites and Brethren in Christ, that we finally turn. In their comparatively high scores on most indices of religious faith and behavior, are they simply behaving like other religious conservatives in America as Stark and Glock thought? Or does their faith produce consequences that are unique to the Anabaptist heritage out of which they come?

Chapter 20

THE SEARCH FOR THE
KEY FACTORS

The church members have been affected by many influences from outside of their groups. They have been influenced not just by urbanization, higher education, greater income, and shifting youth cultures, but the very forms of their faith and involvements in the church have been modified by styles of piety and methodology borrowed from various religious currents in the environment. For example, the GCMC was particularly influenced by the American ecumenical movement, the BIC by the American holiness movement, and all five groups by the American fundamentalist movement.

The authors' way of studying this aspect of Mennonite and Brethren in Christ reality was to treat church membership as a *dependent variable*, especially in Chapters 16-18. The school of thought which interprets religion as a dependent institution ranges from Emile Durkheim, who saw religious rituals to be only a reflection of the social struggle for survival;[1] to H. Richard Niebuhr, who saw American denominations to be the reflection both of the kingdom of God and social struggles of many kinds — national, racial, sectional, ethnic, and economic.[2] Even those who reject the thesis that religion is only a reflection of social needs can read Durkheim and Niebuhr for many helpful insights into how social forces shape its forms and expressions.

In Chapters 19 and 20, the focus shifts to the question of faith as an *independent factor* — reflecting the claim of sociologists like Max Weber[3] and Gerhard Lenski[4] that religion is an "intervening" and "autonomous" influence in society. These terms are placed in quotation marks because they are regarded as separate levels of the independent influence of religion. On the lower level of "intervention," Durkheim's assumption that persons are religious for socially conditioned reasons is accepted; but it is observed that once a person becomes a member of a religious group, his membership intervenes to become a new form of social conditioning that affects his life in a way that those who are not members are not affected. On the higher level of influence, Durkheim's assumption is rejected and it is claimed that church membership is "autonomous" of natural forces in its influence upon the member and upon society.

The present chapter will test both levels of influence of faith as an independent variable. On the lower level, certain of the faith variables may have consequences (anti-Semitism, racial prejudice, provincial outlook, etc.) that are not different from what would be expected on the basis of natural forces and social conditioning. On the higher level of influence, faith may have consequences (compassion for underprivileged peoples, universal outlook, etc.) that are different from what one would predict on the basis of social conditioning and that are thus truly autonomous influences in the lives of church members.

As stated in Chapter 1, the overarching theses of the present study are (1) that among the dimensions of faith at work in the lives of the respondents, assent to the Anabaptist vision ranks near the top as an independent influence and (2) that the influence of this vision moves in the direction of transforming life in keeping with biblical norms and thus is autonomous of class or nationalistic values in society.

Anabaptist Vision and Mennonite Reality

In testing these theses with the survey data the authors will be addressing a current debate in the Mennonite family of churches concerning the correlation between what has been termed "Mennonite reality" and "Anabaptist vision." The first of these terms refers to the present patterns of religiosity and ethics in the churches whose members have been studied. The second term refers not primarily to a sixteenth-century episode permanently canonized as the model for later generations but to a transcendent vision of what it means to be authentically Christian.

H. S. Bender, whose definition of this vision formed the basis for the attempt to measure it reported in Chapter 6, believed optimistically that

> American Mennonitism on the whole is still sound at the core, has to a large extent recovered its sense of connection with its great past, has developed a large capacity for self-criticism and understanding of its own problems and needs, and in general has a good balance of faith and works, inner experience and evangelistic outreach and witnessing. It has retained much of the essence of its historic Anabaptist-Mennonite faith, and is learning how to correct its own aberrations and accumulated deficiencies.[3]

This reference to "Anabaptist-Mennonite" as though these terms were synonymous typifies this side of the debate.

On the other side, John H. Yoder, whose writings have also been quoted frequently in this study, has come to the conclusion that "Anabaptist vision" and "Mennonite reality" are not only in considerable discontinuity, but that they are in certain structural aspects incompatible.

> So what we have is not an Anabaptist community when measured by the criteria which we have stated. It is rather a small *Christendom*. . . . Mennonitism still finds its identity most properly on the ethnic community level. . . . Precisely because the language of Anabaptism has so long been used as a reinforcement of Mennonite self-confidence, the Mennonite population is now refractory beyond the average to the Anabaptist message, having been, as it were, vaccinated. Mennonites are less avid in asking to see the novelty of the Anabaptist witness than are Christians of other kinds of backgrounds. This is no reproach; they are struggling to overcome a conception of their inherited distinctness and separateness which is neither biblical nor viable in the modern world or the modern church. But what we are trying to test now is not whether this observation gives reason to scold someone. The question is whether it is

into the root stock of the heirs of Mennonite culture that God is most likely to be able to engraft the new radical reformation reality which is His will for the modern world.[6]

These two ingroup scholars subjectively assessed the condition of the same community of faith in the light of its historic norms and drew opposite conclusions. With their arguments in the background, along with the old controversy in social theory about religion as a dependent or independent variable, we now bring to a climax this audacious effort to test the truth of the matter with scientifically collected data.

Selective Review of Methodology

One of the difficult methodological problems in testing reality is the theoretical and operational definition of terms. Specifically, in this study it is the question of the validity of our scales and whether they actually measure what they are supposed to measure. The careful reader knows by this time what questions went into each scale, or at least he knows that he can look back and review their operational definitions. In this final analysis he will have to judge for himself whether the scales seem valid and the findings convincing, although one additional caveat will be added toward the end of this chapter. We turn now to a review of the methods by which answers have been sought to the basic question of identity in this study.

One method was to compare present respondents with other samples of church members to ascertain whether they are significantly different and different in the predicted direction; i.e., to test John H. Yoder's claim that "Mennonites are less avid in asking to see the novelty of the Anabaptist witness than are Christians of other kinds of backgrounds." This method was used insofar as comparisons were possible, and it was discovered, as reported in the previous chapter, that on Anabaptism and six other faith scales, the present sample of members as a whole scored significantly higher than members of alternative denominational systems. The comparisons were inconclusive, however, on whether these differences could be interpreted as direct consequences of these alternative commitments or whether Mennonites and Brethren in Christ were simply behaving like other evangelical conservatives with or without an Anabaptist orientation.

Another method was to compare the five groups with each other according to some prediction about which has been most faithful and which least faithful to the normative position and whether there is a significant difference in scale scores and in the predicted direction. This was also attempted in the previous chapter and, again, yielded uncertain results. The MC stands closest to the vision on one scale (Anabaptism) and farthest on another (voluntarism). The GCMC is positioned farthest up the secularization ladder on numerous scales but is most loyal to the implementation of the vision on others (support of MCC, social concerns, etc.). The MBC ranked first in Bible knowledge but last in social concerns. The BIC was highest on personal evangelism and fourth on the communal qualities of the faith. The EMC scored first on orthodoxy and fifth on Anabaptist vision. With these ambiguities, the method of rank position was questionable indeed.

In the final analysis to follow, the method most appropriate was to intercorrelate the scales and to report which ones emerge as the best predictors of the behavior and attitudes of church members and to search in this way for the key factors in Mennonite and Brethren in Christ reality.

For the sake of narrowing the search, the scales qualifying as predictors were limited to the ten faith scales and five social background scales. The main focus, of course, will be on the faith variables, and especially on the Anabaptist Scale. But the best gauge of the influence of any single factor is a comparison with the influence of other factors generally recognized to have importance. Certainly these would include the factors of age, education, income, socioeconomic status, and urbanization.

Moreover, the dimensions of behavior and attitude to be predicted will be limited to the scales that have been broadly classified as moral-ethical and work of the church in content. In all, there are twenty-three such dependent variables.

The statistic to be used for this analysis will be the Pearson product-moment correlation coefficient (commonly designated by the letter "r"), a sensitive detector of the power of one variable to predict another when the measurement of both has achieved interval scale.[7] The magnitude of the coefficient will indicate which of the ten faith variables and five social background variables have the most power to predict the twenty-three dependent variables.

A word should be said about the meaning of terms like "predictive power," "correlation," "influence," and "dependent" or "consequential" variables. The idea that if the scores on one variable (*e.g.*, Anabaptism) are known, one can predict the scores on another variable (*e.g.*, pacifism), implies a cause and effect relationship that may not be warranted. This type of analysis is difficult at best and the authors do not want the reader to suppose that it is not. Instead of members' assent to Anabaptism causing them to be pacifists, it could be the other way: members with pacifist leanings may tend to be more interested in Anabaptist doctrines. Or it could be that some third factor like higher education is affecting both Anabaptist beliefs and pacifism. In order to infer that Anabaptist theology is producing pacifist attitudes, such a conclusion should be reasonable in the light of theory, there should be reason to believe that the presumed cause occurred earlier in time than the presumed effect, and there should be evidence that no third variable is the primary cause. To verify a causal relation, the researchers would have to control or neutralize other variables regarded as possibly exercising influence on the dependent variable. In preference for keeping the presentation of the data on as low a level of abstraction as possible, the authors have not done this.

Nevertheless, some of the terms that imply causal relationships will be used in this chapter with the understanding that a speculative type of usage is primarily intended. This is justified for several reasons. Such usage is firmly established in the sociological literature that will be cited for purposes of comparison. It is the basic conceptual framework in sociological theory and in empirical studies in which elaborate statistical controls are sometimes used. Moreover, as indicated earlier in the chapter, the present discussion relates to an ongoing dialogue in the Anabaptist family of churches in which cause and effect language is frequently used. We are searching for the key variables in Mennonite and Brethren in Christ reality without the illusion that there are "magic keys" to be found to unlock all the doors of the inquiry. Church members are far too complicated to warrant that kind of assumption.

Therefore, when the term *correlation* is used, it means simply a statistical relationship between two variables, without implication as to which is the change agent and which is the consequence When the term *predictive power* is used, it refers to a magnitude of correlation gauging the accuracy with which a member's response on one scale can be predicted on the basis of another. When the term *influence* is used, the discussion has moved into the area of speculation about the effect that a so-called independent variable is having on a dependent (or *consequential*) variable.

Not only the *extent* of influence but also the *direction* of influence has to be examined. It would be one thing to say that assent to the Anabaptist vision is a potent influence among the members. It would be quite another thing to say that the influence leads the member in a direction different from what could be readily predicted on the basis of social pressures in society (*e.g.*, socioeconomic status, urbanization, etc.) rather than simply reflecting or reinforcing such pressures. Some way is needed to discern whether or not each faith variable is autonomous of such influences as class and culture.

The best way to test this is to specifiy in advance the kind of consequences of faith one would expect if it was moving a member's attitude or behavior in the direction of truly biblical norms or teachings. Because it would be difficult to secure agreement about this for some dependent variables, the directions test will be limited to those for which agreement would be nearly unanimous — often as specified in officially published statements of denominational position. Most readers will agree that the influence of a given faith variable, if it is functioning as a truly biblical influence, would lead to *high* scores on the scales of moral attitudes, moral behavior, pacifism, race relations, social concerns, welfare attitudes, stewardship attitudes, stewardship performance, personal evangelism, Sunday school attendance, Bible knowledge, ecumenism, shared ministry, role of women, support of MCC, and support of church colleges. Conversely, it would lead to *low* scores on the scales of anti-Communism, anti-Semitism, and anti-Catholicism.[8]

The beauty of the Pearson correlation coefficient is that it reports in one statistic not only the power of one variable to predict another but also the direction of relationship, whether positive (+), negative (-), or nonsignificant (o). By using this statistic, one can come closer than before to a meaningful answer to the unresolved question about "Anabaptist vision" and "Mennonite reality." If assent to the Anabaptist vision ranks high as a predictor of the dependent variables, we have reason to assume at the very least that it is one factor among several in the mix of influences. If, in addition, the direction of that influence is positive rather than negative or neutral in terms of biblical norms, we have reason to conclude that it is autonomous of worldly social influences that may have been assimilated.

Findings

Table 20-1 lists 345 correlation coefficients, taken from the computer printouts. As indicated above, these are the raw data for the analysis to follow, and are included here largely for the reader's reference as the rest of the story unfolds.

Intercorrelations of the Faith Variables. Table 20-2 which adds another 45 coefficients, measures the intercorrelations among the faith variables themselves. This is only incidentally germane to the rest of the analysis but is inserted here for several reasons.

The table shows, first, that there are only two negative intercorrelations among the faith scales. There are slight inverse correlations between the ethical-social conversion scale and the two orthodoxy scales. The rest of the correlations are positive in direction, although six are too low to be significant.

This finding, which suggests a certain degree of integration of the ten indicators of the faith response of the church members, is in keeping with the arguments cited in Chapters 4-6 that a good Anabaptist should attend church regularly, voluntarily, and with a community spirit, that he should have experienced conversion and sanctification followed by a daily discipline of prayer, and that he should subscribe to the historic, evangelical doctrines of the church.

The table reveals, however, that with one exception the intercorrelations of the faith scales are not very high. But how much is high? A correlation should be high enough so that the scores on one variable can be successfully used to predict the scores on another. Stark and Glock specify a coefficient of .7 for minimal success in prediction, since the square of a coefficient is approxi-

TABLE 20-1

Intercorrelations Between 15 Independent Variables and 23 Dependent Variables

Independent Variables	Moral Attitudes	Moral Behavior	Pacifism	Race Relations	Social Concerns	Welfare Attitudes	Anti-Communism	Anti-Semitism	Anti-Catholicism	Church-State Separation	Political Action	Political Participation	Anti-Labor Unions	Stewardship Attitudes	Stewardship Performance	Evangelism	Sunday School Participation	Bible Knowledge	Ecumenism	Shared Ministry	Role of Women	Support of MCC	Support of Church College
	Moral-Ethical Scales													*Work of the Church Scales*									
Age	317	216	056	296	123	077	077	173	234	282	097	181	237	203	278	386	153	132	173	352	232	028	142
Education	227	122	132	257	180	105	285	261	273	240	294	283	278	138	022	040	035	298	240	253	299	165	090
Income	095	110	002	055	068	078	072	110	096	248	078	067	074	059	242	065	012	081	081	096	095	064	042
Socioeconomic Status	199	010	172	248	175	090	276	255	274	105	252	239	216	172	028	085	047	301	254	230	294	154	154
Rural-Urban Residence	165	134	041	034	068	084	033	046	117	114	208	206	181	068	066	029	205	064	119	026	153	005	020
Associationalism	376	382	118	092	041	024	133	040	051	151	133	012	130	412	375	461	758	331	059	079	149	125	258
Voluntarism	380	214	023	156	149	098	112	161	168	140	113	111	132	255	204	353	270	051	172	309	260	012	183
Communalism	274	280	177	071	015	049	049	103	114	142	198	153	226	166	190	189	236	114	186	154	163	094	245
Moral-Personal Conv.	301	155	029	029	053	068	017	129	118	178	140	076	086	163	104	216	227	101	095	140	208	006	132
Ethical-Social Conv.	042	045	162	087	181	123	125	063	076	198	082	031	020	015	041	059	002	062	000	062	086	054	054
Sanctification	367	196	014	085	109	069	017	132	102	223	141	068	128	220	220	458	286	070	128	138	195	027	179
Devotionalism	466	433	059	044	083	029	006	126	150	352	194	039	240	344	399	553	460	265	153	215	258	040	250
General Orthodoxy	501	325	163	150	184	178	150	198	199	276	255	072	148	303	220	284	351	068	207	294	373	014	159
Fundamentalist Orth.	572	392	265	276	300	248	330	292	323	405	375	185	280	226	175	242	322	070	317	418	523	106	060
Anabaptism	445	389	385	056	085	068	216	146	141	346	346	332	405	244	262	282	333	229	205	075	230	136	302

*The Pearsonian coefficients, r, are given for each correlation. Decimals are omitted to conserve space. Direction signs are given in Table 20-4.

TABLE 20-2
Intercorrelations of Faith Variables

	Chapter 4			Chapter 5				Chapter 6			Average Intercorrelation	Rank Order
	Associationalism	Voluntarism	Communalism	Moral-Personal Conversion	Ethical-Social Conversion	Sanctification	Devotionalism	General Orthodoxy	Fundamentalist Orthodoxy	Anabaptism		
Associationalism	X	288	222	187	019	315	538	272	222	273	260	7
Voluntarism		X	216	218	013	278	392	356	353	240	262	6
Communalism			X	090	007	151	258	122	160	391	180	9
Moral-Personal Conversion				X	32ⁿ	356	282	347	306	267	265	5
Ethical-Social Conversion					X	103	031	-016	-067	117	078	10
Santification						X	425	354	346	257	287	4
Devotionalism							X	350	332	358	330	1
General Orthodoxy								X	721	186	303	2.5
Fundamental Orthodoxy									X	220	303	2.5
Anabaptism										X	257	8
									Overall Average		252	

*The decimals in front of each Pearson coefficient have been omitted to simplify presentation. A coefficient, to be significant at the .01 level, must be .081 or greater.

mately equal to the percentage overlap between the two variables, and since $.7^2$ would mean that roughly 50% of the scores on the second scale could be successfully predicted by the scores on the first.[9] Only one coefficient in Table 20-1 achieves this minimal level of relationship — namely, the correlation between general orthodoxy and fundamentalist orthodoxy. The overall average correlation is only .252, which means that, in general, the faith variables coincide only about 6% of the time and vary independently about 94% of the time. This confirms the findings of Lenski[10] and Stark and Glock[11] that these types of religiosity seem to be independent dimensions rather than measurements of the same thing. In fact the average intercorrelation in the latter study was .272, slightly larger than ours. This indicates that Mennonites and Brethren in Christ exhibit even less patterning in their faith than do Protestants generally.

Members who are acquainted with the prophetic writings of some of their leaders will not be shocked by this finding. Seventy-five years ago an MBC leader in South Russia wrote the following:

> Although I am no Old-Mennonite myself, yet for years I have been tired . . . of the outside influences . . . and should like to call out urgently to all reformers (and I mean General Conference as well as Mennonite Brethren) . . . to stop a little and ask yourselves, What is Mennonitism? Have we after all forgotten something which it would be good to relearn as a reaction against this endless new, new, new? Are we not perhaps losing a large or essential and good part of our Mennonite soul? What does God expect of us as a group? — That we, who call ourselves Mennonites, should become a conglomerate of Lutheran, Baptist, Plymouth Brethren . . . traits (I mean in our understanding and expressions of our Christianity)? What is the particular unique character which God has assigned to us through our original heritage of faith, our history, and our present situation?[12]

Although most of the types of faith response of Mennonites examined in the present study were part of an Anabaptist synthesis in the sixteenth century, the synthesis shifted in subsequent generations through acculturation and assimilation. Certainly associationalism was part of the commitment of the Anabaptists, but associations tend in history to become formal, impersonal, and routinized. Communalism, similarly, was part of the Anabaptist commitment; but in relatively closed, rural, ethnic communities, the communal dimension tended to change the constitutive principle of the church from voluntarism to involuntarism. Although conversion and prayer were dominant teachings of Menno Simons, with their reintroduction in later reformation movements (MBC, BIC, EMC) came "a change in type of piety in the direction of a warmer, more expressive, more verbalized spirituality and an emphasis upon crisis conversion together with some change in theological emphasis in the direction of more attention to conversion and status, rather than ethics and discipleship." H. S. Bender, who wrote these words, believed that some of these changes produced "a significantly different Mennonitism."[13] Similarly, Robert Friedmann analyzed the changes in devotionalism among Mennonites through the centuries, showing how the piety of the Anabaptists shifted from the hard principle of the "fear of God" whose Word had to be obeyed to the soft principle of "godliness," which he concluded "was no longer 'Anabaptist' in character."[14] Finally, these same leaders pleaded for a type of doctrinal orthodoxy purged of the diluting character of modernism, on one hand, and the militant spirit of fundamentalism on the other. "From the vantage point of 1956. . . , Mennonites . . . see more clearly than before that they belong neither in the Modernist nor the Fundamentalist camps, but have a satisfactory biblicism and evangelicalism of their own with its unique Anabaptist heritage."[15]

Having reviewed historically the shifts in the patterning of faith among Mennonites, we return to the sociological analysis with which we began. The response of members on the questionnaire divulged a wide range of attitudes in the areas of morals, ethics, and church concerns. This information is germane and crucial to the inquiry about the consequences of various types of faith. Given the complexity of the inquiry and the diverse effects of time on these people, one might expect to find no faith variable entirely positive or negative in its consequences for morals, ethics, and other churchly concerns. One might expect, however, that some dimensions of the faith response will turn out to be more positive in their "biblical" consequences than others.

The Church Participation Scales. On the basis of the correlation

statistics in Table 20-1, Table 20-3 summarizes the overall power
of each independent variable to predict the scores of members on
twenty-three dependent variables *when grouped.* Table 20-4 specifies
whether the *direction* of correlation in each case is positive, negative, or neutral, with respect to the accepted biblical norm. One can
observe, first, that communalism ranks tenth for power to predict
the dependent variables (see right column of Table 20-3). This
finding seems to contradict John H. Yoder's thesis, quoted earlier
in the chapter, that "Mennonitism still finds its identity most properly on the ethnic community level." In order properly to assess
the significance of this contradiction, the reader would have to compare Yoder's definition of communalism with that of the present
study. The writer has argued elsewhere[16] that the concepts are comparable but that the communalism scale constructed for the
present study is more precise for the purpose of scientific measurement. Among the church participation scales, communalism ranks

TABLE 20-3

**Overall Average Correlations and Rank Order of Power
of Independent Variables to Predict Dependent Variables**

Independent Variables	Moral-Ethical Mean Corr.*	Moral-Ethical Rank Order	Work of the Church Mean Corr.	Work of the Church Rank Order	Overall Total Mean Corr.	Overall Total Rank Order
Age	.182	6	.208	6	.193	7
Education	.226	3	.158	11	.196	6
Income	.077	15	.079	13	.077	14
Socioeconomic Status	.204	5	.172	10	.190	8
Rural-Urban Residence	.109	12	.076	14	.095	13
Associationalism	.127	10	.301	1	.202	5
Voluntarism	.151	8	.207	7	.176	9
Communalism	.141	9	.174	9	.155	10
Moral-Personal Conv.	.103	13	.139	12	.119	12
Ethical-Social Conv.	.084	14	.043	15	.066	15
Sanctification	.124	11	.192	8	.153	11
Devotionalism	.159	7	.294	2	.217	4
General Orthodoxy	.211	4	.227	5	.218	3
Fundamentalist Orthodoxy	.322	1	.246	3	.289	1
Anabaptism	.253	2	.230	4	.243	2

*All coefficients are Pearsonian r.

TABLE 20-4
Direction of Correlation Between 15 Independent Variables* and 19 Dependent Variables

INDEPENDENT VARIABLE	Moral Ethical Scales									Work of the Church Scales									
	Moral Attitudes	Moral Behavior	Pacifism	Race Relations	Social Concerns	Welfare Attitudes	Anti-Communism	Anti-Semitism	Anti-Catholicism	Stewardship Attitudes	Stewardship Performance	Evangelism	Sunday School Participation	Bible Knowledge	Ecumenism	Shared Ministry	Role of Women	Support of MCC	Support of Ch. College
Age	+	+	+	-	-	-	-	-	-	+	+	+	+	+	-	-	-	o	+
Education	-	-	+	+	+	+	+	+	+	+	o	+	o	+	+	+	+	+	+
Income	-	-	o	+	+	-	+	+	+	+	+	-	o	o	+	+	+	+	o
Socioecomonic Status	-	o	+	+	+	+	+	+	+	+	o	+	o	+	+	+	+	+	+
Rural-Urban Residence	-	+	o	o	+	+	o	+	+	+	-	o	-	+	+	o	+	o	o
Associationalism	+	+	+	+	-	o	+	-	-	+	+	+	+	+	-	-	-	+	+
Voluntarism	+	+	o	-	+	-	-	-	-	+	+	+	+	+	-	-	+	o	+
Communalism	+	+	+	-	o	o	+	-	-	+	+	+	+	+	-	-	-	+	+
Moral-Personal Conv.	+	+	o	o	-	-	o	-	-	+	+	+	+	+	-	-	-	o	+
Ethical-Social Conv.	o	-	+	+	+	+	+	+	+	o	o	+	o	o	+	+	+	+	+
Sanctification	+	+	o	-	-	-	o	-	-	+	+	+	+	+	-	-	-	o	+
Devotionalism	+	+	+	-	-	o	o	-	-	+	+	+	+	+	-	-	-	+	+
General Orthodoxy	+	+	-	-	-	-	-	-	-	+	+	+	+	+	-	-	-	o	+
Fundamentalist Orthodoxy	+	+	-	-	-	-	-	-	-	+	+	+	+	-	-	-	-	-	+
Anabaptism	+	+	+	+	+	+	+	-	-	+	+	+	+	+	-	-	-	+	+

* A positivie or negative sign indicates a correlation that is statistically significant at the .01 level of probability (P .0, the assumed direction of biblical norms (see text). A neutral sign (o) means that the correlation failed to achieve the .01 level of probability (P .01). The signs on the anti-Communism, anti-Semitism, and anti-Catholicism intercorrelations were reversed so that a positive sign indicates a favorable attitude toward Communists, Jews, and Catholics.

lower in predictive power than associationalism or voluntarism. This is a rather surprising finding, considering that 65% of the members surveyed still live on farms or in small rural towns. It appears that the communal influences are dissolving and the ethnic factor among Mennonites and BIC is not as great as is commonly thought.

As reported in Chapter 4, the measurements of associationalism and communalism were similar to those of Gerhard Lenski in the Detroit study. It is worthwhile now to take those comparisions a step further. In his summary of their intercorrelation with the attidudes and behavior of Detroit respondents, Lenski wrote that

> By and large, our evidence leads us to the conclusion that religious subcommunities tend to foster and encourage a provincial view of the world. In Chapter 2 we noted that unfavorable images of other groups are consistently linked with a high level of communal involvement, but not with a high level of associational involvement. In fact, there was some evidence that a high level of associational involvement, among Protestants at least, had the opposite effect. . . . In short, involvement in socio-religious subcommunities seems to promote many of the virtues and vices which Töennies and others have identified with the *Gemeinschaft*, the folk community, or the little community as it has been variously designated. However, what is startling about our present study is the finding that communalism survives, and even thrives, in the heart of the modern metropolis, though admittedly in a guise which makes its recognition difficult for those accustomed to associating communalism with geographically isolated and numerically small populations.
> The discovery of socio-religious subcommunities is also significant from one other standpoint. Many of the critics of the churches have often charged them with promoting intolerance, narrow-mindedness, and similar characteristics. Our findings suggest that these critics have been a bit wide of their mark, since it is the subcommunities rather than the churches which seem to foster these traits.[17]

The particular contrasting consequences of communalism and associationalism to which Lenski referred in the above passage do not hold for Mennonites and Brethren in Christ. Table 20-4 shows that both types of church participation are positively correlated with pacifism, nonmilitancy toward Communists, and personal evangelism, and that both are negatively correlated with social concerns, ecumenism, attitudes toward Jews, and attitudes toward Catholics. The two variables contrast only in their correlation with attitudes toward race relations. Associationalism is positively related to this dimension while communalism is negative. Thus, on associationalism only is Lenski's comment pertinent that the subcommunities rather than the churches as such appear to foster race prejudice and indecision about speaking out on social issues.

The churches should be encouraged, not just because associationalism ranks fifth overall in extent of influence, but because its impact is positive in twelve out of nineteen areas of ethics and church work. It should be noted, however, that together with eight out of nine of the other faith variables, associationalism is negative on the concepts of shared ministry and the equal participation of women in the work of the church. Moreover, while associationalism ranks first for extent of correlation with the work of the church variables, it ranks only tenth in its relationship to the ethics variables.

On first observation the consequences of voluntarism are somewhat puzzling. The noncoercive aspect of faith has been so closely linked to the Anabaptist vision of discipleship that it comes as something of a surprise to find the Voluntarism Scale positively related to only eight dependent variables, six of them are in the area of the work of the church. Voluntarism is less related to Anabaptism ($r = .240$) than to devotionalism ($r = .392$) or general orthodoxy ($r = .353$), and it follows their pattern of relationships more than that of the Anabaptism Scale. On reflection, one may reasonably suppose that voluntarism can undergird one dimension of faith as well as another, and that a member can be doctrinally conservative and follow a devotional discipline with as much or more voluntarism as he can be voluntarily committed to the Anabaptist vision. The consequence of such mixed linkage is that voluntarism has a negative influence in nine of the correlations that were measured.

The Religious Experience and Practice Scales. Conversion and sanctification are not very high predictors of the attitudes and behavior of twelfth-generation Anabaptists. The index of initial conversion, which is not an interval scale and hence is not included in tables in this chapter, ranked fourteenth in predictive power when measured by a nonparametric statistic of correlation (the contingency coefficient). Inasmuch as the extent and direction of its intercorrelations were nearly identical to that of the moral-personal conversion and sanctification scales, these scales can be examined together.

The interesting finding with regard to the scales of sanctification and moral-personal conversion is not the extent but the direction of their influence. For some reason, the direction of whatever influence the moral-personal type of conversion has upon church members is almost entirely opposite to that of ethical-social conversion. When the direction of influence of the former was positive in the biblical sense, the latter became negative or neutral; and when the former was negative or neutral in the direction of its influence, the latter bore a commendable kind of influence. Certainly these findings are mixed, but at least one can say that it makes less difference whether or not conversion is definitely experienced than how it is conceptualized by the church member. Conversion conceptualized in terms of a private struggle with guilt and an individual yearning for redemption is linked with unbiblical attitudes on seven out of nine scales in the area of ethics; and conversion defined in terms that are social rather than individual, outward rather than inward, is linked to scores that are positive on seven out of nine of the ethics-area scales. It appears, moreover, that a moral-personal type of conversion experience is oriented more toward general orthodoxy ($r = .347$) than to Anabaptism ($r = .267$) while an ethical-social type of conversion is more congenial to the Anabaptist vision ($r = .117$) than to general orthodoxy ($r = -.016$).

The devotionalism scale, the fourth most powerful predictor, is certainly more influential and not quite as negative in its correlations as in moral-personal conversion or sanctification. On pacifism and support of MCC, with which the latter two scales were negatively linked, devotionalism was linked positively. In every other connection, however, devotionalism functioned like the other two dimensions of the faith response. Since this pattern, by and large, diverged from the findings of Campbell/Fukuyama and of Lenski regarding the consequences of devotionalism, it is worthwhile again to draw the interdenominational comparisons. In their study of members of the United Church of Christ, Campbell and Fukuyama predicted that the consequences of devotionalism would be largely negative in its linkage with interest in public affairs, social acceptance of minority groups, and civil rights for Negroes; but the reverse of their expectations is what they found.[18] Hence, their findings supported those of Lenski, who wrote that among respondents in Detroit

> the devotional orientation is linked with a unified *Weltanschauung*, or view of life, with religious beliefs and practices being integrated with other major aspects of daily life. In particular, the devotional orientation is linked with a humanitarian orientation . . . when confronted with problems of social injustice.[19]

It appears that devotionalism among Mennonites and BIC functions more like that which Campbell and Fukuyama expected but did not find — a type of piety that is negatively or at best neutrally related to race relations, social concerns, welfare for the poor, attitudes toward Communists, toward Jews, toward Catholics, ecumenism, shared ministry, and the equal participation of women in the work of the church. Its role is more effective in the area of the work of the church (second rank and positive in seven out of ten correlations) than in the area of ethics (seventh and positive in only three out of nine correlations).

The Variables of Belief and Doctrine. The faith variables that rank in first, second, and third positions for predictive power are fundamentalist orthodoxy, Anabaptism, and general orthodoxy, respectively.

The correlation between the two orthodoxy scales is very high (r = .721), and the direction of their influence is nearly identical, with only one interesting exception. General orthodoxy and fundamentalist orthodoxy are correlated in the opposite direction with Bible knowledge — the former positively and the latter negatively. Since both correlations, however, are very small for purposes of the present analysis, the two variables can be treated together. Perhaps fundamentalist orthodoxy in the way it was measured in this study, is simply a more discriminating index of the same belief dimension. Certainly by virtue of its first rank as a predictor it can be said that few leaders of these denominations have adequately acknowledged the influence of fundamentalism upon their members.[20]

Assent to the Anabaptist vision ranks second for overall predictive power. This finding is important even though by itself it tells nothing about direction of influence. It is important because it supports the first of the two overarching hypotheses of the present study — namely, that assent to the Anabaptist vision is a potent influence among Mennonites and BIC. Among the independent factors known to account for behavioral differences among people, those of age, education, and socioeconomic status rank high. Yet the Anabaptism Scale exceeds all three factors of social background for predictive power.

This is not to claim that Anabaptism is such a potent factor among Mennonites and Brethren in Christ that knowledge of a member's score on this scale is sufficient for predicting accurately how he will vote, how he will treat blacks, how he will feel about Communists, how much money he will give to the church, how well he knows the Bible, or how open he is toward women in the pulpit. No attempt is made here to substitute a doctrinal determinism for an ethnic communal determinism. Our model for analysis is one of multiple rather than unitary causation; and our conclusions, therefore, stand in contrast to the one-factor theological determinists who argue that ethnic communalism or some other single factor is the determining self-image of Mennonites. As Lenski wrote, "Despite the fond hopes of the . . . determinists, there are no 'magic keys' that open all doors. Human beings and the social organizations which they create are far more complex phenomena than the determinists credit them with being."[21]

What is claimed, first of all, is that differences on the consequential variables associated with assent to the Anabaptist vision are substantial and of an overall magnitude exceeded only by fundamentalist orthodoxy, among the selected list of predictors.

Second, with regard to direction of influence our data have empirically demonstrated that fundamentalist orthodoxy undermines the pacifist commitment, racial tolerance, a focused social witness by Christians, concern for the welfare of the poor, ecumenical openness, shared ministry, and support of MCC. It is also associated with anti-Semitism, anti-Catholicism, anti-Communism, and lack of biblical knowledge. Although some of its influences are in the "right" direction (moral attitudes and behavior, Sunday school participation, evangelism, and stewardship attitudes and performance), it has, for the most part, a negative impact on twentieth-century Anabaptists in terms of the historic norms which they cherish. The evidence confirms the fears of the late Harold S. Bender that the assimilation of the polemic spirit of fundamentalism was eroding the nonresistance and love ethic of his people.

Assent to the Anabaptist vision, on the other hand, is positive in its correlation with fourteen out of nineteen consequential variables, including all but two of the moral and ethical scales and all but three of the work of the church scales. It is negatively oriented only to the scales for shared ministry and role of women, and to ecumenism and its two correlates — anti-Semitism and anti-Catholicism. Moreover, on the five negative intercorrelations, its coefficient of correlation is not nearly as high as for fundamentalist orthodoxy:

	Fundamentalist Orthodoxy	*Anabaptism*
Shared Ministry	-.418	-.075
Role of Women	-.523	-.230
Ecumenism	-.317	-.205
Anti-Semitism°	-.292	-.146
Anti-Catholicism°	-.323	-.141
°Computer signs reversed		

With this evidence we are ready to speak to the second of the overarching hypotheses of the study. Both fundamentalism and Anabaptism have a strong influence among the church members surveyed. The influence of fundamentalism, however, cannot properly be interpreted as an autonomous factor but rather as one that reinforces many of the prevailing prejudices and mainstream tendencies that plague society. On the other hand, with a few noted exceptions, doctrinal adherence to the Anabaptist vision has moved twelfth-generation Anabaptists to a position that stands against the stream of society on most of the indicators employed in the study and hence may properly be called an autonomous variable of considerable importance.

Summary and Caveat

The portrait of positive and negative consequences of faith unveiled here is not new to behavioral scientists. As early as 1902 William James described "sin-sick" and "healthy-minded" types of religious experience.[22] More recently, in a study of prejudice, Gordon Allport distinguished between extrinsic and intrinsic types of faith, theorizing that it is not church membership as such which produces prejudice but the kind of faith practiced by members.[23] The member with extrinsic faith *uses* his religion for personal comfort and social security, separates religious considerations from everyday affairs, prays for himself, believes God to be primarily the provider of a future heaven, and interprets faith as conferring a sense of status. The member with intrinsic faith *lives* his faith, tries hard to apply it to every aspect of life, prays for others, believes God gives meaning to everyday life, and interprets faith as an obligation. Allport believes that it is extrinsic faith that causes bigotry, not intrinsic faith.

The present researchers observe, in summary, that extrinsic and intrinsic aspects are present in all ten faith variables studied, but that in their consequences each one tends to move in one direction or the other. Arranged in the order of their predictive power and whether more or less than half of the consequences were in the positive direction, the variables divide as follows:

Intrinsic Faith	*Extrinsic Faith*
Anabaptism	Fundamentalist Orthodoxy
Devotionalism	General Orthodoxy
Associationalism	Voluntarism
Communalism	Sanctification
Ethical-Social Conversion	Moral-Personal Conversion

Of course, the validity of such findings depends much on the way the questions were asked and the scales defined. There is a sense, however, in which their meaning transcends the researchers' ability to control the instrument. Church members responded to over three hundred questions and gave a wide range of answers on many subjects. When a conglomerate of information is fed into the computer and it reports plus and minus correlations of various magnitudes, we are pushed to make sense of the reports whether or not we have defined the factors in advance. For better or for worse, the print-outs did report these correlations. Whatever names are given to the factors shown to be related, these relationships stand as indubitable facts of faith and life, whether or not we fully comprehend their meaning.

Chapter 21

SUMMARY AND IMPLICATIONS
FOR THE CHURCHES

Provided the analogy is not pushed too far, sketching a sociological profile of a religious population is not unlike the product of the artist whose media are canvas and brush. The study began with some bold strokes outlining the major historical lines and the contemporary proportions of the people called Mennonites and Brethren in Christ. Then the detail was painted in, the church members appearing in a wide variety of hues and shades, describable only because some colors were more predominant than others. Now comes the time for stepping back from the canvas to view the picture as a whole, with the detail receding out of focus.

In this final chapter, some of the principal findings will be summarized. The main thrust, however, will be to pull together some of the major themes and patterns of thought that ran through the previous pages, and that need to be tied together in some meaningful fashion. Beyond this there will be some effort to project the findings into the future, not so much in the sense of a risky attempt to forecast future trends, but to suggest the issues and themes that the churches should be dealing with in the years immediately ahead.

Underlying the entire work is the attempt, using the techniques of survey research, to answer the question, Who are the Mennonites and Brethren in Christ? The goal has been not only to provide descriptive data bearing on this question, but also to seek helpful interpretations of the data that speak to the larger trends and issues in contemporary church life.

A Profile of the Church Members

The 3,591 church members who completed the lengthy questionnaire have provided us with a portrait of the 200,000 Americans and Canadians who claim membership in the five denominations that were studied. Compared to the national populations of the two countries, these are a rural people, with about one third living on farms and another third in rural nonfarm places. Their educational achievement is on a par with the national populations, and their economic position, as measured by the income distributions, is a little above the national levels. Age and sex distributions are not much different from the national populations. The occupational distribution differs significantly from the national populations, primarily due to the presence of larger proportions of farmers and professional persons, and smaller proportions in the urban blue-collar occupations.

Although a knowledge of the demographic characteristics of the church members was of some value, the primary concern was with their religious characteristics — their beliefs, their moral and ethical attitudes and behavior, and the patterns of participation in the life and work of the congregations. Hence the major thrust of the study involved the measurement and analysis of some 34 different religious dimensions, each of which was transformed into a scale of numerical values amenable to statistical treatment. Some comparisons with other denominations — Protestant, Catholic, and Jewish — were possible because of a number of surveys that have been published in recent decades. Without such benchmarks for comparisons, the profile of twentieth-century Anabaptists would have been less discernible.

The present-day descendants of the sixteenth-century Anabaptists emerge from the study as a religiously conservative group. Their scores on two doctrinal orthodoxy scales placed them near the most orthodox end of the liberal-orthodox continuum, with about 90% of the respondents choosing the most orthodox response. This portrays Mennonites and Brethren in Christ as more orthodox than all other major denominations that have been studied, both Protestant and Catholic, with one notable exception, the Southern Baptists. Contemporary Anabaptists seem to have emerged from the first half of the twentieth century relatively unaffected by the theological development of that period referred to as "modernism." They were affected substantially, however, by the movement called "fundamentalism," which will be referred to later in this chapter.

About four fifths of the members recognized a definite point in their lives when they had a conversion experience. Of those who had such a definite experience, over half reported having at least two such experiences, and some reported four or more. About two thirds of these experiences occurred in a "public church meeting," while the remainder occurred in a variety of private or group settings. The personal piety of the members was further explored through a scale called "devotionalism," a measure of the respondent's involvement in worship, Bible study, and prayer, and his personal relationship to God. This dimension of faith proved to be one of the most significant in respect to its relationship to other desirable aspects of faith and life. That is, persons scoring high on the devotionalism scale tended to score significantly higher on such other dimensions as church and Sunday school participation, doctrinal orthodoxy, moral attitudes and behavior, stewardship attitudes and behavior, and personal evangelism. It is not possible from the data to determine whether devotional practices are an antecedent or a consequence of these other dimensions. However, the implications for pastors and denominational leaders are that, while encouraging members to make devotionalism a part of their lives, they will be promoting a broader pattern of characteristics of growth in Christian discipleship.

A scale called "associationalism" measured the extent of a member's church participation, that is, his attendance, interest, and leadership in the local congregation. Relative to other denominations, a pattern of high attendance was observed. Within the most recent three-year block of time, at least half of the members were involved in some type of leadership responsibility in the congregation such as council member, officer, Sunday school teacher, committee chairman, or youth group officer or sponsor. In general, the smaller the congregation, the larger the proportion of members involved in leadership responsibilities.

Three classes of church members were compared — ordained persons, lay leaders, and other members. On most of the variables, ordained persons scored substantially higher than others, and lay leaders scored somewhat higher than nonleaders. Regular Sunday school participation is characteristic of over 80% of the church members, with teenagers having the highest attendance rate. The findings reveal that high Sunday school participation has been successful in promoting greater Bible knowledge, higher devotionalism, and higher moral attitudes and behavior, but there has been less success in the area of social ethics and concern for minorities and the poor.

Members of Mennonite and Brethren in Christ churches take marriage vows very seriously. Three fourths view marriage as binding until the death of a partner. Apparently less than two percent of present members have experienced divorce or separation. There is a wide range of opinion on whether divorced and remarried persons can be accepted in full fellowship in the congregation. Strong "in-groupness" is evidenced by three fourths of members choosing their spouses from the same denomination. A substantial minority evidence racial prejudice in opposing interracial marriage even if both persons are Christians. There is work to do in the years ahead if members are to discover the full meaning of "unity in Christ."

Church members exhibit a lot of uncertainty on the issue of abortion. A substantial majority oppose "abortion on demand" as allowed under the recent Supreme Court decision. On the question of the morality of sexual intercourse outside of marriage, 85% view this as "always wrong."

Anabaptism

An integrating theme in this study was the question of the extent to which twentieth-century Anabaptists still bear the marks of their sixteenth-century forebears. Can present-day Mennonites and Brethren in Christ validly claim the name of Anabaptists? The findings lean in the affirmative direction although not in all the details. To be sure, a minority do not assent to the distinguishing principles which set the early Anabaptists apart from the other reformers. But a substantial majority do.

The early leaders emphasized the need for the church to be separated from the state, taught love and nonresistance, opposed military service and the swearing of legal oaths. They taught that membership in the church should be based on a voluntary decision, and symbolized by adult baptism. They emphasized a thorough church discipline so that unfaithful members could be restored to, or in exceptional cases, excluded from, church fellowship. They taught and exemplified a rigorous discipline in personal morality, eschewing the vices so easily tolerated by the state churches.

From sixty to eighty percent of the present church members express agreement with these basic principles of Anabaptism. An additional ten to twenty percent indicate uncertainty on these issues. Ten to twenty percent definitely disagree with the Anabaptist position.

The Anabaptists discouraged their members from seeking justice in the civil courts. Currently Mennonites and Brethren in Christ are about equally divided on whether it is right to bring suit in court to reclaim damages. This issue needs further study by the churches.

Contemporary Anabaptists are weak in their support of the early Anabaptist principle of the "priesthood of the laity." The Anabaptists emphasized that all members of the congregation are ministers and should share in the ministerial functions of the congregation. Although a bare majority agreed to this in principle, a majority also accepted the idea that a congregation cannot be complete without an ordained minister. If we assume that the early Anabaptists expressed the biblical norm on this issue, then the contemporary churches need to examine further whether, and how, this principle can be more widely accepted among the brotherhood.

Commitment to a "shared ministry" among the laymen of a congregation has a number of ramifications, one of which is the role which women can, and should, fill in congregational leadership. The study revealed that traditional views on women's roles prevail, among both men and women. The churches need to explore new ways by which the resources of women can be more fully utilized in the work of the church.

A basic question is whether a commitment to Anabaptism makes any significant difference in the life and witness of contemporary church members. Is there any evidence that those committed to Anabaptism score higher on the other religious dimensions than those who are not so committed? A summary comparison of those rating high and those rating low on the Anabaptism Scale reveals the following: Those rating high are also higher on all the faith scales, especially associationalism, communalism, conversion, devotionalism, and doctrinal orthodoxy. Those strongly Anabaptist also rate higher on moral attitudes and behavior, pacifism, and the idea of separation of church and state. In several areas of social ethics, notably attitudes toward racial minorities and toward welfare programs, those committed strongly to Anabaptism are not much different from others. Those committed to Anabaptism are slightly more prejudiced against Catholics and Jews, and are more opposed to labor unions.

Those strongly committed to Anabaptism also evidence greater attainment on "work-of-the-church" variables, especially evangelism, stewardship attitudes and performance, and support of church colleges. However, a negative association ($r = -.21$) exists between Anabaptism and ecumenism, a fact that will be expanded later. Something of a tension is also posed by a negative association between Anabaptism and political participation, also discussed later. The negative relationship between Anabaptism and the scales measuring favorableness toward a shared ministry and an expanded role of women in the church have already been mentioned.

Some Unresolved Tensions

Although commitment to Anabaptism has been shown to be associated with most of the biblical norms advocated by the Christian churches, some tensions or dilemmas between Anabaptism and other values are not yet resolved. Brief comment is given on several of these.

Sectarianism versus Ecumenism. The negative association between Anabaptism and ecumenism (favorableness toward increased interdenominational cooperation and merger of church programs) poses a basic question: Is it possible for a people to have a strong commitment to a particularistic faith and still be open to full fellowship with those Christians whose faith is different in certain ways?

From a psychological standpoint, this may be difficult, on the grounds that if commitment *to* something has real meaning, it must result in diminished interest and loyalty to the alternatives. Only when the differences are relatively inconsequential can a person be committed to two positions or groups at the same time. It is the old tension between particularism and universalism that we are facing here. Sectarianism tends to emphasize the differences between sects and churches. Yet Jesus specifically prayed "that they may all be one" (John 17:21).

As pointed out at the beginning of Chapter 15, the early Anabaptists did not seek to withdraw from the state churches, but persisted in maintaining a dialogue with the church and civil leaders. However, even if they had not been "pushed out" of the reformed church, the Anabaptists probably could not have long retained an organic unity with the state church. Ecumenism for the Anabaptists meant primarily conversation and dialogue rather than organic unity. The negative association that we have documented may mean any one or more of the following: (1) Mennonites and Brethren in Christ reject an ecumenism defined as possibly including a merger of church organizations and programs for fear of loss of their distinctiveness. (2) There is an irreconcilable psychological antithesis between a strong particularistic commitment and the achievement of a Christian universalism. (3) Contemporary Anabaptism simply contains too much ethnic and religious sectarianism to admit the universal Christian oneness for which Christ prayed. The continuing agenda for contemporary Anabaptists is to find more ways of working cooperatively with each other and with other Christian denominations, and to put the goal of organic unity into the larger perspective of the Anabaptist vision.

Anabaptism versus Political Participation. For the early Anabaptists, a break with the church meant a break with the state government. Furthermore, the state soon became their persecutor. It is not surprising, therefore, to find contemporary Anabaptists cautious about becoming involved in politics, as is evidenced by the negative correlation of Anabaptism with the Political Participation Scale (r = -.33) and the Political Action Scale (r = -.35). The negative relationship is illustrated by the fact that the Mennonite Church, strongest of the five groups on Anabaptism, is lowest on the political scales. Are modern Anabaptists a political cop out, refusing to lend their interest and support to the development and maintenance of enlightened and responsible (if not Christian) government?

Within the framework of twentieth-century representative government, providing both separation of church and state and religious freedom, the principles of sixteenth-century radical Anabaptism tend to look much less radical and the faithful are not being threatened with a martyr's death, at least not in the nations where this study was made. As indicated in Chapter 9, some Mennonites have strongly advocated participation in the political sphere, and, indeed, three percent of the church members reported having held political office. If Mennonites have any concern for love and justice in the world, then because government is designed to obtain justice, Mennonites should not hide their political lights under a religious bushel. Speaking to this issue, Elmer Neufeld suggests that "when we are thoroughly motivated by the love of Christ of the cross — when we all actually take our neighbors' interests as seriously as our own — our concerns will appropriately find expression in actions that do have political relevance."[1] Yet the situation is complicated by troubling experiences. Within the lifetimes of many present church members, not only in the United States and Canada, but also in Russia and Germany, the political power of national government has been used in attempts to crush the opposition of Anabaptists to participation in the military forces.

All this study says is that contemporary Anabaptists are leery of political powers, and tend to express this in terms of a considerable withdrawal from the political process. What the sixteenth-century Anabaptists would do if they were here at this moment, we cannot tell. It is simply a dilemma of contemporary Mennonites and Brethren in Christ to know which is most Anabaptist — to participate or not to participate in the political processes. On the basis of the data, nonparticipation appears to be the most Anabaptist.

Personal Piety versus Social Concerns. The data revealed a number of low correlations, and even some negative correlations between measures of personal piety on the one hand and measures of social concerns and social ethics on the other. This is illustrated by the MBC which is highest on the Devotionalism Scale and lowest on the Social Concerns Scale. The fact that the tension exists among Mennonites and BIC indicates that the impact of Anabaptism has not succeeded in the resolution of the tension. The early Anabaptists were noted for their piety. They were also noted for their concern for the poor and the needy, and they developed means of sharing their material resources with those in need. Were they able to effect a synthesis of these two, often antithetical emphases? Twentieth-century Anabaptists have been weak in finding a synthesis, being pulled in two directions by the fundamentalists and the social gospelers.

Through worldwide missions and service programs, the Mennonite and Brethren in Christ churches have merged the proclamation of the gospel with aid for the suffering and oppressed peoples. Yet at home we have not been able to achieve fully a synthesis of the worshiping heart and the helping hand. Those who score high on the Anabaptism Scale should also score high on the anti-prejudice scales and on the scales expressing concerns for the poor and the minorities. But this did not turn out to be the case, and we can take little comfort from the fact that the correlations that did obtain were close to zero.

The Enigma of Fundamentalism. Within the wider orbit of Christendom, Anabaptism has been an enigma. For Anabaptists, however, the enigma is fundamentalism. It is not that fundamentalism and Anabaptism are in polar opposition to each other. In fact, a correlation of .26 was obtained between the Anabaptism and Fundamentalist Orthodoxy scales. As pointed out in Chapter 6, during the twentieth century Mennonites and Brethren in Christ have been attracted by the fundamentalist emphasis on personal piety, Bible teaching, and evangelistic fervor. And yet, among those most attracted by fundamentalism, the ties to Anabaptism tend to weaken the most. The EMC is highest on the Fundamentalist Orthodoxy Scale and lowest on the Anabaptism Scale. The EMC further illustrate the tension between evangelistic outreach, where they have been more successful than the other four groups, and low adherence to the Anabaptist vision.

A part of the tension grows out of the fact that fundamentalists have been militaristic and nationalistic, both of which are a threat to the essence of Anabaptism. Furthermore, fundamentalism has too often aligned itself with political conservatism and its related unconcern for the welfare of the downtrodden and dispossessed of the earth, whose cause has been championed by those of a more liberal political and religious persuasion. Anabaptists need to be wary, lest in borrowing from the religious zeal and enthusiasm of the denominations and interdenominational agencies that are strongly aligned with fundamentalism they sell their souls to the very militant nationalism and social unconcern that Anabaptists of the sixteenth century would have strongly condemned.

The Threat of Assimilation. Recent generations of Mennonites and Brethren in Christ have given considerable attention to forces of social and economic change in the larger society, fearing that, caught up in those changes, they might somehow lose their historic faith. A central concern was whether Anabaptism could endure urbanization and its concomitant individualism and economic affluence. Perhaps the threat is real; perhaps it is overstated.

Chapter 18 revealed that the rural-urban differences with respect to the variables of faith and life were "real but relatively unimportant." Adherence to Anabaptism was only slightly stronger among rural members than among urban members. Rural and urban respondents did not differ in their support of pacifism. As measured by a Socioeconomic Status Scale, increased social status appears to be related to decreasing fundamentalism, increasing political participation, and some diminution in personal moral restrictiveness. In general, increasing urbanization and increased socioeconomic status have mixed effects on the central doctrines of Anabaptism, in some instances slightly reinforcing and in other instances slightly undermining the distinctives of Anabaptism. This does not mean that contemporary Anabaptists should be unconcerned about these major social processes. The impact of a secular order is always threatening to religious particularism.

Anabaptism Four Centuries Later: Myth or Reality? Some readers may feel that the study has cast the modern heirs of the Anabaptist movement into too bad a light. They may feel like Walter Wagoner that "a reading of contemporary sociology of religion . . . is a maddening experience . . . too much truth for comfort and too much overstatement."[2] Other readers may feel that we have too easily assumed that the people in the study are Anabaptists by any definition and that by using the label as a

shorthand for MC, GCMC, MBC, BIC, and EMC, we have unfortunately contributed to what Bernard Bowman, a spokesman for
the younger generation, called

> the worst kind of religiosity or pietism which may very well bend
> and mold the will to adherence to the prescribed forms but it
> never really reaches the core of the problem — the spirit. This,
> as I see it, has been a major problem in the Mennonite
> Church. Our heritage has become the myth by which we
> justify our existence and the vision has become, at times, a
> "luxury" possessed by only a few "elite" while the majority
> know it only as a myth.[3]

It may be too much to hope that the statistics have spoken for
themselves, presenting a portrait that is neither all positive nor all
negative with respect to the normative vision, and revealing less
faithfulness to that vision than some readers may have expected
and more genuine commitment to that vision than other readers
may believe to be true to reality.

At least it should be clear by now that the authors are committed to Anabaptism as a faithful expression of New Testament
Christianity. What we have conveyed implicitly, we now state
explicitly: The leadership of the denominations that participated in
this study should more rigorously promote the principles of Anabaptism as an essential part of the larger Christian gospel and
witness. Evidence that this is already happening is found in the
current preparation of the "Anabaptist curriculum" for use in the
Sunday schools. Other avenues are open and are being explored.

If Anabaptism is to speak with freshness and relevance to the
here and the now, it cannot be freighted with too much cultural
baggage from the past. The younger generation is looking for a
message that will speak to the latter part of the twentieth century.
The message from the "left wing of the Reformation" does speak
to the contemporary world, but it must be freed from the en-
crusted cultural forms within which it so easily becomes encased
by the passage of time and the generations.

The findings of this research should suggest avenues of study
and work which will help achieve a firmer commitment to the
Anabaptist faith and witness. There is much to be done, and the
hurts of the world cry out for the message of love and Christian
service set forth by the Anabaptist reformers four centuries ago.

NOTES

Introduction

1. Paul M. Lederach, *Mennonite Youth,* Herald Press, 1971.
2. Elkhart: Mennonite Biblical Seminary, 1970.
3. Newton: General Conference Mennonite Church, 1970.

Chapter 1: Anabaptists Yesterday and Today

1. Harold S. Bender, *Conrad Grebel 1498-1526: The Founder of the Swiss Brethren Sometimes Called Anabaptists* (Goshen, Ind.: Mennonite Historical Society, 1950), p. xiv.
2. "Anabaptist," *The Mennonite Encyclopedia* (Scottdale: Mennonite Publishing House, 1957), I, pp. 113-115.
3. The name "Anabaptist" is generic, since there have been few bodies which were officially called by that name or some close derivation of it. In Holland and in Switzerland, the names *Doopsgezind* and *Taufgessint,* meaning literally "baptism-minded," were used as early as the seventeenth century in preference to the name Mennonite. Currently the official name of the main conference of Mennonite churches in the Netherlands is *Algemeene Doopsgezinde Societet.* In Switzerland the name is *Konferenz der Altevangelische Taufgesinten-Gemeinden der Schweiz.* Elsewhere, most of the churches following in the Anabaptist train and dispersed from Europe to North and South America by the mid-twentieth century carried the label "Mennonite" in one form or another. Three notable exceptions are the Hutterian Brethren, the Brethren in Christ Church, and the Old Order Amish. For information on all of these groups see the articles by these names in *The Mennonite Encyclopedia, op. cit.,*
4. C. J. Dyck, ed., *An Introduction to Mennonite History* (Scottdale: Mennonite Publishing House, 1967), pp. 96, 114.
5. Levi Miller, ed., *Mennonite Yearbook and Directory,* 1973 (Scottdale: Mennonite Publishing House, 1973), p. 80.
6. *Ibid.,* p. 77 (corrected to include Canadian members of the Brethren in Christ Church).
7. The statement is found in Guy F. Hershberger, *War, Peace, and Nonresistance* (Scottdale: Herald Press, 1944), Appendix 10, pp. 388-389.
8. Quoted in H. S. Bender, "The Anabaptist Vision," *Mennonite Quarterly Review,* 18:2 (April 1944), p. 81.
9. See Emile Durkheim, *The Elementary Forms of the Religious Life,* tr. Joseph W. Swain (New York: Collier Books, 1961).
10. See Max Weber, *The Protestant Ethic and the Spirit of Capitalism,* tr. Talcott Parsons (New York: Charles Scribner's Sons, 1930).
11. Ernst Troeltsch, *The Social Teaching of the Christian Churches,* Vol. I (New York: Harper Torchbooks, 1960), pp. 331-343; Max Weber, *From Max Weber: Essays in Sociology,* tr. H. H. Gerth and C. Wright Mills (New York: Oxford University Press, 1958), pp. 302-306.
12. C. Richard Niebuhr, *The Social Sources of Denominationalism* (New York: Meridian Books, Inc., 1957), Chapters 2 and 3.
13. *Ibid.,* p. 20.

14. J. Milton Yinger, *Religion, Society, and the Individual* (New York: The Macmillan Co., 1957), p. 152.

15. For the precise statistical effects of this computerized trickery, see Appendix, "How the Study Was Conducted."

Chapter 2: Historical Profiles of the Denominations

1. Robert Friedmann, *Mennonite Piety Through the Centuries* (Goshen: Mennonite Historical Society, 1949), p. 251.

2. Harold S. Bender, "Outside Influence on Mennonite Thought," *Mennonite Life*, X:1 (January 1955), p. 47.

3. *Ibid.*

4. Harold S. Bender, "John Horsch, A Biography," *Mennonite Quarterly Review*, XX:2 (July 1947), p. 142.

5. C. J. Dyck, ed., *An Introduction to Mennonite History* (Scottdale: Herald Press, 1967), p. 179.

6. Grant M. Stoltzfus, "A People Apart and a People Involved — The 'Old' Mennonites," *Christian Living*, 17:6 (June 1970), p. 20.

7. *Ibid.*

8. J. C. Wenger, *The History of the Mennonites of the Franconia Conference* (Scottdale: Mennonite Publishing House, 1938), pp. 53-56.

9. Grant Stoltzfus, *op. cit.*, p. 22.

10. Melvin Gingerich, *Mennonite Attire Through Four Centuries* (Breinigsville, Pa.: Pennsylvania German Society, 1970).

11. Daniel Kauffman, *Fifty Years in the Mennonite Church* (Scottdale: Mennonite Publishing House, 1941), p. 67.

12. Harold S. Bender, "Mennonite Church," *Mennonite Encyclopedia*, III, p. 613.

13. C. J. Dyck, *op. cit.*, p. 192.

14. Paul E. Whitmer listed twelve congregations and fifteen ministers who transferred from the MC to the GCMC for either or both of these two reasons. See *The Autobiography of Paul E. Whitmer* (published by the author, 1952), pp. 94, 96.

15. Heinz Janzen, "The Patchwork Quilt of the Mennonites," *Christian Living*, 17:3 (March 1970), p. 25.

16. Robert Friedmann, *op. cit.*, p. 260; John A. Hostetler, *The Sociology of Mennonite Evangelism* (Scottdale: Herald Press, 1954), p. 257; Grant Stoltzfus, *Mennonites of Ohio and Eastern Conference* (Scottdale: Herald Press, 1969), p. 294, fn. 8.

17. H. P. Krehbiel, *The History of the General Conference of the Mennonites of North America* (published by the author, 1898), p. 1.

18. "A Statement of the Position of the General Conference of the Mennonite Church of North America," first published in *Official Minutes and Reports of the Twenty-Ninth Session of the General Conference* (Souderton, Pa., 1941), p. 163.

19. Leland Harder, *GCMC Fact Book of Congregational Membership* (Elkhart: Mennonite Biblical Seminary, 1970), p. 30.

20. Minutes of a Meeting of the Executive Committee, Mennonite I-W Coordinating Board, Elkhart, Ind., Sept. 18, 1961, reported by John E. Lapp, I-W Coordinator.

21. Elmer and Phyllis Martens, "Mennonite Brethren: Does the Name Fit?" *Christian Living*, 17:9 (September 1970), p. 3.

22. *Ibid.*

23. Franklin H. Littell, *The Origins of Sectarian Protestantism* (New York: The Macmillan Co., 1964), pp. 46 f.

24. Rudy Wiebe, "The Meaning of Being Mennonite Brethren," *Mennonite Brethren Herald*, 9:8 (April 17, 1970), p. 3.

25. Acts 8:38, 39.

26. Romans 6:3, 4; Colossians 2:12.

27. A. E. Janzen, *Mennonite Brethren Distinctives* (Hillsboro: Mennonite Brethren Publishing House, n.d.), p. 14.

28. Frank C. Peters, *Your Church and You* (Hillsboro: Mennonite Brethren Publishing House, n.d.), p. 14.

29. *Mennonite Weekly Review*, 50:1 (January 6, 1972), p. 1.

30. Leland Harder, *Steinbach and Its Churches* (Elkhart: Mennonite Biblical Seminary, 1970), p. 50.

31. Elmer and Phyllis Martens, *op. cit.*, p. 6.

32. *Ibid.*, p. 4.

33. Virtually all of the authorities consulted on the BIC and cited below referred to this synthesis as the most distinctive aspect of BIC history.

34. Norman A. Bert, *Adventure in Discipleship* (Nappanee: Evangel Press, 1968), p. 105.

35. C. O. Wittlinger, *History of the Brethren in Christ* (unpublished manuscript) Archives of the BIC Church, Grantham, Pa.), p. 8.

36. *Ibid.*, pp. 5, 14.

37. Bert, *op. cit.*, p. 79.

38. Robert J. Baker, "The Calling and Destiny of the Brethren in Christ," *Christian Living*, 16:12 (December 1969), p. 4.

39. Martin H. Schrag, *The Brethren in Christ Attitude Toward the World* (unpublished PhD Dissertation, Temple University, 1967), p. 293.

40. *Origin, Confession of Faith, and Church Gocernment, Together with an Abstract of the Most Important Decisions Made by General Council of the Brethren in Christ* (Abilene: Brethren in Christ Church, 1901), pp. 5-11.

41. Schrag, *op. cit.*, pp. 295, 296.

42. John E. Zercher, "The Brethren in Christ Accent" (unpublished paper presented to a conference of BIC Seminary Students, Elkhart, Ind., June 4, 1973), p. 6.

43. Harry F. Weber, *Centennial History of the Mennonites of Illinois* (Goshen: Mennonite Historical Sociaty, 1931), p. 337, italics added.

44. In this connection, mention should also be made of the emergence of the "Stucky Amish" in central Illinois and northern Indiana, a similar renewal movement that took the name of Central Illinois Mennonite Conference. As will be pointed out in the text, the "Egly Amish" and "Stucky Amish" cooperated in a number of missionary and service projects.

45. See *1970 Annual Report and Directory*, H. A. Driver, ed. (76th Annual Convention, Aug. 15-21, 1970), p. 13.

46. Article IV in the EMC Constitution reads as follows: "We are prepared to study sympathetically plans for closer affiliation with groups of like faith and emphasis if such relationship would open to us mutual opportunities of richer fellowship and wider, more effective avenues of witness and service in our age of supreme challenge."

47. Personal interview, Elkhart, Indiana, Dec. 18, 1972. In a similar vein, although with reference to other doctrinal issues. Charles Zimmerman, past president of the EMC, wrote: "There is needed today a balance in the approach of our fathers and the current emphasis among us. In the 'good old days' each one knew . . . what he believed and what was right because the church said it for him in both doctrine and practice. . . . A form of tradition and legalism was often the practical end. Every effort must be made to avoid over-reaction. When all convictions are neutralized and commitments minimized, one has nothing left which is either positive or valuable. Can a proper balanced approach be achieved and maintained? . . . The

effect might be a clearer sense of identity. What are we? Who am I?" (Paper presented to EMC ministers, April 26, 1971).

48. Evangelical Mennonite Church Manual of Faith and Practice (1970), pp. 31, 32.

49. David E. Hostetler, "Anabaptist Churchmen Discuss Cooperation," *The Mennonite*, 87:42 (November 21, 1972), p. 688. See also *Gospel Herald*, 65:46 (November 21, 1972), p. 966.

Chapter 3: Characteristics of the Church Members

1. 1970 U.S. Census data reported in this chapter are taken largely from U.S. Bureau of the Census, *Census of Population 1970, General Social and Economic Characteristics*. Final Report, PC (1)-C1, "United States Summary," June 1972. For Canadian data, *1971 Census of Canada: Population, Urban and Rural Distributions*, Bulletin 1.1 — 9, Ottawa: Statistics Canada, February 1973, p. 2. The Canadian percentages have been adjusted to conform to U.S. definitions of rural and urban. Canada counts as urban all persons residing in places over 1000 population, which results in 76.1% urban and 23.9% rural by Canadian definitions.

2. Merton P. Strommen, *et al*, *A Study of Generations* (Minneapolis: Augsburg Publishing House, 1972), p. 49; Anthony Campolo, Jr., *A Denomination Looks at Itself* (Valley Forge, Pa.: Judson Press, 1971), p. 57.

3. A tally of nonrespondents indicates that 50.1% of them were male. Thus females responded in slightly better proportions than males. This may be due to a general tendency of females to be more cooperative in respect to requests or expectations for assistance that are presented to both sexes.

4. The loss of members primarily in the age span of 20-29 was reported in John A. Hostetler, *The Sociology of Mennonite Evangelism* (Scottdale: Herald Press, 1954). The study was limited to the MC.

5. U. S. Bureau of the Census, *Current Population Reports*, Series P-60, No. 90, "Money Income in 1972 of Families and Persons in the United States," U.S. Government Printing Office, Washington, D.C., p. 31.

6. U.S. Department of Commerce, *1970 Census of Housing, General Housing Characteristics, U.S. Summary*, p. 9.

Chapter 4: Church Participation

1. Paul Peachey, "The Modern Recovery of the Anabaptist Vision," *The Recovery of the Anabaptist Vision*, ed, G. F. Hershberger (Scottdale: Herald Press, 1957), pp. 337, 338.

2. "Organization of the Church," written about 1527. *Mennonite Quarterly Review* XXIX (April 1955), p. 164. In *The Legacy of Michael Sattler*, John H. Yoder claims that this document, which he entitled "Congregational Order," was in the same handwriting as the copy of the famous Schleitheim Articles and was probably circulated with them. Yoder's full translation of this article was as follows: "The brothers and sisters should meet at least three or four times a week, to exercise themselves in the teaching of Christ and His apostles and heartily to exhort one another to remain faithful to the Lord as they have pledged." (p. 44).

3. J. C. Wenger, *The Mennonites in Indiana and Michigan* (Scottdale: Herald Press, 1961), p. 14.

4. A. E. Janzen, *Mennonite Brethren Distinctives* (Hillsboro: Mennonite Brethren Publishing House, n.d.), pp. 14, 15.

5. Norman A. Bert *Adventure in Discipleship* (Nappanee: Evangel Press, 1968), pp. 37, 38.

6. J. Milton Yinger, *Religion, Society and the Individual* (New York: The Macmillan Co., 1957), p. 12.

7. Rodney Stark and Charles Y. Glock, *American Piety: The Nature of Religious Commitment* (Berkeley: University of California Press, 1968), p. 84.

8. Gerhard Lenski, *The Religious Factor* (Garden City: Doubleday & Co., 1961), pp. 32-37.

9. Merton P. Strommen, *et al, A Study of Generations* (Minneapolis: Augsburg Publishing House, 1972), p. 46. The figure 56% is given on p. 176.

10. Anthony Campolo, Jr., *A Denomination Looks at Itself* (Valley Forge: Judson Press, 1971), p. 63.

11. George Gallup, Jr., and John O. Davies, *Religion in America* 1971: *The Gallup Opinion Index,* Report No. 70 (Princeton: Gallup International, 1971).

12. See Chapter 12 for a more detailed survey of Sunday school participation.

13. See Chapter 11 for a more detailed survey of leadership in these churches.

14. Campolo, *op. cit.,* pp. 68-70.

15. W. Robertson Smith, *The Religion of the Semites* (New York: Meridian Books, 1956), p. 28.

16. Ernst Troeltsch, *The Social Teaching of the Christian Churches,* Vols. I and II (New York: Harper Torchbooks, 1960), pp. 339, 703.

17. Leo James Garrett, ed., *The Concept of the Believers' Church* (Scottdale: Herald Press, 1969), p. 316.

18. Bert, *op. cit.,* p. 74.

19. Melvin Gingerich, "The Mennonite Family Census of 1963" (Goshen, Indiana: Mennonite Historical and Research Committee mimeographed report, 1965), p. 2.

20. The position statement adopted August 27, 1959, was published in Ernest D. Martin, *The Story and Witness of the Christian Way* (Scottdale: Mennonite Publishing House, 1971), pp. 81-83.

21. Martha Wagner, "Is Adult Baptism Enough?" *Gospel Herald,* LVIII:8 (September 8, 1964), p. 788.

22. H. S. Bender, "The Mennonite Conception of the Church," *Mennonite Quarterly Review,* XIX:2 (April 1945), p. 1.

23. J. Lawrence Burkholder, "Social Implications of Mennonite Doctrines," *Proceedings of the Twelfth Conference on Mennonite Educational and Cultural Problems* (Elkhart, 1959), p. 103.

24. Lenski, *op. cit.,* pp. 10, 11, 17-22, 32-50.

25. Stark and Glock, *op. cit.,* pp. 163-164.

26. *Ibid.,* p. 166.

27. Lenski, *op. cit.,* pp. 34-36.

28. J. C. Wenger, "Dordrecht Confession of Faith," *Mennonite Encyclopedia,* II, p. 92. Wenger reprints the entire text in his *History of the Mennonites of the Franconia Conference* (Scottdale: Mennonite Publishing House, 1938), pp. 435-463. The MC has reiterated the Dordrecht view on endogamous marriage in its 1955 "Christian Separation and Nonconformity" statement, its 1960 declaration on "The Christian View of Marriage and Christian Parenthood," and its 1963 "Confessions of Faith." The nonconformity declaration asserts that "Christians shall enter into this relationship only with those of like precious faith."

29. Janzen, *op. cit.,* p. 10.

30. *Minutes of General Conferences of Brethren in Christ from 1871-1904* (Harrisburg, 1904), pp. 16, 17.

31. Lenski, *op. cit.,* p. 48.

32. *Ibid.,* pp. 33-35.

33. *Ibid.*, pp. 35, 49.

34. *1962 Minutes of the General Conference Mennonite Church*, 36th Session, August 8-15, 1962, Moravian College, Bethlehem, Pa., pp. 10, 27.

35. Leland Harder, *The Sectarian Commitment: Patterns of Faith in the Mennonite Church* (Elkhart, Associated Mennonite Biblical Seminaries, 1968, multilithed), pp. 102-104.

36. John H. Yoder, "Anabaptist Vision and Mennonite Reality," *Consultation on Anabaptist Mennonite Theology*, ed., A. J. Klassen (Fresno: Council of Mennonite Seminaries, 1970), p. 6.

37. *Ibid.*, pp. 31, 32.

38. Rudy Wiebe, "The Meaning of Being Mennonite Brethren," *Mennonite Brethren Herald*, 9:8 (April 17, 1970), p. 4.

Chapter 5: Religious Experience and Practice

1. *The Complete Writings of Menno Simons*, tr. Leonard Verduin, ed. J. C. Wenger (Scottdale: Herald Press, 1956), p. 92.

2. Delbert Wiens, *New Wineskins for Old Wine* (Hillsboro: M. B. Publishing House, 1965), p. 2.

3. Francis L. Strickland, *Psychology of Religious Experience* (New York: Abingdon Press, 1924), p. 109.

4. William James, *The Varieties of Religious Experience* (New York: The Modern Library, 1902), p. 186.

5. *Ibid.*, pp. 79, 355, 477.

6. Elmer T. Clark, *The Psychology of Religious Awakening* (New York: Macmillan, 1929), pp. 47, 48.

7. Michael Argyle, *Religious Behaviour* (Glencoe: The Free Press, 1959), p. 60.

8. *Ibid.*, p. 62.

9. Gordon W. Allport, *The Individual and His Religion* (New York: The Macmillan Co., 1961), p. 33.

10. The statement adopted on August 27, 1959, was entitled 'The Nurture and Evangelism of Children." See Chapter 4, footnote 20.

11. A. C. Underwood, *Conversion: Christian and Non-Christian: A Comparative and Psychological Study* (London: George Allen & Unwin Ltd., 1925), pp. 143-152.

12. *Manual of Doctrine and Government of the Brethren in Christ Church* (Nappanee, Ind.: Evangel Press, 1961), p. 22.

13. *Ibid.*

14. Rodney Stark and Charles Y. Glock, *American Piety: The Nature of Religious Commitment* (Berkeley: University of California Press, 1968), pp. 125-140.

15. *Ibid.*, p. 127.

16. *Ibid.*, pp. 131, 133, 139.

17. See John H. Yoder, *The Legacy of Michael Sattler* (Scottdale: Herald Press, 1973), p. 44. Yoder notes (fn. 105, p. 54) that this may be another trace of an inheritance from monasticism.

18. Tieleman Jansz van Braght, *Martyrs Mirror* (Dordrecht, 1660).

19. Robert Friedmann, "Devotional Literature, Anabaptist and Mennonite," *Mennonite Encyclopedia*, II, p. 46.

20. *Minutes of General Conferences of Brethren in Christ from 1871 to 1904* (Harrisburg, 1904), p. 308.

21. Lenski, *op. cit.*, p. 52.

22. Stark and Glock, *op. cit.*, p. 121.

23. Merton P. Strommen, *et al*, *A Study of Generations* (Minneapolis: Augsburg Publishing House, 1972), p. 390.

24. A. E. Janzen, *Mennonite Brethren Distinctives* (Hillsboro: M. B. Publishing House, 1966), p. 8.

25. Stark and Glock, *op. cit.*, p. 110.

Chapter 6: Belief and Doctrine

1. M. Marie Diller, *An Historical Study of the Development and Growth of the Evangelical Mennonite Church* (unpublished MRE thesis, Biblical Seminary of New York, 1951), p. 64.

2. H. S. Bender, "Outside Influences on Mennonite Thought," *Mennonite Life*, X:1 (January 1955), p. 48.

3. Daniel Kauffman, *Fifty Years in the Mennonite Church* (Scottdale: Mennonite Publishing House, 1941), pp. 69, 70.

4. See Lewis J. Sherrill, *The Gift of Power* (New York: The Macmillan Co., 1957), p. 66.

5. See Norman A. Bert, *Adventure in Discipleship* (Nappanee: Evangel Press, 1968), p. 44; John E. Zercher, "The Brethren in Christ Accent," (unpublished paper, June 4, 1973), p. 9.

6. Grant M. Stoltzfus, "A People Apart and a People Involved — the 'Old Mennonites,' " *Christian Living*, 17:6 (June 1970), p. 24.

7. J. C. Wenger estimates that one eighth of the membership of the Indiana-Michigan Conference of MC withdrew to form three congregations that joined GCMC. See *The Mennonites in Indiana and Michigan* (Scottdale: Herald Press, 1961), p. 43. Grant Stoltzfus reports that three congregations in Ohio were expelled, two of which joined the GCMC and one of which disbanded, its members joining an existing GCMC congregation. See *Mennonites of the Ohio and Eastern Conference* (Scottdale: Herald Press, 1969), pp. 192, 193.

8. S. F. Pannabecker, *Faith in Ferment: A History of the Central District Conference* (Newton: Faith and Life Press, 1968), pp. 223-227.

9. Heinz Janzen, "The Patchwork Quilt of the Mennonites," *Christian Living*, 17:3 (March 1970), p. 26.

10. Elmer and Phyllis Martens, "Mennonite Brethren: Does the Name Fit?" *Christian Living*, 17:9 (September 1970), p. 9.

11. Shailer Mathews, *The Faith of Modernism* (New York: Macmillan Co., 1924).

12. See H. S. Bender, "Fundamentalism," *Mennonite Encyclopedia*, II, p. 418.

13. H. Richard Niebuhr, "Fundamentalism," *Encyclopedia of the Social Sciences*, Vol. 5, 1944 ed., pp. 526, 527.

14. Stewart G. Cole, *The History of Fundamentalism* (New York: Richard R. Smith, Inc., 1931).

15. W. E. Garrison, "Fundamentalism," *Encyclopaedia Britannica*, Vol. 9, 1960 ed., pp. 919, 920.

16. John Horsch, *Is the Mennonite Church of America Free from Modernism?* (Scottdale: Mennonite Publishing House, 1926), pp. 4, 28.

17. Ernest R. Sandeen, *The Origins of Fundamentalism: Toward a Historical Interpretation* (Philadelphia: Fortress Press, 1968), p. 25. See also Sandeen's larger work, *The Roots of Fundamentalism* (Chicago: University of Chicago Press, 1970).

18. John H. Yoder, *The Ecumenical Movement and the Faithful Church*, (Scottdale: Herald Press, 1958), pp. 39, 40.

19. Merton P. Strommen, *et al*, *A Study of Generations* (Minneapolis: Augsburg Publishing House, 1972), pp. 378-381.

20. Thomas C. Campbell and Yoshio Fukuyama, *The Fragmented Layman* (Philadelphia: Pilgrim Press, 1970), p. 234.

21. John H. Yoder, *op. cit.*, p. 40.

22. See C. H. Moehlman, "Confessions, Formal, of the Christian Church," *An Encyclopedia of Religion*, ed. V. Ferm (New York: The Philosophical Library, 1945). pp. 193-195.

23. One prior instrument, however, was most useful as a model for the construction of the Anabaptism scale. See Russell Dynes, "Church-Sect Typology and Socio-Economic Status," *American Sociological Review*, 20:5 (October 1955), 555-560. Article based on author's doctoral dissertation, *Church-Sect Typology: An Empirical Study* (Ohio State University, 1954.

24. H. S. Bender, "The Anabaptist Vision," *Church History*, XIII:1 (March 1944), pp. 3-24.

Chapter 7: Moral Issues

1. Harold S. Bender, "Walking in the Resurrection," *Mennonite Quarterly Review*, XXXV:2 (April, 1961), pp. 96-110.

2. John H. Yoder, "A People in the World: Theological Interpretation," in James Leo Garrett, Jr., editor, *The Concept of the Believers' Church*, (Scottdale: Herald Press, 1969), p. 263.

3. Bender, *op. cit.*, p. 96.

4. William M. Arnett, "Current Theological Emphases in the American Holiness Tradition," *Mennonite Quarterly Review*, 35:2 (April, 1961), p. 120.

5. Quoted in Harold S. Bender, "The Anabaptist Vision," in Guy F. Hershberger, editor, *The Recovery of the Anabaptist Vision* (Scottdale: Herald Press, 1957), p. 44.

6. Robert Friedmann, *Mennonite Piety Through the Centuries* (Goshen, Ind.: The Mennonite Historical Society, 1949), pp. 14-18.

7. J. W. Fretz, "The Growth and Use of Tobacco Among Mennonites," *Proceedings of the Seventh Annual Conference on Mennonite Cultural Problems* (Tabor College, Hillsboro, Kan., 1949), pp. 87-100. Also Harold S. Bender, "Tobacco," *The Mennonite Encyclopedia*, IV: 732-734.

8. Harold S. Bender, "Alcohol," *The Mennonite Encyclopedia*, I:36-42.

9. James D. Smart, *The Teaching Ministry of the Church* (Philadelphia: Westminster Press, 1954), pp. 77-80.

10. James Leo Garrett, Jr., *op. cit.*, p. 316.

11. *Manual of Doctrine and Government of the Brethren in Christ Church*, Revision of 1973 (Nappanee, Ind.: Evangel Press, n.d.).

12. Lawrence K. Kersten, *The Lutheran Ethic* (Detroit: Wayne State University Press, 1970), pp. 94-97.

13. Gerhard Lenski, *The Religious Factor* (Garden City, NY: Anchor Books, 1963), pp. 164-167.

Chapter 8: Social Ethics

1. H. S. Bender, "The Anabaptist Vision," *Church History*, XIII:1 (March 1944), p. 21.

2. Guy F. Hershberger, "Nonresistance," *Mennonite Encyclopedia*, III, p. 898,

3. "Peace and the Christian Witness," adopted by General Conference of MC, August 27, 1957. See Ernest D. Martin, *The Story and Witness of the Christian Way* (Scottdale: Mennonite Publishing House, 1971), pp. 59-67.

4. "A Christian Declaration on Peace, War, and Military Service" adopted by the GCMC, August 22, 1953. See *Reports and Official Minutes of the 33rd Session of the GCMC*, pp. 245-246, 267-271.

5. MBC Confession of Faith, *Yearbook of the 52nd Session of General Conference* (Hillsboro: Mennonite Brethren Publishing House, 1972), p. 22.

6. BIC *Manual of Doctrine and Government* (Nappanee: Evangel Press, 1968), p. 32.

7. EMC *Manual of Faith and Practice* (Fort Wayne: EMC, 1960), p. 31.

8. See Footnote 3.

9. "The Way of Peace" adopted by the GCMC, August 19, 1971. See *Minutes 1971 General Conference Mennonite Church*, p. 21.

10. See Footnote 7.

11. H. S. Bender, "Outside Influences on Mennonite Thought," *Mennonite Life*, X:1 (January 1955), p. 48; "Fundamentalism," *Mennonite Encyclopedia*, II, pp. 418, 419.

12. "The Way of Peace," *op. cit.*, p. 19.

13. "The Way of Christian Love in Race Relations," adopted by the MC August 24, 1955 (published in Ernest D. Martin, *The Story and Witness of the Christian Way* (Scottdale: Mennonite Publishing House, 1971), pp. 70-74; "A Christian Declaration on Race Relations," adopted by the GCMC on August 17, 1959. See *The General Conference Mennonite Church Minutes 1959*, pp. 10, 23, 24.

14. "Resolutions re Ministering to Underdeveloped Areas and Underprivileged Peoples of Our World," *Ninety-eighth Annual General Conference Minutes* (Nappanee: Brethren in Christ, 1968), pp. 81-82.

15. "Resolution on Proclamation of the Gospel and Christian Social Responsibility," *Yearbook of the 52nd Session of the General Conference of MB Churches* (Hillsboro: Mennonite Brethren Publishing House, 1972), p. 8.

16. "Resolution on Poverty in North America," *Minutes of the General Conference Mennonite Church*, 38th Session (Newton, 1968), p. 26.

17. "Communism and Anticommunism," adopted by the MC August 24, 1961, at Johnstown, Pa.; "A Christian Declaration on Communism and Anti-Communism," adopted by the GCMC at Bethlehem, Pa., August 13, 1962.

18. "A statement of Position Adopted by the General Conference of the Brethren in Christ Church and by the Mennonite General Conference in 1941" published as Appendix 6 in Guy F. Hershberger, *War, Peace, and Nonresistance* (Scottdale: Herald Press, 1946), pp. 378-381.

19. *Yearbook of the 51st Session, General Conference of MB Churches* (Winnipeg: Christian Press, 1969), pp. 17, 18.

20. John C. Bennett, *Christian Ethics and Social Policy* (New York: Charles Scribner's Sons, 1946), pp. 42-46.

21. H. Richard Niebuhr, *Christ and Culture* (New York: Harper & Brothers, 1951), p. 56.

Chapter 9: Political Participation

1. For an excellent summary of sources as well as the essential elements in the Anabaptist political ethic, see H. S. Bender, "The Anabaptist-Mennonite Attitude Toward the State," *Mennonite Encyclopedia*, IV, pp. 611-618.

2. *Ibid.*, p. 613.

3. *Ibid.*, p. 612.

4. Hans J. Hillerbrand, "The Anabaptist View of the State," *Mennonite Quarterly Review*, XXXII:1 (January 1958), 28-47. See also E. D. Martin, *The Story and Witness of the Way* (Scottdale: Mennonite Publishing House, 1971), p. 54.

5. H. S. Bender, *op. cit.*, p. 615.

6. "Regarding Political Involvement," *Yearbook, 50th Session, General Conference of Mennonite Brethren Church* (Hillsboro: MB Publishing House, 1966), p. 24.

7. J. C. Wenger, *History of the Mennonites of the Franconia Conference* (Scottdale: Mennonite Publishing House, 1938), pp. 53-55, 433. Although some of the rules date from 1880, most of them were reaffirmed in July, 1933, in a reissuance of "Rules and Discipline of the Franconia Conference of the Mennonite Church."

8. *Minutes of General Conferences of Brethren in Christ from 1871 to 1904* (Harrisburg, 1904), pp. 13, 22, 30, 55, 72, 73, 94.

9. J. Winfield Fretz, "Should Mennonites Participate in Politics?" *Mennonite Life*, XI:3 (July 1956), p. 144.

10. H. P. Krehbiel served in the Kansas Legislature in 1909. E. W. Ramseyer, a member of the Pulaski, Iowa, Mennonite Church, served 18 years in Congress (1915-1933) and then as Commissioner in the U.S. Court of Claims at Washington, D.C. E. C. Eicher, a member of the Eicher Mennonite Church near Wayland, Iowa, served 6 years in Congress (1933-1939), and then as Chief Justice in the District Court of the District of Columbia. The former was a Republican, the latter a Democrat.

11. Elmer Ediger, "A Christian's Political Responsibility: A Personal Analysis of Two Major Views," *Mennonite Life*, XI: 3 (July 1956), p. 144.

12. "Regarding Political Involvement," *op. cit.*, p. 25.

13. *Ibid.*

14. The two questions cited in Table 1 had five responses, scored from zero to four: strongly disagree, disagree, uncertain, agree, and strongly agree. The third question had only three choices: disagree, scored zero; uncertain, scored one; and agree, scored two.

15. A respondent received two points for agreeing that members should vote, two points for disagreeing that members should *not* hold government office, and two points for agreeing that members should write to legislators. The "uncertain" response was given one point. Then on the question of how many were the recent elections in which he voted, he got 1 point for "few," 2 points for "some," 3 points for "most," and 4 points for "all."

16. See Barry Goldwater, "Conservatism," *The World Book Encyclopedia*, Volume IV (Chicago: Field Enterprises Educational Corp., 1965), p. 795.

17. See Hubert H. Humphrey, "Liberalism," *The World Book Encyclopedia*, Volume XII (Chicago: Field Enterprises Educational Corp., 1965), p. 204.

18. Frank H. Epp, *Mennonite Exodus* (Altona: D. W. Friesen & Sons Ltd., 1962), pp. 103-105. Prior to King's government, further Mennonite immigration to Canada was hindered by a May 1, 1919, order of Privy Council prohibiting entry into the country of any Mennonites, Doukhobors, and Hutterites. Mackenzie King, whose Liberal Party came into power in 1921, had promised that if elected, his government would rescind this order, a promise he speedily implemented.

19. At the time of going to press, the authors had not fully researched the sources and consequences of political party identification, using the independent variables of the study. A last-minute check revealed that American members scoring high on Anabaptism were no more likely to take an independent political position than members scoring low. However, American members scoring high on Fundamentalist Orthodoxy were five times less likely to take an independent position than members scoring low. Moreover, of those American members who take a position, 81% of the high scores on Fundamentalist Orthodoxy declare themselves to be Republicans compared to 11% who are Democrats; but 43% of the low scorers on Fundamentalist Orthodoxy are Democrats compared to 11% of the high scores. In its relationship to political partisanship, the Anabaptism variable acts like Fundamentalist Orthodoxy, except that the association is less significant (chi square of .125, compared to .595 respectively).

20. John H. Redekop, *Making Political Decisions: A Christian Perspective* (Scottdale: Herald Press, 1972), p. 25.

21. "Regarding Political Involvement," *op. cit.*, p. 25.

Chapter 10: Marriage and the Family

1. *Mennonite Confession of Faith,* Herald Press, 1963) MC). Evangelical Mennonite Church, *Manual of Faith and Practice,* 1970. Statement on "The Christian Family" adopted by the General Conference (of the GCMC) in 1962. Sixth Revised Draft of the "Mennonite Brethren Confession of Faith," under further study and revision in 1973. Brethren in Christ Church, *Manual of Doctrine and Government,* 1973. Minutes of the General Conference of the Brethren in Christ, 1972, p. 7.

2. "The Way of Christian Love in Race Relations," a position statement adopted by the Mennonite General Conference (MC) on August 24, 1955. Copies available from Herald Press, Scottdale, Pa.

3. See current numbers of the *Monthly Vital Statistics Report* published by the Public Health Service, U.S. Department of Health, Education, and Welfare.

4. Judson T. Landis and Mary G. Landis, *Building a Successful Marriage,* Fifth Edition (New York: Prentice-Hall, Inc., 1968), p. 85.

5. *1971 Census of Canada: Population, Age at First Marriage* (Ottawa: Statistics Canada), Bulletin 1.5 — 10, March 1974, p. 1, U.S. Bureau of the Census, *Statistical Abstract of the United States: 1972* (Washington, D.C., 1972), p. 63.

6. J. Howard Kauffman, "A Comparative Study of Traditional and Emergent Family Types Among Midwest Mennonites," unpublished dissertation, University of Chicago, 1960, p. 102.

7. U. S. Department of Commerce, *Population Characteristics, Household and Family Characteristics,* March 1972, Current Population Reports No. 246, February 1973, p. 83.

8. U. S. Department of Commerce, *1970 Census of Population, General Social and Economic Characteristics,* United States Summary, p. 369.

9. *1971 Census of Canada: Population, Women Ever Married by Number of Children Born* (Ottawa: Statistics Canada), Bulletin 1.2 — 6, October 1973. pp. 24-31.

10. No question asking the respondent to report on his behavior in regards to sexual intercourse outside of marriage was included in the questionnaire. It was feared that to do so would engender ill will toward the study on the part of older respondents. A study done in 1968 on Mennonite College students led to an estimate that not more than 20 percent of both males and females would have experienced sexual intercourse before their marriage ceremony. (Theodore Larrison and Glenn Smucker, "A Survey of Sexual Attitudes and Behavior of Mennonite College Students," unpublished paper, Department of Sociology, Goshen College, 1968.) This proportion is substantially less than estimates for college and university students in the general population. (See Atlee L. Stroup, *Marriage and Family,* New York: Appleton-Century-Crofts, 1966, pp. 154, 155 for a summary of studies on premarital sexual intercourse among students and other populations.)

Chapter 11: Leadership in the Congregation

1. Franklin H. Littell, *A Tribute to Menno Simons* (Scottdale: Herald Press, 1961), p. 42.

2. Franklin H. Littell, *The Origins of Sectarian Protestantism* (New York: The Macmillan Co., 1964), p. 94.

3. Hendrik Kraemer, *A Theology of the Laity* (Philadelphia: The Westminster Press, 1958), p. 63.

4. "Brotherly Union of Some Children of God," written at Schleitheim in Switzerland in 1527. Tr. John H. Yoder, *The Legacy of Michael Sattler* (Scottdale: Herald Press, 1973), p. 39. In footnote 73, p. 52, Yoder writes, "Perhaps 'installed' would be less open to the sacramental misunderstanding. *Verordnet* has no sacramental meaning."

5. Franklin H. Littell, "The Radical Reformation," *The Layman in Christian History,* ed. Stephen Neill, and Hans Ruedi Weber (Philadelphia: The Westminster Press, 1963), pp. 263, 264.

6. Littell, *The Origins of Sectarian Protestantism, op. cit.,* p. 93.

7. David Ewert, "The Covenant Community and Mission," *Consultation on Anabaptist Mennonite Theology,* ed. A. J. Klassen (Fresno: Council of Mennonite Seminaries, 1970), pp. 130-134; Delbert Wiens, *New Wineskins for Old Wine* (Hillsboro: Mennonite Brethren Publishing House, 1965), pp. 12-15.

8. The new MC constitution puts the congregation rather than the district conference into the center of "the life and witness of the denomination." As the bylaws put it, "All that God intends the church to be and do must first be experienced in the local congregation. Any agency or program beyond the congregation is intended to assist the congregation in fulfilling its function." In the BIC, bishops are now elected for five years. They can be reelected but must move to another district after two terms.

9. Ross T. Bender, *The People of God: A Mennonite Interpretation of the Free Church Tradition* (Scottdale: Herald Press, 1971), pp. 154-156.

10. Joseph H. Fichter, *Social Relations in the Urban Parish* (Chicago: University of Chicago Press, 1954), pp. 21-30.

11. Thomas C. Campbell and Yoshio Fukuyama, *The Fragmented Layman* (Philadelphia: Pilgrim Press, 1970), p. 228.

12. Walter Kloetzli, *The City Church — Death or Renewal* (Philadelphia: Muhlenberg Press, 1961), pp. 203. 204.

13. Merton P. Strommen, *et al., A Study of Generations* (Minneapolis: Augsburg Publishing House, 1972), p. 376.

14. See David O. Moberg, *The Church as a Social Institution* (Englewood Cliffs: Prentice-Hall, Inc., 1962), pp. 414-418.

15. Murray H. Leiffer, *The Effective City Church* (New York: Abingdon Press, 1955), p. 159.

16. John H. Yoder, "Theses on the Definition of the Free Church Vision," (unpublished paper presented to the Dean's Seminar, Associated Mennonite Biblical Seminaries, 1968).

17. Franklin H. Littell, "The Radical Reformation," *op. cit.,* p. 271.

18. John H. Yoder, *op. cit.*

19. Ernest D. Martin, *The Story and Witness of the Christian Way* (Scottdale: Mennonite Publishing House, 1971), p. 51.

20. Ross T. Bender, *op. cit.,* p. 155.

21. H. S. Bender, "Lay Preachers," *Mennonite Encyclopedia,* III, p. 301.

22. The three questions in Table 3 had five responses, scored zero to four in the direction of affirming shared ministry. The first two questions listed in Table 5 had three responses scored zero to two in the same direction. Combining all five produced a top possible score of sixteen.

23. H. S. Bender, "The Status of Women," *Mennonite Encyclopedia,* IV, p. 972.

Chapter 12: Christian Education in the Local Church

1. H. S. Bender, *Mennonite Sunday School Centennial, 1840-1940* (Scottdale: Mennonite Publishing House, 1940), p. 8. This pamphlet was prepared to observe the 100th anniversary of the first MC Sunday school in a congregation in Ontario, a school that lasted only a short time. In 1963, a few months after Bender's death, J. C. Wenger reissued this pamphlet with additions to commemorate the 100th anniversary of the first permanent MC Sunday school in West Liberty, Ohio. It bore the new title, *The Church Nurtures Faith* (Scottdale: Herald Press).

2. H. S. Bender, *op. cit.*, mentions John F. Funk, Abraham Wambold, Benjamin Eby, Nicholas Johnson, and others. Among BIC leaders with early Sunday school experience were Henry Brubaker, J. I. Long, William Rosenberger, Monroe Dourts, and Walter Winger. See A. W. Climenhaga, "History of the Brethren in Christ Sunday Schools," *Forward with Our Sunday Schools*, V (Spring Issue, 1953), p. 2.

3. Bender, *op. cit.*, p. 12.

4. *Ibid.*, p. 21

5. *Minutes of General Conferences of Brethren in Christ from 1871-1904* (Harrisburg, 1904), p. 44. The minute reads: "Art. 10. Should Sabbath-schools be encouraged among the brethren? Ans. Yes, if properly conducted by the brethren, and God's word be used as a basis of teaching, and that no picnics or celebrations be allowed."

6. Quoted from Oberholtzer's letter to friends in Germany, *Mennonite Quarterly Review*, XI:2 (April 1937), p. 161. See also S. F. Pannabecker, *The Development of the General Conference Mennonite Church in the American Environment* (unpublished doctoral dissertation, Yale University, 1944), p. 157. H. S. Bender, *op. cit.*, pp. 26, 27, reports similar hostile comments: "These Sunday schools are the work of the devil" and "These English Sunday schools are all pride."

7. Bender, *op. cit.*, p. 27.

8. *Ibid.*, p. 31.

9. Harold E. Bauman, *The Believers' Church and the Church College* (unpublished doctoral dissertation, Teachers College, Columbia University, 1972), pp. 66, 67.

10. See J. C. Wenger, "Dordrecht Confession of Faith," *Mennonite Encyclopedia*, II, pp. 92, 93; A. W. Climenhaga, *History of the Brethren in Christ* (Nappanee, 1942), p. 101.

11. Martin H. Schrag, *The Brethren in Christ Attitude Toward the World* (unpublished doctoral dissertation, Temple University, 1967), pp. 195-210.

12. H. S. Bender, *op. cit.*, p. 55.

13. Anthony Campolo, Jr., *A Denomination Looks at Itself* (Valley Forge: Judson Press, 1971), pp. 68-70.

14. Walter Kloetzli, *The City Church — Death or Renewal* (Philadelphia: Muhlenberg Press, 1961), p. 203.

15. H. S. Bender, *op. cit.*, p. 47. Italics added.

16. *Ibid.*

17. See Thomas Roy Pendell, "Biblical Literacy Test," *The Christian Century*, LXXVI:42 (October 21, 1959), pp. 1212, 1213.

18. H. S. Bender, *op. cit.*, p. 48.

19. *Ibid.*

20. James D. Smart, *The Teaching Ministry of the Church* (Philadelphia: The Westminster Press, 1954), p. 77.

21. Harold Bauman, *op. cit.*, p. 71.

22. H. S. Bender, *op. cit.*, pp. 49, 50.

23. *Ibid.*, pp. 50, 51.

24. The question that gave this information was, "In your childhood and youth, were your parents members of the church denomination to which you now belong?" The five denominations were ranked by the percentage of members answering that neither mother nor father were members of the Mennonite or BIC denomination to which the respondent now belongs.

25. *Minutes 1971 of General Conference Mennonite Church, 39th Session,* pp. 18-21.

Chapter 13: Denominational Schools

1. The Mennonite Church has three colleges: Eastern Mennonite College and Sem-

inary, Harrisonburg, Virginia; Goshen College, Goshen, Indiana; and Hesston College, Hesston, Kansas. The GCMC has four colleges: Bethel College, North Newton, Kansas; Bluffton College, Bluffton, Ohio; Freeman Junior College, Freeman, South Dakota; and Canadian Mennonite Bible College, Winnipeg, Manitoba. The MBC has three: Tabor College, Hillsboro, Kansas; Pacific College and Seminary, Fresno, California; and Mennonite Brethren Bible College, Winnipeg, Manitoba. The BIC denomination operates Messiah College, Grantham, Pennsylvania, but has no seminary. Conrad Grebel College, Waterloo, Ontario, one of several denominational colleges attached to the University of Waterloo, is supported by several Mennonite conferences in Ontario. In addition to the two seminaries above, there is the Associated Mennonite Biblical Seminary, Elkhart, Indiana, a joint program of the Mennonite Biblical Seminary (GCMC) and the Goshen Biblical Seminary (MC). The Evangelical Mennonite Church operates no schools.

2. Data from the office of the Mennonite Board of Education, Goshen, Ind.

3. C. Robert Price, *Education and Evangelism: A Profile of Protestant Colleges* (New York: McGraw-Hill Book Co., 1972), p. 14.

4. Daniel Hertzler, *Mennonite Education: Why and How?* (Scottdale: Herald Press, 1971), p. 22.

5. *Ibid.*, p. 29.

6. Merton P. Strommen, *Profiles of Church Youth* (St. Louis: Concordia Publishing House, 1963), pp. 49, 60.

7. Paul M. Lederach, *Mennonite Youth* (Scottdale: Herald Press, 1971), pp. 56-67, 94-97.

8. Gerhard Lenski, *The Religious Factor* (Garden City: Doubleday and Co., Anchor Books edition, 1963), pp. 270, 271.

9. Andrew M. Greeley, *Religion and Career* (New York: Sheed and Ward, 1963), pp. 80-82.

10. Andrew M. Greeley and Peter H. Rossi, *The Education of Catholic Americans* (Chicago: Aldine Publishing Co., 1966), pp. 7, 17.

11. *Ibid.*, p. 166.

12. *Ibid.*, p. 119.

13. Otto F. Kraushaar, *American Nonpublic Schools* (Baltimore: The Johns Hopkins University Press, 1972), pp. 354, 355.

Chapter 14: The Stewardship of Church Members

1. *Giving, USA, 1972*, American Association of Fund-Raising Council, New York, N.Y. Also see Douglas W. Johnson and George W. Cornell, *Punctured Preconceptions* (New York: Friendship Press, 1972).

2. Data are from page 244 of the *Yearbook of American and Canadian Churches, 1973* (New York: Abingdon Press, 1973), except for the MBC and EMC; data for these are from denominational headquarters.

3. Evangelical Mennonite Church, *Manual of Faith and Practice*, Revised 1970, pp. 26, 27.

4. *Manual of Doctrine and Government* of the Brethren in Christ Church, Part 2, Article 19.

5. Douglas W. Johnson and George W. Cornell, *Punctured Preconceptions* (New York: Friendship Press, 1972), p. 152. The study was conducted by the National Council of Churches. The MC was one of the 15 denominations whose members were surveyed, but the report does not provide a breakdown of data for the separate denominations.

Chapter 15: Parochial and Ecumenical Attitudes

1. 1 Cor. 1:11-13a.

2. 2 Cor. 6:14.

3. Paul Erb, "Church Practices We Can Do Without," *Christian Living*, 19:1 (January 1972), p. 4.

4. The following writings have been consulted: (1) John H. Yoder, *The Ecumenical Movement and the Faithful Church* (Scottdale: Mennonite Publishing House, 1958); (2) John H. Yoder, "A Historic Free Church View," *Christian Unity in North America*, ed. J. Robert Nelson (St. Louis: The Bethany Press, 1958); (3) John H. Yoder, "The Free Church Ecumenical Style," *Quaker Religious Thought*, X:1 (Summer 1968), pp. 29-38. (4) H. S. Bender, "Inter-Mennonite Relations," *Mennonite Encyclopedia*, III, pp. 44-48; (5) Harold E. Bauman, *The Price of Church Unity* (Scottdale: Herald Press, 1962); (6) Calvin Redekop, *Brotherhood and Schism* (Scottdale: Herald Press, 1963); (7) Ross T. Bender *The People of God* (Scottdale: Herald Press, 1971), pp. 156-160.

5. John H. Yoder, "The Prophetic Dissent of the Anabaptists," *The Recovery of the Anabaptist Vision*, ed., Guy F. Hershberger (Scottdale: Herald Press, 1957), p. 95, footnote 2.

6. See footnote 4, item 1, p. 31.

7. Yoder, "Prophetic Dissent," *op. cit.*, p. 94.

8. See footnote 4, item no. 2, p. 90.

9. See footnote 4, item no. 1, p. 33.

10. See footnote 4, item no. 3, p. 32.

11. Grant M. Stoltzfus, "A People Apart and a People Involved — the 'Old' Mennonites," *Christian Living*, 17:6 (June 1960), p. 24.

12. *Mennonite General Conference Proceedings*, 1967 (Scottdale: Mennonite Publishing House, 1967), pp. 59-70.

13. *Mennonite General Conference Proceedings, 1969* (Scottdale: Mennonite Publishing House, 1969), pp. 54-62.

14. 1967 MC proceedings, *op. cit.*, p. 69. With regard to the intentional establishment of parallel "Interchurch Relations Committees" in the MC and GCMC at the same time, the MC committee reported that "there is clearly an impression held by some that this is, probably by design, preliminary to an eventual complete merger of the two bodies." The committee took action to correct such an impression so as not to jeopardize relations with groups other than the GCMC. For the GCMC reaction to this, see below.

15. *The General Conference Mennonite Church Minutes 1959*, p. 15.

16. *Minutes 1968 General Conference Mennonite Church*, p. 30.

17. Elmer and Phyllis Martens, "Mennonite Brethren: Does the Name Fit?" *Christian Living*, 17:9 (September 1970), p. 6.

18. *Ibid.*, p. 9.

19. *Yearbook 50th Session General Conference of MB Churches* (Hillsboro: MB Publishing House, 1966), p. 33.

20. See "Subject of Merger Tabled by E.M.C.," *Mennonite Weekly Review* (May 23, 1974), p. 1.

21. *Yearbook 50th Session General Conference of MB Churches*, p. 22.

22. See Walter M. Abott, ed., *The Documents of Vatican II* (New York: America Press, 1966), pp. 336-370.

23. Charles Y. Glock and Rodney Stark, *Christian Beliefs and Anti-Semitism* (New York: Harper & Row, 1966), pp. 66-74, 131-135.

24. Merton P. Strommen, *et al.*, *A Study of Generations* (Minneapolis: Augsburg Publishing House, 1972), pp. 208-212.

25. Source for the comparisons on the first question: Glock and Stark, *op. cit.*, p. 64. Source for the second question comparisons: Strommen, *op. cit.*, p. 374; Glock and Stark, *op. cit.*, p. 111. Source for the third question comparisons: Lawrence K. Kersten, *The Lutheran Ethic* (Detroit: Wayne State University Press, 1970), p. 79.

Chapter 16: Sex and Age Differences

1. Michael Argyle, *Religious Behavior* (Glencoe: The Free Press, 1959), pp. 72-79.

2. Charles Y. Glock, Benjamin B. Ringer, and Earl R. Babbie, *To Comfort and to Challenge* (Berkeley: University of California Press, 1967), p. 41.

3. Thomas C. Campbell and Yoshio Fukuyama, *The Fragmented Layman* (Boston: Pilgrim Press, 1970), pp. 81.

4. Lawrence K. Kersten, *The Lutheran Ethic* (Detroit: Wayne State University Press, 1970), pp. 35-49.

5. Anthony Campolo, Jr., *A Denomination Looks at Itself* (Valley Forge: Judson Press, 1971), pp. 63-69.

6. Because of the large number of cases (3,591 respondents) in the study, statistical significance at the .01 level results from sample proportions differing as little as three percent. Only those differences (even when referred to as "slight") that are great enough to be statistically significant are reported as differences. Otherwise the results are reported as of no difference between the sex, age, or other categories of respondents. Kendall's Tau C, with computations of significance level, was used to measure the degree of association between sex and other variables in the Contingency Tables upon which these reported findings are based.

7. For a summary of these theories see David O. Moberg, *The Church as a Social Institution* (Englewood Cliffs, N.J.: Prentice-Hall, Inc., 1962), pp. 396-401.

8. Gordon W. Allport, *The Individual and His Religion* (New York: Macmillan Co., 1961), pp. 28-46.

9. Argyle, *op. cit.*, pp. 65, 66.

10. Glock, Ringer, and Babbie, *op. cit.*, p. 55.

11. Merton P. Strommen, *et al*, *A Study of Generations* (Minneapolis: Augsburg Publishing House, 1972), particularly Chapter 10.

12. Campbell and Fukuyama, *op. cit.*, p. 77.

13. Strommen, *op. cit.*, p. 232.

Chapter 17: Education and Social Class

1. The ranks utilized, in order, are: (8) professional, (7) business management, (6) sales and clerical, (5) farm operator, (4) craftsman or foreman, (3) machine operators, (2) service workers, and (1) laborers. Since only "employed" occupations were included, housewives and students were excluded from the respondents to whom an SES ranking was assigned. This has the desirable effect of eliminating most teenagers from the SES scale. Most teenagers have not yet reached their ultimate educational ranking, and their current income ranking is not their own but that of their parents. A true ranking of a person's socioeconomic status cannot really be made until he has completed his education, entered an occupation, and has his own income.

2. In studying "Jonesville" (Morris, Illinois), Warner and his associates used four readily available status criteria to construct an "Index of Status Characteristics": occupation, source of income, house type, and location of residence (area of the city where the family lived). They concluded that only about three percent of the city's residents were "upper class." W. Lloyd Warner, *Democracy in Jonesville* (New York: Harper and Brothers, 1949), p. 51.

3. Russell R. Dynes, "Church-Sect Typology and Socio-Economic Status," *American Sociological Review*, October 1955, pp. 555-560.

4. H. Richard Niebuhr, *The Social Sources of Denominationalism* (New York: Henry Holt & Co., 1929), Chapters II and III.

5. Charles Y. Glock, Benjamin B. Ringer and Earl R. Babbie, *To Comfort and to Challenge* (Berkeley: University of California Press, 1967), pp. 76-79.

6. *Ibid.*, p. 86.

7. Michael Argyle, *Religous Behavior* (Glencoe: The Free Press, 1959), p. 133.

8. Gerhard Lenski, *The Religious Factor* (Garden City: Doubleday & Co., 1963), p. 59.

9. Merton P. Strommen, *et al, A Study of Generations* (Minneapolis: Augsburg Publishing House, 1972), p. 296.

10. Lawrence K. Kersten, *The Lutheran Ethic* (Detroit: Wayne State University Press, 1970), p. 40.

Chapter 18: Residence: Rural-Urban, Regional, National

1. *1970 Census of Population: General Social and Economic Characteristics, United States Summary* (Washington, D. C.: U.S. Bureau of the Census, June 1972), pp. 1: 380, 381.

2. *1971 Census of Canada: Population, Urban and Rural Distributions,* Catalogue 92-709, Vol I-Part 1 (Ottawa: Statistics Canada, February 1973), p. 1.

3. 1970 Census of Population, *op. cit.,* p. 1:411.

4. Charles P. Loomis and J. Allan Beegle, *Rural Social Systems* (New York: Prentice-Hall, Inc., 1950), pp. 3-38, 789-824; Rockwell C. Smith, *The Church in Our Town* (New York: Abingdon Press, 1955), pp. 15-26.

5. Smith, *op. cit.,* p. 20.

6. Richard Dewey, "The Rural-Urban Continuum: Real but Relatively Unimportant." *American Journal of Sociology,* LXVI:1 (July 1960), 60-66.

7. John R. Mumaw, "Current Forces Adversely Affecting the Life of the Mennonite Community," *Mennonite Quarterly Review,* XIX (April 1945), pp. 101-116.

8. Harvey Cox, *The Secular City* (New York: The Macmillan Company, 1965), p. 41. Note especially the comment on page 51, "By and large, the mobile man is less tempted than the immobile man to demote Yahweh into a Baal."

9. Egon Bergel, *Urban Sociology* (New York: McGraw-Hill Book Co., 1955), p. 308.

10. Paul Peachey, *Die Soziale Herkunft der Schweizer Taufer, 1525-1540* (PhD Dissertation, University of Zurich, 1954), summarized in "Social Background and Social Philosophy of the Swiss Anabaptists 1525-1540," *Mennonite Quarterly Review,* XXVIII (April 1954), 102-127. And Robert Kreider, "Vocations of Swiss and South German Anabaptists," *Mennonite Life,* VIII (January 1953), 38-42.

11. H. Richard Niebuhr, *The Social Sources of Denominationalism* (New York: Meridian Books, Inc., 1957), p. 34. J. Milton Yinger, *Religion in the Struggle for Power* (Durham: Duke University Press, 1946), pp. 30, 31.

12. The term "Agrartypus" was employed by Ernst Correll in his doctoral research concerning the social development of Swiss Anabaptism into a rural type. See *Das Schweizerische Tauffermennonitentum: Ein Soziologischer Bericht* (Tübingen, 1925).

13. *The Complete Writings of Menno Simons 1496-1561,* ed. J. C. Wenger (Scottdale: Herald Press, 1956), p. 451.

14. See J. Lawrence Burkholder, "Social Implications of Mennonite Doctrines," *Proceedings of the Twelfth Conference on Mennonite Education and Cultural Problems* (Elkhart, Ind. 1959), p. 102.

15. Guy F. Hershberger, *War, Peace, and Nonresistance* (Scottdale: Herald Press, 1946), p. 291.

16. Paul Peachey, "Early Anabaptists and Urbanism," *Proceedings of the Tenth*

Conference on Mennonite Educational and Cultural Problems (Chicago, 1955), pp. 75-83.

17. Murray H. Leiffer, *The Effective City Church* (New York: Abingdon Press, 1955), Chapter IV.

18. Peachey, *op. cit.*, p. 76.

19. The Pearson coefficient of correlation between the scores on this scale in its uncollapsed 0-32 interval form and the rural-urban variable (assuming underlying continuity) was .08, significant at the .001 level.

20. Frank H. Epp, "Time to Rearrange Relationships," *The Mennonite*, 88:42 (November 20, 1973), pp. 682-683.

21. A significant relationship was defined as a contingency coefficient of .10 or greater.

Chapter 19: Denominational Patterns of Faith and Life

1. Robert Friedmann, *Mennonite Piety Through the Centuries* (Goshen, Ind.: Mennonite Historical Society, 1949), pp. 260,251.

2. John A. Hostetler, *The Sociology of Mennonite Evangelism* (Scottdale: Herald Press, 1954), pp. 257,248, 170, 178, 179.

3. Elmer and Phyllis Martens, "Mennonite Brethren: Does the Name Fit?" *Christian Living*, 17:9 (Sept. 1970), p. 5.

4. Robert E. Park and E. W. Burgess, *Introduction to the Science of Sociology* (Chicago, 1924), p. 873.

5. Based on the analysis by Karl Baehr, "The Secularization Process Among Mennonites," *Conference on Mennonite Cultural Problems* (Newton, Kan.: Bethel College Press, 1942), pp. 35-40.

6. The most recent argument with this line of reasoning is John H. Yoder's "Anabaptist Vision and Mennonite Reality," *Consultation on Anabaptist Mennonite Theology* (Fresno, Calif.: Council of Mennonite Seminaries, 1970), pp. 1-46.

7. See Ralph Linton, "Diffusion," *Sociological Theory*, ed. Borgatta and Meyer (New York: Alfred A. Knopf, 1956), p. 498. This was originally a chapter in Linton's *A Study of Man* (1936).

8. Calvin Redekop, "Patterns of Cultural Assimilation Among Mennonites," *Proceedings of the Eleventh Conference on Mennonite Educational and Cultural Problems* (North Newton, Kan.: Bethel College, 1957), pp. 99-101. Redekop's definition of secularization would be unacceptable to a new group of "secular theologians" who see this as a process of liberation which is authentically biblical and Christian. See Harvey Cox, *The Secular City* (New York: Macmillan, 1967), pp. 15-32, who distinguishes between secularization and secularism. Our use of the term "secularization" corresponds essentially to what Cox meant by "Secularism," although the "Secular city debate" is far from finished.

9. *Ibid.*, pp. 101-108.

10. E. K. Francis, *In Search of Utopia* (Glencoe, Ill.: The Free Press, 1955), pp. 276, 277.

11. See J. Lawrence Burkholder, "The Anabaptist Vision of Discipleship," *The Recovery of the Anabaptist Vision*, ed. Guy F. Hershberger (Scottdale: Herald Press, 1957), pp. 135-151.

12. See Chapter 6, footnote 2.

13. See Chapter 2, footnote 14.

14. Elmer and Phyllis Martens, *op. cit.*, p. 9.

15. H. S. Bender, *op. cit.*, p. 48.

16. E. G. Kaufman, "General Conference Mennonite Church," *Mennonite Encyclopedia*, II, p. 469.

17. J. H. Quiring, "An Analysis of the Present," *A Century of Grace and Witness*, ed. Walter Wiebe (Hillsboro, Kan: M. B. Publishing House, 1960), pp. 75-77; A. E. Janzen, *Mennonite Brethren Distinctives* (Hillsboro: M.B. Publishing House, 1966), p. 27. Quiring writes, "There is a great need today for establishing principles of right and wrong in the minds of our people and stating them in such a way that they do not need a revision every time that some evil comes to us dressed in a different garb."

18. Elmer and Phyllis Martens, *op. cit.*, p. 6..

19. *1969 Yearbook*, 51st Session, p. 13, Resolution II on "The Individual Member and Guidelines of the Church."

20. Grant Stoltzfus, "A People Apart and a People Involved — the 'Old' Mennonites," *Christian Living*, 17:6 (June 1970), p. 24.

21. Elmer and Phyllis Martens, *op. cit.*, p. 9.

22. John H. Yoder, *The Ecumenical Movement and the Faithful Church* (Scottdale: Mennonite Publishing House, 1958), p. 31.

23. Paul Erb, "Church Practices We Can Do Without," *Christian Living*, 19:1 (January 1972), p. 4.

24. Of course, in comparing the Anabaptist denominations with Protestants as a whole, the variations within Protestantism are ignored. The number of "high ratings" would be fewer if, for example, the comparisons were between Anabaptists and Southern Baptists, since the Stark and Glock study revealed that Southern Baptists were sometimes as high as, or in some cases higher than, the scores which Anabaptists made on similar scales.

25. Rodney Stark and Charles Glock, *American Piety: The Nature of Religious Commitment* (Berkeley: University of California Press, 1968), p. 73.

26. Benton Johnson, "A Critical Appraisal of the Church-Sect Typology," *American Sociological Review*, XXII (February 1957), p. 90.

27. *Ibid.*, p. 91.

Chapter 20: The Search for the Key Factors

1. Emile Durkheim, *The Elementary Forms of the Religious Life* (New York: Collier Books, 1961).

2. H. Richard Niebuhr, *The Kingdom of God in America* (New York: Harper & Row, 1937), and *The Social Sources of Denominationalism* (New York: Henry Holt, 1929).

3. Max Weber, *The Protestant Ethic and the Spirit of Capitalism*, tr. Talcott Parsons (New York: Charles Scribner's Sons, 1930).

4. Gerhard Lenski, *The Religious Factor* (Garden City: Doubleday & Co., 1961).

5. H. S. Bender, "Outside Influences on Mennonite Thought," *Mennonite Life*, X:1 (January 1955), p. 47.

6. John H. Yoder, "Anabaptist Vision and Mennonite Reality," *Consultation on Anabaptist Mennonite Theology*, ed. A. J. Klassen (Fresno: Council of Mennonite Seminaries, 1972), pp. 6, 34, 40.

7. For the interested reader the following brief explanation of the Pearson coefficient of correlation is offered. The coefficient measures the extent to which the scores on one scale can predict the scores on another, for instance, the extent to which a member's score on Anabaptist vision successfully predicts his score on pacifism. A perfect correlation would give a coefficient of *one*, but perfect correlations in the behavioral sciences are almost never achieved. Therefore, the correlation coefficient almost always falls somewhere between *zero* and *one*, expressed as a decimal figure

(*e.g.,* + .263). A positive sign in front of the coefficient indicates that as the scores on one scale increase, the scores on the other also increase. A negative sign would indiciate that as the scores on the first scale increase, the scores on the second decrease. One may think of two scales as represented by two circles. When the two circles completely overlap one another, the correlation is perfect (r=1). When the correlation is zero (r=0), the circles do not overlap at all. Correlation coefficients between zero and one indicate the extent to which the circles overlap. Generally speaking, if as much as one percent of the circles overlap, it is unlikely that even that low amount of correlation would have occurred by chance alone. In a sample of 1,000 persons, a correlation coefficient of .081 would be statistically significant at the one percent level of significance, which means that even a coefficient as low as that (with less than one percent of the circles overlapping) would be expected to occur by chance alone in less than one time out of 100.

8. The following scales were omitted from the list of dependent variables when doing the directions test: political participation, political role of the church, and labor-management attitudes. As indicated in the text, the reason for their omission is the low level of agreement concerning the application of the Anabaptist ethic in these areas of life in the modern world.

9. Rodney Stark and Charles Y. Glock, *American Piety: The Nature of Religious Commitment* (Berkeley: University of California Press, 1968), pp. 179, 180.

10. Lenski, *op. cit.,* pp. 20, 52, 53.

11. Stark and Glock, *op. cit.,* pp. 180. 181.

12. P. M. Friesen, *Die Alt-Evangelische Mennonitische Bruederschaft in Russland* (Halbstadt, 1911), p. 265. Quoted in H. S. Bender, *op. cit.,* p. 45.

13. H. S. Bender, "Evangelism," *Mennonite Encyclopedia,* II, p. 269.

14. Robert Friedmann, "Devotional Literature, Anabaptist and Mennonite," *Mennonite Encyclopedia,* II, p. 47.

15. H. S. Bender, "Outside Influences . . .," *op. cit.,* p. 48.

16. See Leland Harder, "An Empirical Search for the Key Variable in Mennonite Reality," *Mennonite Quarterly Review,* XLV:4 (October 1971), pp. 333, 334.

17. Lenski, *op. cit.,* p. 296.

18. Thomas C. Campbell and Yoshio Fukuyama, *The Fragmented Layman* (Philadelphia: Pilgrim Press, 1970), pp. 141, 145, 147, 162-164, 167.

19. Lenski, *op. cit.,* pp. 291, 297.

20. For a confirmation of this judgment, see Gerald Studer, "The Influence of Fundamentalism on the American Mennonite Church" (unpublished thesis, Goshen College Biblical Seminary, 1949).

21. Lenski, *op. cit.,* p. 295.

22. William James, *The Varieties of Religious Experience* (New York: The Modern Library, 1920), pp. 77-162.

23. Gordon W. Allport, *The Nature of Prejudice* (Garden City: Doubleday and Company, 1958), pp. 413 ff.

Chapter 21: Summary and Implications for the Churches

1. Elmer Neufeld, "Christian Responsibility in the Political Situation," *Mennonite Quarterly Review,* XXXII:2 (April, 1958), pp. 141, 142.

2. Walter Wagoner, *Bachelor of Divinity* (New York: Association Press, 1963), p. 18. Wagoner was reacting specifically to the writings of Gibson Winter and Peter Berger, whom he called "sociological Jeremiahs."

3. Bernard Bowman, "Is the Anabaptist Vision a Myth?" *Gospel Herald,* 66:36 (September 11, 1973), p. 692. Bowman was a student at Eastern Mennonite College when this article was published.

APPENDIX

How the Study Was Conducted

Some readers will want to know more about how the study was conducted than was told in the introductory parts of the book. It is the purpose of this appendix to supply considerable detail on the research methodology so that the interested scholar can make a better judgment of the validity and reliability of the procedures and findings. The authors will welcome the opportunity to supply additional information to anyone desiring it.

The study was launched in the spring of 1971 after more than a year of planning and negotiations for funding. Consultations with representatives of a variety of church boards and committees were carried out in the summer of 1971. Preparation of the research instrument and selection of the sample congregations and sample members were completed by the following March. The field work (administering the questionnaires) was conducted from March through June of 1972. With work limited mainly to the summer months, it required nearly two years for the authors to process the data, write the research report, and prepare it for publication. Meanwhile a series of advance reports were given to various denominational boards and committees. This yielded useful feedback for the analysis and interpretation of the findings.

Objectives and Scope of the Study

As set forth in the research proposal, the purpose of the study was to obtain a profile of the beliefs, attitudes, and religious practices of Mennonite and BIC church members. The more specific objectives were to determine (1) the extent of attendance and participation of members in the local congregation, (2) attitudes of members toward their denomination, (3) private and family religious practices, (4) degree of acceptance of the theological positions of the churches, (5) attitudes and practices in relation to social and political issues, such as war, race relations, poverty, welfare programs, and so on, (6) position of members on moral issues, (7) extent of interest in and support of denominational programs, and (8) attitudes toward interdenominational cooperation.

It was recognized that each participating denomination might wish to explore areas of interest or concern unique to its own situation. Thus the questionnaire was developed so as to include five sections of items unique to a particular denomination, one section each for the five participating churches. However, most of the questionnaire was designed to be answered by the members of all five denominations.

The basic objective in determining the scope of the study was to obtain information that would be of most use to the various boards and committees of the participating denominations. This necessitated a series of consultations with agency personnel. Over a period of several months, the study directors consulted approximately 175 board and committee officers and staff executives in some 18 different meetings held at various places in the United States and Canada.

From these meetings a long list of topics was derived for possible inclusion in the study. Many of these topics were subsequently worked into the content of the questionnaire. However, the necessity of keeping the questionnaire length within reasonable limits made it impossible to include many of the suggested topics. Whether a questionnaire item was ultimately included or excluded was basically determined by: (1) the number of agencies interested in the item, (2) the item's relevance for testing basic hypotheses about the faith and life of church members, and (3) its relation to basic theories about the relationship between faith and life.

Basic theories of interest to the authors have already been elaborated in early chapters. Of central concern was the extent to which twentieth-century Anabaptists still reflect the theology and social ethics of the sixteenth-century Anabaptists. Another primary focus was upon the "spiritual health" of church members as evidenced by their private and public worship practices, their strength of faith, the commitment of their resources to the work of the church, etc.

A third area of interest relates to assimilation theory. Like all religious or ethnic minorities, Mennonites are subject to the tendency to modify their beliefs and cultural norms in the direction of the beliefs and norms of the larger society of which the minority is a part. But individuals and groups within the Mennonite and BIC ethnic populations vary greatly in the degree to which their beliefs and values conform to those of the larger society. An effort was made to discover the factors that seem to explain these variations in conformity or nonconformity with the values of the larger society.

In summary, the scope of the study was determined by two somewhat conflicting interests: (1) The need to obtain information on a wide variety of topics of concern to a variety of church agencies. This focus, while producing useful information of a practical nature, tends toward a non-integrated, eclectic research product. (2) The desire to test certain basic theories and hypotheses of interest to scholars in the field of the sociology of religion. This approach, aimed at exploring in depth a narrower range of related topics, yields a more closely, reasoned, integrated analysis, shorn of eclectic miscellanea.

This research report represents a compromise between these two conflicting objectives. Much of the material selected for inclusion does relate to a central core of relevant theory. Other data are included because of their usefulness for denominational policy-making and action planning. Hopefully most persons will find both types of data valuable.

A word needs to be said about the data-gathering method used in the study. There are basically two methods for gathering survey data: (1) a personal interview with each respondent, and (2) use of a questionnaire, either sent to the respondent by mail or administered to respondents individually or in groups.

Much can be said for the interview method. The personal contact with the respondent facilitates the establishment of good rapport, gives opportunity for a full explanation of the research goals, secures proper answers to questions since the interviewer can rephrase and interpret the question if necessary, and allows for depth probing. Above all, the interview method secures the highest rate of response, since a personal contact yields fewer refusals. The difficulty, of course, is that interviewing is very time-consuming and therefore highly expensive. If a survey covers a large geographical area, much time and money would be required for travel. Moreover, interviewing is a skill for which considerable training and experience is required.

The use of a questionnaire usually makes possible a much larger number of returns for a given cost than can be obtained by interviewing. Consequently nearly all church member surveys have been done by questionnaire. A notable exception is the Baptist study (Anthony Campolo, Jr., *A Denomination Looks at Itself,* Judson Press, 1971) in which 1,000 church members were interviewed by a professional polling agency. Moreover, the anonymity of the respondent can be assured by questionnaires mailed to respondents or administered in group settings. The weakness is that there may be a serious problem of non-response.

To gather reliable data from five denominations required the use of a large sample. Thus cost considerations ruled out interviewing in favor of the use of a questionnaire. To avoid the high non-response rate associated with mailed questionnaires, an alternative method of administering questionnaires was sought. The possibility of administering questionnaires in the local congregation during the Sunday school hour was considered. This idea was abandoned on the grounds that (1) the Sunday school hour may not provide sufficient time to complete a questionnaire, (2) since only a fraction of the congregation was to be included in the sample, there would be some difficulty in finding separate space for the respondents, and (3) some respondents might object to missing the study of the Sunday school lesson.

The final decision was to administer the questionnaire to the respondents in each sample congregation in a group setting. This was done by calling the respondents together at the church building on some evening when there was no conflict with another church program or activity. This method made possible a significant cost efficiency while providing a personal contact with the respondents. The latter was achieved by the presence of a "research visitor" who went to the congregation to administer the questionnaire. He was able to establish rapport, provide an explanation of the nature and purpose of the study, and offer encouragement to each respondent to fully complete the lengthy questionnaire.

Development of the Research Instrument

The ideas and items ultimately incorporated into the questionnaire were drawn from many sources. The directors of the Lutheran research project (*A Study of Generations*, 1972) were particularly helpful in allowing certain items to be borrowed from their questionnaires. Research by Glock and Stark (*Religion and Society in Tension*, 1965; *American Piety*, 1968) suggested items for probing the respondent's position on theological and ethical issues. Other sources of items and ideas, which we gratefully acknowledge, include Lenski (*The Religious Factor*, 1961), Campbell and Fukuyama (*The Fragmented Layman*, 1970), Hadden (*The Gathering Storm in the Churches*, 1969), Glock, Ringer, and Babbie (*To Comfort and to Challenge*, 1967), and the Mennonite Youth Research. Some items borrowed from other sources could be used without alteration, thus enhancing comparability between studies. Other items were modified in an effort to improve them, or to adapt them more appropriately to a Mennonite context.

It was necessary for the authors to create *de novo* a large number of items for gathering information on specific concerns of the church agencies. Many of these applied only to Mennonite settings or circumstances, and therefore would not have been used in research in other denominations. This was particularly true of those sections of the questionnaire having to do with Anabaptist doctrines, evaluation of church agency programs, attitudes toward Mennonite parochial schools, and attitudes toward inter-Mennonite cooperative agencies and programs.

Questions requiring written answers ("open ended" questions) were generally avoided as being more difficult for the respondent and considerably more time-consuming and costly in the data tabulation phase. "Categorized" responses were almost uniformly used for ease of answering and tabulating.

A major goal was to include items that apply equally well to both sexes, all ages, single and married, and other respondent variants. For example, certain types of questions regarding family relationships would have required different wording for single and married persons, for parents and children, and for husbands and wives. To introduce different sets of questions for different types of respondents might have caused respondent confusion and subsequent error. Two exceptions were made to the principle of formulating questions applicable to all respondents: (1) the unique items for the members of each participating denomination referred to above, and (2) several items referring to politcal matters that had to be worded differently for Canadian and American respondents.

The questionnaire sections went through several revisions. A draft of the questionnaire was submitted for criticism to about fifty denominational leaders, which resulted in numerous helpful suggestions for improvement. As a pretest, the instrument was administered to 38 church members selected to represent a wide range of age and educational levels. This permitted an item analysis test on scale items, and those items evidencing low validity were dropped from the scales.

A matter of considerable concern was the length of the questionnaire. The pretest experience indicated that respondents would persist in answering questions for at least two hours, not without some strain, however, in the case of elderly persons and persons with low educational achievement. The Lutheran survey succeeded even though the average respondent was required to work for nearly three hours to complete the questionnaires. It was decided that the Mennonite questionnaire should require not more than two hours for the average respondent to complete. This would permit the gathering of as large a quantity of data as possible, which was desired because of the large investment of resources in the project. With a "coffee break" between the two hours of work, it was assumed that few respondents would be unable to complete the questionnaire on the appointed evening. The questionnaire required the respondent to work through about 27 large pages of questions.

Various efforts were made to assure the respondent's anonymity, to minimize any anxiety he may have, and to urge care and diligence in responding to the questionnaire items. These can perhaps best be indicated by quoting the letter appearing on the inside cover of the questionnaire:

Dear Fellow Church Member:

Welcome aboard! You are about to become a participant in the most extensive study ever made of the members of Mennonite and Brethren in Christ congregations throughout the United States and Canada. We are grateful for your willingness to be a part of this significant study.

Try to imagine a leader of your denomination reaching a major decision on some church project (evangelistic emphasis, Christian education, finances, etc.) and asking himself, "How do people in our churches really feel about this?" Now you and over 4,000 other church members of all ages have the opportunity to help answer many of his questions. You will help to paint a portrait of our churches in the 1970s.

If you have any anxiety about filling out a questionnaire, we would like to put you at ease. First of all, this is not a test of your knowledge, so there is no sense in which you could "fail." You are asked mainly to express your opinions and beliefs on a large variety of matters simply by putting check marks in blank spaces.

You will not sign the questionnaire, so the information you give will be strictly anonymous. The data will be processed by a computer. The results will be reported only for *large groups* of respondents, not for either individuals or congregations. The number that appears on the front of this questionnaire is a *congregation* number and is the same for all members of your congregation. It does not identify you as a person.

This may be the longest questionnaire you have ever answered, but do not dismay! The material should be sufficiently stimulating to keep your interest high to the end, even if it should take as much as a couple of hours to finish. Frankly, the investment in time and resources to do this major survey argues for covering as much ground as possible in this one time around.

It is expected that the results of the study will be reported in book form, and thus be available to all interested persons. Perhaps some portion of the findings can reach you through articles in the denominational papers.

Following the letter, a page of instructions for answering the questions was presented, as follows:

To the Respondent

1. *Easy Answering.* This questionnaire has been constructed so that answers can be given very easily — simply by making a check mark in a blank space. There is no time limit, but do not spend too much time on any one item. Give your first impression and move quickly to the next item.

2. *At the beginning of each section* you will find specific instructions for answering the questions in that section. Please read and follow these carefully. In a few places you will be asked to check more than one answer.

3. *Please answer every question* that applies to you. Unanswered questions cause problems in tabulating and processing the data.

4. *Frankness and honesty in answering.* A study of this kind is useful only if the respondents are wholly frank and honest in expressing their beliefs and opinions. Answer all questions accurately and as you truly believe, not as someone else might wish you to answer.

5. Do your best to answer the questions as they are written. Do not attempt to change the wording of questions or responses.

6. The word "Americans" should in all cases be understood to mean members who are living in the United States, whether citizens or not. Persons living in Canada are uniformly referred to as "Canadians" whether citizens or not. Although nearly all items in the questionnaire are for both Americans and Canadians, a few are to be answered only by one or the other.

7. Respondents who are *temporarily* living away from home (in college, in service, etc.) will need to answer questions pertaining to their relationships to their home congregations by recalling the situation during their most recent period of living at home.

Selection of the Participants

At the end of the questionnaire, the respondent was invited to add any parting comments he might have. Among those who wrote comments, a few expressed negative criticisms, for example, "I personally think more time should be spent in winning souls instead of studying the members of churches." Most, however, indicated favorable reactions. Two of the latter were: "It was very interesting. I had never as much as thought about a lot of these questions before." "It made one examine himself and his relationship with God and the church."

Assuming that other respondents also had such reactions, it could be argued that maximum benefit to the churches would have resulted if all members had been asked to complete a questionnaire. To print, administer, and tabulate the results from nearly 200,000 questionnaires, of course, would have required resources far beyond those available. Obviously the study required the use of a properly chosen sample of all church members.

The assignment given to the study directors was to study church members in the United States and Canada. Because of language differences, and problems related to geographic distance, members belonging to congregations affiliated with the participating denominations but located in countries other than the United States and Canada, including Puerto Rico, were not to be included. Any member of a church located in the U.S. and Canada, but living abroad, was to be included if his name was drawn from the membership list of his participating congregation. What was needed therefore was a sample of the church members of all congregations located in the United States and Canada and affiliated with one of the five participating denominations.

Actually five samples were needed, one for each of the five denominations. Since the total membership of these denominations varied widely (from nearly 90,000 for the MC to about 3,000 for the EMC) the sample size or the sample proportion, or both, would need to vary from church to church. Separate samples were needed in part because denominational leaders wanted separate tabulations of data for their respective denominations.

The determination of sample size must necessarily represent a compromise between two conflicting desiderata: (1) maximum reliability of the sample data, which is achieved by using as large a sample as possible, and (2) minimum cost, which is achieved by keeping the sample as small as possible. In order to keep the sample variance at a desirable level, and to keep within the budgeted financial resources a target sample of 5,000 members was established, with estimated returns of 75% or 3,750 completed questionnaires. The total was distributed so that the smallest denomination would be represented by not less than 500 respondents and the largest by not less than 1,000. The distribution of members, churches, and sample estimates for the five denominations is given in Table A-1. The data on members and churches were for the most recent years available (1970 or 1969) at the time the sample was drawn (1971).

How can a target sample of 5,000 best be selected? Once again attention had to be given to cost/benefit considerations. From a strictly scientific standpoint, the best sample would be a simple random selection of 5,000 names from a listing of the total of nearly 190,000 members. This would involve selecting one sample member for every 38 (190,000/5,000) church members, an average of about three persons for every congregation. Such a procedure would be highly inefficient, however, as it would necessitate working with all 1,646 congregations in order to list names of all members, draw a sample, and administer questionnaires to one or more

TABLE A-1
Members, Churches, and Sample Estimates for the
Five Denominations, United States and Canada

Denomination	Total Members*	Total Churches*	Average Members Per Church	Target Sample	Estimated Respondents
Mennonite Church	89,273	957	93	1400	1000
General Conf. Mennonite	55,623	286	194	1100	900
Mennonite Brethren	31,327	211	148	1000	750
Brethren in Christ	10,589	175	61	800	600
Evangelical Mennonite	2,950	17	174	700	500
Total	189,762	1646	115	5000	3750

*For churches in United States and Canada only. (Puerto Rico is excluded.)

sample members in each congregation. Consequently a two-stage sampling process was adopted, with a selection of approximately 200 congregations in the first stage, followed in the second stage by a random selection of 25 to 30 sample members from each sample congregation.

The Sample of Congregations. The first step was to establish a "sampling universe" of congregations, *i.e.*, a listing of all "eligible" congregations in each denomination. For the sake of efficiency, small congregations were omitted. In the Lutheran study all congregations of less than 50 members were omitted, resulting in a reduction of persons of less than one percent (Strommen, *et al*, 1972, p. 321). For the MBC, GCMC, and EMC, all congregations with less than 50 members were omitted. Due to the fact that the MC and the BIC have much larger proportions of small churches (average membership per church being only 93 and 61 respectively) it seemed necessary to use a smaller cutoff point. Consequently for these two churches all congregations with less than 25 members were omitted. As a result of these omissions of small churches, the number of "eligible" congregations was reduced from 1,646 to 1,265, a reduction of 23%. However, the reduction of eligible church members was much less — from 189,762 to 182,463, or 4%. This small percentage loss cannot be expected to have significantly altered the research findings, even on those variables on which congregation size has some noticeable effect.

Another criterion of eligibility was whether the congregation was formally affiliated with a conference — district or general. Certain arbitrary decisions were reached by denominational officials, since the situation varied from church to church. In the BIC and MBC there was no problem of determining eligibility. All eligible congregations were members of a district (regional) conference and *ipso facto* members of the denominational general conference. In the EMC there are no district conferences, all 17 congregations being members of the denominational organization.

In the GCMC, a congregation is normally affiliated with both a district (regional) conference and the General Conference. Some congregations, however, are members of one or the other, but not both. It was decided that only those congregations that were affiliated with the General Conference would be included in the sampling universe.

In the MC, congregational affiliation is with a district conference only, and not with the Mennonite General Conference, whose membership is comprised of district conferences. Thus congregations in the MC were included in the sampling universe only if they were affiliated with a district conference. This ruled out over 100 congregations who are "independent" Mennonite congregations.

Table A-2 gives the distribution of the 1,265 eligible congregations by denomination. The table also indicates the proportion of total members included in the sampling universe after the exclusion of small churches.

TABLE A-2
Congregations in the Sampling Universe
by Denomination

Denomination	Number of Churches	Number of Members Included	Percent of Total Members Included	Target Churches Selected
Mennonite Church	734*	86,003	96.3	70
General Conf. Mennonite	245**	54,323	97.7	50
Mennonite Brethren	146**	29,409	93.9	40
Brethren in Christ	125*	9,848	93.3	30
Evangelical Mennonite	15**	2,880	97.6	15
Total	1265	182,463	96.2	205

*All churches under 25 members omitted.
**All churches under 50 members omitted.

Since there were only 15 eligible congregations in the EMC, all of these were included in the sample. In the other four denominations a stratified random selection was made. The yearbook for each denomination lists the congregations alphabetically within conference districts. After the ineligible congregations were crossed off, the remaining congregations were listed (alphabetically) and the congregational membership was listed in a second column. An accumulative membership total was added as a third column, by successively adding each congregation membership to the previous total.

When the eligible churches for a denomination had all been listed and total membership accumulated, the total membership was divided by the number of target sample congregations for that denomination. This yielded a "skip interval." A "random start" was obtained by selecting (from a table of random numbers) a number from one to the skip interval. Beginning with the number of the "random start," the skip interval was successively added and each resulting "selection number" was noted in a fourth column beside the congregation whose cumulative membership numbers contained the selection number. This was continued to the end of the listing, and resulted in the selection of the desired number of sample congregations.

This process of selection is illustrated in Table A-3, which contains the initial portion of the congregational listing for the BIC. This process is desirable because it gives to each congregation a probability of selection in proportion to its size. For example, a congregation of 500 members has ten times the chance of being selected as a congregation of 50 members. (See Leslie Kish, *Survey Sampling*, 1965, Chapters 7 and 10, for an explanation of this method of multi-stage "area" sampling.) Thus *each member* of a large congregation has the same chance of being selected as each member of a small congregation (provided the second stage of the sampling

TABLE A-3
Initial Portion of Sample Congregation Selection Table
for the Brethren in Christ Church

Conference and Congregation	Congregation Membership	Cumulative Membership Total	Selection Number
Allegheny Conference:			
Air Hill	155	155	152*
Altoona	33	188	
Antrim	154	342	
Baltimore	47	389	
Big Valley	48	437	
Carlisle	261	698	480**
Cedar Grove	62	760	
Cedar Springs	71	831	808
Chambersburg	242	1073	
Clarence Center	123	1196	1136
. . .	. . .	. . .	. . .
Welland	36	9843	

*Random start 152
**Skip interval   9,843 members divided by 30 target churches   328

process selects the *same number* of sample members from each congregation regardless of size, as noted later.) This is important because it is a sample of *members*, not a sample of churches, that was ultimately needed. Every member of a denomination should have the same probability of being selected for the sample as every other member if the sample is to be properly representative of the denominational membership.

The process resulted in the selection of a much larger proportion of the large congregations than of the smaller congregations. This was properly offset, however, by the fact that in the second stage, much larger proportions of the members of small sample congregations than of the members of large congregations were chosen.

Of the 205 congregations selected, two were discovered to have recently severed their ties to their district conferences. This ruled them ineligible, resulting in only 203 eligible sample congregations. The pastor (or lay leader, in a few cases) of the congregation was contacted by correspondence to elicit the congregation's participation in the survey, and to request a list of the members of the congregation. Ultimately 174 congregations (85.7%) participated. The other 29 congregations declined to participate for a variety of reasons. A number of MBC and GCMC pastors in the western provinces of Canada insisted that too many of their members were German-speaking and would not be able to complete a questionnaire in English. Twelve Canadian churches refused participation at least in part for language reasons. Several pastors refused on the basis of personal disinterest in surveys, for reasons of being too busy, or for fear that involvement in the study would require too much time. A few congregations pleaded inability to participate due to a temporary lack of pastoral leadership. In a couple cases the congregation was in the process of disintegration. The pastors of a couple churches insisted that their members, having largely come from non-Mennonite backgrounds, will be ill prepared to answer questions about their denomination.

The Sample of Congregation Members. The second stage of the sampling process involved a selection of sample members from each sample congregation. If all members of the sample churches had been included in the survey, the number of respondents would have been much too large — on the order of 20,000, or four times too great. This might have been offset by taking only one fourth the number of sample congregations, say 50, but this would have reduced the number of sample congregations in each denomination to a very low number (e.g., only seven for the BIC). This would seriously threaten the reliability of the sample, since the probability of choosing a good cross-section of churches would be greatly reduced. On the other hand, it would be a financial advantage, since it would cost much less to send "research visitors" to 50 churches instead of 200.

A further disadvantage that would have accrued if all members of a congregation were included in the survey was the difficulty of administering questionnaires to large groups. Probably the greater efficiency is achieved when a supervisor is in charge of a "classroom size" group of from 15 to

30 persons. Smaller groups cause the respondent unit cost to be greater than necessary. Larger groups lead to problems of administering the questionnaire — finding a room large enough and adequately equipped for all to be accommodated, and finding it possible for the administrator to supervise adequately that many people.

Consequently it was decided that the number of sample members to be selected from each congregation should not be more than 35 nor less than 25. Allowing for absentees and nonresidents, the number of respondents appearing on a given evening would likely run from 15 to 25, a desirable number from the standpoints of efficiency and effectiveness of administration.

A simplification of the sample selection process (and therefore a slight advantage) results when a uniform number of sample members is chosen from each sampling unit (congregation, in this case). This policy was adopted within denominations, with some variation in sample size between denominations. The number of sample members needed from each denominational sampling unit was determined by dividing the target sample for that denomination by the estimated number of participating churches. Table A-4 indicates the estimates and computations used in arriving at the number of sample members to be drawn from each congregation in each denomination.

Membership lists were received from the 174 participating congregations. The pastor was asked to up-date the list as of the time he mailed it in. The list was to include *all* members, whether active or inactive, resident or nonresident in the local community. Persons regularly attending the

TABLE A-4
Computation of Number of sample Members Needed from Each Congregation

Denomination	Target Sample	Number of Churches Selected	Estimated Number of Participating Churches	Number of Sample Members per Church
Mennonite Church	1400	70	60	25
General Conf. Menn.	1100	50	42	28
Mennonite Brethren	1000	40	34	31
Brethren in Christ	800	30	25	32
Evangelical Menn.	700	15	12	58
Total	5000	205	173	...

church but not yet members were to be excluded from the list. Most membership lists were arranged alphabetically by members' last names, sometimes grouped by families.

The first step in the selection process was to number the members from 1 to N (the total number). The "selection ratio" was then determined by dividing the total number by the number of sample members to be chosen from the congregation. If a congregation had 200 members and 25 were to be selected, then the selection ratio would be 200/25 or eight members for every one to be selected. The method used was to take every "nth" number on the membership list, in this case every eighth name would be selected. The name to be started with was randomized for each list by taking (from a table of random numbers) a "random start," a number from one to the "selection ratio" number. In the case of the illustration, the random start was some number from one to eight. Beginning with the random start, every nth name was selected and listed on a sample form sheet for the congregation.

The sampling procedure for the EMC congregations was different, since all churches, rather than a sample, had been included in the first-stage selection process. In order that all church members would have equal probability of selection, a constant selection ratio had to be applied in *all* congregations in selecting the sample members. Since the 15 eligible congregations contained 2,880 and the target sample for the denomination was 700, a selection ratio of four (2880/700) was adopted. Thus, for the EMC congregations, every fourth member was selected for the sample.

As mentioned earlier it was decided that the pastor of each congregation should be included in the survey. If the pastor's name was not obtained in the random selection process, it was added to the congregation sample list. There were two main reasons for this: (1) to involve the pastor in the study so as to hopefully increase his understanding and interest in the research program, and (2) to increase the number of ordained persons in the sample in order to increase the reliability of comparisons between ordained and non-ordained church members. The 129 pastors thus arbitrarily added had the effect of raising from 5% to 9% the proportion of ordained persons within the total sample.

It should be noted that no substitutions were made for refusals in either of the sampling stages. Both the original number of congregations selected (205) and the target number of sample members (5,000) were set at a large enough figure to allow for expected refusals and still have sufficient remaining congregations and members. This no-substitution strategy proved satisfactory, since the number of cooperating churches (174) and the number of respondents (3,670) turned out to be close to original expectations (168 and 3,750 respectively).

Participation of Congregation Sample Members. It was assumed that, for various reasons, some of the congregation sample members would not be able to participate. Indeed, in none of the congregations did every sample member participate, although in a few congregations all but one or two members succeeded in filling out a questionnaire.

Two copies of the congregation sample list were sent to each pastor, one copy to keep and one to return to the research office. The purpose of this was to have the pastor verify the sample list and to indicate which sample members would not be able to come to a meeting to complete a questionnaire. The latter were not to be sent the form letter of invitation to attend the meeting. The pastor was asked, "If any sample member falls into one or more of the following categories of persons whose ability or availability for completing a questionnaire may be in question, please place the *letter* of the category in the blank space in front of the name." The categories were:

A. Not presently a member of this congregation. (The person may have died or withdrawn from membership in the several months interim since the membership lists were originally submitted; or the name may appear by error.)

B. Member *under* the age of 13. (It was assumed such individuals might have difficulty comprehending some parts of the questionnaire.)

C. Has a physical or mental disability, serious illness, or other incapacitation that might prevent completing a questionnaire.

D. Cannot read English well enough to complete a questionnaire.

E. Is temporarily absent from the community due to attending college, in service, or other reason.

F. Is no longer resident within commuting distance of the church.

G. Inactive member, still resident in the community, possibly attending elsewhere.

H. Other reasons: Please write the reason following the name.

The pastor was further requested to add the full address of any member who was not presently living in the community (the "nonresidents," designated "E" or "F"). These addresses were then used in mailing a questionnaire from the research office to each nonresident member. Where pastors failed to provide these addresses on the returned sample form, further correspondence was necessary to obtain the addresses.

In designating the persons unable to participate in the survey, we were at the mercy of the judgment of the pastor, since there was no other feasible way to obtain such information. We have no check on the accuracy of the pastor's judgments. On the other hand, we have no reason to believe that the pastors made improper judgments, except possibly by unwitting error.

The policy of selecting the congregation sample at the research office proved to be a wise step in retaining objective control over the sample selection process. It would have been possible to place responsibility for congregation sample selection in the hands of the pastor by providing him with a set of instructions for carrying out the process. However, it is probable that numerous errors would have been made due to the intricacies of the process. Also we detected in some cases some tendencies of pastors to shield inactive or disloyal members from inclusion in the sample. It was necessary in some cases to emphasize the necessity of including all types of members, inactive as well as active, aberrant as well as faithful members, if the final sample was to be as free as possible from bias in a favorable direction.

Field Procedures

A vital link in the research chain was the role played by each of the 44 "Research Visitors" who traveled to the 174 congregations to administer the questionnaires. These were, for the most part, staff members of various denominational boards, committees, and institutions who volunteered their time without remuneration. Typically a research visitor visited from four to six congregations located within 100 to 200 miles from his home. In a few cases, the research visitor had to travel large distances to reach remote congregations, such as in Florida or central Saskatchewan.

Each research visitor (R.V.) participated in a "training session" conducted by the study director. To minimize travel, three such all-day sessions were held in different parts of the United States. The purpose of the training session was to fully inform the research visitors of the background, nature, and goals of the research project, and to work out in detail the strategy and procedures for visiting the churches and administering the questionnaires. A Research Manual, prepared by the study director, was supplied to each research visitor for use during the training session and to serve as a guide and reminder of the details that needed to be carried out in the field work.

The first task of the research visitor was to contact (normally by phone) the pastor of each sample congregation assigned to him. Between them a date was determined for the research visit; also any details on the time of the research meeting, facilities available, etc., could be discussed. The plan was for the sample members in each congregation to be invited by letter to come to the church building on the appointed evening. When the pastor and the R.V. had agreed on a date, the pastor mailed to each sample member a form letter announcing the study and giving details on time and place of the meeting. Enclosed with the letter was a brochure explaining the Church Member Profile project in some detail. Both the form letter and the brochure were supplied the pastor by the central research office, although the pastor added his name to the bottom of the letter.

The pastor was instructed to send these letters only to those members who should be able to attend the meeting. A person on the sample list did not receive a letter if he was no longer a member, was under 13 years of age, was incapacitated due to physical or mental illness or disability, could not read English, or was not currently resident in the community. The pastor was instructed to send a letter to all inactive members and was urged to make every possible effort to elicit their participation. As a follow-up procedure, the pastor was urged to make a personal contact to encourage the participation of any person who might be reluctant or anxious about becoming involved in the study. The goal of maximum particiation was stressed.

The R.V. was in full charge of the research meeting from start to finish. Meetings normally began at 7:00 P.M. and were held in a large Sunday school room or a fellowship hall. The R.V. was expected to arrive considerably ahead of meeting time in order to check with the pastor on last-minute details and to see that facilities· for seating, writing, proper lighting, ventilation, etc., were in order. In nearly all cases a "coffee break" had been arranged by the pastor or pastor's wife. After a solid hour of work, coffee and cookies proved to be a valuable strain reliever and energy restorer.

At the start of the meeting it was the R.V.'s duty to welcome the participants, help them to find seats and be at ease, briefly review the nature, purpose, and importance of the project, distribute the questionnaires, try to answer any questions about procedures, and encourage the respondent to seek his assistance if anything was not clear.

At the end of the meeting the R.V. received the completed questionnaires, checked attendance on a copy of the sample list, and arranged for the pastor or some other person to place a questionnaire copy and return envelope in the hands of each absentee (any person invited but who did not appear). The R.V. was also instructed to obtain any nonresident's address which had not already been obtained.

When a respondent had completed his questionnaire he was free to leave. The most speedy respondents were able to complete the questionnaire in an hour or slightly longer. The average time requirement was about two hours. Slower respondents took up to three hours. In a few cases, a person still laboring after three hours was given a mailing envelope, with the suggestion that he complete the questionnaire the next day and mail it in.

Following the visit, the R.V. returned the following by mail: (1) the completed questionnaires, (2) the congregation sample list, on which attendance had been marked, and on which it was indicated for which absentees a blank questionnaire was left for later return, and (3) a "Research Visit Report Form" on which the R.V. reported the number in attendance, number of absentees, and the name and address of the person who agreed to give questionnaires to the absentees.

Upon receipt of the R.V.'s report of visits, the research office compiled a list of names and addresses of all nonresident sample members. These persons were then mailed a brochure, questionnaire copy, return envelope, and a cover letter encouraging them to complete and return the questionnaire. Of the 661 nonrespondents, returns were received from 257 (38.9%). These returns seem to justify the effort to reach them, since they do provide useful information about this special category of church members.

An effort was also made to follow up on absentees, who had been given questionnaires to complete at home and mail in. An "absentee" was a resident member, presumably able to appear at the meeting, but who did not appear. In many cases, of course, his absence was due to some conflicting activity. Several weeks after the date of the research visit, a follow-up on these persons was made in the hope of adding to the returns already received.

The research visitor's report indicated which persons were absentees. Although a numbering system was used to determine how many absentee returns had been received from each congregation, it was not possible to know *which* absentees had, and which had not, returned a questionnaire. By comparing the number of absentees with the number of absentee returns it was possible to determine how many had not yet returned a questionnaire. In a congregation where this difference was more than two, a follow-up was made. The R.V. had listed on his report form the name and address of the follow-up designate. This person (usually the pastor) was sent a letter with an enclosed list of absentees for his congregation, and was urged to contact each absentee and encourage completing and re-turning of the questionnaire by anyone who had not already done so. There was evidence that this effort did yield additional returns.

A summary of the sampling results is given in Table A-5. The data indicate a congregation participation rate of 85.7%. By denominations, the congregation participation rate ranged from 75.5% for the GCMC to 91.3% for the MC.

A total of 5,202 eligible sample members was obtained in the 174 participating congregations. Questionnaires were received from 3,670 respon-dents, a rate of 70.5%, somewhat below the hoped-for rate of 75%, but comparing favorably with other denominational studies. Congregational participation and sample return rates for the Lutheran study were 85% and 65% respectively. (Strommen, 1972, pp. 322-330.) Questionnaire returns as a percent of the total samples by denominations ranged from 60.9% for the GCMC to 75.6% for the MC.

Compared to the results for all denominations, the MC and BIC con-gregation and member participation rates were higher than average, GCMC rates were lower than average, and the MBC and EMC were about average.

The tabulated data are based on 3,591 adequately completed ques-tionnaires. Although there were 3,670 returns, 79 of these were rejected on the basis of being inadequately completed, i.e., several sections or numerous items had not been answered. The 3,591 usable returns are 69.0% of the 5,202 eligible members on the original membership lists of the 174 participating congregations. If a subtraction of persons unable to participate (ill, incapacitated, or unable to use English) is made, the number of usable returns is 73.9% of all persons eligible and able to participate. These data are summarized in Table A-6.

Finally, of the 3,591 usable returns, 2,577 (71.8%) were completed at meetings, 761 (21.2%) were mailed in by absentees, and 253 (7.0%) were returned by nonresidents to whom questionnaires had been mailed.

TABLE A-5
Analysis of Sampling Results

	Denomination					
	MC	GCM	MB	BIC	EMC	Total
A. Congregation Sample:						
Churches selected	70	50	40	30	15	205
"Eligible" churches	69	49	40	30	15	203
Participating churches	63	37	34	27	13	174
Participating churches as % of eligible churches	91.3	75.5	85.0	90.0	86.7	85.7
B. Member Sample:						
Total eligible sample members in participating congregations*	1588	1049	1048	856	661	5202
Questionnaires returned	1228	639	723	631	449	3670
Questionnaires returned as % of total sample	77.3	60.9	69.0	73.7	67.9	70.5
Average sample members per participating cong.	25.2	28.4	30.8	31.7	50.8	29.9
Average questionnaires returned per participating congregation	19.5	17.3	21.3	23.4	34.5	21.1

°Not included: 46 members under 13 years old and therefore ineligible, and 89 persons no longer members.

Analysis of Data

Each completed questionnaire was assigned an identifying five-digit code number. The first digit identified the denomination; the second and third digits the congregation and the district conference with which it was affiliated. The fourth and fifth digits were respondent numbers. The first three digits were placed on the questionnaires before they were used, so that when they were returned, the congregation to which the respondents belonged would be known. The fourth and fifth digits were added when the questionnaire was returned. The fourth digit indicated whether the respondent completed the questionnaire at an evening meeting, or whether he was an absentee or a nonresident.

TABLE A-6
Analysis of Usable Returns

Category		Number	Usable returns (3,591) as a per- cent of category
1. All names drawn in the sample		5,337	67.3
Less ineligible names: Recently deceased or otherwise withdrawn from membership	89		
Under age 13	46	135	
2. All eligible names		5,202	69.0
Less persons unable to participate: Chronically ill, or mentally or physically incapacitated	239		
Unable to read English adquately	104	343	
3. All persons able to respond		4,859	73.9

Each returned questionnaire was examined to determine whether it was adequately completed, and therefore could be included in the data tabulation. As mentioned in the previous section, 79 (2.2%) were discarded for the reason of having too many uncompleted sections or items. A tabulation of these 79 questionnaires revealed that these respondents were much older on the average, and had lower average educational achievement than the other respondents. For example, the median age of all respondents was 41.2 years, but was 71.1 years for the 79 respondents returning incomplete questionnaires. This would suggest that failure to respond adequately was related to low ability rather than carelessness or neglect.

Data Processing. All questionnaire item responses were assigned numerical codes, and the coded responses were punched into data cards for computer processing. Eight cards were required to contain the data of one questionnaire. The services of the Computation Center at the University of Chicago were utilized for all data processing. This involved, first of all, the transfer of the card data to magnetic tape, and then the preparation of tabulations and statistical computations from the tape. The SPSS (Statistical Package for the Social Sciences) system of data processing provided highly efficient methods of preparing tables, assembling scale data and producing percentage distributions, correlations, tests of significance of association between variables, and other statistical measures. Staff members of the National Opinion Research Center, located at the University of Chicago, served as consultants on data processing. These persons had earlier been consulted on various aspects of the sampling design.

After the data were transferred from cards to magnetic tape, the data were "cleaned" of all "illegitimate" codes that had resulted from errors in coding and punching. Illegitimate codes were transformed into "missing data" (combined with nonresponse codes). For most items, the missing data frequencies tended to run below two percent.

Most computer printout of data was obtained in the form of two- and three-variable cross-tabulations, providing both raw frequencies and percentage distributions. In working with nonparametric variables, the chi-square test of independence of relationship between variables was commonly used.

Significance Level. An alpha level of .01 was used to determine significance of association between variables. That is, no relationship was assumed to be significant unless there was less than one chance in 100 that the observed relationship resulted from chance factors in sampling. Thus a relationship identified as significant can, with high confidence, be assumed to actually exist in the denominational populations which the sample presumes to describe. Actually, due to the large sample and subsamples, the level of significance for most cross-tabulations proved to be a probability of less than .001. Indeed, many cross-tabulations resulted in a probability of less than .00001.

Denominational Weighting Procedures. For certain parts of the data analysis it was necessary to weight the responses of each respondent according to his denomination. This was not necessary when data were tabulated for the denominations separately. However, when tabulations were needed for the entire sample, each denomination needed to carry no more nor no less than its proportional weight in the total response. Since the five denominations are not represented in the total sample in the proportions which they represent in the total populations, it was necessary to make an adjustment that would bring the respondents of each denomination into line with the proportion which that denomination obtains in the total combined membership of the five churches. For example, the GCMC constitutes 29.3% of the total membership of the five denominations, but only 17.1% of the respondents. By weighting the GCMC responses by a factor of 1.71, the GCMC responses then carry their proper weight in the sample. By applying a weight factor of 0.13 to the 444 EMC responses, their weight is reduced to the 1.6% of total adjusted responses, the same proportion that EMC membership obtains in the membership of the five denominations. The data for these adjustments are given in Table A-7.

The table indicates that the MC and the GCMC are underrepresented in the sample, and the other three churches are overrepresented. The "adjusted sample" column gives the distribution of 3,591 respondents if each denomination were represented by its proper proportion in the sample. The "weight factor" is the amount by which the actual number of respondents for a denomination needs to be multiplied to bring the

TABLE A-7
Derivation of Weight Factors for Adjusting
Denominational Responses

Denomination	Total Membership		Sample		Adjusted Sample*	Weight Factor**
	N	%	N	%		
MC	89,273	47.0	1202	33.5	1688	1.40
GCM	55,623	29.3	614	17.1	1052	1.71
MB	31,327	16.5	712	19.8	593	0.83
BIC	10,589	5.6	619	17.2	201	0.32
EMC	2,950	1.6	444	12.4	57	0.13
Total	189,762	100.00	3591	100.0	3591	

*Obtained by multiplying the percentages in the total membership column by 3,591 (total sample).
**Obtained by dividing, for each denomination, the adjusted sample by the actual sample.

denominational weight into its true proportion in the total population. Whenever cross-tabulations, or other computations, were made for the entire sample, these weight factors were assigned to the responses. Fortunately this adjustment, an impossible task if it were to be done by hand, can be done very simply by the computer.

Derivation of Scales. Many of the principal variables in the study have been measured by means of a scale or scales, rather than by the responses to a single item. A scale provides a measure of a variable in terms of a range of numerical values from the lowest score to the highest. A respondent's scale score is derived by adding together the coded values of the responses to the items that comprise the scale.

The rationale for the use of a scale is largely that a dimension (variable) can be measured more accurately by several items than by one. For example, "Adherence to Anabaptism" can be more reliably measured by a scale of six or eight items than by reliance upon a single item. This is because there are many tenets of Anabaptism, and if a measure of adherence to Anabaptism was to rely on any one of them alone, there would be considerable error, since a respondent that agrees with one aspect of Anabaptism may not agree with others. The best measure of the individual respondent's adherence to Anabaptism would be that incorporates most, or at least the more important, of the tenets of Anabaptism. Thus his scale rating, or score, represents a composite of his agreements (or disagreements) on a series of significant items.

A total of 34 scales and subscales were used in this report. Some of the scales were derived from sets of items that were used in other research projects. Others were developed *de novo* to fit the needs of this study. Following are the names of the scales, listed according to the chapter in which the derivation of the scale is explained:

Chapter		*Chapter*	
4	Associationalism.	8	Social Concerns
4	Voluntarism	9	Separation of Church and State
4	Communalism	9	Political Participation
5	Moral-Personal Conversion	9	Political Action
5	Ethical-Social Conversion	11	Shared Ministry
5	Sanctification	11	Role of Women
5	Devotionalism	12	Sunday School Participation
6	General Orthodoxy	12	Bible Knowledge
6	Fundamentalist Orthodoxy	12	Evangelism
6	Anabaptism	13	Support of Church Colleges
7	Moral Attitudes	14	Stewardship Attitudes
7	Moral Behavior	14	Stewardship Performance
8	Pacifism	15	Ecumenism
8	Race Relations	15	Anti-Semitism
8	Welfare Attitudes	15	Anti-Catholic
8	Anti-Communism	15	MCC Support
8	Anti-Labor Union	17	Socioeconomic Status

An "Item Analysis Test" was relied upon as the principal method of testing the validity of scale items. This test, developed by Rundquist and Sletto (*Personality in the Depression,* Univ. of Minnesota Press, 1936), determines the power of each item to discriminate between those respondents who score high and those who score low on the scale. If an item was found to have low "discriminative power" it was dropped from the scale. This test of scale items was used on data obtained from the pretest, and then again on the final data. An additional validity check was made by computing a coefficient of correlation between the scores for each item and the total scores for the scale of which the item was a part.

A functional advantage of a scale is that the range of possible scores is usually large enough to justify the use of parametric statistics in the analysis of data. Consequently Pearsonian "r" was frequently utilized as a measure of the association between scales.

INDEX

Abortion, 122-123, 179-181
Abott, Walter M., 359
Accommodation, 38, 300
Acculturation, 300, 304, 321
Africa, 20
Age characteristics, 55-58
Age differences, 72, 128, 137, 158, 160, 162, 180-181, 188-189, 205-206, 215, 220, 230, 234, 240, 249, 251, 256, 261-274, 295, 315, 319, 347, 359
Age of accountability, 89
Age of baptism, 70
Age of conversion, 71-72, 87-88
Agrartypus, 360
Agricola, Franz, 23
Alexanderwohl, 75
Algemeene Doopsgezinde Societet, 344
All-Mennonite Conventions, 47, 247
Allport, Gordon, 89, 265, 331, 349, 359, 363
Alsace, 20
Alternative service, 133
American Association of Fund-Raising Council, 234, 357
American Baptists, 55, 66, 68, 99, 205, 263
American Independent Party, 164
American Journal of Sociology, 360
American Protestantism, 298
American Sociological Review, 351, 359, 362
American Sunday School Union, 200-201
Amish, 19, 120
Amish schism, 244
Ammann, Jacob, 20
Amsterdam, 49, 291
Anabaptism, 16th century, 19, 20, 22, 23, 26, 27, 32, 34, 39, 40, 50, 64, 69-70, 84, 92, 96, 102, 103, 111, 115-116, 118-119, 129, 130, 144, 150-151, 170, 183-185, 190, 194-195, 201-202, 210-211, 243-245, 253, 256, 277, 289, 290-292, 299-300, 301, 304, 310, 314, 321-322, 336, 339, 341, 342, 344, 360, 365
Anabaptism Scale, 27, 115, 129, 135, 137, 138, 143, 146, 149, 158, 160, 162, 168, 189, 194, 197, 205, 214, 216, 224-225, 227, 230, 242, 249, 251, 257, 259, 268, 278, 280-281, 295, 301-303, 305, 308, 315, 319, 320, 321, 323, 324, 325, 327, 328, 329, 331, 338, 341, 342, 353, 385,
Anabaptist curriculum, 202-203
Anabaptist Curriculum Project, 217
Anabaptist-Mennonite concept, 313
Anabaptist type, 253
Anabaptist Vision, The, 42, 114, 136, 292, 301, 312-314, 317-318, 339, 344
Anglican, 26
Anti-Catholic Scale, 137, 143, 194, 197, 214, 216, 249-252, 272, 281, 289, 302, 304, 308-309, 317, 319, 324, 325, 328, 329, 330, 338, 385
Anti-Communism Scale, 135, 137, 143-144; 149, 189, 194, 272, 280-281, 289, 302, 304, 317, 319, 321, 325, 328, 329, 385

Anti-Labor Union Scale, 146, 149, 280-281, 287, 302, 304, 319, 338, 385
Anti-Semitism Scale, 135, 137, 143, 194, 214, 216, 249-252, 269, 272, 281, 302, 304, 308-309, 317, 319, 324, 325, 328, 329, 330, 338, 385
Argyle, Michael, 88, 262, 264, 266, 279, 349, 359, 360
Aristotle, 284
Arnett, William M., 351
Asia, 20
Assemblies of God, 309
Assimilation, 300, 305, 307, 342, 365
Associated Mennonite Biblical Seminaries, 185, 192, 349, 355, 357

Associationalism concept, 64-69, 74, 76, 81, 222
Associationalism Scale, 67-68, 82, 129, 136, 137, 188-189, 205, 213, 224-227, 242, 259, 267, 281, 289-290, 302, 308, 318, 319, 320, 321, 323, 324, 325, 331, 335, 338, 385
Attendance at church schools, 220-221
Attendance at public worship, 66
Attendance at Sunday school, 68
Austria, 20
Autonomy of religion theory, 25, 27, 312, 330
Average members per church, 371

Babbie, Earl, 263, 360, 367
Baehr, Karl, 298, 301, 361
Baker, Robert, 44, 346
Baptism, 20, 22, 46, 115, 245, 337
Baptism, age of, 70-72
Baptism by immersion, 32, 40
Baptism of Holy Spirit, 91
Baptists, 110, 121, 126, 247, 307
Baptists, Southern (see Southern Baptists)
Baptists, American (see American Baptists)
Baptist study of members, 366
Bartholomew, 208
Basel, 49
Bauman, Harold, 202, 356, 358
Beachy Amish Mennonite, 21
Beards, 33
Beck, Ervin, 8
Beechy, Winifred, 8
Beegle, J. Allan, 360
Behavioral norms, 305-306
Belief, 101-117
Believers, 22
Believers' Church concept, 184, 190, 202
Believers' Church Conference, 122
Bender, Harold S., 19, 32, 35, 74, 114, 118, 130, 135, 194-195, 203, 205, 208, 209, 211, 214, 218, 305, 313, 322, 330, 344, 345, 348, 350, 351, 352, 355, 358, 362, 363
Bender, Ross T., 355, 358
Benevolences, 234
Bennett, John C., 146, 148, 352
Bergel, Egon, 360
Berger, Peter, 363

Bert, Norman, 45, 70, 346, 347, 350
Bethel College, 111, 357
Bethesda Mennonite Colony Conference, 21
Bible, Doctrine of, 112
Bible Institutes, 220-221
Bible Knowledge, 203, 207-210
Bible Knowledge Scale, 143, 188-189, 208-299, 216, 224-225, 227, 230, 242, 268, 280-281, 302, 304, 308, 315, 317, 319, 324, 328, 329, 336, 385
Bible study, 98-99
Biblical norms, 317-318, 338
Birth control (see Contraception)
Bluffton College, 109, 111, 357
Bourgeois class, 291
Bowman, Bernard, 343, 363
Braght, Tieleman van, 349
Brekke, Milo, 8, 12
Brethren in Christ Church, 9, 21, 42-45, 52, 55-56, 58, 59, 62, 66-67, 71, 77, 87, 94, 98, 106, 112, 116, 124, 132-133, 139, 142, 144, 147, 148, 153, 157, 159, 161, 164, 167, 179, 191, 196, 200, 204, 209, 213, 220, 229, 234, 236, 239, 248, 250, 255, 258, 276, 284, 295, 343, 344, 346, 349, 351, 352, 353, 371, 372, 375, 381, 384
Brotherhood, 23
Brotherly Union of Some Children of God (see Schleitheim Articles)
Brubaker, Henry, 356
Brubaker, Merle, 8, 10
Budget, annual, 239
Budget, denominational, 217-218
Bullinger, Heinrich, 119
Burgess, E. W., 298, 361
Burkholder, J. Lawrence, 74, 348, 360, 361

Calvin, John, 70, 118
Calvinist, 116
Campbell, Thomas C., 113, 187, 327-328, 350, 355, 359, 363, 367
Camp meeting, 87, 89
Campolo, Anthony, 66, 263, 347, 348, 356, 359, 366
Campus Crusades, 247
Canada, 20, 51-52
Canada East Region, 295-296

Canada West Region, 295-296
Canada-U.S. differences, 293-296
Canadian Mennonite Bible College, 358
Canadian politics, 162-166
Capital punishment, 148, 157, 281, 288
Card-playing, 306
Category, concept of, 32
Causal relation, 316
Central (Illinois) Conference of Mennonites, 47, 48, 346
Central District Conference, 36
Characteristics of church members, 51-63
Charismatic movement, 92
Child evangelism, 72
Chi-square test, 278, 383
Chortitz Mennonites, 21
Christ-against-culture, concept of, 146
Christ, doctrine of, 106
Christendom, 313
Christian Century, 356
Christian education, 199-218
Christian Living, 345, 346, 350, 358, 362
Church attendance, 268, 270
Church, doctrine of, 64
Church History, 351,
Church Member Profile, 10, 28
Church of the Brethren, 43, 104
Church of Christ, 309
Church of God, 309
Church of God in Christ (Holdeman), 21
Church participation, 64-82
Church participation scales, 323-326
Church-Sect theory, 26, 277
Church schools, type of, 220
Church-state relationships, 157-159
Clark, Elmer T., 87, 349
Climenhaga, A. W., 356,
Closed theocratic community, 74, 298
Coffee, use of, 122-123
Cole, Stewart G., 110, 350
College attendance, 220-221
College support, 241, 229
Colleges, denominational, 222-224, 293
Columbus, Ohio, 278
Committee chairman, 187

Committee on Christian Concerns, 109
Communalism, 73-81, 222
Communalism Scale, 77, 80-81, 82, 129, 135, 146, 188-189, 205, 214, 216, 225-227, 230, 251, 256, 257, 259, 281, 287, 302-303, 308, 315, 318, 319, 320, 321, 323, 324, 325, 331, 338, 385
Communion, 32, 35, 46
Communism, 133, 143-144
Communism, attitudes toward (see Anti-Communism Scale)
Communist Party, 164-165
Conclusions of the study, 333-344
Conference headquarters, 293
Confessions of faith, 64-65, 92, 184, 202, 245, 304
Congregationalists, 66, 95, 98, 99, 107
Congregational polity, 185
Conrad Grebel College, 357
Consequences of church membership, 261-332
Consequential variable (see Dependent variable)
Conservatism, political, 162-163, 353
Conservatism, religious, 261-262, 281
Conservative-Liberal continuum, 298-299, 303, 334-335
Conservative Party, 164-165
Contingency Coefficient, 327
Contingency tables, 359
Contraception, 122-123, 179-180
Conversion, 21, 26, 39, 42, 44, 70, 84-91, 335
Conversion, frequency of, 87-88
Conversion Index, 86-88, 215, 302, 308, 318, 326
Conversion, place of, 87-89
Conversion, type of, 90-91
Cooperation, interchurch, 253-255
Corn belt, 293
Cornell, George, 237, 357
Correlation, concept of, 316-317
Council member, 187
Council of Mennonite Seminaries, 355, 361
Covering, prayer, 33
Cox, Harvey, 289, 360, 361
Creation, doctrine of, 112
Creedalism, 104
Cultural Conference Proceedings,

348, 351, 360, 361
Cultural diffusion, 299-300
Culture borrowing, 299
Curitiba, Brazil, 49
Curriculum, production of, 216-217

Dancing, 122-123, 281, 288, 300
Data-gathering method, 366
Data processing, 382-383
Danzig, 49
Davies, John O., 348
Dean's Seminar (AMBS), 355
Defenseless Mennonite Brethren, 48
Defenseless Mennonite Church, 46
Democratic Party, 163-165
Demographic characteristics, 51, 234
Demonstrations, peaceful, 148
Denominational merger, 254-255
Denominational patterns, 297-310
Denominational schools, 219-232
Dependent variable, faith as, 25, 27-28, 311
Detroit Study (see also Lenski, Gerhard), 125, 223, 279, 308, 325, 328
Devil, 94, 106
Devotionalism, 96-100
Devotionalism Scale, 98, 100, 129, 146, 188-189, 209, 213, 216, 223, 227, 242, 251, 263, 268, 281, 295, 302, 308, 318, 319, 320, 321, 323, 324, 325, 327, 331, 335, 336, 338, 341, 385
Dewey, Richard, 288, 360
Dick, H. H., 10
Diggers, 26
Diller, M. Marie, 103, 350
Direction of correlation, 317-318, 323, 324
Discernment, Christian, 201-202
Disciples of Christ, 99, 110
Discipleship 22, 145, 202, 303, 322
Discipline, 115
Dispensationalism, 32
Divorce, 122-123, 170-174
Divorce, incidence of, 175-176
Doctrinal norms, 304-305
Doctrine, 101-117
Document of Secession (MBC), 40
Doopsgezind, 344
Dordrecht Confession, 33, 78, 102
Doukhobors, 353
Dourts, Monroe, 356

Dress, distinctive, 34, 35, 46, 65, 298-299
Drinking, 123, 281, 288, 306
Driver, Harvey, 8, 10, 347
Drugs, 122-123
Drunkenness, 123
Dunkards, 43
Durkheim, Emile, 311, 344, 362
Dutch Mennonites, 33, 102, 120
Dyck, C. J., 8, 344, 345
Dynes, Russell, 278, 359

East Pennsylvania Conference, 36
Eastern Mennonite College, 357, 363
Eby, Benjamin, 356
Ecumenical attitudes, 243-260
Ecumenical attitudes, type of, 252-253
Ecumenical movement, 246, 311
Ecumenical norms, 306-307
Ecumenism, 338-339
Ecumenism Scale, 137, 194, 197, 214, 216, 224-225, 227, 249, 251, 254-256, 259, 269, 272, 281, 290, 302, 304, 306, 319, 324, 325, 328, 329, 330, 338, 385
Ediger, Elmer, 155, 353
Educational Attainment, 58-59
Education Index, 135, 137, 143, 146, 149, 158, 160, 162, 168, 169, 180-181, 188-189, 194, 197, 205, 214, 215, 240, 249, 251, 256-257, 259, 275-285, 295, 315, 319, 323, 324, 329
Education, elementary, 240-241
Education, secondary, 240-241
Egly Amish, 46-47, 346
Egly, Henry, 46
Eicher, E. C., 353
Elder, 187
Elections, political, 161
Elementary schools, 220-221
Employment (see Occupation)
Employment of women, 178
Encyclopaedia Britannica, 350
Encyclopedia of Religion, 351
Encyclopedia of the Social Sciences, 350
Engle, Jacob, 43
Episcopalians, 99, 126, 168, 263, 279-280
Epp, Frank, 294, 361
Erb, Paul, 358, 362

Eternal punishment, doctrine of, 112
Eternal security, 32
Ethics, 322, 328
Ethical-Social Conversion, 86, 90-91
Ethical-Social Conversion Scale, 91-92, 135, 143, 193-194, 214, 249, 251, 301, 302, 318, 319, 320, 324, 327, 331, 338, 385
Ethnic solidarity, 79-80
Euthanasia, 281
Evangelical conservatives, 110-111
Evangelical Free Church, 48
Evangelical Mennonite Brethren (see also Defenseless M.B.), 21, 41, 48
Evangelical Mennonite Church, 9, 21, 45-48, 52, 55-56, 58, 59, 62, 66-67, 71, 77, 87, 94, 106, 112, 116, 124, 132-133, 139, 142, 144, 147, 148, 157, 159, 161, 164, 167, 179, 191, 196, 204, 209, 213, 220, 229, 234, 236, 239, 248, 250, 258, 276, 284, 295, 343, 348, 349, 354, 371, 372, 375, 381, 384
Evangelical Mennonite Conference, 21
Evangelical Mennonite Mission Conference, 21
Evangelism, 80, 212
Evangelism Scale, 135, 188-189, 213-215, 216, 227, 242, 268, 270, 281, 290, 302, 308, 315, 317, 319, 324, 325, 329, 335, 338, 385
Ewert, David, 185, 355
Excommunication, 299
Exile, The, 208
Extramarital sex, 336
Extrinsic faith, 331

Family characteristics, 174-178
Family Life Education, 241
Family worship, 98-99, 178-179
Farming, 298
Farm population, 54
Farm residence, 234
Federal Council of Churches, 37, 246
Female-male differences, 262, 265
Ferm, Virgilius, 351
Fertility, 177-178
Fichter, Joseph H., 187, 355
Field procedures, 378, 382
Finance, church, 233-234

Flood, doctrine of, 112
Foot washing, 35
Foundation Series, The 202-203
Francis, E. K., 300, 361
Franconia Conference, 33, 35, 44, 49, 153, 201
Free churches, 26
Free participation position, 154
Freeman Junior College, 357
Fretz, J. Winfield, 154, 351, 353
Friedmann, Robert, 32, 298, 301, 322, 345, 349, 351, 361, 363
Friendships, 76
Friesen, Dorothy, 8
Friesen, P.M., 362
Friesland, 290
Fukuyama, Yoshio, 113, 187, 327-328, 350, 359, 363, 367
Fundamentalism, 109, 110, 322, 335, 341-342
Fundamentalist-Modernist Controversy, 305
Fundamentalist Movement, 311
Fundamentalist Orthodoxy, 107-114
Fundamentalist Orthodoxy Scale, 111-114, 129, 135, 136, 137, 143, 146, 149, 158, 160, 162, 168, 188-189, 193-194, 197, 205, 214, 216, 225, 227, 242, 251, 256-257, 259, 263, 268, 280-281, 289-290, 295, 302, 303, 315, 318, 319, 320, 321, 323, 324, 328, 329, 330, 331, 334, 342, 353, 385
Fundamentals Conference, 108
Funk, John F., 200, 356
Full Community, 74

Gallup, George, 348
Gallup Poll, 66
Gambling, 122-123, 281
Garrett, James Leo, 348, 351
Garrison, W. E., 111, 350
Gemeinschaft, concept of, 325
General Conference Mennonite Church, 9, 21, 35-39, 48, 52, 55-56, 58, 59, 62, 66-67, 71, 77, 87, 94, 98, 106, 112, 116, 124, 132-133, 139, 142, 144, 147, 148, 157, 159, 161, 164, 167, 179, 191, 196, 204, 209, 213, 220, 229, 234, 236, 239, 247, 250, 255, 258, 276, 284, 295, 343, 344, 345, 350, 351, 352 ,

371, 372, 375, 381, 384
General Orthodoxy, 101-108
General Orthodoxy Scale, 106, 107, 129, 135, 136, 137, 143, 158, 160, 168, 193-194, 197, 205, 214, 216, 225, 227, 242, 251, 256-257, 263, 268, 280-281, 289-290, 302, 303, 304, 305, 308, 315, 318, 319, 320, 323, 324, 325, 327, 328, 331, 334, 338, 385
Generation gap, 273-274
German Baptists, 42-43
German Lutheran Pietists, 39, 43
German-speaking, 53
Germany, 20, 340
Gerth, H. H., 344
Gethsemane, 208
Gingerich, Melvin, 70, 72, 345, 348
Giving, estimated, 237-238
Giving per member, 234
Glock, Charles, 66, 76, 85, 95, 97, 99, 105, 107, 140-141, 249-252, 263, 266, 279-280, 308-310, 318, 321, 348, 349, 350, 358, 359, 362, 363, 367
God, doctrine of, 105-106
Goldwater, Barry, 353
Goshen Biblical Seminary, 357
Goshen College, 10, 108, 111, 357
Goshen, Indiana, 49
Gospel Herald, 34, 347, 348, 363
Gospel Light Sunday School Materials, 109
Government grants, 159
Grace (prayer), 178-179
Grace Bible Institute, 109
Graham, Billy, 247
Great Awakening, 203
Great Britain, 262
Grebel, Conrad, 19, 344
Greeley, Andrew M., 223-224, 357
Grossmünster Church, 290
Guaranteed income, 287

Hadden, Jeffrey, 367
Harder, John, 8
Harder, Leland, 10-11, 345, 346, 349, 363
Healing, Divine, 46, 94
Hein, Marvin, 8, 10
Hershberger, Guy F., 344, 347, 351, 352, 360, 361

Hertzler, Daniel, 357
Hesston College, 357
Hiebert, Paul, 8
Higher Education, 241
Hillerbrand, Hans, 151, 352,
History of denominations, 31-50
Holiness, 22
Holiness Movement, 121, 311
Holland, 20, 120
Holy Spirit, doctrine of, 91, 92, 94
Home Missions, 240-241
Homosexuality, 122-123
Horsch, John, 108, 109, 111, 350
Hostetler, David E., 347
Hostetler, John H., 298, 301, 345, 347, 361
Humphrey, Hubert H., 353
Hutter, Jacob, 277
Hutterites, 20, 21, 74, 277, 344, 353
Hypotheses, 28, 365

Illinois, 47
Immersion baptism (see Baptism by immersion)
Implications of study, 333-344
Income, 62-63, 128
Income Index, 158, 188-189, 224, 285, 315, 319, 323, 324
Income taxes, 133
Income tax evasion, 122-123
Independent, Political, 163-166
Independent variable, faith as, 312
Index of Initial Conversion (see Conversion Index)
India, 275
Indiana, 36, 46, 47, 65, 79, 201
Indiana-Michigan Conference, 108-109
Indianapolis, 38
Induction, refusal of, 133
Industrial Relations, 144
Influence, concept of, 316-317
In-Group marriage, 78, 299
Instruction, Christian, 200
Interchurch Relations Committee (GCMC), 247
Interchurch Relations Committee (MC), 246
Intercorrelations of faith variables, 318-321
Intercourse, premarital, 179-180
Inter-Mennonite I-W Coordinating

Board, 38
International Sunday School Lesson Series, 212
Interracial marriage, 172-173, 336
Interval scales, 315
Interview method, 367
Intrinsic faith, 331
Iowa, 36
Item analysis, 68, 385

James, William, 85, 86, 331, 349, 363
Janzen, A. E., 41, 99, 306, 346, 347, 350, 362
Janzen, Heinz, 9, 10, 36, 346, 351
Janzen, Lester, 8, 10
Jesus, 22, 64, 80, 84-87, 93-94, 102, 104, 106-107, 112, 115, 118-119, 122, 131-132, 141, 146, 151, 152, 195, 202, 212, 214, 222, 243, 253, 300, 304, 339, 340
Jewelry, 34, 35
Jews, 125-126, 210, 307-310
Jews, attitude toward (see also Anti-Semitism Scale), 248-252
Johnson, Benton, 309, 362
Johnson, Douglas, 237, 356-357
Johnstown, Pennsylvania, 143

Karlsruhe, Germany, 49
Kauffman, Daniel, 34, 345, 350
Kauffman, J. Howard, 10-11, 354
Kaufman, Edmund G., 362
Kendall's Tau C, 281, 359
Kersten, Lawrence, 125, 222, 252, 263, 281, 309, 351, 359-360
Key factors, 311-332
King, Mackenzie, 165, 353
Kirchliche, 39, 41
Kish, Leslie, 373
Kitchener, Ontario, 49
Klassen, A. J., 355, 362
Kleine Gemeinde, 39, 41
Kloetzli, Walter, 187, 355, 356
Knox, John, 118
Konferenz der Altevangelische Taufgesinten-Gemeinden, 344
Kraemer, Hendrik, 184, 354
Krauschaar, Otto, 232, 357
Krehbiel, H. P., 154, 345, 353
Kreider, Robert, 360

Labor Unions, 145-147
Lancaster Conference, 33, 42, 44
Landis, Judson T., 176, 354
Lapp, John E., 345
Large city residence, 284-290, 292
Larrison, Theodore, 354
Lawsuits, 115, 287, 337
Lay leader, 186-188, 203, 211, 336
Lay member, 211
Layman's Profile, 9
Leaders, 336
Leadership, 183-198
Leadership and Age, 269-270
Leadership position, 186-187
Lederach, Paul, 8, 10, 223, 344, 357
Left wing of Reformation, 343
Legalism, 121
Leiffer Murray H., 189-190, 292, 355, 361
Lenski, Gerhard, 66, 76, 78, 79, 85, 97, 125, 223, 279, 308, 312, 321, 325, 329, 348, 349, 351, 357, 360, 362, 363, 367
Levellers, 26
Liberal-Conservative continuum, 234-235, 298-299, 303
Liberal Party, 164-165, 353
Liberal views, 281
Liberalism, political, 163, 363
Liberalism, religious, 110, 261-262
Life after death, 106
Limmat River, 290
Linton, Ralph, 361
Literature, church, 241
Literature, Sunday school, 241
Litigation (see also Lawsuits), 115
Littell, Franklin, 40, 184, 190, 345, 354, 355
Long, J. I., 356
Loomis, Charles P., 360
Lordship of Christ (see also Discipleship), 22
Lord's Prayer, 65
Lot, called by, 46
Low German, 39
Luther, Martin, 70, 92, 118, 184
Lutherans, 26, 43, 55, 66, 92, 98, 113, 118, 125-126, 140-141, 187, 205, 222, 223, 249-252, 266-267, 279-280, 308-209, 321
Lutherans, American, 11
Lutherans, Missouri, 99

Lutheran "Study of Generations," 8, 263, 266, 272, 367

Macedonian Call, 208
Macedonians, 233
Male-Female differences (see also Sex Index), 262-265
Manitoba, 293, 300
Manz, Felix, 19, 245, 290
Manual of Doctrine and Government (BIC), 103, 122, 248, 351, 357
Manual of Faith and Practice (EMC), 248, 347, 354
Marijuana, 122-123
Marital status, 175-176
Marriage, 122-123, 170-182
Marriage, age of, 176-177
Marriage, attitudes toward, 171-173, 336
Marriage, incidence of, 175-176
Marriage, In-Group, 78, 299
Marriage, Interfaith, 177
Martens, Elmer and Phyllis, 40, 42, 109, 298, 303, 305-306, 345, 346, 350, 358, 361, 362
Martin, Ernest D., 348, 351-352, 355
Martyrs Mirror (see also Braght, Tieleman van), 349
Mass communications, 240-241
Masturbation, 122-123
Mathews, Shailer, 109, 350
Mean scores (find specific table listed on pp. 14-17)
Median Age of marriage, 176-177
Median education, 59
Median income, 62-63
Median number of conversion experiences, 87
Median scores on Sanctification Scale, 94
Meetinghouse, 65
Members, Baptized, 21
Membership of denominations, 371
Menno Simons (see Simons, Menno)
Mennonitism, 19, 41, 80
Mennonite, The, 347, 361
Mennonite Biblical Seminary, 10, 344, 345, 346, 357
Mennonite Brethren Bible College, 357
Mennonite Brethren Church, 9, 21, 39-42, 48, 52, 71, 77, 87, 94, 98, 106, 112, 116, 124, 132-133, 139, 142, 144, 147, 148, 155, 157, 159, 161, 164, 167, 179, 191, 196, 200, 204, 209, 213, 220, 229, 234, 236, 239, 247-248, 250, 255, 258, 276, 284, 295, 343, 346, 351, 352, 358, 371, 372, 375, 381, 384
Mennonite Brethren Herald, 345, 349
Mennonite Brethren in Christ, 48
Mennonite Board of Missions, 9
Mennonite Central Committee, 9, 21, 45, 47, 49, 136, 254, 257-259
Mennonite Central Committee Peace Section, 48
Mennonite Church, 9, 21, 32-35, 52, 55-56, 58, 59, 62, 66-67, 71, 77, 87, 94, 98, 106, 112, 116, 124, 132-133, 139, 142, 144, 147, 148, 157, 159, 161, 164, 167, 179, 191, 196, 200, 204, 209, 213, 220, 229, 234, 236, 239, 246, 250, 255, 258, 276, 284, 295, 343, 345, 348, 350, 352, 371-372, 375, 381, 384
Mennonite Church By-Laws, 246-247
Mennonite Cultural Conference (see Cultural Conference Proceedings)
Mennonite Disaster Service, 258
Mennonite Encyclopedia, 344, 345, 348, 349, 350, 351, 352, 355, 356, 358, 362, 363
Mennonite Family Census, 70
Mennonite I-W Coordinating Board, 345
Mennonite Life, 345, 352, 353, 360, 362
Mennonite Mutual Aid, 9, 10, 287, 288
Mennonite Mutual Aid Association, 7
Mennonite Publishing House, 9, 10, 12
Mennonite Quarterly Review, 344, 345, 347, 348, 351, 352, 356, 360, 363,
Mennonite reality, 312-314
Mennonite Research Fellowship, 116
Mennonite Sunday School Centennial, 355
Mennonite Weekly Review, 346, 358
Mennonite World Conference, 45, 47, 49
Mennonite Yearbook, 21, 344

Merger, attitude toward, 254
Methodist (s), 99, 110, 121, 126, 201, 208
Midwest region, 293
Migration, 51-54
Military force, 144
Military service, 133
Miller, D. D., 201
Miller, Levi, 344
Mills, C. Wright, 344
Minimum annual income, 142
Ministry, pattern of, 184-185
Miracles, doctrine of, 106
Missionary Church Association, 48
Missionary movement, 203
Missions, 240-241
Mixed marriages, 172-173, 177
Moberg, David O., 355, 359,
Mobility, social, 277
Modernism, 37, 108, 109, 322, 335
Moehlman, C. H., 351
Moral Attitudes Scale, 124, 126-127, 194, 197, 210, 216, 225, 227, 230, 256-257, 263, 269, 271-272, 281, 289-302, 305, 306, 308, 317, 319 324, 329, 336, 338, 342, 385
Moral Behavior Scale, 126-127, 189, 210, 216, 224-225, 227, 263, 281, 289, 302, 317, 319, 324, 329, 336, 338, 385
Moralism, 121, 210-211
Moral issues, 118-129, 210
Moral life, 203
Moral-Personal Conversion Scale, 86, 90-92, 205, 214, 251, 295, 302, 318, 319, 320, 323, 324, 327, 331, 338, 385
Moravia, 20
Movies, 35, 123, 287, 288
Mumaw, John R., 360
Musical instruments, 35
Mutual aid (see Mennonite Mutual Aid)

National Association of Evangelicals, 45, 248
National Conference identity, 294
National Council of Churches, 357
National Holiness Association, 44, 121
National Opinion Research Center, 8, 12

National place of residence, 293-296
Neill, Stephen, 355
Nelson, J. Robert, 358
Netherlands, 102, 291, 344
Neufeld, Elmer, 340, 363
Neufeld, William, 42
New Democratic Party, 164-165
Newton, Kansas, 49
Niebuhr, H. Richard, 26-27, 110, 146, 148, 279, 282, 311, 344, 350, 352, 360, 362
Noncombatant service, 133
Nonconformity, 22, 34, 35
Nonparticipation position, 152-153
Nonregistration for draft, 133
Nonresident members, 285
Nonresistance, 22, 23, 115, 131, 141, 143, 330, 337
Nonviolence, 145
Number of churches per denomination, 372
Nurture, Christian, 199-200

Oaths, 35, 115, 337
Oberholtzer, John H., 36, 201, 356
Objectives, research, 30, 364-366
Occupation, 60-62
Occupation Index, 188-189, 285
Occupations of Anabaptists, 291
Ohio, 36, 47
Ohio Conference, 200
Old Order Amish, 21, 46, 47, 120-121, 298, 344
Old Order Mennonites, 21, 121, 201
Old Colony Mennonites, 21
Ontario, 36, 53, 293
Open Community, 38, 74
Ordained ministers (leaders), 186-188, 211, 336
Ordination, 190-192
Organs, 34
Orthodoxy, Fundamentalist (see Fundamentalist Orthodoxy)
Orthodoxy, General (see General Orthodoxy)
Ottawa, Canada, 258
Otterbein, Philip, 43
Oyer, Becky, 8

Pacific College, 357
Pacifism, 132-136
Pacifism Scale, 134-135, 137, 138, 143,

149, 209, 216, 227, 251, 259, 263, 269, 271, 280-281, 302, 304, 317, 319, 324, 325, 327, 329, 338, 342, 385
Pacifist movements, 246
Pannabecker, S. F., 350, 356
Paraguay, 74
Park, Robert E., 298
Parochial attitudes, 243-260, 361
Parsons, Talcott, 344, 362
Particularism, 114, 309, 339, 343
Pastors, 11
Patterns of faith and life, 64-182
Paul the Apostle, 233, 243, 262, 291
Peace education, 241
Peace Section Washington Office, 258
Peachey, Paul, 347, 360
Pearson correlation coefficient (r), 281, 315, 317-319, 320, 323, 361-362, 385
Pendell, Thomas R., 356
Pennsylvania, 33, 36, 120, 200
Pennsylvania-German origins, 293
Pennsylvania Mennonites, 42
Pentecost, 208, 233
Permissiveness, 38
Peters, Frank, 41, 346
Philosophy of Education (MC), 222
Pietism, 66, 92
Pietists, German, 120
Piety, 322, 335, 340-341
Pingjum, Friesland, 290
Plymouth Brethren, 321
Poland, 291
Political Action Scale, 166-169, 197, 256-257, 263, 289, 302, 304, 319, 339, 385
Political candidates, 167
Political issues, 167
Political office, 161
Political participation, 34, 35, 150-169, 339-340
Political Participation Scale, 135, 160-166, 189, 216, 263, 269, 280-281, 289, 295, 302, 304, 319, 338, 339, 342, 385
Political Party preference, 162-165
Poverty, 141-143
Prayer, 98, 178-179
Prayer covering, 33, 35
Prayer meetings, 34

Predictive power, 316-317
Pregnancy, 181
Prejudice, 331
Premarital intercourse, 179-180
Premillennialism, 32
Presbyterian(s), 99, 110, 116
Pre-Test of questionnaire, 368
Price, C. Robert, 357
Priesthood of believers, 337
Primitivism, 40
Product-Moment Correlation Coefficient (see Pearson r)
Proportional giving, 236-238
Protest marches, 148
Protestant Reformation, 244
Protestant Reformers, 84, 86, 92, 119, 130
Protestants, 95, 97, 99, 107, 125, 140, 191, 234, 251-252, 267, 279, 307-310, 321, 325
Protestant denominations, 237
Psychology of religion, 85
Public welfare, 142 (see also Welfare Attitudes).
Publishing and Editorial Councils, 217
Publishing houses, 293
Pulpit, 167
Purpose of the study, 364-366
Pyramid, Age-Sex, 56-57

Quakers, 26
Quaker Religious Thought, 358
Questionnaire, 366, 367-369
Questionnaire returns, 382
Quiring, J. H., 306, 362

Race relations, 136-141
Race Relations Scale, 135, 138-141, 143, 149, 189, 194, 197, 209, 214, 216, 251, 256-257, 263, 269, 271-272, 280-281, 289, 302, 304, 308, 317, 219, 324, 325, 328, 329, 338, 385
Radio, 240-241
Raikes, Robert, 200
Ramseyer, E. W., 353
Random start, 376
Rank order of denominations, 300-307
Rape, 181
Reckless driving, 122-123
Redekop, Calvin, 8, 300, 358, 361

Redekop, John H., 166, 353
Reformed Churches, 26, 43, 119
Reformed Mennonites, 21
Reformers, Protestant (see Protestant Reformers)
Regional place of residence, 293-296
Registration for draft, 133
Reinland Mennonites, 21
Relief program, 241, 255
Religion as dependent variable, 25, 311
Religion as independent variable, 25, 312
Religious beliefs, 222 (see also Doctrinal norms, Doctrine, Orthodoxy)
Religious experience, 83-96
Religious experience scales, 326-328
Religious knowledge, 222
Religious practice, 83, 96-100, 222
Religious practice scales, 326-328
Remarriage, 173-174
Repentance, 22
Republican Party, 163-166
Research instrument, 367-369
Research methodology, 314-318, 364-385
Research visitors, 11, 379
Residence, 51-55, 128
Residence, Index of Rural-Urban, 146, 158, 160, 162, 168, 169, 179, 205, 214, 230, 256, 283-296, 319, 323, 324, 342
Restitution, concept of, 184
Resurrection, doctrine of, 106
Rich, Jarvis, 8, 12
Ringer, Benjamin, 263, 360, 367
Ris, Cornelis, 102
River Brethren, 43
River Mennonites, 43
Role categories, 186-188
Role of women, 194-197
Role of Women Scale, 146, 196-197, 214, 216, 280-281, 287, 295, 302, 304, 317, 319, 324, 325, 328, 330, 337, 338, 385
Roman Catholics, attitudes toward (see Anti-Catholic Scale), 248-252
Roman Catholics, 20, 26, 23, 50, 66, 91, 95, 99, 107, 125-126, 140, 187, 191, 223, 224, 234, 252, 279, 307-310

Roper Research Associates, 263
Rosenger, William, 356
Rossi, Peter H., 224, 357
Rundquist, 385
Rural farm residence, 59, 284-290, 292
Rural life hypothesis, 291-292
Rural nonfarm residence, 59, 284-290, 292
Rural residence, 54-55, 59, 234, 283-296
Russia, 20, 74, 103, 291, 321, 340
Russian Baptists, 41
Russian Mennonites, 36, 39, 40, 41, 51

Salaried ministers, 191
Samaritans, 208
Sample members per denomination, 375
Sample of congregations, 371-372
Sample of members, 374-375
Sample selection, 369-378
Sampling results, 381
Sanctification, 26, 32, 42, 91-96, 119
Sanctification Scale, 94, 95, 146, 188-189, 205, 209, 213-214, 251, 302, 308, 318, 319, 320, 323, 324, 326, 327, 331, 385
Sandeen, Ernest R., 111, 350
Saskatchewan, 293
Sattler, Michael, 347, 349, 354
Scales, derivation of, 29, 384
Scales, list of, 385
Schism, 34, 35, 46
Schleitheim, Switzerland, 354
Schleitheim articles, 102, 151, 156, 347
Schrag, Martin, 44, 45, 202, 346, 356
Schrock, Paul, 12
Schwarzenau, Germany, 43
Scope of study, 364-366
Scripture Press, 109
Second Coming of Christ, 106
Second Vatican Council, 249
Second work of grace, 32
Secondary schools, 220-221
Secret societies, 35
Sectarians, 244
Sectarianism, 338-339
Sects, 309
Sect-Cycle theory, 298-301, 303, 304,

306, 309
Secularism, 361
Secularization theory, 37, 296-298, 300, 306, 307, 309, 315, 361
Selection ratio, 376
Selective Participation Position, 154-155
Self-Identity, Church, 207
Seminaries, denominational, 220, 293
Seminary support, 241
Separation of Church and State, 23, 115
Separation of Church and State Scale, 135, 137, 151, 157-159, 160, 197, 302, 319, 338, 339, 385
Separatist Party (FLQ), 165
Service programs, 240-241, 255
Sex, extramarital, 288
Sex Index, 55-58, 60-61, 181, 189, 197, 215, 234, 261-274
Sex, premarital, 281, 287
Sex ratio, 56
Sexual intercourse, 123
Sexual standards, 179-180
Shafer, Donald, 8
Shakespeare, 298
Shared ministry concept, 190-192
Shared Ministry Scale, 135, 137, 138, 143, 149, 193-194, 211-212, 216, 249, 251, 256-257, 302, 317, 319, 324, 325, 328, 329, 330, 337, 338, 385
Sheatsley, Paul, 8, 12
Shenk, Betty, 8
Sherrill, Lewis J., 350
Short, Reuben, 48
Siemens, H. K., 42
Significance level, 383
Simons Menno, 20, 39, 49, 84-85, 97, 119-120, 184, 290-291, 303, 304, 322
Simplicity, 35
Singlehood, incidence of, 175-176
Size of household, 287
Small city residence, 284-290, 292
Smart, James, 210, 351, 356
Smissen, Carl van der, 102
Smith, Rockwell C., 361
Smith, W. Robertson, 69, 348
Smoking, 281, 288, 306
Smucker, Glenn, 354
Social causation theory of religion, 25, 27, 311
Social class, 275
Social class of Anabaptists, 291
Social class of members, 275-282
Social concerns, 340-341
Social Concerns Scale, 135, 137, 138, 143, 146-149, 194, 197, 210, 214, 251, 259, 281, 288-289, 295, 302, 304, 315, 317, 319, 324, 325, 328, 329, 341, 385
Social Credit Party, 164-165
Social ethics, 130-149
Social gospelers, 341
Social welfare attitudes, 141-143
Socialist Party, 164-165
Socioeconomic Status Scale, 135, 137, 146, 158, 160, 162, 168, 189, 197, 230, 249, 251, 256-257, 259, 275-277, 281, 295, 315, 319, 323, 324, 329, 342, 385
Sommerfelder Mennonites, 21
Souderton statement, 102
Sources of church membership, 261-332
South America, 20
Southern Baptists, 66, 95, 99, 107, 335, 362
Soviet Central Asia, 41
Space exploration, 148, 288
Speaking in tongues, 94
Spiritual life, 203
Spiritual maturity, 208
Spiritualist type, 253
Spouse, 77-78
Sletto, 385
St. Francis of Assisi, 277
Stark, Rodney, 66, 76, 85, 93, 97, 99, 105, 107, 140-141, 249-252, 308-310, 318, 321, 348, 349, 350, 358, 359, 360, 362, 363, 367
State, function of, 156-157
Steinbach, Manitoba, 11, 41
Stereotype, 32
Stewardship, 23, 233-242
Stewardship Attitudes Scale, 189, 230, 237-238, 239, 241-242, 263, 268, 280-281, 290, 302, 317, 319, 324, 329, 335, 338, 385
Stewardship Performance Scale, 225, 227, 238-239, 241-242, 281, 290, 302, 308, 317, 319, 324, 329, 335, 338, 385

Stock holding, 133
Stoltzfus, Grant, 33, 108, 246, 306, 345, 350, 358, 362
Strategy of withdrawal, 146
Strickland, Francis, 85, 349
Strommen, Merton, 8, 12, 66, 98, 113, 140, 188, 223, 249-252, 279-280, 282, 308, 347, 348, 349, 350, 355, 357, 358, 359, 360, 367
Stroup, Atlee, 354
Stucky Amish, 346
Studer, Gerald, 363
Style of life, 285-288
Subculture, 278
Suffering, 23, 115
Summary of study, 333-344
Sunday school, 200-201, 203-216
Sunday school attendance, 68
Sunday School Participation Scale, 189, 203-206, 242, 281, 289-290, 302, 317, 319, 324, 329, 335, 336, 385
Sunday school teachers, 187, 215-216
Sunday school teaching, 68-69, 204
Support of Church Colleges Scale, 224-225, 227, 228-230, 281, 302, 317, 319, 324, 338, 385
Support of Mennonite Central Committee Scale, 135, 143, 258-259, 269, 281, 302, 304, 315, 317, 319, 324, 327, 329, 385
Supreme Court (see U.S. Supreme Court)
Susquehanna Brethren, 43
Swain, Joseph, 344
Swamp Mennonite Church, 201
Swearing oaths (see Oaths)
Swiss Anabaptists, 43
Swiss Brethren, 19, 20, 119-120, 344
Swiss immigrants, 36
Switzerland, 344

Tabor College, 111, 357
Taufgessint, 344
Tea, use of, 122-123
Teachers, Sunday School, 187, 215-216
Teaching, 23
Television, 240-241, 287
Temperance, 120-121
Testimonies, 65
Tests of significance, 359
Theater, 35

Theocratic type, 253
Theory, 25
Theories underlying study, 365
Tithing, 236
Tobacco, 122-123
Töennies, Ferdinand, 325
Troeltsch, Ernst, 25, 69, 277, 344 348
Type of conversion, 90
Tyrol, 20

Underwood, A. C., 90, 349
Unemployment, 142
United Brethren in Christ, 42
United Church of Christ, 113, 187, 263, 270, 327-328
United Methodist Church, 42
United States, 20, 51-52
United States Supreme Court, 138, 180, 336
USA East Region, 295-296
USA West Region, 295-296
Unity, 38
Universalism, 339
University of Waterloo, 357
Unruh, G. H., 42
Urban-Industrial Region, 293
Urban life hypothesis, 292
Urban residence, 54-55, 59
Urbanization, 283-285, 342

Variables of belief, 328-331
Variables of doctrine, 328-331
Verduin, Leonard, 349
Vietnam War, 133
Virgin Birth of Christ, 112
Virginia Conference, 200
Voluntarism, 69-73, 81
Voluntarism Scale, 71, 73, 82, 129, 137, 193-194, 205, 214, 251, 281, 294, 301, 302, 318, 319, 320, 321, 323, 324, 325, 331, 385
Voluntary service, 300
Voting, 161, 167, 329

Wagner, Martha, 348
Wagoner, Walter, 342-343, 363
Wambold, Abraham, 356
War, 133, 159
Warner, W. Lloyd, 359
Washington, D.C., 258
Waterlanders, 20

Way of Peace Statement, 214
Weber, Hans Ruedi, 256
Weber, Harry F., 346
Weber, Max, 25, 277, 312, 345, 362
Weighting procedures, 383
Welfare Attitudes Scale, 135, 137, 138, 142-143, 149, 197, 214, 251, 269, 271, 280-281, 287, 302, 304, 317, 319, 324, 328, 329, 338, 385
Weltanschauung, 328
Wenger, J. C., 32, 65, 108, 345, 347, 348, 349, 350, 352, 356, 360
Wesley, John, 44
Wesleyans, 26, 42, 43, 45, 92, 121
Whitefield, George, 43
Whitmer, Paul E., 346
Widowhood, incidence of, 175-176
Wiebe, Rudy, 40, 80, 345, 349
Wiebe, Walter, 362
Wiens, Delbert, 34, 185, 349, 355
Winger, Walter, 356
Winter Bible Schools, 220-221
Winter, Gibson, 363
Wisler Mennonites, 21
Withdrawal, point of, 155
Witmarsum Theological Seminary, 109
Witness, evangelistic, 23, 213
Witness to state, 161

Wittlinger, C. O., 43, 346
Women in church leadership, 196
Women, ordination of, 196
Work of the church, 183-260
World Book Encyclopedia, 353
World Christian Fundamentals Association, 110
Worship, family, 178-179
Worship, Public, 66
Writing to legislators, 161

Yearbook of American and Canadian Churches, 234, 358
Yinger, J. Milton, 66, 345, 347, 360
Yoder, John H., 8, 80, 82, 111, 118, 190, 244-246, 313, 314, 323, 347, 349, 350, 351, 354, 355, 358, 361, 362
Youth group leader, 187
Youth Research Center, 12

Zaccheus, 208
Zehr, Howard, 9, 10
Zercher, John E., 45, 346, 350
Zimmerman, Charles, 346
Zollikon, 19
Zurich, 19, 49, 64, 290
Zwingli, Ulrich, 19, 70, 118, 245, 290

Kauffman   Harder

J. HOWARD KAUFFMAN was born in Champaign County, Ohio, in 1919, and educated at Goshen College (BA), Michigan State University (MA), and the University of Chicago (PhD).

He is Professor of Sociology at Goshen College, chairman of the Department of Sociology, Social Work, and Anthropology, and executive director of Social Research Service.

Kauffman served on the Mennonite Commission for Christian Education for more than a decade and is past president and treasuere of Mennonite Historical Society. He holds membership in the American Sociological Association, the National Council on Family Relations, and the African Studies Association. He has authored numerous professional articles and papers.

He and his wife, the former Verda Lambright, are the parents of four daughters, and members of the College Mennonite Church, Goshen, Indiana.

LELAND HARDER was born in Hillsboro, Kansas, in 1926, was educated at Bethel College (BA), North Newton, Kansas; Michigan State University (MA); Bethany Theological Seminary (MDiv); and Northwestern University (PhD). He has also studied at the Medical College of Virginia, Richmond, and the Irish School of Ecumenics, Dublin, Ireland. He is director of field education and Professor of Practical Theology at Mennonite Biblical Seminary, Elkhart, Indiana.

Harder is an ordained minister and elder in the General Conference Mennonite Church. He has served on its Commission on Home Ministries. Committee on City Churches and Board of Missions. He has authored numerous professional articles and papers.

He and his wife, the former Bertha Fast, are parents of two sons, John David and Thomas Lee.